WE NEED MEN

WE NEED MEN

The Union Draft
in the
Civil War

James W. Geary

NORTHERN ILLINOIS UNIVERSITY PRESS/DEKALB
1991

© 1991 by Northern Illinois University Press
Published by the Northern Illinois University Press, DeKalb, Illinois 60115
Manufactured in the United States using acid-free paper
Design by Julia Fauci
Casebound editions of Northern Illinois University Press books are
smyth-sewn and printed on permanent and durable acid-free paper.

Library of Congress Cataloging-in-Publication Data

Geary, James W.
We need men : the Union draft in the Civil War / James W. Geary.
p.   cm.
Includes bibliographical references and index.
ISBN 0–87580–157–9
1. United States—History—Civil War, 1861–1865—Manpower.
2. Draft—United States—History—19th century.   3. United States.
Army—History—19th century.   4. United States. Army—Recruiting,
enlistment, etc.—History—19th century.   I. Title.
E491.G42   1991
973.7'41—dc20   90–21636
CIP

For Linda Leigh

CONTENTS

PREFACE

As a young man subject to the draft in the mid-1960s, and later as a student of conscription in graduate school and beyond, I have been involved with the question of compulsory service for most of my adult life. In deciding whether to add still another book to the genre of Civil War literature, and in formulating the direction that such a study might take, I recalled one night from almost a quarter century ago. A midwesterner by the name of "Old Man" Sloan had recounted how he happened to be drafted. Most of us present were nineteen or twenty and, at that time, not old enough to vote. Sloan was around twenty-five, and, through our eyes, an "Old Man."

Sloan had worked in a junkyard. One day he received a message from his local postmaster that an urgent letter was waiting for him. Not accustomed to receiving any important mail, Sloan hurried to the post office and discovered his induction notice. In his typically quiet manner, he remarked something along the lines of "once I get out of this man's army, I ain't never going to leave my junkyard again."

Sloan's tale reflects the ambivalent attitude that most American men have toward conscription. They dislike military life, view it as an imposition on their personal lives; but in the best tradition of the citizen-soldier, they usually go when called and, at the earliest opportunity, return to their civilian pursuits.

The Selective Service System that temporarily took Sloan from his familiar environs had its origins in the Civil War. Within two years after the firing on Fort Sumter, both the Union and the Confederacy had enacted draft laws. Taken together, these governments had established the principle of national conscription for their generation and for those to follow. Other influences notwithstanding, the state from that point on possessed the unequivocal right to take a citizen from hearth and home and subject him to military discipline under national authority.

Some individuals believe that an imbalance exists in the "nation's historiography" because of the numerous studies on the American Civil War. Most people do not share this view. At the opposite end of the spectrum are those who support the need for still more works on this pivotal period in the nation's past, particularly in view of a trend that began in the late 1960s "to read the Civil War out of American history."[1] Regardless of the merits in support of either position, the literature is indisputably massive. In addition to countless journal articles and dissertations, over fifty thousand books have appeared on several of the war's aspects.[2]

Despite this abundance of secondary source material, there is no "adequate" study on the Civil War draft in the North or South, as James M. McPherson identified recently in his *Battle Cry of Freedom*.[3] The reasons for this void are understandable. Any conscription system influences all sectors of a society; its impact is not confined solely to political and military decisions. A draft affects all individuals and their families in one form or another. In turn, this human dimension generates certain perceptions and emotions, and adds to the multitude of contemporary opinions on what the draft means to these people and to the society in which they live. By virtue of conscription's all-encompassing nature, and given its complexity, a definitive analysis by a single individual often cannot be achieved. Instead, it requires cumulative knowledge through the contributions of many persons over time.

This problem is compounded by the availability of primary source material. Where it is virtually nonexistent, few good studies, if any, can result. Where it is abundant, a consensus of historical opinion on a particular issue often proves elusive.[4] An important factor too is that certain unfounded contemporary opinions are perpetuated in later studies and historians, even with the benefits of time and distance, sometimes find it difficult to separate myth from reality. These continuing differences of opinion nevertheless add to the body of literature. The central purpose of this book, which draws partly on past contributions and relies on various collections of primary source material, is to provide a general, but analytical, history of the Civil War draft in the North.

The debts I have incurred since the inception of this study are numerous. Like others who have labored in the arcane windings of archives, libraries, and manuscript repositories, I need not emphasize the deep gratitude that we have for those archivists, curators, and librarians who go above and beyond the call of duty to find the sources we need. They are the unsung heroes who collect, preserve, and help locate those materials that provide the nucleus for scholarly studies. Rather than risk offending a single person through the unintentional omission of a name, I wish to extend a collective thank-you to all who helped me along the way.

My appreciation extends as well to the Kent State University Libraries and other university agencies for support over the years while this work was in progress. This assistance came in many forms including the award of a sabbatical in the spring of 1989 so I could finish some remaining research and begin writing this study. The Office of Research and Sponsored Programs also deserves special mention for providing a series of matching grants so I could hire qualified student assistants to help with extracting the extensive data that I had arranged to microfilm at the National Archives. Without the diligent assistance of students Joyce Moore, Mary Morris, and Maria Murray, this extended phase of my research probably would not have seen completion.

Of the individuals (including anonymous readers) who examined earlier versions of the manuscript, three in particular—John Whiteclay Chambers II, John T. Hubbell, and James M. McPherson—warrant special thanks for taking time from their own busy schedules to offer comments and detailed analyses on various occasions. The final product has benefited immensely from their suggestions. They are, of course, absolved from any blame because any remaining errors are mine alone.

The aforementioned persons and agencies made this study possible. However, the following five individuals contributed in one form or another to the probability of it being done. John F. Gorman made me aware that all things were possible. Aunt Mal and Uncle "Dutch" Rice opened their home to generations of nieces and nephews and, in my case, provided the opportunity to continue my education at a critical juncture. From the beginning of my work with the draft, John T. Hubbell has been a constant source of assistance and encouragement. I have saved my greatest debt and deepest appreciation for last. Throughout this entire project and other endeavors, my wife, Linda Leigh, has been unwavering in her devotion and support. In my otherwise monastic existence while this work was in progress, she has always been there to remind me that there is a life beyond the Civil War draft.

INTRODUCTION

One of the most significant periods in America's history occurred in the four short years from 1861 to 1865. In many ways, the Civil War represented a watershed between the transition from localism to the nascent nation-state. The emphasis on states' rights was replaced by increasing centralization at the federal level in military affairs, fiscal policy, and other areas. At least in theory, freedom for all Americans had been achieved. The sweeping political, economic, and social changes that took place during the war influenced the nation's destiny well into the twentieth century.

The principle of national conscription was established during this conflict, but many of the system's peculiar features, such as commutation, were abandoned in favor of other policies and the needs of the moment. As so ably described by John Whiteclay Chambers II in *To Raise an Army: The Draft Comes to Modern America,* an American citizen's military obligation is constantly changing. It has evolved through a series of six distinctive stages beginning with the "*Settlement Model*" through the current "*World Power Model.*" Accordingly, each generation has had to redefine its policy and develop a system compatible with various pressures, including external threats, socioeconomic needs, and perhaps most important, the extent to which a distasteful program is acceptable to those faced with the prospect of being drafted.[1]

Civil War conscription falls within Chambers's "*New Nation Model*" phase of American military history. This stage ranges from the 1790s until 1917, when the Great War ushered in the "*Nation State Model: wartime national mass mobilization.*" Structurally, the "*New Nation Model*" represented a blend of locally and nationally organized units consisting of three basic components: a small regular army, local militias, and federally controlled U.S. Volunteers. The tradition of voluntarism in particular provided the federal government with the flexibility for expanding its manpower base and creating a wartime army whenever the need arose. Before World War I, the only significant aberration from this pattern came in the last three years of the Civil War, when both the Union and the Confederacy chose to "confront national conscription as a means of raising their wartime armies."[2]

On a limited scale, drafting had been used locally before 1861 to meet a variety of military predicaments. During the Revolutionary War some areas resorted to local drafts, but most relied on citizen-soldier volunteers to fill quotas. Enticements included bounties in the form of land or money.[3] Where local drafting was necessary, many areas allowed their citizens to avoid actual service in the militia by furnishing a substitute or by paying the equivalent of a commutation fee in the form of a fine.[4] These practices were accepted and, in varying degrees, were utilized in both the North and South when they instituted their more federalized drafting systems. In deference to the ingrained tradition of the citizen-soldier, Civil War drafting never totally replaced recruiting but instead proceeded on a parallel course with voluntarism.[5]

When the United States Congress turned its attention to a nationalized form of conscription in July 1862, it had only weak precedents on which to draw. The militia acts of May 8, 1792, and February 28, 1795, reflected the cautious attitude that Americans had toward a standing army and a strong executive. The first enactment authorized the enrollment of all able-bodied men between the ages of eighteen and forty-five for service in local militia companies. These companies were subsequently organized into larger military units under the direct command of the state governors. The president, however, was not empowered to call the militia into federal service.

Some of the weaknesses in the 1792 law were rectified three years later. The act of 1795 explicitly authorized the executive to order the militia into federal service for suppressing internal rebellion or for repelling foreign invasion. Permission from the legislatures of the affected states was required, or if they were not in session, from the respective governors. The act further stipulated that no militiaman was to serve under federal authority for longer than three months in any one year. Nor did the law give the executive any power to order a draft in dire emergencies when volunteering alone failed to meet troop requirements.[6]

The need for this authority surfaced at a critical hour during the War of 1812. When some New England states refused to provide their assigned quotas, President James Madison asked Congress to enact a conscription law that would have authorized him to draft eighty thousand militiamen into the regular army for two years. But before the proposed legislation cleared Congress the war ended, along with any further discussion on the subject. Between the battle of New Orleans and the attack on Fort Sumter, the militia system fell into disuse in many regions, and the United States depended solely on volunteers to meet its extended military needs. Indeed, the regular army, which was augmented by volunteer regiments, had done "so well in Mexico" that the government saw no need to consider any changes in the raising of troops between the Mexican and Civil wars.[7]

*S*imilar to the mobilization systems that emerged to meet America's military manpower needs in the twentieth century, the Union draft followed an evolutionary pattern. By the second summer of the war, the Thirty-seventh Congress had passed the first of two pieces of enabling legislation. It authorized the Union government to conscript men for a limited period in those states that had deficient or nonexistent laws. After a few days of debate, Congress endorsed a final version of the Militia Act and President Lincoln approved it on July 17, 1862. A weak measure, it had to be replaced the following winter with the Enrollment Act of March 3, 1863. Like its predecessor, the 1863 law also required substantial revision. It contained so many deficiencies that the Thirty-eighth Congress substantially altered the original Enrollment Act three times in less than fifteen months.

The legislative course of the Civil War draft in the North is discussed in my dissertation, "A Lesson in Trial and Error: The United States Congress and the Civil War Draft, 1862–1865." The detailed, and at times protracted, analysis of the various draft laws, roll calls, and voting behavior has helped to correct misconceptions about the passage of these laws. Nevertheless, the political machinations that occurred in Congress are only one part of the Union conscription system. For information on the parliamentary maneuvering that transpired, or for detailed accounts of the debates and the substantive basis for my roll call analyses, exact page references to my dissertation or the *Congressional Globe* are provided when the individual laws are discussed in this book.[8]

The present study is much broader in scope than my dissertation and fundamentally concerns how the Union draft evolved, and how it affected Northerners and their attitudes toward the draft. The principal focus is on matters directly related to conscription rather than on other mobilization issues, such as logistics and general recruitment policies and practices. Various scholars have covered these subjects at length, particularly Eugene C. Murdock, Fred A. Shannon, Herman Hattaway, and Archer Jones. Others, such as John Whiteclay Chambers II, Theodore Hershberg, Gerald F. Linderman, James M. McPherson, and Bell I. Wiley, have contributed in other substantial ways, especially in their discussions of general trends and specific events. Draft resistance continues to attract the attention of scholars, and dissertations by Grace Palladino and Robert E. Sterling proved of particular value.

In an effort to assess how the draft affected Northern citizens, I relied heavily on manuscript collections, archival records, and other primary material. Among the more important of the printed sources is the massive set of *Official Records of the Union and Confederate Armies* and the full *Final Report* of Provost Marshal General James B. Fry. An abridged version of Fry's report is available in the *Official Records,* and it is cited whenever possible because it is more readily accessible to researchers.[9] Through the use of these sources, this study addresses one question in particular—namely, whether the draft made the Civil War "a rich man's war and a poor man's fight." My search for usable data on this subject was much more involved than I had anticipated and, for the benefit of those who later venture forth into the voluminous records of the provost marshal general, I have recorded some of my experiences in the appendix.

This study also attempts to chronicle the influences that culminated in the peculiar aspects of the Northern conscription system. In a way, the development of the federal draft policy mirrored President Abraham Lincoln's approach to emancipation. Although national conscription was a revolutionary concept, it was an evolutionary process. This is not to suggest the existence of a conscious, long-term Northern plan for compulsory military service. Quite the contrary! Federal officials favored a short-term approach that emphasized placing men into the Union army in the least objectionable way possible and with a minimal impact on Northern industry. They seldom initiated any measure that ran counter to this rather pragmatic view; but when necessary, they could and did respond to pressures from various groups who demanded changes. The Union conscription system, however, appeared harsher than it really was. Despite contemporary beliefs, the actual draft did not disproportionately fall on Union men to any great extent, although it placed a tremendous burden on communities.

To capture the essence of this gradualism, chapters 3, 4, 5, 9, 10, 12, and, to some extent, 1 and 11, follow a chronological format. In addition to a brief history of conscription in the Confederacy, chapter 1 identifies the key events between the attack on Fort Sumter and July 1862 that set the stage for the Union draft. Chapters 3 and 5, and parts of chapters 10 and 12, discuss the legislative aspects of the draft system. The chronological order, however, is not intended solely to provide a narrative history in the strictest sense of that term. Besides telling the story, this approach serves to identify and elucidate certain trends that occurred over time.

Certain subjects transcend narrow chronological limits, and they are addressed in the remaining chapters. An overview of the bounty system and the importance of Massachusetts senator Henry Wilson are examined in chapter 2. The focus is not on the bizarre and colorful incidents of bounty jumpers and the competitive nature of the bounty system (these subjects are covered extensively in Eugene Murdock's works), but rather the emphasis is on key developments that influenced conscription in the North. In chapter 6, Provost Marshal General James Fry, an overview of how the draft worked, and general recruiting practices are discussed. One of the most problematic areas in Civil War studies is the conflicting information that exists on quotas and credits. Chapter 7 seeks to resolve some of the aspects of these confusing figures. Chapter 8 contains tables and general data on Union recruits, drafted men, and those who failed to report. Based in part on these profiles, it addresses the extent to which the draft affected men of various occupations, age groups, and nationalities. In a related vein, the impact of commutation's repeal on working men is examined in chapter 11. Within a broader context of American history, the issues of "a rich man's war and a poor man's fight" and whether the draft "worked" are among the subjects examined in the conclusion.

Brief historiographical surveys appear in certain chapters where appropriate, but my article, "Civil War Conscription in the North: A Historiographical Review," should be consulted for the most complete survey.[10] Also, throughout this study I have avoided the use of twentieth-century terms such as "draftee," "inductee," and "commuter." I have relied instead on nineteenth-century terminology that defines a "drafted man" as one who was actually held to service before he exercised an option of paying commutation, providing a substitute, or entering the army as an actual conscript.

In considering the various directions I could have taken with the present study, I selected one that I hope will add to the earlier works done by my predecessors. No doubt some of my conclusions, like theirs, will place this study in that genre of works that "promise to elude consensus for generations to come."[11]

WE NEED MEN

VOLUNTARISM

Raising an Army the "Old Way"

T he Union government suspended volunteering "just when the rebels commenced their conscriptions . . . [and] the results are before the country," complained the Democratic editor of the *Chicago Times* in early July 1862.[1] Much had happened in the months between April Fool's Day and Independence Day. Within two weeks after the North closed its recruiting offices on April 3, the Confederacy had enacted a conscription law. That same month General George B. McClellan began marching his Army of the Potomac toward the Confederate capitol at Richmond. This combination of events led Northerners to believe the South was on its last legs and that the conflict pitting brother against brother would soon be over. All that remained was for McClellan's army to administer the final blows.

The North's hope for an early victory had all but died by July, McClellan's army had suffered tremendous casualties in some of the severest fighting to that point in the war, and his troops had retreated toward Harrison's Landing. Almost three years would pass before the Union army was as close again to Richmond. A turning point in the war had occurred, and by mid-July the North too would take its first step toward national conscription.

Almost four months before President Abraham Lincoln approved the North's first draft law on July 17, the Confederate Congress passed its first conscription act at the instigation of President Jefferson Davis.[2] The South could not rely on high bounties in raising troops because it lacked the financial resources of the North, and the Confederacy was desperate for men.[3] This need was reflected in the enabling legislation of April 16, 1862. Among its major provisions was a clause that arbitrarily extended the service term of one-year volunteers for another two years. Under the terms of their original enlistments, these soldiers were due for discharge in May 1862. The law was also designed to "force other able-bodied men into service."[4]

Unlike the North, which ultimately relied on a system of *universal* liability for men in specified age groups, the Confederacy pursued more of a *selective service* approach through the explicit exemption of men in certain occupations. This basic philosophy surfaced when the Confederate Congress passed supplementary legislation on April 21 that exempted governmental officials, certain clerks, various individuals in the transportation and communication sectors, workers in some industries (such as mines and foundries), hospital personnel, ministers, one druggist per apothecary, and many of those employed in the field of education. The secretary of war was authorized further to excuse men in other pursuits, such as cotton and wool production, if he deemed it necessary.

The passage of the April 21 measure opened the floodgates to other groups who appealed for special consideration. In an effort to meet the diverse demands for raising troops, while also attempting to ensure that certain classes of individuals remained on the home front, the Confederate Congress repeatedly "made and unmade exemption laws" during the next three years. Some workers lost their special status only to regain it later. Soldiers in certain occupations were furloughed to work in the civilian sector after they had been drafted. Many abuses also surfaced. Teaching suddenly became a "popular" pastime, numerous apothecaries opened that resembled little more than "variety stores or produce depots," and the competition for an appointment to a minor sinecure led to corruption. Some men even paid as much as five hundred dollars for the privilege of becoming a bailiff or a postmaster in some remote locality.[5]

Money could be used in other ways, as well. No other section of the Southern draft caused greater difficulty than a provision in the original exemption act that authorized substitution. This action, and a change in October 1862 that excused individuals who were responsible for supervising twenty or more slaves, lent credence to the charges of "a rich man's war and a poor man's fight." The apparent class discrimination resulting from these policies understandably offended those Southerners who had no choice but to go to war.[6]

To further complicate matters, the machinery for drafting was not established in some areas of the South for more than a year after the legislation was passed. Much to the displeasure of the Bureau of Conscription, field commanders began raising troops on their own initiative. The bureau also had to compete with a recruiting system that coexisted with the draft. Overt challenges to the system came as well from influential governors, such as Zebulon B. Vance of North Carolina and Joseph E. Brown of Georgia. Vance objected most strenuously to the conscription of those individuals who were needed in the home guard, while Brown attacked the very essence of this nationalized approach to raising an army by claiming that it violated states' rights.[7]

National conscription in a governmental system that rested on the preeminence of states' sovereignty was a paradox with which Davis constantly wrestled. In addition to complaints from governors, Davis's vice-president, Alexander H. Stephens, openly criticized the system for "being radically wrong in principle and in policy." Complaints not only contributed to public criticism but also led to more substantive actions. By the war's end, numerous legal suits calling the draft system into question had been filed. These suits culminated in judicial reviews by the supreme courts of Alabama, Georgia, Mississippi, North Carolina, Texas, and Virginia. All of them sustained the constitutionality of the Confederate draft system.[8]

Aside from these challenges, the most important consideration that the Confederate government faced in sustaining its army was how to reconcile the needs of its army with the needs of the home front. Efforts to resolve this issue resulted in repeated changes to the conscription and exemption laws, particularly in September and October 1862, May 1863, February 1864, and March 1865. At the same time, the government recognized an ever-pressing need to expand the existing pool of available manpower. This continuing effort assumed a variety of forms including the repeal of the substitution privilege in 1863, and a gradual increase in the ages of liability from a range of 18 to 35 to a broader range of 17 to 50.

Although these changes demonstrated the dire need for more men, the most dramatic indication surfaced in February 1864 when the Confederate Congress finally authorized the use of free blacks and slaves in noncombatant capacities. Although some high-ranking officials, such as General Patrick Cleburne, had proposed arming blacks as early as 1863, this radical proposal did not receive serious attention until the winter of 1865. By that time the need for troops had become so critical that General Robert E. Lee lent the prestige of his position to the desirability of using blacks in a combatant role. As an incentive to entice them into the ranks, he further recommended emancipating any slaves who served and extending freedom to their families as well.[9] The cycle of desperation in the quest for men had come full circle but arrived too late to be of any consequence for Confederate forces in the field.

Despite the North's fundamental differences in the approach to drafting, especially in determining whether men were liable on a *selective* or a *universal* basis, it would later experience many of the same difficulties that plagued the Confederate conscription system. In raising and sustaining an army, both regions had much in common. Many of the same influences that motivated Northern men to enter the ranks in the early days of the war also had encouraged Southern men to do likewise. Not only did they share a common heritage and culture, but men in both areas believed they were fighting for "freedom," although they defined it differently.[10]

Immediately following the attack on Fort Sumter, more men had volunteered than could be accommodated. In the North, new recruits were caught up in a festive air created by rallies and speeches that were organized in their wards and townships. As the soldiers marched off to war, communities turned out en masse to see them leave on what was expected to be a brief sojourn to the South.[11] While local pride was important, other communal influences were also at work. Some men wanted to serve with friends and neighbors who shared common interests. They joined special units that were organized around activities such as temperance or education. Most conspicuous of all were numerous ethnic units, particularly among the German and Irish populations. At least in the early days of the war, they competed with each other to fill regiments in an effort to demonstrate the intensity of their patriotism.[12]

A belief that the war would end in a few months had encouraged many short-term enlistments of three months' duration. The Union defeat at the First Bull Run in July 1861, however, awakened the North to the possibility of a protracted conflict. Although the battle helped to stimulate enlistments that summer, it also contributed to dissatisfaction in some federal units.

One episode in particular had long-term ramifications on the federal government's authority to continue recruiting soldiers for three years "unless sooner discharged." The First Minnesota Volunteers, who later served with distinction at Gettysburg, in July 1861 consisted of green troops with a mix of enlistment terms ranging from three months to three years. At Bull Run, these inexperienced men were poorly led and suffered more casualties than any other federal unit on the battlefield. In addition to a general dislike toward their commanding officer, men with families came to realize the effect that an absence of three years would have on their "farms and jobs." Consequently, some of the three-year men in the regiment attempted to have their enlistments nullified on the pretext that recruiting officers had failed to follow proper procedures. Their efforts led to litigation that culminated in *United States v. Colonel Gorman*. This decision essentially upheld the constitutionality of legislation that Congress had passed on August 3, 1861, which had retroactively authorized President Lincoln's May 3 call for three-year men. Equally as important, the validity of the three-year "enlistment contract" was sustained.[13] Had the decision been reversed, other unhappy soldiers would have followed suit. Fortunately for Union authorities, the legality of their recruiting methods was upheld early in the war and they did not have to consider other alternatives, such as arbitrarily extending the enlistment terms of their soldiers, as the South did in the spring of 1862.

Length of service was only one among several immediate concerns that the North faced in that first critical year in sustaining its army.[14] Poor field conditions were one of the most important factors in deterring enlistments. Although homesick soldiers have always complained, the grievances of the early Union soldier were generally justified. Disease ravaged many units because of inadequate accommodations, shoddy equipment, and inferior supplies. One surgeon attributed the loss of over half the men in his unit to fatigue, malaria, measles, typhoid fever, and other sicknesses brought on as a result of the men sleeping "on wet ground in wet clothing, without tents." In a virulent letter home, the commander of this brigade was especially critical of the Quartermaster Department for the "neglect, mismanagement, incompetency, & probably dishonesty" in its failure to provide properly for his troops.[15] Another officer advised a friend to stay at home rather than idle away his time "in camp."[16]

Such letters home contributed to the erosion of the volunteer spirit. Enlistments had begun to slow by September 1861, and by the winter of 1861–62, virtually all incentive to enlist was gone. The Midwest had exceeded its assigned quotas in 1861, but a general disgust with the progress of the war to that point had begun to permeate the region. The malaise was exacerbated by an economic depression that had resulted from the closing of the Mississippi River.[17] Another influential factor was the inactivity of the Union army in the eastern theater. In response to constituents, one Ohio congressman promised to oppose any further increases for General George B. McClellan's "comparatively useless" Army of the Potomac until it moved forward and accomplished something besides endless drill.[18] At the turn of the new year, one Ohioan wrote that "unless the army does something [,] no more volunteers can be obtained . . . a Bull Run is better than the do nothing policy."[19] The human toll of war also was becoming more and more salient; one person observed that "I never pass the express companies without seeing one or more coffins."[20]

Reality had set in and Northern men gradually became less willing to enlist. In addition to the war's visible human cost and military inactivity, other reasons also contributed to this change in attitude. Accusations of mismanagement began emerging when troops arrived at rendezvous points and found insufficient arms and clothing for them, while other fully organized units were turned away. In December 1861, U.S. secretary of war Simon Cameron issued instructions that governors were not to send any more regiments forward unless they were requested to do so.[21] Other individuals were convinced that the war was designed solely to benefit corrupt contractors and overpaid officers, who disregarded the needs of the real fighting men.[22] Indeed, charges of fraud had become so pervasive by late 1861 that Simon Cameron finally resigned as the secretary of war.

Confidence in the Union army was restored with the appointment of Edwin McMasters Stanton as the new secretary of war in January 1862.

Although Stanton was an abrasive and generally difficult personality, his presence proved to be a vital addition to the Union cause. His organizational skills brought much-needed direction to War Department operations, and many of the obstacles that hindered recruiting were overcome.

Stanton nevertheless came close to irrevocably eroding public confidence in his ability when he made a critical error in judgment. In the twilight hours of April 3, a message arrived over the telegraph wires in communities throughout the North that gave residents reason to pause and express sighs of relief. After a year of uncertainty in which Union fortunes periodically rose and fell, Stanton issued General Order 33, which effectively discontinued further recruiting for the Union army throughout the North.[23]

The reasons given for this strange order range from "general mismanagement" to cost economy, but, whatever the motive, it proved to be "one of the colossal blunders of the war." One of Stanton's biographers believes that the secretary planned for the suspension to remain in effect for no longer than two months.[24] However, Stanton's intent was never communicated as part of the official order. Instead he required recruiting personnel to close their offices and sell the furnishings before returning to their regiments. In the interim between this order and June 6, when he formally rescinded it, Stanton on May 1 directed army commanders to requisition troops through the states. Eighteen days later, he requested the governors to begin raising new infantry regiments.[25] Despite these actions, the focus remained on General Order 33, and the reactions to it were predictable. Soldiers in the field doubted its wisdom and timing, particularly since existing regiments were understrength.[26] At home, newspapers criticized Stanton for the general confusion he had created and suggested that he was attempting to undermine the popular McClellan. Most important was the effect the order had on enlistments—they slowed to a "trickle."[27]

General Order 33 was the coup de grâce as far as Northern recruiting was concerned. Stanton avoided making a similar mistake again, and not until the end of the war did he issue another order suspending enlistments. Although he could control the flow of official mandates, he experienced more difficulty in finding remedies in other areas that influenced morale in the army and on the home front. The two most important issues involved timely pay and prisoner-of-war exchanges. These issues emerged in the first year of the war and, except for brief periods, remained uncorrected throughout the conflict. Both directly and indirectly they affected desertions, quotas, bounties, recruitment, and the draft.

On the prisoner-of-war issue, the Lincoln administration pursued a policy that generally discouraged any regular exchanges. In 1861 the principal motive behind this policy was a fear that any formal agreement on the release of prisoners would provide the Confederacy with a pretext for diplomatic recognition from various European governments. Congress was more responsive to the plight of Union prisoners, however, and on December 11, 1861, adopted a resolution that called on the administration to change its policy.[28] With some exceptions, the administration nevertheless remained firm in its position on general exchanges. This intransigeance stemmed in part from a policy of attrition that precluded contributing to the Southern army in any way, especially through the release of its battlefield veterans confined in Northern camps. Another important factor was the treatment of black Union soldiers in Southern prison camps. In May 1863 the Confederacy threatened to execute or enslave all blacks who were captured. Lincoln's reaction was immediate and forceful. He suspended further exchanges and threatened to retaliate. For every Union soldier who suffered abuse at the hands of Confederate authorities, Lincoln promised to respond in kind.[29]

The administration's prisoner-of-war policy made sense in terms of overall wartime strategy and, in retrospect, was probably appropriate if the war was not to be prolonged. Although the official position on exchanges deterred some men from enlisting, no other government policy had a greater effect in discouraging married men from volunteering than the indefinite postponement of soldiers' pay. In February 1862, for example, one unit had been in the field for almost six months but had not received a penny.[30] During the first year of the war, delayed payments did not create as much of a problem as later because many communities took it upon themselves to sustain a soldier's family in his absence. But these sources of local charity began to disappear as the war continued. Added to this trend was the fact that a Union private's pay of thirteen dollars a month remained unchanged from August 1861 to July 1864. This small sum could not begin to compete with wages in the civilian sector, which were steadily rising in response to increasing prices.[31] So acute was inflation that even most civilian salaries fell behind the cost of living in the Civil War North.[32]

Irregular pay periods and the difficulties they created for soldiers' families remained unabated until the end of the war. Indeed, as late as February 15, 1865, the government continued to follow the practice of deliberately postponing payments. In response to an inquiry from General Ulysses S. Grant on why his troops before Richmond had not been paid, Army Chief of Staff Henry W. Halleck replied that some of those in the West and South had been without pay for as long as eight months. He lectured Grant about the "want of money in the Treasury," the need for more military victories, and concluded that "if we pay the troops to the exclusion of the other creditors of the Government, supplies must stop, and our armies will be left without food, clothing, or ammunition."[33]

*T*he most important factor affecting Union morale stemmed from the battle-field, and by late June 1862 the evaporating hope for an early military victory had turned the Northern mood to one of despair. In the wake of the enormous casualties that the army had incurred in the Peninsular Campaign and McClellan's subsequent failure to take Richmond, an air of despondency came over the North and even penetrated the ranks of the Union army.[34]

In an effort to restore public confidence, Lincoln called upon various state governors for assistance in issuing a proclamation for three hundred thousand volunteers. In late June, he asked Secretary of State William H. Seward to meet with certain governors in New York City and have them jointly request that the president issue the call. If Lincoln had assumed this action on his own initiative, he could have created a public "panic," partly because of the criticism and confusion resulting from General Order 33.[35] But even at this late hour, the president had not lost all hope that victory was still possible that summer. Within days of his July 1 troop call, he cabled the governors that "if I had fifty thousand troops here *now*, I believe I could substantially close the war in two weeks."[36] Predicting the successful use of bounties, a few state executives replied with promises of prompt action.[37] But one member of Lincoln's cabinet did not share in this optimism. In a letter to a close associate on July 8, the same day that a conscription bill was introduced in Congress, William Seward confided his fear that a draft might be necessary. Before such an action could be taken, however, he cautioned that "we . . . first prove that it is so, by trying the old way."[38]

Seward's perceptive assessment of the situation was on the mark.[39] In a culture that valued voluntarism and a reliance on citizen-soldiers, these traditional methods of raising an army could not easily be abandoned in favor of conscription.[40] Despite a sentiment in some quarters as early as September 1861 that the North needed to begin moving in the direction of a draft, any attempt to do so before July 1862 would have foundered.[41] Voluntarism was a strong tradition, and nothing in those first fifteen months of war suggested that any other system was necessary. After all, Stanton had suspended enlistments at a time when the South found it necessary to enact a conscription law. Union men had flocked to the colors, and the problem was not so much in the number of men recruited. Rather, Northerners questioned how their soldiers were being utilized by generals who seemed to prefer drilling troops over committing them to battle. Most important, no attempt was forthcoming from governmental leaders to alter the faith placed in the sanctity of voluntarism. Instead, Lincoln and other leaders shared the public view that volunteering alone could furnish the necessary number of troops.

Unlike Jefferson Davis, Lincoln evidently never directly initiated a request for any conscription legislation or subsequent changes in the laws. After a measure was passed he defended various aspects of the system, and once he met privately with the House Committee on Military Affairs and the Militia concerning a proposed policy change. After his visit, he concurred in an official recommendation from Stanton concerning the repeal of commutation.[42] This endorsement occurred in June 1864, and on the basis of this singular quasi-initiative, one biographer traces Lincoln's silence on the draft to his belief that "Congress held the powers and the President was no dictator. . . . He was limited to *advising* Congress what the draft law should say."[43]

The lack of evidence on the president's role in "*advising* Congress" on the draft is lamentable, and his attitudes must remain open to speculation. Accordingly, the extant evidence suggests that on July 3 he believed the arrival of enough new volunteers could quickly end the war; and perhaps by July 8 he came to share Seward's private observation that a draft might be necessary. Certainly, he became aware of the prodraft sentiment among some of the governors who, as early as July 9, telegraphed him to urge his support for the draft law pending in Congress.[44]

Regardless of the level of Lincoln's direct involvement in moving the Union toward a federalized system of drafting, Northern practices in the mobilization of military manpower would never be the same again after the spring of 1862. Bell Wiley, one of the most astute and respected students of the Confederacy, believes that the South experienced its first serious morale crisis that season, and that "the turning point in the struggle [for the South] probably came in the spring of 1862 rather than in July 1863."[45] A turning point had also occurred for Northerners that season because it marked the last time for the duration of the war that they could virtually forget about military needs and quotas. Henceforth, they would be faced with continuous demands for more and more men. Communities still had the option of trying to meet these requirements through the timeworn methods of recruiting drives and volunteering; but, unlike the past, two new elements of drafting and a runaway competitive bounty system would be injected into the process.

THE SUMMER OF 1862

The Bounty System and the
Men from Massachusetts

W ithin the space of a few weeks in the early summer of 1862, Congress and various federal officials instituted two programs that had long-term ramifications for mobilizing Northern manpower. One fell within the framework of American tradition because it reinforced the reliance on bounties as the principal means for enticing men into the ranks. The other, the Militia Act of July 17, represented a departure from the past because it indirectly marked the first step toward national conscription in the North. To varying degrees, Henry Wilson, chair of the Senate Committee on Military Affairs and the Militia, would be involved in both of these programs. More than any other person, Wilson, through the development of the Militia Act, set the tempo and determined the general direction that the draft took in the North. He had a less pivotal but nonetheless important role in affecting the way in which future bounty payments were distributed.

The bounty system, which originated in the colonial period, was reinstituted within a month after the battle at Fort Sumter. In addition to monthly pay, each man who enlisted for three years became eligible for a one-hundred-dollar federal bounty upon his discharge. Many communities supplemented this incentive with programs of their own. Some made special efforts to ensure that their troops received certain amenities from home, such as socks, quilts, and dried fruit.[1] Many more chose to furnish extra pay. Wisconsin provided five dollars per month to soldiers with dependents, and Vermont granted an additional seven dollars and New Jersey an extra six dollars per month to their soldiers.[2] As the war dragged on, these supplemental allowances became critical to men with families, especially because of the slowness of military pay. Soldiers from states or communities that sponsored these programs knew that their dependents would have a minimal level of subsistence until the men returned home. Until July 1862 the bounty system functioned reasonably well because of the methods that were used in distributing bounty payments. Most sums were paid either in regular installments or in the form of a promissory note that became due on a soldier's release from service.

Historians often overlook this early bounty system and focus instead on the modified system that began to emerge by midsummer 1862 when a variety of widespread abuses characterized later Civil War recruiting practices. Foremost among the perpetrators were substitutes who deserted and bounty jumpers, who collected money in one locality only to desert at the earliest opportunity so they could enlist elsewhere for another amount. In one of the more extreme examples, one individual allegedly jumped bounty on thirty separate occasions before he and two other repeat offenders were apprehended and executed. These events, which often took place before full field formations, had a disturbing effect on soldiers who had to witness these "scene[s] of horror."[3]

Although these executions apparently helped to deter desertions and bounty jumping among those who had to observe them, the Union army as a whole was the system's greatest loser. Bounties affected army morale because men who had enlisted earlier in the war for a comparatively small sum often resented many of these newcomers.[4] In early September 1864, General William T. Sherman complained to Henry W. Halleck that "it has been very bad economy to kill off our best men and pay full wages and bounties to the drift and substitutes." A few days later, General Ulysses S. Grant noted that desertions accounted for the fact that the army was receiving less than one in every five new men who had been recruited.[5]

In certain instances bounty men were victims of the system because it fostered the rise of a professional class of brokers. For a fee, these agents found substitutes for individuals and often arranged to fill a local quota with men from other areas. As Eugene Murdock describes in detail, brokers often cheated many of these prospective recruits or substitutes out of a large portion or all of their substitute fee or bounty money. Also, the practice of retaining agents to fill a local quota usually led to higher bounties, which resulted in eligible recruits from poorer communities enlisting elsewhere. Unable to draw on a full complement of native manpower, poorer townships had no choice but to increase the burden of drafting on their remaining eligible residents. Communities ultimately became more concerned over filling quotas with paper credits than with physically qualified men.[6] This problem became so serious by February 1865 that Ohio's governor, John Brough, criticized the federal government in a sharply worded letter. Not only did he blame it for the abuses of the bounty system, but he also demanded that it eliminate all local bounties and impose a residency requirement for recruiting purposes.[7]

In an unusual display of unanimity on a draft-related issue, historians rarely depart from Brough's critical assessment of the bounty system. Emory Upton, in his seminal study of United States military policy, claimed that bounties were "vicious" and "were at all times potent factors of evil and discontent." Later scholars have added to this opprobrium. Ella Lonn, in her classic study of Civil War desertion, found that "the bounty, intended as an inducement to enlistment, became an inducement to desertion." Recruits were "noticeably inferior after 1862," and bounties became one of the nine major causes that enticed one in every ten Union soldiers to desert. Fred Shannon devoted parts of his two-volume study along with an entire chapter on the "mercenary factor" to the problems, and Eugene Murdock published three monographs that chronicle the numerous abuses of the system and activities of bounty jumpers who were little more "than common criminals."[8]

These and other scholars have left no doubt that pecuniary rather than patriotic motives dominated Civil War recruiting, particularly in the last two-and-a-half years of the war. Many questions nevertheless remain unanswered. For example, who were the typical bounty jumpers? Certainly some were the dregs of society and "common criminals," but bounty men came from all classes. George W. Peck, who later gained renown as the author of *Peck's Bad Boy*, was a bounty soldier who did not desert. The son of the American minister to Prussia, however, found himself writing from a guardhouse after his capture and detention for bounty jumping in the fall of 1863.[9] Likewise, some substitutes were scoundrels but others served honorably.[10]

Equally important issues are the number of bounty jumpers and the incidence of this activity during the war. Murdock, the foremost authority on the bounty system, concludes that statistics would be difficult to compile but suggests that "the great majority of them [paid soldiers] . . . intended to serve patriotically and did so serve."[11] While Murdock is correct that determining "how many bounty soldiers jumped" would be impossible, the evidence suggests that the problem became most acute in the last nine months of the war. By that time, the resident manpower resources of many communities were exhausted, and the nonresidents who filled local quotas felt no close ties or affinity with the communities that sponsored them. Indeed, as Grant remarked in early September 1864, the army was receiving less than 20 percent of all new recruits at that time.

Although figures vary on the total number of Union deserters, certain evidence confirms Grant's observation that the army was receiving relatively few recruits in the late summer of 1864. After the war, Provost Marshal General James B. Fry gave a final estimate of 268,530 deserters, but he cautioned that this sum included soldiers who had been absent for other causes, such as sickness and overstaying furloughs. Rather than deliberately avoid service, these soldiers voluntarily returned to their units. Fry believed that these unintentional

absentees comprised approximately one-fourth of all men who had been classified as deserters and that the true miscreants numbered 201,397. Ella Lonn
subsequently confirmed Fry's calculations when she arrived at an adjusted sum
of 197,247.

The number of unauthorized absences recorded by regimental commanders
during the war was slightly higher than Fry's figure of 268,530. In their monthly
reports, the commanders identified 278,644 men as deserters; 154,833 of these
absences occurred between April 1863 and April 1865. Consistent with Fry's
estimate and Lonn's later finding, and adjusting for a 25-percent reduction
in the subtotals, approximately 116,125 men actually deserted in the last two
years of the war. In the sixteen-month period from April 1863 to July 1864,
61,465 desertions took place at a monthly average of 3,842. After the third
federal draft call was issued in July 1864, 54,660 men deliberately left their
units with no intention of returning in the next nine months, for a monthly
average of 6,073.[12] Regardless of the calculations used, desertions increased
over 63 percent during the last nine months of the war, and high competitive
bounties were partly to blame.

Little is known too about the general policy that fostered the bounty system.
For example, historians agree with Civil War contemporaries that the purpose
behind bounties was to stimulate enlistments. Theoretically, only those men
who volunteered were entitled to bounty money, not those who waited to be
drafted. Section eleven of the Enrollment Act, however, specified that drafted
men "when called into the service shall be placed on the same footing, in
all respects, as volunteers . . . including advance pay and [federal] bounty
as now provided by law." Either through an oversight or as a humanitarian
gesture, Congress had inserted this curious provision and retained it until July
4, 1864.[13]

Why the federal government, especially by July 1862, continued relying
on bounties rather than reforming the military pay system remains unclear.
Alternatives might have included increasing monthly pay and ensuring that
the troops were paid in a more timely manner. A complete answer to this
question goes well beyond the scope of this study, but certain aspects need
to be identified because of the impact that government policy had on recruiting
and drafting. Aside from a general belief in the spring of 1862 that volunteering
and bounties could fill the armies, the government may have had more pragmatic reasons for avoiding significant modifications in the existing pay system.
Not the least of these was the dire straits of the federal treasury. In the spring
of 1862 many soldiers had not been paid for months because of other financial
obligations of the government. Not until the passage of the second Legal Tender
Act on July 11, which authorized the issue of another $150 million in green-
backs, did the Union government enjoy a respite from its financial woes.[14] This
reprieve did not last. By July 22, Secretary of the Treasury Salmon P. Chase

was concerned that he could not "meet necessary expenses. Already there were $10,000,000 of unpaid Requisitions, and this amount must constantly increase." Chase was hoping that Lincoln would remove General McClellan and thereby possibly restore public confidence in the financial sector.[15]

Given these financial circumstances, the government probably had no choice but to pursue a shortsighted policy that deferred payments to soldiers for as long as possible. This postponement largely accounts for the heavy reliance on bounties as opposed to increased military compensation and regulated pay periods. By the end of the war, however, the cost of bounties would assume astronomical proportions. In Murdock's most recent study he observed that "the amount [of a soldier's total bounty] went up as the war went on"; in his earliest work, Murdock calculated that the government ultimately distributed $300,223,500 in federal bounty payments.[16] This enormous sum was in addition to an estimated $286,000,000 that various states and communities expended in recruiting men to fill their quotas.[17]

Another factor was the belief in the spring of 1862 that the war would soon be over. Therefore, the long-term cost of the bounty system was neither anticipated nor was it a major consideration, because the federal bounty remained at $100 until late 1863 when it increased to $300 for new recruits and $400 for veterans who reenlisted. Furthermore, the program of recruiting at the local level caused communities to absorb a significant portion of the cost in filling their quotas. Whatever the primary reason, it is plausible to assume that these factors may have combined in June and July 1862 to preclude any concerted effort by the federal government to abandon or reform the existing system.

Despite the inconsistency in paying a bounty to drafted men, and the various factors that probably favored retaining the bounty system over other methods of payment, the original guiding philosophy behind the Union bounties at all governmental levels was to encourage enlistments. Even so, this inducement was limited to the army, and not to naval recruits, before February 24, 1864.[18] Although the methods used in distributing bounty payments through July 1862 worked from the perspective of curtailing abuses, Fred Shannon believes that bounties were "rather ineffectual as a stimulus to recruiting" in the predraft period. He bases his conclusion on the ground that recruits wanted cash in hand rather than a promise of future payment.[19] His finding has even more validity if the element of delayed military pay is considered. Certainly, by the spring of 1862, soldiers had begun to realize that they simply could not depend on the federal government to make timely payments.[20]

*B*y late May 1862, the Union pay policy was having such a detrimental effect on recruiting that Governor John Andrew of Massachusetts decided to force changes in federal policy. He became convinced that men were reluctant to enlist for a three-year term, and he insisted that the general government allow advance payments from federal funds to prospective recruits. Secretary of War Simon Cameron had suggested a similar policy in December 1861, but his recommendation remained in limbo until May 19, 1862, when Stanton asked the governors to begin raising additional infantry regiments. During the next week, Stanton vacillated between accepting some three-month men or holding firm on his desire for three-year men. By May 27, placing the onus on Lincoln, he directed that only three-year men would be accepted. Stanton also indicated that these new recruits would probably be discharged in no more than a year because of the progress of the war. Three days later, Governor Andrew proposed that all new three-year recruits be granted at least a month's advance pay, and the two-dollar premium that customarily went to a broker or person who encouraged a man to enlist. In a later communiqué, he also requested that these payments be made when a company was organized, rather than after a full regiment had been mustered. When Stanton quickly refused both requests, Andrew contacted Henry Wilson, the junior senator from Massachusetts, and asked him to intercede. On June 21, Wilson secured congressional approval of a resolution that authorized these two practices.[21]

Within weeks Andrew, with the help of William Seward, brought still more pressure to bear on Stanton. Unless a recruit could receive an advance payment of $25 from his $100 federal bounty, Andrew would refuse to join the other governors in asking Lincoln to issue his July call for three hundred thousand more volunteers. In a July 1 telegram a frantic Seward pleaded with Stanton to do something, even though he lacked congressional authorization. The "$25 is of vital importance. We fail without it," wired Seward. Given this urgency, Stanton capitulated and authorized the advance payment to be drawn against a nine-million-dollar allocation he had for organizing and drilling volunteers. Congress belatedly approved Stanton's action on the advance bounty in the following weeks. In this same section of the Militia Act, Congress also reaffirmed the intent to give each recruit a month's advance pay when his company was full. Through the person of Henry Wilson, Andrew had attained all of his desired changes for recruiting troops.[22]

The advance-bounty provision, however, returned to haunt both Stanton and Congress because it established the precedent that advance payments were permissible. Although Congress's intent was to authorize only a partial sum, with the balance payable in installments, the provision encouraged communities to add still more money to their coffers and to pay the entire sum in advance.

The effect of this policy quickly became apparent. A final report from Simeon Draper, the army's provost marshal general, to Secretary Stanton is particularly revealing. On December 6, 1862, he noted that approximately one hundred thousand men were absent without leave, and "many of them have received bounties, deserted, reenlisted, and deserted several times. Frauds to an enormous amount have been committed upon the Federal and State Governments . . . in connection with the bounty system."[23] According to Shannon, the Militia Act ultimately led "the states [and localities] into the era of competitive bargaining for recruits."[24] His assessment is correct but limited in scope. Had the communities adhered to a policy of partial advances, there still would have been competition for men. The environment that fostered bounty jumping, however, would have been greatly diminished through the use of installment payments.

Unlike most governors, who welcomed federal intervention in removing the politically sensitive issue of conscription from their shoulders, Andrew wanted to retain control over the state recruiting system.[25] He made his position very clear on August 7, 1862. Although he did not question the right of the government to order a draft, he indicated that the "new act is unconstitutional so far as it provides for officering militia, otherwise than as reserved to the States by the Federal Constitution."[26]

Andrew had different motives than most of his peers in resisting federal intervention. As the chief executive of the "most highly industrialized state in the Union," he wanted to make sure that he protected the state's business interests and supply of labor from being drained into the ranks of the Union army. The Bay State had a dearth of available manpower, but it had plenty of money and could afford to recruit men from other areas to fill its quotas. Accordingly, Andrew endorsed numerous schemes that promised to reduce his state's levies at the expense of other areas. He sent agents to Europe to enlist foreigners, to states that could not compete with Massachusetts's high bounties, and to the Southern states to recruit recently freed blacks. By the end of the war, Massachusetts would exceed its quotas, but the methods employed left the state "with a tarnished reputation for patriotism."[27] However, Andrew could not have successfully raised so many troops if not for the presence of Henry Wilson in his capacity as chair of the Senate Committee on Military Affairs and the Militia.

Henry Wilson epitomized the Horatio Alger legend. One of several children, he was born into poverty as Jeremiah Jones Colbrath at Farmington, New Hampshire, on February 16, 1812. By the age of ten he worked as an indentured servant on a farm, then later became a shoemaker's apprentice. Sometime between these experiences, he changed his name to Henry Wilson.

Largely self-educated, he gradually accumulated enough money to study law. This pursuit coincided with a nascent interest in politics. By 1840 he was elected to the Massachusetts State Legislature and became a Free-Soiler; he edited the *Boston Republican* from 1848 to 1851. During the next four

years, he joined the Know-Nothing party and led his state's antislavery delegation away from that group. In the early 1850s he entered the Massachusetts
Militia and eventually rose to the rank of brigadier general. In 1855, he was
elected to the United States Senate, where he remained until 1872 when he
became vice-president of the United States. He died in 1875 while in that
office.

One of the most significant periods of Wilson's political career came during
his tenure in the Civil War Senate. Identified as a radical Republican, he es-
poused an abolitionist philosophy that he demonstrated through his support
of various emancipationist measures. Among his colleagues, he enjoyed a reputation for hard work and persistence, especially as chair of the Senate Committee on Military Affairs and the Militia in the Thirty-seventh and Thirty-eighth
Congresses.[28] Although this committee was relatively unimportant in the prewar
years, it quickly became one of the most influential bodies in Congress with
the outbreak of hostilities. Indeed, it generated so many pieces of legislation
that some senators objected to the need to consider still another military bill;
but, at least during the Thirty-seventh Congress, Wilson usually gained approval for the substantive measures that his committee recommended. There were
a few significant exceptions. In August 1861 he managed to convince his colleagues to give retrospective approval to Lincoln's May 1861 call for three-year
men, but they rejected a proposal that would have sanctioned the president's
suspension of the writ of habeas corpus.[29] One summer later, he also failed
to persuade enough senators to approve a clause in the Militia Act that would
have freed the immediate family of *any* slave who served in the Union army
in any capacity.

Wilson's most thorough biographer, Richard H. Abbott, concurs with the
opinion that Wilson accomplished much as the chair of the Senate Military
Committee, but he believes that Wilson was tied too closely to the Bay State's
economic and political interests to be objective. Based on his experience in
the state militia, Wilson was convinced that voluntarism worked. This attitude
coincided with John Andrew's reluctance to relinquish any control over his
state militia and recruiting. When Wilson was "caught between the need for
troops and the need to protect Andrew's prerogatives," he "compromised"
first with the Militia Act, and more important, with the Enrollment Act. By
essentially abdicating his principal responsibility, Wilson left the North without
an "effective national" draft policy by March 1863.[30]

Abbott presents a persuasive case for explaining why Wilson was reluctant
to push for a stronger conscription system. Nevertheless, his generally valid
assessment is too severe in view of other circumstances. For example, he asserts
that Wilson tried to protect the militia system above any other consideration
when he first introduced the Enrollment Act in February 1863. However, other
senators "insisted on a stronger measure," which Wilson subsequently reported

out. A more recent view finds that Wilson had no choice but to prepare a revised bill because some senators insisted on protecting the state militias "from absolute presidential control." The original, not the later, version of Wilson's proposed federal conscription bill was much stronger. There is little doubt that Wilson compromised on draft legislation in the summer of 1862 because of John Andrew; but in the winter of 1863, he responded to the demands of Senate Democrats and Unionists.[31]

Wilson had to balance various concerns at any given time. Politically, he had to assuage John Andrew's wish to retain control of state recruiting. Most governors, particularly in the Midwest, were eager to transfer the politically sensitive draft issue to the national level. Wilson bowed to Andrew's desires in the summer of 1862, but he did not bend as far six months later in the wake of governors' complaints over quotas, overt resistance to the draft in some states, and a general reluctance on their part to order a draft of the state militias.

In the economic arena, Wilson also followed Andrew's wishes whenever he could. To minimize any disruption of the native industry, the governor sought to retain state control over recruiting so that Massachusetts, not the federal government, could decide who would enter the army in the event of a draft. The ever-diligent Andrew also looked to every conceivable source for recruits from outside the Bay State to fill his quotas. As part of this process, he and various influential businessmen constantly pressured Wilson to remain vigilant. Accordingly, Wilson resorted to a variety of tactics, which included introducing legislation, running interference with the Provost Marshal General's Bureau, trying to reduce his state's troop quotas through recruitment of Southern blacks, and supporting programs such as one that credited naval recruits to the place where they enlisted and not where they resided.

One of Wilson's most controversial actions involved his close association with the policies of commutation and substitution.[32] There was never any danger that he would forget his state's interests and needs. On more than one occasion when he defended these exemption practices, he commented that they had several virtues, including "the ability to retain at home the skilled labor necessary to carry on the industrial pursuits of the country."[33]

Wilson's approach to the draft and the exemption fee, however, were not driven solely by the need to protect his state's business interests. He also believed that commutation benefited the poorer classes because it held down the price of substitutes. Even Fred A. Shannon, one of the most ardent critics of these provisions and no fan of Wilson's, concedes that the fee suppressed substitutes' prices.[34] Contemporaries of Wilson also came to share his view that commutation helped the poorer classes. Democratic opinion in the summer of 1862 supported an exemption fee. The *New York Herald* and the *Cleveland*

Plain Dealer favored it as a means of contributing to a generous bounty fund for those who were drafted.[35]

Wilson had historical precedent and favorable opinion on his side when he first proposed an exemption fee in February 1863. Charges of class discrimination surfaced that spring and were largely a figment of the Democrats' imagination. Indeed, in one of the most dramatic reversals in public opinion during the Civil War, the Democratic press, which in March 1863 had assailed the exemption fee as "$300 or Your Life," became one of its strongest supporters by 1864.[36]

Wilson's origins and lack of formal education made him extremely sensitive, and he never forgot his working-class roots. He also respected individuals, and they reciprocated. One biographer, for example, notes that when Wilson operated his shoe manufacturing company, he enjoyed the "confidence and devotion" of his employees.[37] Had Wilson been interested solely in protecting his state's economic and middle-class interests, he would have supported the provision for substitution alone because the Bay State had ample funds to purchase the men needed. Until the end of commutation in July 1864, however, he tenaciously defended the fee as the only way that a poor man could avoid service. Indeed, by the winter of 1864 he was the only member of the Senate Military Committee who favored the fee's retention.

Commutation was not the only issue where Wilson could blend motives that were both pragmatic and personal. As an abolitionist he was committed to pushing the Lincoln administration in the direction of emancipation. The Militia Act provided such an opportunity and, accordingly, he persisted in his efforts to free any slave and his family who performed any service for the Union army. Perhaps Wilson hoped that slaves who worked in constructing fortifications might be credited ultimately against his state's quota. Nevertheless, given his ability to "compromise," Wilson's actions not only had the potential of achieving political aims but also ideological and personal goals.

THE MILITIA ACT
AND THE SUMMER
OF LOST OPPORTUNITY

The "late reverses at Richmond are very terrible and sad," wrote Senator Lafayette S. Foster on July 8, 1862. Other congressmen echoed similar sentiments, which reflected the general mood of gloom prevailing in the Union.[1] In the wake of McClellan's defeat, partisanship gave way to consensus as both the Republican and Democratic press called for stronger measures. In early July, the *Cincinnati Daily Commercial* declared, "Let us have a draft and that instantly." At the other end of the political spectrum, the *Chicago Times*, which was suppressed a year later for allegedly discouraging enlistments, appeared in the vanguard of Northern opinion when it suggested that the Union follow the South's example by invoking conscription.[2]

The atmosphere was ideal for changes that might enable the North to regain its momentum in prosecuting the war, and on July 8 Henry Wilson reported S. 384. After the Senate debated and amended the measure on July 9, 10, and 11, Wilson introduced a revised version, S. 394, which the Senate discussed and modified over a two-day period. On July 15, the Senate passed the Militia Act and sent it to the House of Representatives, where it passed with little difficulty.

This act, which marked the North's first step toward national conscription, provoked intense discussion, but not because of its military features.[3] Ostensibly, its main purpose was to enable the federal government to order drafting in certain states, but the measure was designed primarily to help guarantee blacks emancipation in exchange for Union service. Toward that end, Wilson and his fellow radicals wanted policies for employing blacks in the Union army as laborers; arming them for use as soldiers; emancipating (along with their families) those who served in the army, regardless of whether a loyal or disloyal master owned them; and compensating loyal owners who lost their slaves as a result of any of these policies.[4]

Had Wilson and his colleagues confined this legislation to the draft, rather than use it as a pretext for advancing their antislavery program, the Committee of the Whole, consisting of 12 Democrats, 4 Unionists, and 32 Republicans, would have spent little time on the measure. Much of what they wanted had already been incorporated into the Second Confiscation Act, but President Lincoln was threatening a veto.[5] To protect certain key provisions, Wilson and his fellow radicals surmised that Lincoln probably would support a conscription law even though it might contain certain disagreeable sections on emancipation. But most senators refused to endorse the Militia Act as a vehicle for wholesale manumission without some restrictions. With the assistance of conservative Republicans, particularly from the border states and the Midwest, the Senate Democrats and Unionists successfully prevented Wilson and his colleagues from gaining all of their primary objectives.

Wilson followed a strategy of introducing a bill that simply authorized the president to call the militia into service for as long as he deemed necessary and to have them conform to the standards of the volunteer forces. Once on the floor, the measure was opened to discussion and amendment. Shortly after Wilson presented the legislation, two of his fellow radicals, James Grimes of Iowa, who was a powerful member of the Senate Naval Affairs Committee, and Preston King of New York, who was a member of Wilson's military committee, offered amendments. On an "intensely hot" July 9, Grimes sparked the controversy when he moved changes to enroll all men between the ages of eighteen and forty-five, to authorize the president to organize black units, and to grant black troops equal pay with white soldiers.

Willard Saulsbury, a Delaware Democrat, demanded an immediate roll call. John S. Carlile, a Virginia Unionist, consoled his angry colleague with the observation that Grimes's amendment would be impractical because only the states possessed the power to determine the character of their militias. Preston King quickly rectified this oversight and moved three new changes. The most important of these proposals would have allowed the president to recruit blacks into United States service rather than state militias and to use them as laborers or in other "competent" service. This nebulous language, which the opposition correctly interpreted as authority to arm blacks, was made even more disagreeable when opponents of the measure learned of King's second modification. Under this amendment, any black who served in the Union army would be freed along with his wife, children, and mother. The third change would have appropriated ten million dollars to carry the first two provisions into effect.[6]

King had opened a Pandora's box. Saulsbury immediately denounced these changes as nothing more than "a wholesale scheme of emancipation." During the next three days of heated discussion, this general issue, and the arming of black slaves, became the crux of the controversy in the Senate. No senator would substantively question the desirability of employing blacks to relieve white soldiers from constructing fortifications and performing other arduous chores. The army's health was in a deplorable state because of soldiers having to work and serve in unfavorable climates.[7] Trouble surfaced within Republican ranks only when it was proposed to free those slaves who served the Union, to extend emancipation to their families and, to a lesser extent, to arm blacks for use as soldiers.

John Sherman of Ohio, a leading spokesman for the conservatives, initially favored manumission for those whom the government actually employed. During the first day of discussion, he stressed the right of the government to "deprive a father of . . . the labor of his son, and the master of the services of his slave." Over the next few days, he modified his original position and proposed to limit emancipation only to male slaves and their families who were owned by disloyal masters. He also objected strongly to the potential cost of compensated emancipation. Days later during the discussion on S. 394, he defended his position on the grounds that "if a slave of a loyal master is engaged one day in the employment of the United States, it will cost the Government $1,000 to pay him for that day's work."[8]

Conservative Republicans, however, were not of a single mind on the manumission issue. Jacob Collamer of Vermont believed that a slave's dependents could not be freed because a slave technically had no family, but he favored emancipating males who served and compensating their owners. Edgar Cowan opposed any form of monetary payment, while Orville Browning advised his colleagues to be careful in their application of some "mysterious . . . war power" as a pretext for transgressing on local institutions. Nor did they agree on the question of using blacks in other "competent" service. Browning, who had conferred with Lincoln on this issue just a few days earlier, and Cowan were firmly opposed to arming blacks. Collamer, however, strongly favored the authorization of black soldiers. Democrats and Unionists were generally opposed to arming blacks. Garrett Davis of Kentucky referred to earlier insurrections when otherwise docile blacks became "excited" once they had weapons. John B. Henderson of Missouri echoed Davis's concern but favored using blacks on construction projects.[9]

These diverse attitudes surfaced when the Senate voted on various amendments to S. 384. With the exception of a motion to postpone the bill indefinitely, the Democrats were highly unified in their votes on the six remaining roll calls. Republicans demonstrated a high degree of discipline on the questions of opposing indefinite postponement, limiting emancipation to males alone, and favoring the use of black soldiers. Sectional loyalty also played an important role in deciding these issues. Of the senators present for voting, the border state senators voted as a unit against those from New England. Generally, the senators from the Middle Atlantic and midwestern states sided with their eastern colleagues. Except on the issue of using blacks as soldiers, far western Democrats tended to align themselves with the border state men.

The voting on most of these amendments represented a clear victory for the Democrats, Unionists, and some conservative Republicans. In its final form, S. 384 specified that slaves could be employed in Union service, but freedom would be extended only to those who were rebel-owned. Slaves of loyal owners were to be returned to their masters, who would receive compensation for the period that their slaves were used. The only concession the radicals won came on the first roll call, which authorized the president to employ blacks in other "competent" service.[10] On this vote, most of the conservatives sided with their radical colleagues because of their attitude toward the adoption of strong war measures, which included the use of black soldiers.

Wilson was dissatisfied with this turn of events, and on July 12 he exhibited the stubbornness that occasionally surfaced in his dealings on conscription bills. He reported a new measure, S. 394, which incorporated many of the suggestions made over the past week. In deference to senators Cowan and Collamer, for example, Wilson's new proposal restricted the period of service to nine months and not to an indefinite period. It also authorized the employment of blacks as laborers or in other "competent" service to which the Senate had agreed. The proposed legislation went beyond the wishes of the Senate conservatives, however, because Wilson persisted in his quest to extend freedom to the family of any slave who served the Union.[11]

Within minutes after Wilson finished his introductory remarks, Sherman voiced his objection to the proposed legislation. He argued that the Senate had already decided who would be eligible for emancipation, and he moved to recall the controversial section. Lane of Kansas demanded a roll call and further proposed that the Senate authorize compensation to loyal owners rather than return a man to bondage once he had fought for his country. The vote proceeded, but the Senate lacked a quorum and could not take action until the following day. Sherman renewed the issue when the Senate reconvened, but he had significantly modified his position so that emancipation would be granted to any male and his family who met the dual criteria of Union service and rebel ownership. By a single vote, eighteen to seventeen, the Senate sustained Sherman's amendment.[12] The Democrats and the Unionists were unanimous in their voting, but unity among members of the majority party was nonexistent. The conservative elements had emerged victorious once again.

Following Sherman's victory over the persistent Wilson, Orville Browning reopened a question that had earlier divided his party when he proposed to delete the clause authorizing the manumission of a slave's family. A few days earlier he had contended that the measure would be impractical because a male could be owned by a rebel, while his family could be the property of a loyal master. Browning hoped to translate his opinion into law by limiting emancipation to males only. Not all conservatives agreed on the question of emancipation for Union service, and the split in this group became evident when the Senate voted on two proposed amendments. Browning's first proposal was rejected by a vote of twenty to seventeen. He proved more successful in attracting conservative Republican support when he moved to limit emancipation exclusively to rebel-owned slaves.[13]

The two days of discussion and voting on S. 394 were not confined solely to emancipation issues. A few senators mentioned the draft in passing, and one proposed a draft-related amendment. On July 14, Charles Sumner of Massachusetts proposed a modification that would have permitted each township to claim credit for all the men it enlisted, regardless of whether they actually resided in the municipality. Sumner received support only from Henry Wilson, the other senator from the Bay State. Radical Republicans could be very cohesive on emancipation issues, but unity disappeared when it came to troop credits. A fellow radical, James Grimes of Iowa, opposed Sumner's proposition because rich townships with liberal bounties would fill their levies with the citizens of poorer townships. Another radical, John P. Hale of New Hampshire, feared that the men in his state would enlist for the more liberal inducements in neighboring states, and Hale therefore would support Sumner's proposal only if it limited credits to state residents. Sumner's amendment ultimately was rejected without a division, although versions of his proposal would later reappear in other forms when the federal draft bills were being considered.[14]

An Indiana Democrat, Joseph Wright, made the only significant speech on the draft. He indicated his support of the bill, including the provision for black troops, but expressed serious reservations with the provision that authorized bounties. Before the vote on the bill's passage was taken, he urged his colleagues "to make an appeal to the patriotism of the country, uninfluenced by pecuniary considerations."[15]

After all remarks were entered into the record, the radicals made one last attempt to overturn the amendment that restricted emancipation to rebel-owned slaves only. With the Republicans split down the middle, the proposal lost by a fourteen-to-twenty-one vote. The bill, however, passed by a twenty-eight-to-nine margin. The Republicans experienced two defections, and the Democrats recorded their lowest level of party discipline.[16]

An analysis of general voting patterns among the senators on the individual roll calls reveals party loyalty as the dominant factor among the Democrats and Unionists. On nine of the thirteen roll calls taken they voted as a perfect cohesive bloc, then split over the final passage of the bill. Conversely, Republicans did not attain unanimity on any of the roll calls, and sectional cohesiveness proved to be an important factor in influencing Republican voting behavior. Conservative Republicans, particularly from the Midwest, voted along regional lines more than by party affiliation. They were not of a single mind, however, and were often divided on issues such as emancipating the families of slaves.[17]

The Union's first conscription law was never in danger of being lost in the upper house, but the Senate's concentration on manumission eclipsed the issue of drafting in the North. Similarly, it is difficult to gauge what congressional representatives thought about the bill's military aspects. When S. 394 reached the House on July 16, the Republican leadership acted quickly to pass the measure. The opposition displayed only token resistance, in part because of the success of Senate conservatives in limiting emancipation. Also, House Democrats such as Clement L. Vallandigham, who may have wished to consider the measure, had already returned home either to prepare for the forthcoming congressional elections or to assist in recruiting troops. Indeed, of the 108 Republicans, 46 Democrats, and 21 Unionists who were eligible to vote on this bill, only 71, 24, and 12 were present, respectively. The House had other legislation to consider as well before it adjourned the following day. To complicate matters, the remaining hours of the second session of the Thirty-seventh Congress were in danger of being consumed by a reconsideration of the Second Confiscation Act. Lincoln was still considering whether or not to approve this measure.

The opposition did not wish to postpone congressional approval of the Militia Act any longer than necessary, and their actions were merely perfunctory. A Pennsylvania Democrat, Charles J. Biddle, proposed opening the measure to debate. Thaddeus Stevens, the House Republican leader, objected and instead moved the "previous question" on the bill's passage. Before this action could occur, William S. Holman of Indiana moved to table the bill, which motion the House rejected in a seventy-seven-to-thirty vote.[18] This was the only House vote taken on S. 394, and the Republicans presented a solid front against the disunified Democrats.

When Lincoln signed the measure into law on July 17, it signified the first step toward a national conscription policy. The law, however, proved inadequate in many areas. Among the flaws was the vague definition of the relationship that now existed between the president and the governors in the area of drafting. Legally, the president possessed the power to interfere only in those states with deficient or nonexistent conscription laws. Although no state executive ever seriously questioned Lincoln's decision to order a draft on the basis of the Militia Act, the authority for his actions remained doubtful, because a literal interpretation of the act left only the governors, not the president, with the power to conscript citizens.[19] The arrival of the Enrollment Act the following winter resolved this ambiguity and affirmed "the power of the national government to 'raise and support armies' without state assistance."[20]

In its final form, the Militia Act consisted of sixteen sections. It required the enrollment of all male citizens between the ages of eighteen and forty-five for the future draft calls of their respective governors, and it extended the president's power to issue quotas from an earlier act in 1861. It further specified that levies were to be based on population, granted Lincoln the authority to call the militia into federal service for a period not to exceed nine months, and empowered the president to supplement the conscription laws of any state that had deficiencies in its drafting regulations. Other provisions concerned various subjects such as army organization, appropriations, and advance bounty payments. The bill also stipulated that blacks who entered Union service would be given ten dollars per month, which was three dollars less than what white soldiers received. This discriminatory practice was not rectified until the winter of 1864.[21]

Despite all the time consumed on emancipation issues, Wilson and his fellow radicals had achieved only partial success. They had not won freedom for all slaves, even when the provision was tied to compensating loyal owners, but they did manage to include clauses for emancipating slaves who served the Union and who were rebel-owned. Most important, they secured the provision for "competent" service, which had far-reaching ramifications in raising black troops. The language in the Militia Act was more explicit than what was implied in the ninth, tenth, and eleventh sections of the Second Confiscation Act.[22]

The battle over the twelfth section of the Militia Act, which permitted the use of blacks, and the thirteenth section, which restricted emancipation to rebel-owned slaves only, proved a clear victory for the Democrats, Unionists, and conservative Republicans, who wanted to hold the line on further encroachments into the realm of slavery. Nevertheless, Wilson and his colleagues had taken the proper course in approaching these issues. In the event that Lincoln carried through on his threat to veto the Second Confiscation Act, the radicals could always rely on the Militia Act to apply pressure on the president by giving him the necessary authority to use black soldiers and to emancipate at least those who were rebel-owned. Toward this end, the twelfth and thirteenth sections of the new draft law, which Lincoln would certainly sign, served as "insurance" to protect this segment of their antislavery program from possible catastrophe.[23]

The need for added protection and the desire to keep prodding Lincoln in an antislavery direction were the principal motives behind Wilson's decision to sponsor the Militia Act. Lincoln was threatening to disapprove the Second

Confiscation Act, but as president he could not very well veto a bill that resembled a conscription measure for strengthening the army. Further, in early July, Lincoln was reluctant to use black soldiers for fear of alienating white troops and the border states.[24] He revealed as much to Orville Browning on July 9, but by July 22 he had modified his position to allow the recruiting of free blacks. Slaves, however, were not to be used except under the most compelling of circumstances.[25] Lincoln did not communicate this policy very widely and hesitated to exercise his authority completely. He did not, for example, allude to the use of black combatants in his September emancipation proclamation, but he finally did so in his January 1 proclamation.[26]

The most direct piece of evidence that emancipation was the primary reason behind Wilson's introduction of the Militia Act is a June 7 letter from John Murray Forbes to Charles Sedgwick, a radical congressman. Forbes, a leading Boston industrialist, was also a close associate of John Andrew and Henry Wilson. Indeed, Forbes had a major role in recruiting men from other areas to fill Massachusetts's quotas. In his letter, he asked Sedgwick to find "some ingenious Hunker . . . to offer a simple amendment to the emancipation bill that shall provide for the freedom of any slave (and his family) who may serve the United States."[27]

Approximately a month later Wilson, with the assistance of other radicals, became that "ingenious Hunker" and reported such a measure. The Militia Act, while an ineffective conscription law, nevertheless facilitated emancipation for some slaves. Even more important for the future, it was the first measure to clearly authorize the use of black soldiers and was "a giant step along the road away from *Dred Scott* and toward abolition and citizenship status."[28] The subsequent military service of blacks would vindicate Frederick Douglass's judgment that now there would be "no power on earth which can deny that he has earned the right to citizenship in the United States."[29]

The full effect of this policy was not recognized until some eight months later. After that point, public resistance toward black soldiers gradually began to fade away as whites faced the prospect of being taken under federal conscription. The Enrollment Act may have been the "greatest single force" in encouraging black recruitment, but the Militia Act established the right of black men to become Union soldiers.[30] Indeed, after the controversial Negro Troop Bill finally arrived in the Senate on February 2, 1863, it was immediately referred to the Senate Committee on Military Affairs. Eleven days later, Wilson reported it back with a recommendation that the bill be disapproved because the authority to raise black troops already existed under the twelfth and thirteenth sections of the Militia Act.[31]

The measure of July 17, 1862, had laid the foundation for the acceptance of almost 200,000 blacks into the Union military. Approximately 168,000 entered army ranks after March 3, 1863, and roughly 76,000 blacks were recruited in 1863 alone. Aside from any ideological or altruistic considerations, their numbers represented roughly 9 to 10 percent of all Union soldiers.[32] In the last two years of the war, when white males were even more reluctant to enter the army, blacks comprised approximately 13.31 percent of the 1,261,567 estimated new soldiers who were raised. At least in this segment of the population and for the long term, the Militia Act contributed significantly to mobilizing Northern manpower.

Wilson was the wrong person in the wrong position at the right time for sponsoring a conscription bill. Although he had another motive, his subsequent actions do not necessarily sustain the view that he waged "constant warfare" against an effective draft law. In July 1862 he developed a bill that was within the framework of the volunteer tradition. It made enlistments and bounties preeminent and implied a threat of drafting. Had it not been for the issue of emancipation, Wilson might not have introduced a bill at all.

The Massachusetts senator nevertheless missed his greatest opportunity for gaining a strong draft law in the summer of 1862. As reflected in the widespread and bipartisan editorial support for strong measures in July 1862, and compared to later periods in the war, the public was receptive to any policy that would have systematically raised troops and demonstrated Northern resolve to continue prosecuting the war. Wilson alone cannot bear the blame for failing to take advantage of this prevailing sentiment, however, because he received little in the way of advice on what was needed. There was no presidential initiative and William Seward, though he wanted a draft law, did not provide any specific details. But, in fairness to Seward, he may have been dissuaded from offering too much advice. In a July 12 letter to his wife, he indicated as much when he revealed his frustrations in dealing with congressmen who wanted to emphasize the employment of slaves to "fight and work" rather than focus on a conscription bill.[33]

Furthermore, Wilson may not have been on the best of terms with Edwin Stanton in early July 1862. Stanton's authority had been circumvented recently when he was forced to capitulate on the advance pay and bounty questions. This action may have temporarily soured the relationship between Stanton and the chair of the Senate Military Committee. Stanton also was still adjusting to the demands of his new duties and was not in a position to recommend a draft system, though he did assume a more active role by the following December. In addition, Wilson could not draw on his counterpart in the House for support and guidance because Abram Olin was a weak and ineffective chair of the House Military Committee. Nor were Wilson's Senate colleagues of much assistance when the Militia Act was being considered. They offered relatively little comment and few suggestions on the draft-related provisions of the militia bill. They focused on emancipation issues instead, for which Wilson must bear full responsibility; as the bill's author, he decided to make this sensitive matter the primary aim of the measure.

With minimal guidance and constructive criticism, Wilson was left to his own devices, experiences, and preferences in developing the Militia Act. He could not know then, but this proved to be the most advantageous time he had for gaining approval of an effective law. In the months and years to follow, conditions changed dramatically. By the time the third session of the Thirty-seventh Congress convened in December, the mood of the North had changed from one of consensus to one of conflict, and this was reflected in the halls of Congress. To obtain approval of the Enrollment Act, Wilson had to make significant concessions to Democrats in both the House and Senate. His power to persuade with the prestige of his position was further eroded during the Thirty-eighth Congress. Not only did he encounter a new chair of the House Military Committee, who was fresh from the battlefield and anxious to make significant modifications in the draft system, but he also discovered that many of his Senate Republican colleagues shared the views of his counterpart in the House.

"BREATH ALONE KILLS NO REBELS"

The 1862 Militia Draft

ardly had the ink dried on the Militia Act when, on August 4, 1862, Edwin Stanton ordered a draft for three hundred thousand militiamen. Opinions vary on whether volunteering under Lincoln's July 1 call was progressing satisfactorily when the secretary of war ordered the August 4 draft.[1] At a cabinet meeting on July 22 the feasibility of a draft had been discussed, but no consensus had been reached. Later that day, however, Lincoln sent an order to Stanton that revealed he opposed drafting at that point because "we [would] not need more, nor, indeed, so many [men] if we could have the smaller number very soon." In this memorandum, he also gave Stanton the authority to conduct a draft, if necessary, but with the provisos that the men would be part of the three hundred thousand troops already called for on July 1, and that they would be placed in the old regiments.[2]

Whether or not Lincoln and Stanton saw a need to order a draft by early August, they certainly felt pressure to exert their authority. During the debates on the Militia Act, for example, governors urged the president to use his influence to have Congress enact a conscription law.[3] Within days after its passage, an Ohio Republican twice pleaded with Lincoln to order a draft because the present rate of enlistments would never keep pace with the manpower needs of the army.[4] Similar letters were sent to cabinet members in the hope that they could prod the president into acting. One individual suggested to Secretary of the Navy Gideon Welles that the North implement conscription in the border states to reduce the effect of a Confederate draft in that area.[5] Secretary of the Interior Caleb Smith promised to approach the president on the possibility of conscription. In a private memorandum to Stanton, Smith argued that drafting would have to be resorted to sooner or later. The military also pressured the secretary of war to take decisive action. On August 3, Major General Henry Halleck wrote Stanton to suggest that the government issue a call for two hundred thousand more men.[6]

Official support notwithstanding, the threat of drafting citizens during a civil war could have serious ramifications in the public sector. The administration, however, enjoyed widespread editorial support. In this summer of general cooperation, Republican and Democratic newspapers uniformly endorsed the use of conscription as a necessary measure in defeating the South. While the Militia Act was pending approval and weeks after Stanton had issued his August 4 order, the press gave virtually universal support to the administration. In an effort to justify the draft, one Republican newspaper, the *Cincinnati Daily Commerical*, maintained that conscription was beneficial to society because it prevented young, unmarried men from roaming the streets and causing trouble.[7] Another paper, the *Daily Ohio State Journal*, echoed these sentiments and criticized the previous reliance on volunteering because its success depended too heavily on external factors, such as the harvest season and high wages for laborers.[8] Other Republican newspapers in Ohio expressed similar opinions.[9] Dailies in other states also expressed no misgivings over the specter of drafting. The *Boston Daily Journal* contended that the government had finally revealed its desire to prosecute the war in "earnest."[10] The *Washington, D.C. Evening Star* recorded the enthusiastic responses of the various states to the August 4 order.[11] For several weeks, the *New York Times* had been criticizing the slowness of volunteering and emphasized that "if this war is to go on with any hope of success, *the country must resort to a draft of militia, and that immediately.*" It also favored the employment of blacks as authorized under the Militia Act.[12] This provision was a particular favorite of Horace Greeley, the abolitionist editor of the *New York Tribune*. When Stanton's order arrived, Greeley used this occasion to comment that

> nothing is said of the *color* of the conscripts, but 'all able-bodied *citizens* between the ages of 18 and 45' are to be enrolled. This would include Blacks; but as it has not been the custom in this State to enroll them, we presume they will be passed by as exempt. If a few hundreds more of our Democratic friends shall on this account be required to go, they, certainly cannot complain of it, and we shall not.[13]

Greeley's spurious implication was unfair to the Democrats, whose editors generally supported compulsory service during the summer of 1862. Many of them, however, did not share Greeley's advocacy of black soldiers in the Union army. The editor of the *Chicago Times* shuddered at the very thought of arming blacks but supported Stanton's drafting order without reservation. Indeed, the *Times* tended to endorse most administration policy that summer, including the arrest of the *Harrisburg* (Pa.) *Patriot* editors. These individuals had allegedly discouraged enlistments by falsely asserting that the government was planning to integrate blacks into all-white units.[14] Although James J. Faran, editor of the *Cincinnati Enquirer*, disliked the thought of drafting, he voiced no real objection to the Militia Act because "the State military authorities" would retain control of the process.[15] The *Cleveland Plain Dealer*, in its first editorial on conscription, asserted firmly that now "there need be no lack of men to crush out the rebellion." The president not only had the right to adopt but also the duty to enforce conscription and the arming of slaves, if necessary.[16] Another midwestern Democratic paper, the *Detroit Free Press*, defended the necessity for drafting and also supported the use of Negroes, but as laborers only.[17] The *Portland* (Maine) *Eastern Argus* shared these sentiments, while the *New York Herald* favored the draft because it would conscript abolitionists: "Alas, poor Greeley!"[18] Even the irascible Copperhead editor of the *Columbus Crisis*, Samuel Medary, lent his support to the draft during this summer of cooperation. He objected only to the provision for commutation that existed in Ohio law.[19]

In this receptive climate, Edwin Stanton issued General Order no. 94, which called for "300,000 militia . . . to serve for nine months unless sooner discharged." A few days later, on August 9, Stanton's office issued detailed instructions for implementing the draft in states that lacked functioning conscription systems. One of the more important provisions instructed each governor to appoint a commissioner and enrolling officer in each county. These agents were to be charged with preparing enrollment lists of all eligible men between the ages of 18 and 45. After these lists were revised to reflect men who were already in service, the names of the remaining individuals would be placed in a container from which a blindfolded man would select names until the quota was filled. These instructions further specified that the War Department, in consultation with the governors, would appoint a provost marshal for each state who would be charged with apprehending deserters. The order also allowed a drafted man to furnish a qualified substitute and authorized certain occupational exemptions. At least for a brief period that summer, the Union draft system resembled the one in the Confederacy. An itemized list excused high government officials, including members of Congress; workers in government-operated armories; postal and customhouse clerks; and select personnel in the transportation sectors. States with adequate legislation were free to decide what groups to exempt from military duty. Under these guidelines the draft was to commence on August 15 to compensate for any deficiencies remaining from the July 1 and August 4 calls. The responsibility for drafting rested principally in the hands of the governors.[20]

Despite the seeming clarity of these instructions, a series of misunderstandings emerged once the draft was implemented. Much of the initial confusion concerned quotas. The calls of July 1 and August 4 were intended to be distinct activities. The former called for 300,000 three-year men, and the latter required 300,000 nine-month men. Eventually, one three-year man was considered to be the equivalent of four nine-month men. Hence the two calls combined did not necessarily require a total of 600,000 new soldiers, but the equivalent of 375,000 three-year men. To further complicate matters, the original figure of 300,000 was adjusted upward so that the actual quota for each call was 334,835, or an aggregate figure of 669,670 for the two calls. These changes were never communicated properly, thereby increasing the governors' perplexity (This "confusing arithmetic" has also confounded historians).[21] In the final accounting, 87,588 nine-month men were raised under the August 4 call, and 421,465 three-year men volunteered under the July call, for a total of 509,053 new soldiers.[22]

The levies assigned to the individual states proved to be a major headache for the governors. By mid-autumn 1862, some governors were still struggling to determine their actual quotas. On October 31, 1862, for example, Governor Alexander Ramsey of Minnesota asked Governor Edward Salomon for his interpretation of Lincoln's August proclamation that concerned drafting for the old regiments. Ramsey could not obtain a straight answer from the War Department and had "embarrassing doubts" whether he should proceed with the draft scheduled for the following month. On November 4, Salomon replied to Ramsey's inquiry. He too had encountered many difficulties with the War Department and, after much futile correspondence, had decided to formulate his own policy. He advised Ramsey to "disregard the additional call for men to fill old regiments by draft" and to simply deduct the number of volunteers who enlisted in these units from Minnesota's quota. In the absence of clear guidelines from the administration, governors were forced to use their own judgment in filling levies.[23]

When the administration did act decisively, there was no guarantee that the governors would be pleased. Quotas were based on the number of citizens rather than the actual number of able men. This upset Governor Salomon in particular because Wisconsin had a large number of foreigners, and the draft would fall disproportionately on the remaining citizens. Lincoln apparently chose to risk a collision with the governors rather than with foreign nations if their citizens were conscripted.[24]

Many of the governors also were reluctant to enforce a draft. This reluctance stemmed in part from Stanton's orders of August 4 and 9, which specified that a draft would take place on August 15. This date was unrealistic because enrolling officers had to be appointed, enrollment lists had to be compiled and reviewed, and some states simply did not have a mechanism in place to conduct a draft. Governors consequently began asking for extensions on the basis that recruiting was progressing in their states and they hoped to fill all quotas with volunteers. Other reasons for postponement included the onset of the harvest season, a fear of resistance in some areas, and an unwillingness to have a draft before an election. Stanton had no choice but to grant these requests. He also had to rely on officials whom the governors had appointed to implement the draft. These appointees created a host of problems for the secretary because some of them abused their authority under martial law. Indeed, many of the criticisms leveled at the administration during this period "for arbitrary arrests and interferences with civil processes, must be directed to the untamable civilian provost corps." For this reason, Stanton later insisted on the appointment of military officers when district provost marshals were appointed under the Enrollment Act.[25]

The civilian provost marshals, however, constituted only one of several difficulties that Stanton encountered in trying to administer a law that depended so heavily on local custom and initiative. Without some semblance of uniform application, he and the governors often found themselves in awkward positions. A perception of unfairness in administering the draft within certain states, and differences between states, also detracted from public confidence in the militia drafting system.

The variations in exemptions that existed from state to state affected some religious groups in particular. Michigan refused to grant any religious exemptions at all. New York excused Quakers and clerics from service without the payment of a fee, but in Ohio they had to contribute two hundred dollars.[26] This policy finally prompted a group of Ohio Quakers to send an elder to Washington to meet with the president. John Butler arrived in early September 1862 and met with his old friend, Salmon Chase, who arranged for a conference with Lincoln. The president in turn referred Butler to Stanton. A few days earlier the War Department had authorized the exemption of all clerics with "pastoral charge of a church or congregation," but it was unwilling to extend this policy any further because it would lead to members of all sects and denominations demanding an unequivocal exemption. At the same time, Stanton was sympathetic to the plight of the Quakers and agreed to excuse any Friend who submitted an individual application to him. This policy, which essentially required the taking of an oath, was also anathema to Quaker principles, but Butler understood Stanton's delicate position. Shortly after Butler returned to Ohio, however, a military commander of a rendezvous camp in Cleveland held nine drafted Quakers because of their refusal to pay the two-hundred-dollar commutation fee as required by Ohio law. Butler immediately returned to Washington to confer with Stanton. In accordance with their earlier agreement, the elder presented affidavits from the nine men that testified to their conscientious scruples against war. Stanton then instructed Brigadier General C. P. Buckingham, his "chief clerk," to telegraph the wayward commander that "the

orders exempting Quakers from military duty, issued to them from this department must be obeyed, and the parties set at liberty."[27]

In addition to religious exemptions, New York State also excused several
other groups from service, including college professors, teachers, and students.[28]
The absence of such special dispensations in the neighboring state of Connecticut created a furor. Timothy Dwight of New Haven insisted that Yale students
and other university personnel were exempt from the military in accordance
with a 1745 document. That same day, Yale's president threatened legal action
if Governor William A. Buckingham failed to comply with the university's
charter. A student, apparently in attendance at a college outside the state, wrote
the governor and urged him to declare all Connecticut college students exempt
from the draft, regardless of where they matriculated.[29] Other individuals also
requested special consideration. Two private firearm manufacturers pleaded
with Buckingham to grant exemptions to their workers.[30] Another constituent
inquired about the possible release of corporate partners if one or more were
drafted, because serious harm would come to their business if all had to go
to war.[31]

In most states, a man could avoid such potentially disastrous consequences
to a business by simply furnishing a substitute. Although this practice helped
to minimize disruptive effects on home industry during the 1862 drafts, it
created another problem. As the summer wore on, the issue of a "rich man's
war and poor man's fight" began to surface. From Henry Wilson's home state,
the *Boston Daily Journal* attempted to defuse the potential divisiveness of this
issue as early as August 4, 1862. Many rich men were too old to go to war,
the paper contended, and the indispensable occupations of others simply did
not allow them to leave their businesses for very long. They contributed much
more to the war effort by remaining home. Nine days later in the lead editorial,
"Why Should the Poor Enlist?", this Republican paper argued that unlike the
world's poor, America's lower class had a vested interest in preserving society
because of the many benefits it conferred on all of its citizens.[32] Such opinions,
however, did little to alleviate the resentment of the men who were most affected. In late August, for example, Salmon P. Chase was informed that a poor
man in Cincinnati found it financially impossible to procure a replacement.
Men in similiar circumstances, some with as many as eight children, had no
choice but to enter the army.[33] Conversely, some poor men welcomed the substitute provision because they could expect to command sums ranging from two
hundred dollars to fifteen hundred dollars, depending on the geographical area
and at what point they entered the army.[34]

Some individuals who were either unwilling or unable to furnish a substitute relied on other means to obtain an official exemption from the draft. In
one Connecticut town, the selectmen who were responsible for compiling an

accurate enrollment list had conveniently deleted their own names from the sheets. A Vermont woman fearful that her brother would be conscripted wrote her uncle, the governor of New Hampshire, to ask that he use his influence to secure a post office appointment for his nephew. A Pennsylvania man informed his congressman that he had accepted a minor political appointment simply to escape conscription. Once the draft ended in his town, he planned to resign the position.[35]

In the absence of a sinecure, other individuals resorted to deception by obtaining a fraudulent exemption certificate from a dishonest surgeon. One doctor charged a mere five dollars for this service.[36] Part of this problem stemmed from the appointment of examining surgeons in their hometowns. With the welfare of their practices to consider, some bowed to the pressure and granted blanket medical exemptions to their healthy friends and neighbors.[37] In communities where physicians were more ethical, otherwise able-bodied men feigned illness or disability. In Maine, for example, "spectacles" came into vogue to correct sudden visual problems. An Ovid, Michigan, man had predicted that he would develop a severe case of "palsy" before winter. Although men were enlisting at a quick pace in this town, one observer thought that some men between 18 and 45 years of age were suddenly "sick or going to be or . . . [lose] a finger or a thumb or a great toe, anything for an excuse" to escape the draft.[38] These practices added to community anxiety because each irregular medical discharge increased the prospect of being drafted among those who had passed the physical examination.[39]

The uneasiness that accompanied the draft took different forms in Northern townships during the summer and fall of 1862. In the era before quotas were assigned on a district or subdistrict basis, many communities viewed drafting as a disgrace. Conscription carried with it a social stigma that connoted a lack of patriotism.[40] Local pride not only influenced men to volunteer but, depending on the stability of a community, could serve as a powerful deterrent to desertion as well. In two Long Island townships, for example, proportionately fewer men deserted from the more established community of Southhold than from the less cohesive township of Brookhaven.[41] This case study focuses mainly on the men who enlisted in 1862 and cannot be applied to the actions of later recruits because so many of them came from elsewhere and, therefore, had little if any attachment to their sponsors. But in 1862, local pride and community support were important motivating factors in filling quotas. Some townships were uncertain as to the exact quota required of them, however, and occasionally became irritated over the inconsistency between state and federal laws in determining local levies.[42] "Everybody is afraid of the draft" wrote one citizen on August 12. In this letter he also mentioned various bounties that amounted to a "handsome little sum of $200," the town's quota, and the fact that a "good many [men have] gone to Canada from the State."[43]

Draft evasion in the Civil War North was a widespread phenomenon. Under federal conscription, there were 161,244 skedaddlers.[44] The figures are less precise for the militia drafts, but estimates suggest that approximately forty to fifty thousand men evaded the draft prior to 1863.[45] Not all of them deliberately absconded: some were sailors at sea and were unaware that a draft was even being conducted, while others were included on the enrollment lists of two or more townships.

Those who intentionally left prior to 1863 largely did so for personal reasons rather than from any ideological or political motivations. One of the earliest cases of a Civil War skedaddler occurred in September 1861 when a state draft appeared imminent in Iowa. In a letter to a close friend, one citizen revealed that he was making sure he was "accessible to Canada" in case a draft was ordered.[46] This early aversion to military service reappeared with a vengeance within days after Stanton issued his August 4 draft order. Indeed, by August 8 he felt compelled to curtail widespread skedaddling to Europe and Canada by instituting a passport system throughout the North. Under this program, a draft-eligible male had to secure the written permission of his local marshal before venturing outside of his county. To leave his state, he had to obtain similar authorization from his governor.[47]

Although the War Department recalled this order a month later because of the legal difficulties that arose from its enforcement, editorial opinion supported the restrictions on movement.[48] Individuals who were disinclined to enter the military, however, viewed the matter differently. In a series of letters to William Henry Smith, later Ohio's secretary of state, a friend complained that Governor David Tod refused to issue a pass to him until he posted one thousand dollars bond to guarantee his return. He protested that he had no intention of avoiding his duty and either convinced the governor of his integrity, paid the sum required, or simply left the state without a pass.[49] Nine days later he wrote Smith from the safety of Altoona, Pennsylvania, to tell him of his enjoyable vacation. This elusive individual also inquired about the draft. Before returning to Ohio, he wanted Smith to procure a substitute for him.[50] High public officials too may have attempted to circumvent the system. One rumor suggested that Governor Buckingham had sent his two sons to Europe so they could escape the draft in his state.[51]

By the fall of 1862, Republicans had begun to imply that only Democrats evaded their military duty. David Ross Locke (creator of the comedic character Petroleum V. Nasby), for example, employed satire quite effectively in portraying his party's opponents. The fictitious Nasby was drafted and, when he reported for his draft physical, gave ten reasons why he should be exempt. In the vernacular of the semiliterate Democrat, he contended that he was "rupchered in nine places"; but despite his numerous infirmities, Nasby passed the examination. Intent on avoiding service, he left immediately for Canada and into "political eggsile." Instead of receiving a cordial welcome on his arrival, however, Nasby was greeted by a sarcastic Canadian servant girl who asked him if he wanted the window closed. Nasby responded, "Why set it down, gentle maid? Because 'replide she,' I thot perhaps the draft was too much for ye."[52]

Satire merely reinforced what most Northerners already knew by autumn 1862. The spirit of relative cooperation that had characterized the early summer had, by the end of that season, transformed into a climate where partisanship prevailed. Various factors accounted for this shift, but most important was President Lincoln's issuance of the Preliminary Emancipation Proclamation on September 22. Although volunteering had already started to wane, Democratic accusations that the war had become one for the abolition of slavery contributed to dampening enthusiasm in some quarters. Lincoln acknowledged as much in a private letter to his vice-president on September 28, when he noted that "troops come forward more slowly than ever. . . . The North responds to the proclamation sufficiently in breath; but breath alone kills no rebels."[53]

Abolitionists certainly favored the proclamation, although some believed it was not as assertive and all-encompassing as it could have been. Democrats, especially with the approach of the fall elections, pointed to it and other of Lincoln's actions in an effort to show that he had little or no regard for the Constitution. Tax commissioners and draft officials had appeared everywhere. The latter in particular threatened civil liberties, according to the Democrats, because of the power they acquired on September 24 when Lincoln suspended the writ of habeas corpus for any individual who discouraged enlistments, resisted the draft, or gave "aid and comfort" to the enemy in any form.[54] When voters went to the polls that fall, many Northerners revealed the extent of their disenchantment. Disgruntled over taxes, arbitrary arrests, the prospect of being drafted into an abolitionist war, and other complaints, the voters handed Republicans numerous setbacks. Democrats captured gubernatorial races in New York and New Jersey, and several seats in both Congress and the statehouses.[55]

Troubles for the Lincoln administration that fall did not end once the voters had cast their ballots. Challenges to the draft emerged from various quarters. One of the most serious instances occurred in Wisconsin when a lower court ruled that the Militia Act was unconstitutional because Congress had wrongfully delegated its power to raise an army to the executive branch. Although this decision was later reversed in a higher court, a belief had been nurtured that the act was illegal, and this "truly remarkable extension of executive power in a democratic state . . . was a matter of grave question in the minds of many thoughtful men."[56]

Patriotic fervor. The enthusiasm in the war's early days is captured in this scene of New York's 7th Militia Regiment departing for Washington, D.C. on April 19, 1861. It appeared originally in Frank Leslie's *Illustrated Weekly.* (*The American Soldier in the Civil War.* New York: Bryan, Taylor & Co., 1895, p. 37)

Going to the trenches. This scene was sketched sometime in May 1862 at Camp Winfield Scott before the battle at Yorktown, Virginia. Constructing fortifications and digging trenches were part of a Union soldier's duty. Troops complaining of these laborious details in their letters home discouraged enlistments. Part of the rationale that Congress used in justifying a provision for black military recruitment in the Militia Act came from the argument that blacks would relieve white troops from performing arduous tasks in unhealthy climates. (Library of Congress)

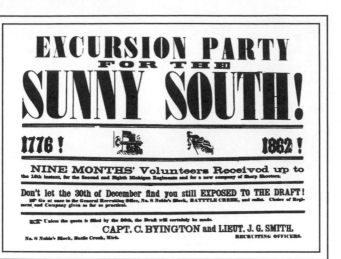

EXCURSION PARTY
FOR THE
SUNNY SOUTH!

1776 !   1862 !

NINE MONTHS' Volunteers Received up to
the 16th instant, for the Second and Eighth Michigan Regiments and for a new company of Sharp Shooters.

Don't let the 30th of December find you still EXPOSED TO THE DRAFT !
Go at once to the General Recruiting Office, No. 8 Noble's Block, BATTLE CREEK, and enlist. Choice of Regiment and Company given as far as practical.

Unless the quota is filled by the 30th, the Draft will certainly be made.

CAPT. C. BYINGTON and LIEUT. J. G. SMITH.
No. 8 Noble's Block, Battle Creek, Mich.   RECRUITING OFFICERS.

Drafting in 1862. There are few extant posters on the 1862 state drafts. This one is particularly interesting because it shows the absence of uniformity in administering the pre-federal draft system. Although men were expected to enlist for three years, they were sometimes allowed to enlist for other lengths of time such as nine months. (Michigan Historical Museum, Michigan Department of State)

Battle-hardened volunteers. A few of the men in this photograph might have entered the army as a result of the 1862 state drafts, but most were experienced volunteers. More than any other picture of the several hundred available on Union soldiers, this one epitomizes the somber mood of men in war after their initial enthusiasm had worn off. Mathew Brady supposedly took this picture at Fredericksburg in December 1862, while others place the image at Petersburg in early April 1865. The noted investigator of Civil War battle photographs, William A. Frassanito, *Grant and Lee: The Virginia Campaigns, 1864–1865* (New York: Charles Scribner's Sons, 1983), pp. 422–23, finds that A. J. Russell was the actual photographer. These troops were from General William T. H. Brook's division and were located in a trench along the west bank of the Rappahannock River just before the battle at Fredericksburg on May 3, 1863. (U.S. Army Military History Institute; reproduction by James Enos, photographer, Carlisle, PA)

Overt resistance to the draft that autumn erupted in some areas of Indiana, Ohio, and most extensively in Wisconsin and Pennsylvania, but federal and state officials acted quickly to restore order. Many of the riots' participants were Democrats and foreign-born. Recent scholarship suggests that the rioters did not necessarily object to being drafted but rather resisted the draft for other reasons. Grace Palladino's study of draft resistance indicates that in 1862 Pennsylvania's coal miners were driven more by a resentment against the local provost marshal than by a desire to escape the draft. This official worked in close concert with local mine owners to discourage miners from organizing. Robert Sterling devotes more attention to the 1862 disorders in the Midwest. He, too, found that the rioters were upset because apparent "injustices in the drafting process" were often ignored. Along with other concerns, potential conscripts feared that their families would suffer with the approach of winter.[57] Even before overt resistance surfaced, some overzealous Republicans may have contributed to the tensions surrounding the draft. As early as August 1862, they suggested that drafting be employed as a political weapon to discourage Democrats from voting.[58]

*D*espite the temptation of bounties, high wages understandably persuaded many a prospective soldier to remain at his regular job, especially given the distinct possibility that his family would become destitute if he went to war.[59] When recently discharged men from one Michigan unit returned home they complained about the lack of military pay, and the local recruiting agent duly noted the adverse effect on enlistments.[60] As always, delayed payments caused particular hardship for married men. In January 1863 one desperate soldier, a machinist in civilian life, asked his New York congressman to use his influence to procure an honorable discharge for him. His wife and six children were poverty-stricken as a result of his absence. To compound matters he could not even send them his "little Earnings [*sic*]," since the government had not paid him in five months.[61]

Soldiers with domestic responsibilities became increasingly aware that they could not rely on the vicissitudes of local charity to provide for the welfare of their dependents while they awaited military pay. By late 1862 in Wisconsin, for example, the wells of local relief began drying up when draft-eligible men, concerned for their families, began hoarding their extra money against the day when they might be conscripted.[62] In the wake of the Union defeat at Fredericksburg, Jane Waldron expressed the feelings of many midwestern women. In one particularly despondent moment, she revealed her deep anxieties over the high cost of living and the distinct possibility that her brothers or "loved husband" might be drafted.[63]

Inflation compounded the problem of low, irregular pay. On November 29,

1862, Governor Oliver P. Morton of Indiana recognized the impact that this dual evil had on enlistments. In a printed petition to Congress, he requested an increase in pay for private soldiers from the existing monthly rate of $13. During the preceding 15 months, or since the last pay raise, the price of food had risen by an average of 60 percent, while other necessary articles recorded a gain in price that approached 120 percent. To support his argument, he included a list of 23 different commodities and compared their earlier costs and present prices. Morton preempted any rebuttals to this request when he added that

> desertion is becoming frequent, and threatens the demoralization and destruction of the army unless it can be promptly arrested. The most potent cause . . . is the condition of the soldier's family at home. He receives letters from his wife, children, or parents, announcing that they are destitute of food, fuel, clothing, or are about to be turned out of doors for [the] nonpayment of rent, and that their neighbors are failing to provide for them, as they are able and ought to do. He becomes maddened and desperate, and finding a furlough impossible, desertion is frequently the result.
>
> Whatever contributes to the speedy termination of the war is economy on a large scale.[64]

In addition to these economic deterrents to volunteering, diverse policies and events coalesced into a pattern by autumn's end that suggested a callous attitude in the federal government toward its men in uniform. Union soldiers continued to complain about poor food, sickness, and fatigue. Even officers were not immune from the effects of harsh conditions in the field. One company commander typified this sentiment when he referred to his present situation as "living death."[65]

The treatment of prisoners of war affected morale both in the army and on the home front. As early as July 13, the *New York Times* predicted that a renewed interest in volunteering would follow a general release of all captives in Southern prisons. On July 22, 1862, the North and South finally reached an accord in this sensitive area, only to have new problems arise. Under the provisions of the cartel, many Union soldiers were paroled to await their formal exchange on a one-to-one basis. Instead of being furloughed home while in this temporary status, they were ordered to camps of instruction. This arrangement proved little better than rebel internment.[66] Like their fellow soldiers in the field, these parolees had to wait months before being paid, and physical conditions in the camps were deplorable.[67] In a particularly irate letter to Secretary of War Stanton, Governor Salomon demanded that the government at least furnish Wisconsin parolees with adequate food, clothing, and quarters, if the men could not obtain permission to go home. The treatment of these former prisoners tended "more than anything else to discourage enlistments" in his state. Within weeks, William H. Hoffman, the commissary general of prisoners, wrote Salomon to assure him that these conditions had been improved.[68]

During the winter of 1862 a new dimension of the government's insensitivity toward its troops emerged. Earlier that year, the public was upset over the inactivity of the Army of the Potomac. In December, however, people were horrified as reports started to trickle in of the Union repulse at Fredericksburg. On December 13, Major General Ambrose Burnside ordered assaults against well-entrenched Confederates on Marye's Heights. By the end of the day, the Union forces had suffered 12,653 casualties, including 1,284 dead. In the wake of this needless carnage, Burnside was criticized for his rashness and lack of an effective strategy. But the damage had been done, and Northern morale plummeted to an all-time low.[69]

The battle of Fredericksburg symbolized the end of any remaining ardor for war in the North. The enthusiasm that came in the wake of Fort Sumter had reappeared only sporadically in 1861 and remained dormant in the first half of 1862. Patriotic fervor temporarily revived that summer after Lincoln issued his call for three hundred thousand men, and when Stanton issued his August draft order. Numerous localities sponsored bond drives and ward meetings to encourage volunteering, and public officials gave freely of their time and money to give speeches and to raise money for local bounties.[70] Even opponents of the Lincoln administration, including Clement L. Vallandigham, made earnest efforts to promote volunteering. Indeed, two days before Stanton's draft order, this outspoken critic of the administration told his audience that in the event of a draft, a citizen "is duty bound, no matter what he thinks of the war, to either go or find a substitute, or pay the fine which the law imposes; he has no right to resist, and none to run away."[71]

These appeals helped to revive a sense of patriotic duty. Men who had held off from enlisting in 1861 did so in the summer of 1862. George Fowle, a 25-year-old builder, decided to enlist in the 39th Massachusetts because of the possibility that England might declare war on the North. Twenty-year-old Rice Bull was reluctant to leave because "those who stayed home had all the opportunities for success," but when he learned that a regiment of local farm boys was forming, he decided to join the 123d New York. In response to Lincoln's call, Harvey Reid, a 20-year-old teacher, thought that "every man who can possibly do so must enlist." He and some of his hometown friends were mustered into the 22d Wisconsin on August 12.[72]

A sense of duty and the desire to enlist with men from their hometowns were the dominant factors that prompted these men to enlist in the summer of 1862. Although the record is unclear as to whether Reid received a bounty,

he had considered enlisting as early as July 3, before the era of runaway bounties. Fowle became part of the "Immortal 33." Had he and 32 others waited
just a few days, they would have received a $125 bounty from their town.
Rice Bull also enlisted too soon, but consequently he was not labeled a "$140
man," a derisive term that was used to describe those who enlisted mainly
for the bounty a few weeks later.[73] These three men, and others, though separated geographically, nevertheless shared a common motivation. They enlisted
at perhaps what might best be described as the "high-water mark" of volunteering in the North for patriotic reasons.

August 1862 inaugurated the period of competitive bidding for recruits,
and from that point on any sense of patriotism gradually diminished until
it reached its nadir later that fall. Recruiting drives and ward meetings continued to be held until the end of the war, but gone was the enthusiasm that
existed before September 1862. In 1863 and after, many of the same themes
and speeches were used in encouraging men to enlist and for soliciting contributions to bounty funds, but these exhortations increasingly fell on deaf ears;
it became evident that "breath alone [would kill] no rebels." Pecuniary motives,
not a sense of duty, had come to replace the traditional reasons for enlisting.[74]
The draft therefore became increasingly important because it stimulated communities to raise local bounties higher and higher in an effort to avoid conscription. At least in 1862, the draft was also a significant factor in encouraging
men to enlist.[75]

Bounties and conscription had combined to influence volunteering in 1862.
Despite the variations in the original quotas, and the confusion brought about
by counting four nine-month men as one three-year man, the most accurate
evidence suggests that seventeen states and the District of Columbia exceeded
their assigned quotas under the July 2 call. Seven states were deficient. Indeed,
in the final accounting, 421,465 men were furnished when only 334,835 were
required.

The success of drafting in the various states is more difficult to assess. This
is due partly to constantly changing regulations that allowed states, for example,
to count a three-year man as the equivalent of four nine-month men. In any
case, of the 334,835 nine-month men who were required under the August
call, 87,588 men were classified as conscripts.[76]

The secretary of war, in his annual report to the Congress on December
2, acknowledged and praised the response of the governors to the two troop
calls. Many had managed to fill their quotas with volunteers, while others had
partially met their obligations through drafting. Stanton revealed further that
a few states were still in the process of devising conscription laws. Despite

this sign of outward success, he went on to indicate that "experience has shown that serious defects exist in the militia law, which should be promptly remedied," and he promised to forward his recommendations to Congress in the near future.[77] The time had arrived to formulate a law that clearly invested the federal government with the principal responsibility for raising the Union army.

MAJORITY STRENGTH VERSUS MINORITY POWER

The Enrollment Act in the Thirty-seventh Congress

T he Thirty-seventh Congress has been rivaled by few in American history for its legislative accomplishments. Laws for land-grant colleges, taxes, and confiscation represent only a few of the areas in which it left indelible marks on the future.[1] Beyond these essentially nonmilitary programs, which one historian has appropriately labeled the "Blueprint for Modern America," the first Civil War Congress also enacted a variety of military measures in its efforts to raise, organize, and maintain the Union forces. Foremost in this group was the Enrollment Act, which President Abraham Lincoln signed into law on March 3, 1863.

Designed to supersede the Militia Act, the Enrollment Act established the principle of national conscription in the North and demonstrated the Union's resolve to continue prosecuting the war. Besides the bill's purely military and symbolic importance, it was also an excellent example of legislative decision making during the war years. Despite various pressures and a preponderance of Republican votes, approval of the act was far from certain. As the bill moved slowly through the arcane windings of the Thirty-seventh Congress, Republicans—who enjoyed numerical dominance in both houses—encountered the latent power that Democrats exercised whenever necessary to force change in pending legislation.

The legislative machinations that occurred as the final version of the Enrollment Act evolved generally have been misunderstood. In some instances, whole series of debates have been ignored, including a movement on the part of some senators to amend important sections of the bill within days after Congress had passed it and before President Lincoln approved it.[2] This later action was important for revealing congressional attitudes on certain aspects of the draft bill, but the focus typically has been on the more colorful aspects of the original

debates, especially the law's impact on states' rights and its alleged discriminatory character.[3] Consistent with this emphasis is an assumption that the Republican majority dominated the entire proceedings. Partially as a result, the effectiveness of the opposition in forcing modifications to the law has been
underestimated, if not completely ignored, while the influence of the Republican
party has been exaggerated.[4]

A national conscription program at this point in the war was needed to
sustain the Union army, but the task of gaining approval would not be easy.
As the Lincoln administration prepared to enter 1863, it faced enormous pressures, both subtle and overt. In the six months since McClellan's abortive
drive on Richmond, Northern fortunes had taken a turn for the worse. Under
the leadership of General John Pope, Union troops converged on Manassas
in late August, but they once again met defeat at the second battle of Bull
Run. A few weeks later, Union forces were able to check Robert E. Lee's
northward advance at Antietam, but this bloodiest day of the war was not
as decisive a Union victory as it could have been, because Lee's army managed
to escape with little opposition from McClellan's army. Tired of "Little Mac's"
dilatory tactics, Lincoln replaced the popular McClellan with Major General
Ambrose Burnside on November 5. Burnside had scarcely settled into the demands of his new assignment when he too came under fire for his tactics at
Fredericksburg. After a single day's fighting on December 13, the Union army
had met defeat at a cost of more than twelve thousand casualties.

Northern morale was devastated. While the North was still recoiling from
this debacle, confidence in the Lincoln administration reached an all-time low.
Lincoln not only had to continue his search for an effective general but also
faced problems within his official family and party. His cabinet was in a weak-
ened condition that December, due primarily to the political machinations of
Salmon P. Chase and the radical Republicans. Both Chase and Secretary of
State William Seward ultimately tendered their resignations, but Lincoln refused to accept them. The division within his party was exacerbated by the
reemergence of a strong partisan spirit that had become even bolder as a result
of the Democratic electoral successes earlier that fall. These victories stemmed
in part from Lincoln's promulgation of the Emancipation Proclamation and
from the administration's use of martial law and the resulting transgressions
on civil liberties.[5]

Pressures mounted on an administration that for a brief period that winter
was viewed by many as incompetent, bereft of leadership, and lacking in resolve.
Despite Lincoln's troubles, one person in his cabinet, Edwin Stanton, had the
energy and presence of mind to begin laying the groundwork for an improved
system for raising an army. He did so without fanfare. Indeed, he moved so

quietly that he neither communicated his recommendations in writing—
although he had promised to do so—nor, as a perturbed Gideon Welles later
noted in his diary, consulted the cabinet on the proposed federal draft law's
"extraordinary provisions."[6]

Whether Stanton realized it or not, intellectuals, the army, and some Republican businessmen were clamoring for extreme measures. Businessmen in the
Midwest preferred drafting over volunteering because they resented having
to contribute constantly to a bounty system through taxes and gifts.[7] The army
favored conscription as a means of replenishing the thinned ranks of its veteran
regiments. Never one to mince words, William T. Sherman even recommended
the disenfranchisement of men who would not serve.[8] In January 1863, an
anonymous article appeared in the influential *Brownson's Quarterly* that demanded "conscription, as the assertion of the authority of the United States
as a sovereign state; and the aggregation of the conscripts to the regular army
. . . as a protest against State sovereignty." Francis Lieber, the probable author,
further objected to the "mercantile spirit" that accompanied the raising of
troops and supported a national conscription system as the most efficient way
of raising an army.[9]

The astute Stanton did not need encouragement from such diverse quarters
to make changes in the existing conscription system. He disliked the militia
draft because of the numerous requests for postponement, a reluctance of the
governors to enforce conscription, the activities of civilian provost marshals
who were accountable only to their respective governors and not to him, and
the absence of uniformity in the militia regulations of the states. Moreover,
the government could draft for only nine months. This was hardly adequate
time for a man to become an experienced soldier; those who had been conscripted in 1862 would be leaving the army the following summer and fall.
Even more important, those who had enlisted for three years in 1861, who
by now were seasoned veterans, would be discharged in less than eighteen
months.

The prospects for retaining or replacing these soldiers seemed dim, and
the need for more men, not less, was growing. The army desperately needed
replacements for conducting new offensive operations and for securing areas
that the Union armies had captured. Although numerous men had enlisted
for three years in 1862, they had done so during a period of renewed patriotism
and with the stimulus of high, competitive bounties. But patriotism and the
goodwill of communities could no longer be depended on to replenish the
army in the future.

Gone was the enthusiasm of the previous summer. The North was tired
of war, and so were many soldiers. To compound the problem of war weariness,
desertions were reaching epidemic proportions. In a December 6 report, Simeon Draper, who served as Stanton's provost marshal general during the militia

drafts, estimated that some one hundred thousand men were absent, and he blamed the bounty system that had been instituted that summer.[10] He was not exaggerating, because "several hundred" desertions were occurring daily by January 1863.[11] Not all of these absences could be attributed to the bounty system. As always the Treasury was suffering from a want of funds in December 1862, and its "resources . . . were inadequate to meet all the current demands."[12] Troops were not being paid as promised and their families were suffering, while those men who remained at home drew high wages.[13] Others were disenchanted with fighting for a cause that promised to end slavery when they had enlisted only to preserve the Union. This disillusionment affected morale but evidently contributed to few desertions.[14]

One of the greatest potential sources for new recruits was the black male population. By the end of 1862, Stanton had begun laying plans to exploit this significant reservoir of manpower. Before the beginning of the new year, he revealed privately that he fully expected to "have 200,000 negroes [*sic*] under arms before June, holding the Mississippi River and garrisoning the ports, so that our white soldiers can go elsewhere." He also indicated that the president had concurred with a policy for more active recruitment.[15] A few days later, Lincoln authorized the use of black soldiers in the Emancipation Proclamation. This pronouncement was followed a few months later by the Enrollment Act, which required "all able-bodied male citizens" between the ages of 20 and 45 to enroll for the draft. This action represented a turning point in white attitudes. Faced with the prospect of federal conscription, more and more whites came to share the opinion that a greater reliance should be placed on the use of black soldiers.[16]

Stanton recognized that extraordinary measures would be needed if the North was to prevail on the battlefield, but time was growing short. The Thirty-seventh Congress would adjourn in March, and the Thirty-eighth Congress would not convene until the following December. However, as Stanton and Henry Wilson learned in the weeks ahead, the timing for obtaining a stronger and more effective conscription law was not as propitious as it had been six months earlier.

Much to the dismay of these Republican leaders, the Democrats prevented a federal conscription law from being rushed through in the last weeks of the Thirty-seventh Congress.[17] Despite attempts to have the law approved as quickly as possible through the use of devious parliamentary tactics, Democrats, especially in the House, responded forcefully with methods of their own. Only after several full days of debate and major amendments did they even permit the measure to come to a final vote. Indeed, the Enrollment Act did not clear the national legislature until February 28, 1863, exactly one month after Henry Wilson introduced the initial version of the federal draft bill into the Senate.

Few could envy Wilson's position in sponsoring this politically unpopular bill, and he had to proceed cautiously. In spite of large Republican majorities in both houses, congressional acceptance of a federal draft law remained far from certain. Although Wilson's party controlled 33 of the 48 seats in the upper house, Senate Republicans were not a monolithic entity in their attitudes and voting behavior; they often divided along East-West sectional lines on economic issues. Opinions vary on the extent to which radical and moderate Republicans generally split over other issues, but the potential for significant disagreement undoubtedly existed among Civil War Republican senators, especially where the South or racial matters were concerned.[18] Their voting on the Enrollment Act also followed a divisive pattern, but only when they did not have to close ranks to protect the federal draft bill from being completely defeated.[19]

Wilson faced yet another potential difficulty. Even more so than his Republican colleagues, a group of 11 Democrats and 3 Unionists posed a challenge for the chairman of the Senate Military Committee. This minority could encumber any piece of legislation in the Thirty-seventh Senate. The basis for this seemingly disproportionate influence stemmed from the Senate's refusal to recognize the right of secession and to make a corresponding change in its rules. Thus, Senate Republicans had no choice but to operate under a quorum principle requiring at least 35 members present before voting on a roll call. This situation was not rectified until months after the convening of the Thirty-eighth Congress.[20] Therefore, even with the assistance of Garrett Davis, a Kentucky Unionist who often aligned himself with the Republicans, the majority party could not muster the minimum number of senators needed if the 14-member opposition chose to withdraw en bloc. To Wilson's advantage, the absence of effective leadership within this group precluded such a catastrophe, providing he did not alienate the entire membership through some thoughtless or precipitous action. Despite its fragmentation, however, the opposition was not powerless. Individuals or factions could always resort to filibustering, if necessary, to obtain desired changes in a bill, since cloture did not become a Senate rule until 1917.[21]

The quorum issue was not as crucial in the House of Representatives, since only one-fifth of the members had to be present for voting purposes. House Republicans encountered a problem of a different sort. During the Thirty-seventh Congress, leaders of the majority party frequently attempted to force bills through on the basis of the "previous question," or the ordering of the vote on a bill's passage. To counter this strategy, Democrats relied on the 42d rule of the House, under which individual members could resort to procedural delays, such as motions to adjourn, indefinite postponement of a bill, and other dilatory tactics. To consume more time, a member could demand a count of the yeas and nays on the last motion introduced. Such a request assumed precedence over all other matters. As a result of these delays, the Republicans often had to withdraw the "previous question," leaving a measure open to debate and amendment. The Democratic strategy was particularly effective on the Negro Troop Bill. Consideration of this measure began on January 27, 1863. After 43 procedural roll calls, the House finally adjourned just before dawn to prepare for the four days of debate that followed.[22] Later that day, Henry Wilson introduced the federal draft bill into the Senate, undoubtedly aware of the obstacles it might encounter once the bill reached the House.

A few days later, on February 4, Wilson reported S. 493 for consideration. This measure authorized the president to draft state militiamen for two years. Other provisions authorized the executive to consolidate understrength military units and to impose severe penalties on any individual who hindered enlistments or sheltered deserters. Sections two and four received the closest scrutiny from the bill's opponents. The first empowered the president to enroll and draft state militiamen directly without the authority of the state governors. Section four placed a conscript, who was still technically a civilian, under military regulations from the date the government drafted him, not from the time he was actually mustered or sworn into the army.[23]

The freezing weather that enveloped the District of Columbia on February 4 and 5 belied the heated discussion that the opposition generated during the two days of debate on S. 493.[24] While members of the majority party concentrated their energies on framing an effective but humane law, many Democrats and Unionists repeatedly questioned the bill's constitutionality as well as its dual threat to states' rights and civil liberties.

Once discussion ended, the Senate proceeded to vote.[25] On the only two roll calls taken on S. 493, party discipline was particularly strong on the question of whether to delete section four. All the opposition members voted to eliminate the section. With one exception, the entire Republican delegation favored retention. On the question of whether to omit the second section, the Republicans demonstrated strong unity once again, and the motion met defeat by a vote of 28 to 13.[26] The majority party had saved both of these controversial provisions, but the military committee ultimately subjected them to significant alteration.

Within days Wilson reported a new measure, S. 511, which laid the foundation for the Enrollment Act. Among the most significant changes in this latest proposal were those that concerned provisions of which the nine Democrats and Unionists had disapproved so strongly in S. 493. Under the provisions of the new bill, which included conscripting men for three years, drafted men would not be subject to military regulations unless they failed to report, either to claim exemption or to enter the service. After a specified period, only delinquent individuals, not all conscripts, would be classified as deserters and hence subject to military law. The second major change involved a new title for the measure. Instead of a bill for the "militia of the United States," S. 511 encompassed the enrollment and drafting of the "national forces." On the surface, this modification seemed to strengthen the federal law because it included all eligible Northern males, not just state militiamen. Beneath this veneer, however, the state militias were left intact and free from absolute presidential control. S. 511 augmented, but did not replace, the state militias. They would continue to serve as an auxiliary arm of the national forces and to enjoy relatively independent status. Indeed, Lincoln acknowledged the legal existence of the state militias and their equivalents on various occasions. Between the debates on S. 493 and S. 511, for example, he approved a bill authorizing Kentucky to raise a special force,[27] and on June 15, 1863, he issued a proclamation activating the militias in the states of Maryland, Ohio, Pennsylvania, and West Virginia. He called these groups into service for a six-month period but did not draft individual militiamen for three years. The governors of New York and Massachusetts also employed their respective militias in activities such as quelling disturbances or assisting the Union army at the battle of Gettysburg.[28]

Protecting the status of the state militias and determining when conscripts would be classified as deserters had been of primary importance to many Senate Democrats during the debates on S. 493. To expedite the federal conscription bill and to improve its chances for passage through the Senate, Wilson conceded these points of contention in exchange for a promise that the opposition would neither mount a filibuster nor withdraw en bloc from voting.[29]

In making these desired modifications, Wilson showed that he understood the opposition. An attempt to force the Republican will on them would have resulted in disaster. By making these substantive changes, Wilson essentially removed any major objections to S. 511, thus permitting its easy passage through the Senate. After the recess during which two roll calls were taken on minor amendments, nine opposition members, either from good conscience or good politics, failed to return to the Senate chamber that night, or at least they did not make their presence known. Of the five Democrats who helped constitute a quorum for voting purposes on the evening of February 16, three came from the draft-free Far West, one was a lame duck, and the last voted with the Republicans on almost one-fourth of the roll calls pertaining to nonmilitary legislation.[30]

The absence of fundamental disagreement over S. 511 soon became apparent. The opposition members confined their speeches to a few perfunctory and partisan remarks. Only one significant matter surfaced—Milton S. Latham, a California Democrat, revived an earlier suggestion that exemption from military service be allowed through the payment of a commutation fee. Ironically, a Democrat had formally introduced the clause that would become the focal point of the Civil War class discrimination controversy in the North, but many Senate Republicans and Democrats supported his proposal.[31]

Latham was a member of the Senate Military Committee and, using a strategy similar to the one Wilson had employed the previous summer, he encouraged potentially controversial changes to the Militia Act to appear on the floor of the Senate rather than to report them out as part of the bill. Once the issue of the exemption fee was on the floor, however, Wilson emerged as one of its strongest defenders among the Republicans. Throughout the day, he took advantage of every opportunity to defend commutation as part of an overall humanitarian and equitable drafting policy. With the exception of exemptions for high government officials, he argued, all exemptions contained in section two favored "the poor and lowly." Furthermore, younger men without families would be the first drafted, since the bill divided enrolled men according to age and marital status for those 35 and older. In his repeated efforts to convince his colleagues of the law's fairness, Wilson even opposed the exemption of the clergy, a group not without influence in the Bay State. Religious leaders were among the "favored few," and he feared the country's reaction if they were excused with the "burden put upon the toiling men of the country." Two weeks later, with the draft bill and commutation safely through Congress, Wilson reversed his position and voted in favor of a proposal to exempt Quakers who had petitioned Congress for relief from conscription.[32]

When senators were not preoccupied with making the bill palatable to the public, they directed their energy to changes aimed at securing benefits for themselves, their states, and their constituents. Edgar Cowan proposed that members of Congress be excused from conscription because they had more important duties to perform. On the first of two roll calls taken that afternoon, Cowan's motion lost by 11 votes.[33] The Senate again refused to exempt state legislators in a second bipartisan vote. It also recorded three other roll calls on amendments to exempt various public officials, particularly at the state level. In not one of these five votes did party discipline or sectional loyalty play an important part. The party divisions that characterized the roll calls taken on S. 493 had dissipated, and senators, especially Republicans in the absence of a threatening opposition, voted with much individual freedom.[34]

A similar pattern emerged in the voting on amendments that affected troop quotas in certain states. Party unity played no role in deciding the questions of granting naval credits, exempting aliens from the draft, reducing the period of service from three years to one, and crediting state troops on federal quotas. Sectional loyalty also was almost nonexistent on these votes.[35] Several other proposals were considered, but no divisions occurred either on these matters or on the passage of S. 511 before the fatigued, overworked senators adjourned at midnight.[36]

A vote on whether to pass the conscription law was unnecessary. The Republicans certainly had no desire to enter their votes in support of a potentially unpopular issue so long as the bill did not require such action. With the state militias protected for all practical purposes, the opposition apparently saw no further need to dignify the proceedings on S. 511 by remaining throughout the day, or even forcing a roll call on the bill's passage. Of the 48 members eligible to vote, 3 of the 33 Republicans, 6 of the 11 Democrats, and 3 of the 4 Unionists failed to appear or did not voice their attitudes on the bill.[37]

With the most vocal opposition absent, Senate Republicans voted in a highly individual fashion. They had not enjoyed such latitude on February 4 and 5 when they had to vote as a partisan bloc to save certain controversial provisions in S. 493. Nor could they vote as they pleased twelve days later, when the House of Representatives returned S. 511 with amendments.

*I*n mid-February 1863, the House of Representatives consisted of 176 individuals. With 105 members, the Republicans clearly enjoyed numerical dominance over the remaining 47 Democrats and 24 Unionists. To inflate the Republican majority even more, 13 of the 24 Unionists tended to vote along Republican lines. Despite this political reality, however, the House Democrats possessed the necessary power to force concessions from the majority party. Just a few weeks earlier, on the Negro Troop Bill, the Republicans had experienced difficulty in obtaining simple approval of a military measure. Moreover, the session was fast drawing to a close, and the Indemnity Bill and other legislation had yet to be considered. Congressmen were also under pressure from their constituents to act decisively. Even lame-duck Republicans received letters from their districts urging them to pass whatever laws were needed for the prosecution of the war.[38] Conversely, Democrats were instructed by their dissatisfied constituents to challenge all questionable measures, including the bill that had cleared the upper house on February 16.[39]

Other factors contributed as well to the tense atmosphere. Foremost among these was the aura of deceit that characterized the actions of Abram Olin, the Republican chairman of the House Committee on Military Affairs and the Militia. Not only did he antagonize the Democratic minority but also a few Republicans. On February 20, Olin merely ordered that S. 511 be printed. The trouble began the next day when John Bingham moved for a third reading and immediate passage of the bill. Another Republican, Thaddeus Stevens, objected because the military committee had reported the wrong bill. Instead of the one containing the Senate amendments to S. 511, Olin expected approval of the measure that Wilson had introduced originally on February 16. After a Democrat protested on similar grounds, Olin interjected quickly that he would postpone consideration of S. 511 until he received the final version of the bill from the printer, providing it could be made a "special order." Clement L. Vallandigham demurred because of the privileged consideration the bill would then receive. The Ohio Democrat alluded to its "accidental" passage through the Senate in a veiled threat that it would not clear the House so easily. When Olin promised to give the minority party an opportunity to discuss the bill in return for an early disposition of the measure, Vallandigham consented to making it a "special order" for Monday, February 23, just two days away.[40]

The harsh winter storm that struck Washington on February 22 was an omen of the acrimonious House debate to emerge later that week. In conjunction with the muddy streets that followed a thaw, the severe weather served to heighten the petulance of the nation's legislators, who by mid-February 1863 were irritable from the conflicts of a long and rigorous congressional session.[41] On Monday, the discomfort brought about by the weather reached a boiling point when Olin violated his promise to open S. 511 to discussion.

At the appointed hour, Olin presented a de facto plan of action. Obviously worried that House Democrats would radically alter S. 511, which might hinder its approval in the Senate "at this late hour of the session," he proposed returning it to the committee. Debate would then occur on this motion, not on the bill itself. After sufficient time elapsed, he would withdraw the referral to permit voting on the bill's passage. In a vain attempt to defuse the opposition, he promised that the military committee would report an amendatory law before the session ended to remedy any defects in the present bill. Olin's ploy failed. Despite his assurance to the contrary, House Democrats were outraged at the prospect of being unable to offer amendments.[42]

William S. Holman, an Indiana Democrat, led the protest. He disliked dilatory tactics but threatened to use them if necessary to permit discussion and amendment of S. 511. When Holman finished, his colleagues began voicing their displeasure. Charles A. Wickliffe proposed a change to prevent the military from actively interfering in elections. Samuel S. Cox followed quickly with a modification to limit the enrollment to Caucasians only. Faced with the threat of a mushrooming filibuster, Olin withdrew into silence until later that evening. Apparently he thought the Democrats would vent their frustrations sufficiently by that time, thereby permitting the measure to come to a vote.

After Olin opened the bill to discussion on February 23, Democrats focused their criticism on the violations to civil liberties that would result from passage of the Enrollment Act. The issue of states' rights received comparatively little attention, since the Senate Democrats had already secured implicit protection for the state militias. House Democrats concentrated instead on sections seven and twenty-five of the bill. The first of these provisions granted district provost marshals authority to report on "all treasonable practices," as well as "to seize and confine spies of the enemy." The twenty-fifth section empowered these same individuals to arrest summarily all persons resisting the draft or hindering enlistments. It further specified that these government agents would hold those charged in confinement until the draft was completed. Primarily as a result of the efforts of the minority party, both these provisions underwent radical alteration by the time the bill cleared the House on February 25.

As the first day of House debate drew to a close, Olin criticized the Democrats for their partisan speech making. He conveniently overlooked similar orations made by his Republican colleagues, who had spoken in defense of the measure. Despite his hostility toward the Democrats, Olin nevertheless reserved a few words of praise for the minority, since they had not questioned the pressing need for such a measure. Once he finished, he called for the "previous question." George Pendleton, a Democrat, quickly demanded a call of the House. Before this proposal could be voted on, Robert Mallory moved for immediate adjournment. Under House rule forty-two, Mallory's proposal had precedence. By a close vote, 61 to 60, the House agreed to adjourn. All but one of the Democrats supported this motion, along with one-fourth of the Republicans present. The decision to adjourn at 27 minutes before midnight ended the first day of consideration on S. 511.[43] Olin had lost the first round.

Debate resumed a few minutes after noon on February 24. Before Olin had an opportunity to renew his call for the "previous question," Vallandigham reintroduced Pendleton's motion for a call of the membership. By a 41-vote margin it met defeat. Olin then gained the floor to offer yet another plan. This latest proposal would have curtailed debate by having all discussion terminated by mid-afternoon. However, before the rules could be suspended so he could introduce his motion, Olin had to secure the approval of at least two-thirds of the members present. He secured this request with little difficulty—95 members favored it while only 36 opposed. Controversy arose, however, the moment he moved to close debate at 3:30 P.M.

Significantly, Olin began to experience a minor rebellion within his own party. Of the three procedural roll calls that members demanded after he introduced his motion, two came from Republicans who called for adjournment. These two men, John Hickman of Pennsylvania and William Kellogg of Illinois, did not want the motions approved, since they voted against both of them. Instead, they introduced them as a means of expressing their displeasure with Olin's vacillating tactics, which could rekindle the Democrats' filibuster. Such a calamity could carry the measure into the end of the session without resolution. Kellogg had already reminded Olin that the House had other legislation to consider. Ostensibly because the Republican "side of the House" desired to consider the measure further, Olin once again withdrew the "previous question" and let debate resume.[44]

The second day of debates again focused primarily on the conscription bill's threat to civil liberties. Robert Mallory led his colleagues with the opening speech. After paying lip service to the adverse effect that the bill would have on states' rights, he addressed its even greater negative impact on civil liberties. He directed some of his harshest criticism at military commissions and the "informer . . . [or] miscalled provost marshal," whose power under the "treasonable practices" clause was infinite. Before finishing, he surrendered the floor to William D. Kelley of Pennsylvania. Reputedly the most able Republican speaker, Kelley proceeded to denounce the Democrats in a speech that drew loud applause from the galleries. This outburst prompted a demand from the Democrats to clear all spectators from the House. In the last procedural roll call on S. 511, the House defeated this motion by a 50-vote margin.[45]

After this roll call, Mallory resumed the floor to continue his tirade. Once he finished, his Democratic and Unionist colleagues came to his rescue in sustaining the filibuster. These individuals undoubtedly intended to delay passage of S. 511 until the Republican majority agreed to certain changes. John B. Steele later implied as much to a fellow New York Democrat when he referred to his rambling speech on the draft bill.[46]

Republicans rose to the defense of the "treasonable practices" clause. Among those who championed the necessity for this section was Thaddeus Stevens. But unlike his Republican colleagues, he refrained from caustic remarks until after he had reached a compromise with the minority party on the matters of terminating debate, offering amendments, and voting on the bill's passage. In the role of pacifier, Stevens was uniquely qualified. As chairman of the Committee of Ways and Means and as floor leader, the energetic Stevens held the two most important positions in the House, excluding that of Speaker. In addition to wanting an opportunity to offer amendments to S. 511, he undoubtedly remembered Olin's attempt a few weeks earlier to have Stevens's Negro Troop Bill referred to his committee. Once there it would have faded into obscurity.[47] In their contempt for the chairman of the House Military Committee, Stevens and the minority party shared common ground.

Regardless of any latent spite toward Abram Olin, Stevens was fully aware of the opposition's power to delay measures. With the Thirty-seventh Congress ending in exactly one week, he wanted the House to begin considering other business. Accordingly, he moved to close debate on S. 511 on the evening of February 24. At first he gave little ground as he pushed to end discussion by 9 P.M., only one-half hour away. When he persisted in this demand, granting only an additional thirty minutes, the Democrats became restless. Rather than risk alienating them, Stevens wisely consented to extend debate to 1 P.M. the next day, after which an hour would be set aside for the offering of amendments. Even Vallandigham agreed to this proposal.[48] After all, Stevens had met the price for Democratic cooperation, as Benjamin F. Thomas of Massachusetts acknowledged in his speech the following morning, and which Olin paid later that afternoon.

Thomas's speech was one of two presented on the morning of February

25. He defended the bill's constitutionality, then yielded the floor to the aging but still lively John J. Crittenden of Kentucky, who opposed the measure as just another emancipationist act of the administration. Before Crittenden finished it was 1 P.M. and, as agreed, all debate ceased as the House began considering proposed changes to S. 511.

The Democrats had wielded power effectively. As the House turned its attention to amending the bill, Olin appropriately recommended the first modification, which eliminated the "treasonable practices" clause. He also moved a change in the twenty-fifth section to require provost marshals to deliver all nonmilitary prisoners to civilian jurisdiction rather than holding them in military custody until the completion of a draft. The chairman then suggested a further modification that would authorize military commissions to try spies only and to impose a mandatory death penalty in the event of conviction. The Democrats offered no objection to this restricted, specified use of military power. They were concerned primarily with protecting legitimate dissent and imposing safeguards on military authority, not with sheltering spies. The House agreed to all these changes without demanding the yeas and nays.[49]

Commutation received the most bipartisan attention. The disunity that prevailed within both parties over this issue emerged most noticeably when William Holman moved its repeal. Party lines disintegrated as the teller recorded the yeas and nays. Of the 95 Republicans present, 29, or almost one-third, voted with the minority party to eliminate the three-hundred-dollar privilege. Democratic party unity fared a little better. Less than one-fifth, 8 of 41, of those present crossed party lines to vote for its retention. Party unity had a more dominant influence on the other four substantive roll calls, including S. 511's passage by a 115-to-49 vote. On this roll call, 11 of the 24 Unionists favored the bill. Thirty-six of the 40 Democrats opposed it, while 98 of the 100 Republicans present supported the measure.[50]

In the twelve roll calls taken in the House on S. 511, sectional cohesion was a negligible factor. When it came to party loyalty, however, the Republicans demonstrated a high degree of discipline on six of the seven procedural votes. The Democrats, by contrast, sustained unity on only three of these seven votes.[51] In deciding the fate of commutation, both parties experienced significant defections from their ranks. On the other four substantive roll calls, both groups displayed a high degree of unity. Contrary to the pattern of general voting behavior in the Thirty-seventh Congress, the Republicans proved more cohesive than did the Democrats.[52]

For all practical purposes, House action on the Enrollment Act ended on February 25, 1863. Three days later, however, two Democrats resurrected the issue when they received permission to present their speeches on the conscription bill. One of them merely covered the same ground as his colleagues had, but with the additional sarcastic note that the Senate would undoubtedly approve the House amendments to S. 511 "about the hour of two o'clock tomorrow morning [when] the holy Sabbath will be desecrated by its passage in the higher branch of the national legislature."[53]

With the end of the Thirty-seventh Congress only four days away, Henry Wilson moved quickly to secure Senate approval of the House amendments. As before, Wilson had to proceed cautiously in order to prevent the bill from being returned to the House. If this occurred a few members of the opposition, such as Clement L. Vallandigham, would have another opportunity to defeat the measure by mounting a filibuster until the Thirty-seventh Congress adjourned. Certainly, at this late hour, Wilson had no desire to jeopardize the entire bill because of some change. He implied as much to a Quaker leader in late February 1863.[54]

Instead of granting carte blanche approval for the modifications, seven members of the opposition and two prodraft senators insisted on presenting speeches; but, fortunately for Wilson, most of his fellow senators shared his view of protecting the draft bill at this juncture. The 14 members of the Senate opposition were generally supportive and had no desire to quash the federal draft law. Although they disliked certain provisions in the measure, they merely acted as the loyal opposition as they dominated the floor throughout the long, 12-hour day. They directed their remarks more to their constituents than to their colleagues, as Henry B. Anthony of Rhode Island wearily pointed out after listening to four hours of constant harangue. The opposition speakers, when they confined their remarks to the subject of the federal draft, expressed concern over the bill's negative impact on states' rights. Unlike their speeches in early February, much of what they said was partisan rhetoric that often bordered on absurdity.[55]

Once the protracted discussion ended, the Senate proceeded to vote on a motion to postpone the bill indefinitely. It lost with 35 opposed and 11 in favor. With that obstacle removed, the Senate approved all but one of the House amendments without a division. The point of contention focused on the newly authorized military commissions, whose jurisdiction Senator Bayard wanted to limit further. The Senate disagreed with his amendment with 10 yeas and 32 nays. The legislators then voted in favor of retaining the original amendment by a vote of 35 to 6.[56] Lazarus Powell then introduced two amendments, which the Senate rejected by wide margins. His first recommendation would have exempted men "conscientiously unable to perform military service," and the second proposal would have reduced the commutation fee from $300 to $150. Significantly, this Democrat did not object to the principle of the exemption fee but only to its present excessive amount.[57]

Party loyalty proved much stronger than sectional unity on these five roll calls. Senate Republicans, rather than risk the bill's return to the House, voted as an extremely cohesive group. The Democrats and the three Unionists, however, demonstrated little discipline on these votes. They were interested more in voicing objections for home consumption than in achieving formal changes.[58]

After the final roll call, the president *pro tempore* announced that the "vote just taken terminates . . . action . . . on the bill." At approximately 12:30 on the morning of March 1, 1863, the Senate adjourned for a well-deserved day of rest. All that seemingly remained now was the perusal of recommendations before deciding which loyal Republicans to nominate for the new offices created under the Enrollment Act.[59] But the official pronouncement that ended further legislative consideration of the draft bill proved to be premature.

The respite from federal conscription lasted only until Monday, March 2, when senators from both parties attempted to attach riders to another military measure. Had any of these proposals been successful, they would have automatically nullified certain provisions of the Enrollment Act even before Lincoln could sign it into law the following day. The movement to effect these changes began within minutes after Wilson introduced H. R. Bill 523, which concerned the ordnance, quartermaster, and engineer corps.

Henry B. Anthony led his colleagues by reviving the question of whether to exempt men who were conscientiously opposed to war. Before delivering a stirring defense of Quaker principles, the New Englander reminded his listeners that he had "voted against nearly all exemptions but those for conscience sake." Despite Anthony's pleas, his fellow Republicans abandoned party lines on this issue. Sectional loyalty also was not a factor, although seven New England senators voted in favor, while four others opposed the amendment.[60]

Another roll call involved the repeal of commutation. Not only did the vote on this issue demonstrate a perfect absence of sectional and party unity, but it also revealed the intraparty strife in the Senate over the status of the exemption fee. Before the vote was taken, Lazarus Powell moved to adjourn, which revealed the lack of a quorum. Once the sergeant at arms obtained the requisite thirty-five members, the vote proceeded on whether to sustain the amendment. Powell, who earlier contended that three hundred dollars was excessive, joined with another Democrat, seven Republicans, and a Unionist in favor of eliminating the commutation clause. Those who wanted to retain the exemption fee included twenty Republicans, three Democrats, and two Unionists.

The only other bipartisan roll call came on the bill's passage. Four other votes on proposed amendments demonstrated that the Democrats and their Unionist allies could become a disciplined unit on the issue of blacks in the Union army. Three of the four amendments pertained directly to the status of blacks in the military, and the opposition closed ranks.[61] But with the Enrollment Act no longer a binding force, Republican party unity disappeared on these roll calls.[62] Further, sectional loyalty emerged as a notable, but not powerful, force in the voting on these amendments. In general, conservative Republicans, particularly from the border states and the Midwest, defected to the opposition to vote against extending any further rights to blacks. Conversely, a group of preponderantly New England senators voted in unison, as they had done on most of the 25 Senate roll calls recorded on the federal draft.[63]

As a group, Republican senators voted in response to a changing set of conditions on the conscription law. When the measure or an important aspect of it was threatened, most of them blended into a cohesive whole. Senate Democrats and Unionists also showed that they were capable of maintaining party discipline on issues threatening states' rights and those concerning blacks in the military. In line with their attitudes on nonmilitary legislation, minority party senators assumed the role of the loyal opposition and supported any reasonable measure that did not encroach unnecessarily into certain areas. Largely because of the actions of Abram Olin, House Democrats were far more cantankerous, but it was not their intent to obstruct the ultimate passage of S. 511. Like their Senate colleagues, most House Democrats comprised a loyal opposition who wanted only to safeguard certain rights and liberties by amending the legislation.[64]

By gaining congressional approval, the Enrollment Act passed its first critical test. During the next two years it, and the federal draft system that it created, faced a variety of challenges. Most of these demands were aimed at correcting certain shortcomings in the enabling legislation, and they ultimately led to three major amendatory measures. As officials tried to respond to these diverse pressures, most reluctantly agreed to any change that promised to raise more men for the Union forces, so long as the draft was not overly burdensome on Northern men.

CREDITS, QUOTAS, AND CONFUSION

Federal Conscription Arrives in the North

President Lincoln's formal approval of the Enrollment Act on March 3, 1863, signaled the onset of national drafting in the North. Although the "old way" of voluntarism endured, the states effectively were bypassed in the process. With bounties as the carrot and the draft as the stick, the same "carrot and stick" approach continued to be used in stimulating communities to fill their quotas with volunteers.[1] Consistent with the pattern that had begun in the summer of 1862, pecuniary rather than patriotic motives increasingly came to dominate recruitment in the final two years of the war.

The initiation of the federal draft coincided with a subtle and gradual change in social attitudes toward recruiting men for the Union army. Part of this transition was caused by war weariness—people were simply tired of the conflict. The most dramatic change, however, occurred in communal responses. Prior to federal conscription, localities were concerned that they would be viewed as less than patriotic if they failed to encourage enough men to volunteer from their resident male populations. Under federal drafting, this social stigma began to fade as it became more socially acceptable to fill quotas through commutation, substitution, and preferably with as many recruits as possible from other areas through the use of competitive local bounties. When these activities failed to produce enough credits, many communities relied on unethical brokers to fill quotas, which in turn spawned the use of "paper credits."

A principal cause for this change stemmed from the Enrollment Act and the system it had created. The law was imperfect, but most of the criticism was aimed at the Provost Marshal General's Bureau, which was responsible for implementing the law. Although General James B. Fry and his subordinates brought some of this antagonism on themselves, a large portion of their difficulties resulted from having to administer a law that was often confusing and that demonstrated little regard for local conditions. Important too in this wartime climate was the belief that the government's demands for men were excessive and unrelenting. Indeed, Fry had to implement major troop calls in October 1863, March 1864, July 1864, and December 1864, which on paper collectively required an additional 1.4 million new soldiers. The initial enrollment process and these levies were concentrated in a two-year period. Throughout this brief span of time, Fry constantly had to respond to various challenges while grappling with a defective system.

In its final form, the Enrollment Act reflected Congress's desire to make the federal draft as acceptable as possible to Northern citizens while instituting the principle of universal liability to military service.[2] Toward this end, it authorized the enrollment and drafting of all eligible male citizens between the ages of 20 and 45. This group included aliens who had declared their intention of becoming citizens. Enrolled men were divided into two classes, with the stipulation that those in the first category, who were between the ages of 20 and 35, would be drafted before those in the second, which encompassed all married men between the ages of 36 and 45.

Outright exemptions were limited to a few individuals. Section two excused the vice-president, cabinet members, federal judges, and state governors. Once a draft was in progress, the act further provided for the release of convicted felons and the exemption of any person with a physical or mental handicap. Hardship exemptions were allowed for reasons that included being the only son of parents who depended on him for their livelihood, a widower with children under 12 years of age, or an older brother of parentless young children who depended on him for support. Among other humanitarian exemptions was one that provided for up to two exemptions in each family if two or more men were already serving in the military. Neither occupational nor religious exemptions were authorized, presumably because every drafted man would have an opportunity to pay a three-hundred-dollar commutation fee or provide a substitute.

Congress could not anticipate the number of exemptions, but the act's fourteenth section precluded a man from claiming one until he was actually drafted. Consequently, enrolling officers had to record the name, address, occupation, and other pertinent information on all men interviewed. As a result of this procedure, obvious physical and mental misfits were included along with those special cases who clearly qualified for exemption under the second section.

This policy necessarily prevented the government from issuing quotas on the basis of the exact number of qualified men in a district. To compensate for the enrolled men who would be excused under section two, and to allow for those who paid commutation or provided a substitute, the law further required an additional assessment of 50 percent on each district's quota; in July 1864, Congress doubled this figure to 100 percent. While any excess of men called would be discharged automatically, the number would be insufficient in some districts and a supplemental draft would have to be conducted. These requirements not only made draft calls appear larger than necessary, but what Congress underestimated was the number of individuals who would qualify under the liberal provisions of section two. Under the 1863 draft call, for example, 65 percent of those examined were released for reasons of physical disability or hardship. Of the 88,171 men who were ultimately held to service, 52,288 paid the three-hundred-dollar fee, and another 26,002 furnished substitutes. Only 9,881 men became conscripts from the 292,441 names drawn in the 1863 draft.[3]

Although the system exempted more men than it drafted, it established the principle of a male citizen's liability to national service. Indeed, the North's first federal conscription law was so universal in its application that Union sailors were held, since the act had not specifically exempted them. Much to the chagrin of Gideon Welles, the Navy Department had to apply to the War Department to secure the release of each conscripted seaman. Secretary of War Edwin Stanton, in extending his vast power into other areas of the government, also required the navy to pay a two-hundred-dollar commutation fee for each of its drafted clerks. This policy particularly irked Welles.[4]

Welles's problems with the Enrollment Act also extended to naval recruitment. Since the law had not authorized troop credits for seamen, most communities did not have any incentive to encourage naval enlistments through local bounties. This lack of enthusiasm combined with other factors to discourage volunteering for the naval service, and the total number of new seamen soon fell far below the minimum required.[5] Not only did potential sailors refuse to enlist because they qualified only for future prize money, not for the federal bounty, but most also had no desire to join an organization that many viewed as less appealing than the army. Low pay, dangerous conditions aboard ships, the elimination of the traditional "grog" ration, and a navy policy that held sailors for as long as six months beyond their original term of service, among other grievances, combined to attract few men to the navy.[6] In the February 1864 Amendatory Act, Congress reacted by trying to entice more men into the naval service. Thereafter, qualified seamen were permitted to transfer from the army to the navy without penalty. Congress further authorized bounties and local troop credits for future naval enlistments.[7]

The Union army was also dissatisfied with certain features of the law. Under the nineteenth section, understrength units were to be consolidated and any excess officers were to be discharged. Despite General William T. Sherman's initial enthusiasm toward the law, he shuddered at the thought of destroying the original structure of his veteran regiments and charged that this particular clause was a "far worse defeat than Manassas."[8] The prospect of being disbanded, however, encouraged many regimental officers to dispatch recruiting details in an effort to bring a unit up to authorized strength. More often than not, these attempts proved futile. One three-man detachment from the 68th Ohio Volunteer Infantry, for example, managed to recruit only fourteen men from December 3 to 29, 1863.[9]

Other provisions also affected the army. Among the more important was the continuation of the federal bounty to all new recruits, including conscripts, but not to prospective sailors. Further, the president was required to issue a proclamation encouraging deserters to return to their units with no penalty beyond forfeiture of their pay for the period of their absence. Thirty-day furloughs were authorized for enlisted men as well, but no more than 5 percent of a unit could receive one at any given time. While this policy was practical from the standpoint of prohibiting too many soldiers from being legally absent at the same time, it portended disaster for morale. Even under the best of conditions, a soldier could expect to return home only once every 20 months. As late as February 1864, one soldier was finally moved to complain that he had not been home since his enlistment more than two years earlier.[10]

Even greater than its effect on the Union army and navy was the impact of the federal draft law on Northern society. Whether or not a community had to resort to drafting, it and all others came into contact with the national government through the Provost Marshal General's Bureau. In several provisions, the Enrollment Act authorized the establishment of this agency and the appointment of numerous officials empowered to establish regulations for enrolling and drafting.

At the apex of this hierarchy was James Barnet Fry. Born on February 22, 1827, in Carrollton, Illinois, he entered West Point when he was sixteen. In 1847 he graduated fourteenth in his class and was assigned to garrison duty in Mexico City as an artillery officer. After service with General Winfield Scott at Vera Cruz, Fry served at various posts in the southern and western United States. In 1853 he was ordered to West Point, where he remained until 1859. In addition to instructional duties during his six-year tenure at the academy, he gained valuable administrative experience as its adjutant under the direction of Superintendent Robert E. Lee. Subsequently ordered to Fort Monroe, he participated in the arrest of John Brown. For a four-month period in 1860, he returned to West Point to assist in revising the curriculum.

When the war began, Fry was already serving as chief of staff for General Irvin McDowell and eventually participated in the first battle of Bull Run. In November 1861 he was reassigned as chief of staff to Major General Don Carlos Buell and served at Shiloh and Perryville before being ordered to the Adjutant General's Office a year later. While in Washington, he encountered some difficulty as a result of his loyalty to Buell. Much to the consternation of generals Ulysses S. Grant and William T. Sherman, Fry defended Buell's actions at Shiloh. Despite Fry's close association with Buell, Grant nevertheless endorsed him as "the officer best fitted" to administer the newly created Provost Marshal General's Bureau. On March 17, 1863, Colonel Fry was appointed to this post, and in April 1864 he was promoted to brigadier general. He retained that rank until his bureau was dissolved on August 28, 1866.[11]

An important source of the disenchantment associated with the draft can be traced to the confusion that Fry created in assigning quotas. Most individuals, ranging from state governors to average citizens, could not comprehend Fry's methodology. Just a few months after his appointment, for example, Governor Edward Salomon lambasted him for his mysterious methods in determining quotas. The provost marshal general responded quickly to this accusation.[12] The difficulties in assigning quotas stemmed in part from the complexities of the system. In fairness to Fry, the law required him to take into account all men who had been furnished previously from each district. Since soldiers had entered the service for periods ranging from three months to three years during the first two years of the war, Fry first had to reduce all credits to a three-year standard. Moreover, he had to resolve conflicts, such as when two states claimed credit for the same man.[13] To add to the confusion, adjustments had to be made whenever new policies were approved. On February 24, 1864, Congress authorized the crediting of seamen who enlisted after that date; but five months later, Congress further mandated that local credits had to be determined for all sailors who had entered the Union navy prior to February 1864. By the end of 1863, Fry also had to begin factoring in credits for any veteran volunteers or blacks that a locality recruited.[14]

Further problems arose when Fry also refused to assign levies on a town basis. Legally he was justified because of a flaw in the Enrollment Act. Under section nine, a district provost marshal was prohibited from dividing his territory into more than two subdistricts without the express permission of the secretary of war. This policy contributed to diminished confidence in the system and placed an unfair burden on many communities—even if a town managed to supply its share of men, it still remained liable to the draft until the entire subdistrict filled its quota. One irate midwestern Republican charged that this system adversely affected the western division of his town, which was solidly Republican and located in one subdistrict, while it benefited the eastern Copperhead section, which was part of another subdistrict.[15]

The Northeast felt particularly victimized by this policy. New Englanders objected because official business had always been conducted on a town, not on a subdistrict, basis, which a few constituents quickly brought to the attention of their public officials.[16] On February 24, 1864, Congress wisely modified this policy by ordering provost marshals to subdivide their districts "as far as practicable." Fry had begun moving in this direction almost two months earlier by ordering his subordinates to try to take into account future credits down to the town level. The convening of the Thirty-eighth Congress undoubtedly had prompted him to respond to the men who would be voting on his bureau in the future. While Fry could afford to ignore the clamor of ordinary citizens, he could not very well shun angry congressmen, some of whom paid personal visits to his office to express their concerns. Administrative problems nevertheless persisted in implementing changes in the subdistrict policy for the remainder of the war.[17]

Although the law eroded local pride, Fry cannot be totally absolved of all blame for some of the difficulties that accompanied the draft's implementation. In his effort to be efficient, he often contributed to the confusion. During the summer of 1863, for example, Lincoln decided to have the draft proceed in areas that had completed their enrollment. Under this policy 20 percent of those enrolled in a district were to be drafted. On October 17 he issued a formal proclamation for 300,000 men, including those raised the previous summer. A draft was then to proceed in all districts that had not filled their quotas by January 5, 1864. With recruiting progressing rapidly because of generous bounties, and with Congress in the process of amending the Enrollment Act, the president decided to postpone the draft. Before it proceeded under the 1863 call, he ordered an additional draft for 200,000 men on February 1, 1864. On March 14, 1864, he issued still another order for 200,000 men. Fry chose to group these three calls together for an aggregate of 700,000 men. On another occasion, however, he combined only the first two—October 17, 1863 and February 1, 1864—for a total of 500,000 men, and separated the March 14, 1864, call for 200,000 troops. Based on the final records compiled by the War Department, the March 14 order was in fact a distinct call, but at the time Northern communities were perplexed over their exact quotas.[18]

As the individual directly responsible for the administration of the North's first national conscription law, Fry bore the brunt of the criticism. With varying degrees of success, he addressed numerous complaints from officials and other individuals, but nowhere were his decisions and the general operations of the bureau scrutinized more closely than in the press. Charges of inefficiency, corruption, nepotism, and abuses of power were made repeatedly, especially after Lincoln issued a new call for more troops. Discontent with the bureau over quotas and a general impression of incompetency reached such a crescendo by February 1865 that there was a public outcry for Fry's removal.[19]

Fry's problems with the draft did not end with the war. In the spring and summer of 1868, he became the focal point of a controversy that arose between congressmen James G. Blaine and Roscoe L. Conkling. At issue was whether western New York had been assigned excessive troop quotas during the late war. The matter escalated largely because of a judgmental error on Fry's part.

Instead of ignoring the allegation, he chose to refute the charges publicly.[20] After this unfortunate episode, Fry avoided becoming embroiled in similar disputes. Between bouts of extended illness in the 1870s, he served in the Adjutant General's Office in Washington and as an adjutant general in various military departments. After the war, he completed various books on topics that included the draft, certain campaigns, and other aspects of the military. Due to failing health, he retired from the army in 1881. He died at Newport, Rhode Island, on July 11, 1894.

Although Fry was accused of incompetence and inefficiency, his integrity was never seriously called into question. Charges of ineptitude, dishonesty, partisanship, and immorality, however, were lodged against numerous officials who were part of the vast bureaucratic machinery Fry directed. To implement the law, Congress had authorized the appointment of various officials in every state and in every congressional district. At the lowest level, the provost marshal was to preside over a local enrollment board consisting of a surgeon and one other appointed official. In deference to Edwin Stanton, who wished to avoid the difficulties he experienced under the militia system, each provost marshal held the rank of a captain of cavalry. Through this action, these subalterns would be responsible only to Stanton, Lincoln, and Fry, and not to state governors or other officials. As a result of this policy, the most powerful figure on the enrollment board was the district provost marshal, who had the authority to hire enrolling officers and other personnel, to arrest deserters, to confine spies, and to follow any other orders and instructions that emanated from the War Department.

Historians usually do not view these officials in a favorable light. Grace Palladino in her study of draft resistance in the Pennsylvania coalfields, for instance, traces much of the miners' animosity toward conscription to the collusion between mine owners and the local provost marshal, who used his power to repress unionizing efforts. This close relationship—not commutation, substitution, or even the prospect of military service—was the cause of discontent among the miners. Robert Sterling in his extensive study of draft resistance in the Midwest attributes part of the dissatisfaction to draft officials, many of whom were insensitive, corrupt, and inefficient. Phillip Paludan views them collectively as nothing more than a group of political hacks consisting of "Republican favorites and narrow-minded partisans totally lacking in tact or judgment."[21]

These functionaries have few defenders. Foremost among them are Harold Hyman and Eugene Murdock. At the far extreme is Hyman, who contends that Fry's bureaucracy "was the most decent the world had known" up to 1863. He attributes much of its success to the centralization of authority, which resulted in "less favoritism and influence-peddling" when it came to drafting and in apprehending spies and deserters. Hyman further asserts that incidences of vigilantism were significantly reduced by the implementation of procedures. Murdock presents a more tempered assessment by explaining in detail many of the difficulties under which these officials had to labor. These men, especially the provost marshals and the examining surgeons, were under constant pressure to grant favors and special exemptions. At times they suffered under enormous work loads, particularly when a draft was under way in their districts. Their contributions often went unrecognized and they were criticized in a number of quarters. Despite some occasional lapses in judgment, Murdock finds that "the vast majority were good, responsible public servants."[22]

These officials unquestionably were under pressure because of their difficult responsibilities, but the negative impressions they left were not without foundation in several instances. Some were the relatives of important Republicans. The cousin of Major General Robert C. Schenck, chair of the House Committee on Military Affairs and the Militia, for example, ultimately received the provost-marshalship in Ohio's third district.[23] On occasion, nepotism even extended to Democratic critics of the Lincoln administration. Undoubtedly in deference to the wishes of Governor Horatio Seymour, the government appointed the son of Samuel Medary, editor of the influential *Columbus Crisis*, as the acting provost marshal for New York's eleventh district.[24] Most of these positions, however, went to political cronies and supporters. The appointment in Benjamin F. Wade's district went to one Darius Cadwell, an old friend of the senator's. Cadwell, who lived in Wade's hometown of Jefferson, regularly kept the senator informed on matters such as Wade's chances for being reelected to the Senate.[25] Other officials were former congressmen who had failed at reelection to the Thirty-eighth Congress. Alexander S. Diven became the acting assistant provost marshal for the western division of New York. William E. Lehman, a maverick Democrat who had supported the Enrollment Act, received the provost-marshalship in Pennsylvania's first district.[26]

All of these individuals apparently executed their duties without incident, but others blatantly abused their authority.[27] One Massachusetts provost marshal made improper advances toward the wives of two recruits. Only in return for their favors would he authorize the release of their husbands' advance bounty money, to which they were entitled.[28] Others accepted bribes. By early 1865, Ohio Republican governor John Brough accused half of the provost marshals in his state, most of whom were fellow Republicans, of being corrupt.[29] Some of these officials were very sensitive to such charges. One surgeon, for example, whose reputation was beyond reproach, considered resigning when he was accused of accepting unfit recruits that the army subsequently rejected. Still another overworked doctor, who placed a high premium on his integrity, chose to resign rather than continue his association with the throng of undesirable elements that daily visited the enrollment board seeking to court his favor and the influence of the other members.[30]

Charges of favoritism, moral turpitude, and corruption were some of the major difficulties with which these officials had to deal. Equally as important was a public impression of incompetency that stemmed from the complexities of draft policies and procedures. In the course of discharging their responsibilities, many of these men conveyed an image of ineptitude because they too were experiencing various problems as the war progressed. Aside from Fry's sometimes conflicting instructions, the Enrollment Act was subjected to three major revisions before the war's end. In the process, administration of the act naturally suffered. By the spring of 1864, local draft officials could no longer file a simple numerical report but instead had to decide whether a conscript was to be credited to the 1863 or a subsequent draft.[31] One perplexed district provost marshal frequently wrote his immediate superior in an effort to obtain answers to questions such as how to credit skedaddlers, whether a man who paid commutation under the March 1864 draft could claim exemption under the supplemental drafts for that particular call, and whether men who furnished three-year substitutes under the 1862 state militia draft were still exempt in 1864, to which one of Fry's representatives gave an emphatic no.[32] Such negative decisions and the lack of decisiveness in other draft-related matters did not endear the district provost marshal to his constituency. Irritated citizens increasingly turned away from these local administrators and relied more and more on their elected officials for assistance.[33]

Considering that some 185 district enrollment boards had to be established, and given the inherent difficulties in administering the law, Fry's bureau performed no mean achievement in implementing the system in 1863. In addition to administering conscription, the agency was also responsible for such diverse duties as arresting deserters and spies, coordinating army enlistments, and conducting the medical examination process. Preparing for the enrollment phase of the drafting process was in itself a major task. Within a few weeks following his appointment, the energetic Fry nevertheless developed a set of detailed procedures in accordance with the law for conducting the enrollment and the draft. With some revisions, this basic document guided the system for the remainder of the war.[34]

After the local boards were in place, the enrolling process began. Officers had to canvass from area to area and door to door to complete their lists, as opposed to having men between specified ages report in person to register on designated dates, as was done in World War I and afterward. The work was also dangerous. Not only did these agents encounter armed resistance in various areas—a few of them were murdered in Indiana. Nor was the process foolproof. One problem in particular was verification of the information furnished. Fictitious names and other false information were sometimes given. In other instances the actual names and ages of dead men, and of Union soldiers and sailors who were in active service, appeared on the lists. Individuals who had moved found themselves listed in two separate districts. Where a man might be exempted or drafted in one area, he would be listed as having failed to report in another.[35] One angry individual even discovered that he was enrolled twice in the same district. He learned of this oversight when his name was drawn in two instances for the same draft. He unsuccessfully appealed for a special exemption on the grounds that his chances for being drafted had increased twofold compared to other men in the district.[36]

After the enrollment process was completed, the names of those to be drafted were chosen. In compliance with the law, the names of enrolled men were placed in a wheel and, at a public gathering, a blindfolded man reached into the receptacle and drew the names of those who were to be drafted. The names were publicized and a designee of the local board personally delivered notices to the men called. If this was not possible, the document was left at the man's last known address. Each prospective recruit then had to report for a physical. If he passed the medical examination, he next appeared before the enrollment board to determine whether he was eligible for exemption for some other reason. Once this phase was completed, a roster was prepared identifying those who were held to service. A drafted man then had ten days in which to pay commutation, furnish a substitute, or in the case of conscripts, arrange his personal affairs before reporting back to the enrollment board. After this ten-day lapse, a conscript was issued a uniform and confined to a holding area before being sent to a general rendezvous for assignment to one of the regiments.[37]

At this point the system became a sour one for conscripts and substitutes. Instead of being treated on a par with volunteers, they were usually confined to a holding area with bounty jumpers and deserters. On the assumption that they would desert at the earliest opportunity, conscripts were kept under guard until they arrived in their units. Although the stigma of conscription began to disappear from communities after March 1863, conscripts and substitutes continued to be ostracized among soldiers in the field. They were viewed as slackers who were not to be trusted under fire.[38] This prejudice derived primarily from the way conscripts and substitutes had been treated and classified once they reported for duty. Twentieth-century draft officials learned from this experience and took a more positive approach in handling conscripts. In World War I, for example, the draft was presented more as a "voluntary affair" in which citizens participated than as a system that forced men into service.[39]

Although Fry's successors in the twentieth century experienced their share of difficulties, especially in responding to pressure from various groups, they largely escaped severe criticism during most of their tenure. In part, this was due to a deliberate policy that placed more importance on the draft than on recruiting. These men also were influential in shaping the enabling legislation. Unlike Fry, for example, Major General Enoch H. Crowder, head of the Selective Service Bureau during World War I, had a major role in the development of the conscription laws. Lewis B. Hershey, whose name is synonymous with Selective Service, inherited the basic principles of this system and refined it over a period of decades. Although volunteering was encouraged, the draft remained as the preeminent method for mobilizing the nation's manpower resources. Not until the Vietnam War era did Hershey even begin to experience the level of virulent criticism that Fry encountered during the latter part of the Civil War.[40]

Waiting for communities to fill their quotas with volunteers caused major delays for the Provost Marshal General's Bureau. In addition, the quotas, the erosion of local pride, and the strain of economic costs increased the discontent that citizens directed toward Fry's agency, as did the subdistrict policy, and Fry had to depend on community goodwill.

The ways in which troops were recruited before and after March 1863 differed little on the surface. Localities still organized recruiting drives, sponsored bond rallies, and held concerts and exhibitions in an effort to raise bounty money; but the enthusiasm and patriotic fervor of the early war years were gone. By the last year of the war, as voluntary contributions began drying up, many localities increasingly turned to real estate assessments. In many instances elected officials simply ordered special taxes that were levied on property owners, or issued bonds for the raising of bounties that could only be redeemed after the war.[41] The cost of these special levies was enormous. The budget in one Massachusetts town, for example, rose from $11,874 in 1861 to $41,596 by 1865, largely as a consequence of paying bounties.[42] These special levies were resented to the point that they sometimes provoked a violent reaction. Near the end of the war in Stow, Ohio, one wealthy farmer refused to pay a $60 tax that had been ordered by a local recruiting committee. When he was visited by a delegation, he drove them from his property and, in his anger, killed two of the members.[43]

This episode represented an extreme response to substituting money for troops during the war's final years. More common was a trend beginning in 1863 that Eugene Murdock best describes as a relationship in which "bounties went progressively upward while the quality of men obtained went progressively downward."[44] Local bounties unquestionably were the key factor in recruiting men after the federal draft arrived, but they also helped undermine confidence in the combined system of drafting and recruiting. As early as the fall of 1863, an attitude of open disdain began surfacing toward the entire process. Michigan's governor, Austin Blair, identified this "prejudice" when he predicted that the draft would yield few soldiers. Blair's prophecy proved true in the coming months when the returns from the 1863 call were tallied for his state. Of the 2,575 Michigan men held to service, 1,644 paid commutation and 651 furnished substitutes. Only 280 became conscripts.[45]

Rather than unifying a community, the federal draft sometimes had a reverse effect. A Michigan woman in November 1863, for example, called it a "failure" and a "disgrace" because only six men in her entire town had been deemed qualified for service. She further noted a similar pattern in surrounding communities. As she lamented the passing of patriotism, she revealed her displeasure with the men who were enlisting solely for the bounty when she asked, "How much would an army like them do toward putting down the rebellion?" She was equally disgusted with older able-bodied men who were encouraging the enlistments of the 15 to 18 boys in her town in an effort to fill the local quota.[46]

As the reservoir of manpower began to evaporate at home, many townships and other political subdivisions retained brokers to canvass other geographical areas. These quests for prospective recruits, of whatever physical or mental caliber, extended into other communities, states, and foreign countries. Some brokers crossed into Canada to enlist Union skedaddlers and deserters, and also escaped rebel prisoners.[47] Other unscrupulous agents simply drugged Canadian citizens before placing them in the Union army. This practice became so widespread that it ultimately prompted a stiff diplomatic response from the British government.[48] Still other European countries were upset with the influx of agents, particularly from New England, who encouraged their citizens to emigrate, ostensibly for good civilian jobs in the North. Once in the United States, most of these individuals found themselves in the Union army after having first been swindled out of their bounty money.[49]

Many agents and some federal officials employed similar methods in obtaining men at home. Brokers relied heavily on higher bounties in enticing men from poorer areas to enlist in wealthier towns. This practice had an especially detrimental effect on those communities that lost men to wealthier ones, because quotas then fell disproportionately on the remaining citizens. Individuals and brokers were the main beneficiaries of the higher bounties, with a few notable exceptions. In certain Southern states, former slaves were simply impressed into service with no regard for the adverse social effects that their absences would have on those they had to leave behind.[50]

After the war, General Fry observed that the "extension of [his] Bureau over the country brought together the Government and the people by closer ties, [and] nurtured that mutual confidence and reliance through which the civil war was conducted to a successful termination."[51] But, as with so many others who were anxious to put the war behind them, Fry exhibited a selective memory, choosing not to remember the North's initial emotional reaction to the draft, which led to overt resistance in some areas. Before the end of 1863, most Union men had acquiesced in the draft as they successfully devised individual ways to circumvent it. Northern communities, however, increasingly came to resent the system and by the summer of 1864 looked upon it with disdain. By the end of the year, their attitude had crystallized into pervasive alienation as they became more and more contemptuous of Fry and the confusing regulations that emanated from his remote headquarters in the Capitol. By the war's end, most communities despised him, his agency, and the army of bureaucrats who were charged with implementing his instructions and filling his never-ending quotas for more troops.

QUOTAS AND OTHER NUMBERS

S
ome of the most perplexing aspects of the Union draft concern the methods that were used in determining quotas and the accuracy of figures in related areas, such as number of men drafted. Estimates vary widely on the number of conscripts who served in the Union army, but based on the extant evidence they comprised no more than 5.54 percent of all Union soldiers. This figure can be misleading, however, and requires further explanation. Under the nine-month state drafts, the 87,588 men who were taken represented 11.31 percent of the total number raised from April 1861 to March 1863. The number declined dramatically when national conscription was instituted. After that point, federal conscripts made up only 3.67 percent of the new soldiers. Little is known about the number of substitutes who entered the army prior to 1863, but 118,010 went as replacements for drafted men from 1863 to 1865. They represented 9.35 percent of the new soldiers in those final years. In the aggregate, federal conscripts and substitutes comprised 13.02 percent of men raised for the Union army in the last two years of the war.

These percentages differ significantly from those usually cited for conscripts, and the bases for them and other figures are explained below. Much of the difficulty in arriving at exact totals stems from conflicting or incomplete records. Part of the problem also can be attributed to the methods that the federal government used in classifying soldiers into categories, and in determining credits and quotas. Throughout the war, periods of service generally ranged from three months to three years. There were also 1,042 men who enlisted for a four-year term of enlistment under the last two calls of the war. To complicate matters further, credits were reduced to a three-year standard that, if followed strictly, correspondingly decreases the total number of men who served. These figures, however, rarely have been subjected to close scrutiny, and some continue to elude a rational explanation.[1]

In discussing the number of men raised under the calls of July 1 and August 4, 1862, for instance, one student has referred to the "confusing arithmetic" that the War Department used in calculating credits for three-year men who enlisted and for nine-month men who were drafted.[2] Each of these calls imposed a quota for 334,835 men. Many scholars believe that most states filled and in some cases exceeded their obligations, but the "confusing arithmetic" has led others to argue that quotas generally were not met.[3] The extant evidence supports the view that the federal government obtained all of the men it requested under these two calls. According to War Department sources, 421,465 and 431,958 are the two figures that appear for the total number of men furnished. The largest one is the most accurate.[4] Assuming a three-year standard, 334,835 three-year men were ultimately expected under the July call, and the equivalent of one-fourth, or 83,709 three-year men, were ultimately required under the August draft call. These subtotals yield an adjusted total of 418,544 three-year men, rather than an aggregate figure of 669,670 new soldiers. Since 431,958 three-year men were actually furnished, along with 87,588 nine-month men, most states evidently were quite successful in meeting federal troop requisitions in the summer and fall of 1862.

Despite the centralization and the implied uniformity that national conscription promised, the uncertainty over the number of men furnished in some categories did not disappear after March 1863. Instead it increased. In Fry's abridged version of his *Final Report*, for example, he gives conflicting figures in various areas. In one instance, 46,347 is given for the number of men actually conscripted; in another, 52,067 appears. Other inconsistencies abound.[5]

As reflected in the discrepancies in the 1862 calls, the need for relatively precise information cannot be underestimated because it directly influences the conclusions that historians draw about Civil War recruiting and the draft. Peter Levine in his study of the 161,244 men who failed to report, for example, asserts that more men chose illegal over legal evasion. In his calculations, Levine included only those men who provided substitutes *after* being held to service and excluded some 44,403 substitutes that men furnished prior to being drafted. Had he included these data, he would have reached a different finding inasmuch that more, not fewer, men either paid commutation or furnished substitutes. The fault is not with Levine's figures, rather it lies with Fry. In one instance he grouped these 44,403 replacements in the substitute category; in another he classified them as volunteers.[6]

Different figures also exist for the number of men who served during the war. Total enlistments in the Union army and navy are set at 2,778,304, and estimates range from 1,550,000 to 2,400,000 for individuals who actually served (after factors such as the reenlistment of certain groups are taken into account).

A major difficulty arises as well in determining the number of bounty jumpers, particularly those who enlisted over thirty times and were counted toward the quotas in over thirty different localities. They are usually factored into the total number of enlistments.[7] After a detailed examination of varying estimates, E. B. Long finally concluded that "there is no accurate means of determining just how many individuals served in the armed forces of either the Federal or Confederate armies."[8]

Total troop credits is one of the most muddled areas where variant information exists. One table in the *Official Records* lists a total of 2,778,034 men, while another gives a figure of 2,324,516 men when reductions to a three-year standard are taken into account. Other figures are sometimes cited as well. The most accurate information appears to be a table that Fry included as part of his full *Final Report*, which he submitted in March 1866, almost a year after the war ended. It consists of lower figures both for quotas assigned and men furnished, and Fry noted that the information was current through June 30, 1865. Among the discrepancies between Fry's *Report* and the one elsewhere in the *Official Records* is a 4,621 difference in quotas. There is also a disparity of 87,903 in the number of men obtained.[9] The origin of the larger figure has not been ascertained, but it may stem from states and communities claiming credit for the same men, or as part of special service forces that Lincoln authorized on occasion.[10] As reflected in his *Final Report*, Fry was quick to sing the praises of his bureau and would have undoubtedly cited the inflated figure if he thought it was valid.

Fry's figures on quotas are presented in table 1, and tables 2 and 3 concern federal conscription. Although table 1 will not provide definitive answers on the exact number of individual men who served in the Union forces, the data in tables 2 and 3 yield more precise figures on those who were drafted. All of them derive from information in Fry's full *Final Report*. Also, the data in tables 2 and 3 were generated from information at the district level and were compared to various facts and figures in Fry's published and abridged report.[11] The tables are arranged in such a way that future students can generate percentages needed for other works.

In some instances the information in table 1 has been consolidated in accordance with certain of Fry's decisions.[12] For example, there were two calls for troops in May and July 1861, and he grouped the figures together. President Lincoln issued three additional calls on October 17, 1863, February 1, 1864, and March 14, 1864. On one occasion Fry grouped all three together, but on another he linked only the first two and kept the March 14 one distinct. The March call is listed separately in the composite table. Finally, a large difference exists between the quota and the number obtained under this call. This stems mainly from a series of supplemental drafts that were conducted in districts that needed to make up deficiences under the first federal draft in 1863.

TABLE 1

Composite of Troop Calls, Quotas, and Numbers Obtained, 1861–1865

Date of Call	Number Called	Period of Service	Quota	Number Obtained
Apr. 15, 1861	75,000	3 months	73,391	93,326
May 3 & July 1861	592,748	3 years	611,827	714,231
May & June 1862	No formal call	3 months	—	15,007
July 2, 1862	300,000	3 years	334,835	431,958
Aug. 4, 1862	300,000	9 months	334,835	87,588
June 15, 1863	100,000	6 months	—	16,361
Oct. 17, 1863	500,000	3 years	467,434	374,807
Mar. 14, 1864	200,000	3 years	186,981	284,021
Apr. 23, 1864	85,000	100 days	113,000	83,652
July 18, 1864	500,000	1, 2, and 3 years	346,746	384,882
Dec. 19, 1864	300,000	1, 2, and 3 years	290,000	204,568
TOTAL	2,952,748	—	2,759,049	2,690,401

Federal conscription was introduced at the midpoint of the Civil War, and data suggest that slightly more than half of the men obtained, 1,348,291, were raised during Fry's tenure as provost marshal general. From this figure, however, should be deducted 86,724 men who paid the exemption fee but who nevertheless were credited as troops furnished. Presumably the War Department was to use this commutation money to purchase substitutes, and in the fall of 1863 it authorized federal bounties to be paid from this fund for the purposes of raising new recruits and encouraging veterans to reenlist. All recruits and veterans so acquired were credited to localities as men furnished. But no matter how Fry tried to slice the pie under this system, the government obtained only one actual man per bounty and not two.[13]

Further, Fry's bureau had no direct involvement in initiating the reenlistment of 136,507 veteran volunteers who would be exempt from the draft once they completed their initial term of service. The bureau also had little to do with encouraging men to enlist for six months in June 1863 or for one hundred days in the spring of 1864, because these 100,013 men initially did not receive exemptions from the draft while in service. Nevertheless, Fry's agency did determine where credits for these men would be assigned and facilitated their enlistments. As such, they can be included under the number of actual troop credits raised during Fry's tenure. When the 86,724 men who paid commutation are deducted from Fry's total of men furnished, his bureau was responsible for either directly or indirectly obtaining no more than 1,261,567 men for the Union army and navy. This adjusted total obviously does not take into account the men who either jumped bounty or deserted prior to arriving in their units.

The majority of men, 1,342,110, joined the Union forces prior to March 1863, when patriotism was still a significant motivation and the needs of the Union army were not as great. Even if an estimated 50,000 three-month men who reenlisted in the summer of 1861 are deducted, leaving a balance of 1,292,110, most men entered Union ranks before Fry assumed the office of provost marshal general. This break is important because it further illustrates that Fry had to keep drawing on a diminishing pool of qualified manpower in a climate that became increasingly hostile where troop calls were concerned.

Conflicting figures were not the only problem that plagued the beleaguered provost marshal general. The Enrollment Act essentially required that a relatively large number of men be drawn to make up anticipated deficiencies in local quotas. Only after a draft was ordered were men then examined and either discharged, exempted for physical disability and other causes, or held to service. While the number drawn in the federal drafts can serve as a barometer on the relative health of Union men, it is not a good yardstick to use for measuring the draft's effect. Also, from a public relations standpoint, this method contributed to misunderstanding because it inflated the quotas assigned rather than specifying the exact number of men needed. Although cumbersome, this system was preferred by Congress over any other method because of its desire to rely as much as possible on stimulating communities to fill quotas with volunteers rather than conscripts.

As indicated in table 2, a total of 776,829 men were drawn under the four major calls ordered between 1863 and 1865. In retrospect, this figure is not as ominous as it appears. At the end of the war, a balance of 2,254,063 men on Northern enrollment lists had not yet had their names drawn from the draft wheel.[14] Further, one recent account argues that approximately one-half of Northern eligible males served in the Civil War, compared to approximately 80 percent for the Confederacy.[15]

Northern society nonetheless believed that quotas were burdensome, and particularly so in those communities that had to conduct a draft. If a citizen was drawn in the draft, however, he stood only one chance in four of being held to service. At that point he could pay a commutation fee, when that program was generally available, or furnish a substitute. There also existed the possibility that he would be among some 93,000 men who were discharged either per special order or because the quota was considered full.[16] Another 848 men were exempted for mental disability, and 159,403 were excused for

TABLE 2
FEDERAL DRAFT CALLS

Date of Call	Number Drawn	Did Not Report	Discharged	Examined	Disability Exemptions	All Other Exemptions	Held to Service
Oct. 1863	292,441	39,415	460	252,566	81,388	83,007	88,171
Mar. 1864	113,446	27,193	1,296	84,957	21,525	18,427	45,005
July 1864	231,918	66,159	27,223	138,536	42,964	39,567	56,005
Dec. 1864	139,024	28,477	64,419	46,128	14,374	14,257	17,497
TOTAL	776,829	161,244	93,398	522,187	160,251	155,258	206,678

TABLE 3
HELD TO SERVICE

Date of Call	Number Held to Service	Paid Commutation	Furnished Substitute	Conscripted
Oct. 1863	88,171	52,288	26,002	9,881
Mar. 1864	45,005	32,678	8,911	3,416
July 1864	56,005	1,298	28,502	26,205
Dec. 1864	17,497	460	10,192	6,845
TOTAL	206,678	86,724	73,607	46,347

a variety of physical ailments. Exemptions were granted to an additional 155,258 men for other reasons. In 1863 certain liable men could escape the draft for hardship reasons, including being the only son of aged parents or the father of motherless children. Other reasons for exemption ran the gamut of being under twenty or over forty-five years of age, having died, being nonresidents, and already being in service with the Union army or navy.

In interpreting subtotals in table 2, the categories of did not report, discharged, and examined, equal the number drawn. The number examined total includes those who received disability exemptions, all other exemptions, and those held to service. In table 3, those who paid commutation, furnished substitutes, or were conscripted reflect the distribution of those held to service.

The subtotal given for substitutes, 73,607, in table 3 represents only those principals who furnished replacements after being drafted. It excludes the 44,403 substitutes that enrolled men placed into service before they were drafted. Unfortunately, the district subtotals in Fry's full *Report* do not reveal the number of these substitutes assigned to each district for the last three drafts. Neither are the manuscript sources in the National Archives of much assistance. Where the information exists at all, this class of substitutes tends to be consolidated according to a district but not delineated by draft call.[17] The important point is that 118,010 draft-liable men hired substitutes in the last two years of the war.

A total of 46,347 conscripts is the most accurate figure, and historians generally have used it rather than the higher figures of 48,209 and 52,067. However, they have inadvertently erred in estimating that the draft obtained only 6 percent of the soldiers for the Union army, because they have based their calculations on the 776,829 who were drawn in the national draft from 1863–1865.[18]

As reflected in table 2, over 160,000 men were listed as delinquent and therefore need to be discounted from the number drawn. They either consciously or unknowingly failed to appear, but they did not make a choice whether to pay commutation, provide a substitute, or render personal service. Also, the number of men who were discharged and those who received exemptions need to be deducted because they too did not have to exercise one of these choices. These adjustments are important because they affect significant conclusions. For example, Hugh G. Earnhart in his study of Ohio argues that commutation's repeal had an adverse effect on workingmen. He bases his finding on the number of men drawn instead of those who were held. As discussed later, the fee's recall did not necessarily discriminate against Ohio workingmen when the analysis is confined to those men who were actually drafted.[19]

In general, the number of men drawn must be used with caution because it is an unreliable index for assessing the impact of federal conscription on Union men. Had those who received discharges or exemptions been drafted, they probably would have selected one of the three choices available to those held to service. They would have done so in similar proportions depending on the geographical area, the draft call, and other factors such as the availability of substitutes.

The extent to which the federal draft directly raised troops for the Union army was not that burdensome on Northern men. Using the revised figure of 1,261,567 actual troops raised between 1863 and 1865, which includes 46,347 conscripts and 118,010 substitutes, the following percentages appear. Federal conscripts comprised 3.67 percent, and substitutes comprised 9.35 percent. With an aggregate of 164,357 men, 13.02 percent of those who entered the Union army did so as a direct consequence of the federal draft.

Among other percentages that can be generated is the total number of conscripts compared to the maximum number of individual soldiers obtained under all calls for the entire war. Here some difficulties arise because this calculation requires adding 87,588 nine-month men who were drafted before March 1863 to the total pool of Union conscripts. Further, an estimated 50,000 men who reenlisted in 1861 and 136,507 veteran volunteers, both of whom Fry counted twice, need to be deducted from his grand total of 2,690,401 men raised. There is also the matter of 86,724 commutation credits. In any case, definitely no more than 2,467,170 men actually served for periods ranging from three months to four years, but even this figure is high. After an untold number of bounty jumpers, men who were counted twice, and approximately 200,000 actual deserters are taken into account, probably just over two million individuals entered Union ranks.

Using the highest possible figure of 2,467,170 men and a total of 133,935 conscripts, it appears that 5.54 percent of the soldiers in the Union army were conscripts. In addition to the uncertainty over the exact number of individuals who entered the army, this percentage must be approached with caution for other reasons as well. Aside from the fact that the 1862 conscripts served only for nine months, compared to the one-to-three-year term required of federal conscripts, only thirteen political entities conducted a draft in 1862. This information invites scrutiny, however, because the Nebraska Territory provided 1,228 conscripts, but it was neither liable to conscription nor assigned any quota. Nevertheless, its men were included in the War Department's total of 87,588 conscripts, even though they should have been classified as volunteers.[20] Also, the 1862 drafts were administered through the states, and their laws varied particularly when it came to substitution and commutation. Some states allowed these practices and others did not. Aside from these differences, little usable data exist on the men who went as substitutes in 1862. Therefore, the total number who entered the army as a direct result of Union conscription from 1862 to 1865 must remain open to conjecture.

The most accurate information that can be generated on the draft's effect derives from the more uniform system of federal conscription. Slightly more than 13 percent of soldiers in the Union army were federal conscripts and substitutes, as compared to estimates of 20 to 21 percent of men who entered the Confederate army in a similar status. Based on the available data, which are also conflicting and incomplete, one study estimates that conscripts made up 11 percent of the Southern army, while substitutes comprised another 10 percent.[21]

Excluding black males, the seceding states, and emigration figures for the war years, estimates suggest that there were 4,559,872 white males of military age among the population of the territories, the border states, and the rest of the North in 1860.[22] Therefore, just over 1 percent (1.01 to be exact) of these men entered the Union army as federal conscripts. Even if the aggregate number of 206,678 men held to service or drafted is used, only 4.5 percent of this group had to exercise an option of either paying a fee, providing a substitute, or going to war under federal conscription. Further, it bears reiterating that the estimate for the four-and-a-half-million eligible men omits blacks. At least in Delaware, some resident blacks paid commutation, furnished substitutes, or served as conscripts.[23] Allowing for such adjustments, a Northern man of military age had less than one chance in a hundred of actually becoming a federal conscript.

The purpose of this analysis has been to clarify some of the conflicting figures rather than to add to the confusion. A corollary aim has been to demonstrate further that complaints of Northern citizens were not without some justification as they tried to interpret Fry's figures. Indeed, more than a century after the end of the Civil War, some of the numbers still continue to befuddle historians who, unlike local officials and community leaders in the Civil War North, enjoy the detachment of time and distance from the Provost Marshal General's Bureau.

YANKEE RECRUITS,
CONSCRIPTS, AND
ILLEGAL EVADERS

Much is known about the general characteristics of the men who served in the predominantly volunteer Union army. Numerous studies discuss why Union men were motivated to enlist, and others describe shifts in attitude toward the war through an adept use of soldiers' diaries, letters, and journals.[1] These primary sources often contain disparaging comments about the men who stayed at home through either commutation or substitution, or about those who went as conscripts. Beyond these personal opinions, however, little is known about the characteristics of Northern men who were drafted for Union service.[2]

A survey of major works that examine traits of Union recruits, as well as composites of the occupations, ages, and birthplaces of 14,336 Union men who were held to service, appears later in the chapter. Occupational data on another 6,453 men who resided in select Northern districts, and who were exempted for reasons such as physical disability, are also presented. This aggregate of 20,789 men whose names were drawn in the draft reveals various patterns, including whether an unskilled laborer or a professional person had a greater possibility of being exempted. Even more important is how the subset of 14,336 men who were actually held to service compared to Union soldiers and the military-age population of the North in 1860. Extant data on men who failed to report are very limited, but an analysis of an additional 497 New York men who were classified as illegal evaders is included also.[3]

Civil War soldiers have been analyzed almost since the opening shot at Fort Sumter. In conjunction with American life insurance companies, the United States Sanitary Commission initiated anthropometric examinations of

Union soldiers during the first year of the war. Among other uses, this information was later applied in making comparisons between the characteristics of white and black soldiers once the latter were accepted for Union service.[4] The Provost Marshal General's Bureau also generated a wealth of data on men who were examined but for composites it limited its tabulations primarily to personal characteristics such as height, weight, and physical infirmities.[5]

Under the auspices of the Sanitary Commission, Benjamin A. Gould published his *Investigations in the Military and Anthropological Statistics of American Soldiers* in 1869. Based on an examination of muster rolls, Gould and an army of assistants constructed tables that described characteristics such as the occupations, ages, nativities, complexions, hair and eye colors, and mean dimensions of the bodies of 666,530 Union soldiers. Gould's tabulations reflected certain distinct biases, particularly in the creation of a separate occupational classification for printers, a tendency to favor the professional and educated classes, and the exclusion of data from Delaware and Maryland. Nevertheless, as later compilations and general surveys on the ages and occupations of typical recruits reveal, Gould drew a fairly good portrait of the average Union soldier.[6]

In the period since Gould's monumental work, historians have reaffirmed some of his findings and have refined or expanded upon others. The two most important and ambitious of these endeavors stem from the work of professors Bell Wiley and James McPherson. Wiley examined the muster rolls of 114 units and extracted data on 13,392 soldiers for age, occupation, and nativity. A study of this material led him to agree with many of Gould's findings and to modify others, which he described in his narrative on *Billy Yank*.[7] Using Wiley's extensive research as a basis and that of Ella Lonn for nativity data, McPherson constructed a useful matrix in which he classified the men in Wiley's sample according to occupation. He included a similar table based on the occupational data of Northern males from the 1860 census (see table 4).[8]

As McPherson explains, the figure for unskilled workers can be misleading because of the age factor. The Union army was a young one, as reflected in the median age of 23.5 years. Equally as important, 40 percent of the soldiers were 21 years of age and under when they entered the service. Wiley further calculates that, halfway through the war, three-fourths of all Union troops were under 30, and at least half had not reached 25 years of age.[9] In addition, various studies on occupational mobility in the nineteenth century have shown that a significant number of men who started out as unskilled workers eventually moved into white-collar positions. When the mobility factor is taken into account, McPherson speculates that it was not "a rich man's war and a poor man's fight" in the North. Except for unskilled workers who did not serve

TABLE 4

OCCUPATIONAL COMPOSITE OF UNION SOLDIERS, 1861–1865

Occupational Category	Union Soldiers, U.S. Sanitary Commission Sample (%)	Union Soldiers, Bell Wiley Sample (%)	All Males, 1860 Census (%)
Farmers & farm workers	47.5	47.8	42.9
Skilled workers	25.1	25.2	24.9
Unskilled workers	15.9	15.1	16.7
White-collar & commercial	5.1	7.8	10.0
Professional	3.2	2.9	3.5
Miscellaneous and unknown	3.2	1.2	2.0
TOTAL	100	100	100

From *Ordeal by Fire: The Civil War and Reconstruction* by James M. McPherson.
© 1982 by Alfred A. Knopf, Inc. Reprinted by permission of the publisher.

to the extent that their numbers warranted in the total population, men from all classes were proportionately represented in the military.[10]

The ethnicity of Union soldiers has also been examined. Approximately 25 percent of the army's ranks were filled by immigrants or by men who were born abroad, but the foreign-born actually comprised 30 percent of men of military age in the North. Foreigners generally were not as well represented in the army as they might have been. These broad generalizations must be used judiciously, however, because, as McPherson points out, some groups such as German Protestants furnished more than their fair share of soldiers; others, especially German and Irish Catholics, did not participate as fully as their numbers warranted.[11]

Wiley's and McPherson's painstaking efforts have given students an accurate and extensive data base on the occupation, age, and nativity of the average Union soldier. In the absence of further evidence, they have shown beyond a reasonable doubt that the Union military was a citizen's army because it reflected the Northern male population at large, especially in the areas of age and occupation. Their combined work provides the closest approximation available of a reasonable national standard. In turn, it can prove useful as a framework for certain studies that examine the occupational composition, age distribution, and nativity of men who enlisted in a particular unit or from a particular locality. There are, of course, some obvious exceptions. More than 92 percent of soldiers in the predominantly ethnic 12th Missouri Infantry, for example, were foreign-born. Limitations also exist where information is nonexistent or has little value, as in the case of the USS *Cairo,* where 48 percent of the ship's complement listed no previous occupations.[12]

McPherson's and Wiley's data also can be used as a beacon to chart how the war affected men in various occupational and age categories and, for the later war years, how recruiting may have altered the socioeconomic composition of Northern communities. To a limited extent their work has been considered, but the full potential of the data has yet to be realized. W. J. Rorabaugh in his study of Concord, Massachusetts, for example, cites McPherson and Wiley, raises appropriate questions about the reliability of occupational data recorded in the nineteenth century, and goes beyond their analyses by controlling for property ownership. Contrary to their findings, Rorabaugh determines that the preponderance of recruits were young propertyless clerks and farm laborers, and skilled workers in their thirties. He suggests, but indicates he cannot prove, that this trend stemmed from "economic frustration and a social malaise" whose origins lay in the antebellum period.

Rorabaugh's analysis of Concord men who became soldiers covers the entire war period, and the men are not subdivided according to whether they entered the army prior to March 1863. Of the 203 individuals who were credited to this town, only 97, less than 48 percent, appeared both in military records and in the manuscript census. He concentrates on these 97 men and also excludes the Irish from his sample.[13] The omission of the other 106 men is important because a strong possibility exists that many of them were not Concord residents at all if they entered the army after 1863. Instead, several of them undoubtedly were imported to fill local quotas. Emily Harris identifies the extent to which this activity occurred in Deerfield, Massachusetts. As the war dragged on, this town became less and less willing to commit its native sons to battle. Indeed, of the 303 men ultimately credited to Deerfield, only 167, roughly 55 percent, were residents. The other 136 came from elsewhere.[14]

Harris's and Rorabaugh's studies contain some valuable data, but their work could be enhanced through the inclusion of other important variables. One mentions and then differs from the data that McPherson and Wiley generated, while the other does not refer to this information at all. Neither study controls for the institution of the federal draft in the spring of 1863, a factor that has some bearing on their conclusions. In Deerfield, for example, eleven men were drafted in January 1863 and are included in the aggregate of drafted men in Harris's study. There existed distinct differences between conscripts who were taken for nine months under the 1862 militia draft, and which was still in progress in early 1863, and the men who subsequently became federal conscripts for one to three years. Aside from the shorter period of service, some semblance of local pride still existed in many communities in early 1863. Concurrent forces were also at work, especially as "the grim reality of war" was being brought home. Although Harris believes that recruiting took place throughout the war in a "context of constant local patriotism," she implicitly acknowledges the important role returning veterans had in discouraging other men from going to war. In a particularly poignant story she tells of Alden Spout, whose soldier brother Dana became seriously ill and was sent home to die. Confronted with this reality in the summer of 1863, Alden decided to avoid the draft by paying the commutation fee.[15]

Harris charts many important shifts that occurred in raising troops, and this information can be applied to other Northern communities. Conversely, Rorabaugh's data cannot be accepted at face value because he grouped all of the men in his sample together for the entire war period. Had he separated Concord soldiers by chronological enlistment periods, he probably would have discovered, based on trends that were occurring elsewhere, that many of those who enlisted or were drafted in 1861 and 1862 were residents and property owners. More likely than not, those who were credited in the last two years of the war were nonresidents and non–property owners. It is possible too that there were some Concord residents enlisted from 1863 to 1865, or went as substitutes. Rather than "economic frustration," perhaps their motivation was high local bounties or fees for relatively short periods of service. Such financial incentives may have proven more attractive than the wages these men could earn as clerks, skilled workers, or farm laborers. Perhaps some residents, responding to competitive bounties, enlisted in neighboring towns for larger sums of money. Another possibility, though doubtful, is that Concord represents an aberration from recruiting practices that were occurring elsewhere after 1863.

Another Massachusetts town and its recruits also have been the object of recent inquiry. In a sweeping essay, Maris A. Vinovskis legitimately calls for more local studies of the war's effect on individuals both during and after the war. In an analysis of enlistments in Newburyport, his work goes beyond the scope of Rorabaugh's and discusses ethnicity, occupation, wealth, school attendance, and educational attainment as "predictors of enlistment." Of the 1,337 men who appeared on the town's rosters as recruits, 728, or 55 percent, were residents (Vinovskis confines his analysis to residents alone). Among his major findings are that the highest percentage of enlistments occurred among the young, that the working classes were not disproportionately represented, and that the foreign-born were less likely to enlist. All of these findings are generally in accord with McPherson's, but as with similiar works, this study ignores the federal draft as a factor in determining the type of recruit who entered the Union army after the midpoint of the war.[16]

Federal conscription is only one of the important variables that must be considered when examining trends in the raising of Northern troops at the local level. Also significant for assessing any major changes that transpired is the selection of a community that furnished men both before and after 1863.[17] Within the context of these methodological considerations, additional local studies are needed to more precisely assess the war's effect on Northern communities and civilians. Greater reliance also must be placed on the mass of data that McPherson and Wiley compiled and made available on the typical Union soldier. Among more important uses, these data can identify the effect that troop calls may have had on certain occupational classes and the extent to which a community differed from the national norm in furnishing troops for the Union army. Local studies also would add indirectly to the depth of our knowledge on the factors that influenced men to go to war.

*H*istorians usually agree on why Northern men volunteered for the army. Community pride, patriotism, a desire to participate in preserving the Union and to prove one's manhood on the battlefield rank among the dominant reasons that motivated men in the early part of the war. High bounties were a primary influence for many of those who waited until later to enlist.[18] Little is known, however, about why so many men waited to be drafted. High wages at home dissuaded some men from enlisting. A reluctance to go to war combined with the visual effects of disabled veterans returning home was another deterrent. Other men had little reason to fear the draft because of the availability of commutation and substitution. "Hear well," wrote James Bamon in a rather nonchalant letter to a friend, "I am drafted into the survice [*sic*] of the united [*sic*] States. I am gointo [*sic*] put a man in for one year" for a thousand dollars.[19]

Data have been analyzed from the "Descriptive Books" and their equivalents in the Records of the Provost Marshal General's Bureau at the National Archives in an effort to better understand how federal conscription affected Northern men. As in any historical study, the availability of extant and useful source material is a major consideration. In Record Group 110, unfortunately, not all district records are complete. Of the six draft districts in Michigan, for example, only the second and third districts contain relatively thorough information. Of the 435 men who paid commutation in Delaware under the 1863 call, usable information is available on only 4 of them. Consequently, this group was deleted entirely rather than inflating the category of unknowns. The first-district records for Rhode Island contain information on conscripts, which is included, but no data are provided on those who paid commutation or furnished a substitute.[20]

Within the limitations of extant material, localities are included that not only reflect geographical diversity but also urban-rural and political differences. In addition to Delaware, Michigan, and Rhode Island, there are sources from the states of Iowa, Kansas, New Hampshire, and the thirtieth district of New York.[21] Not all of these areas were liable to all four federal drafts, but in the aggregate the results from the four calls appear in the tables. The placement of individuals into occupational clusters relies mainly on the classifications developed by Theodore Hershberg and Robert Dockhorn for 1860 American society.[22] For ease in comparing data, table 5 follows the same general format and arrangement of categories as McPherson's table on Union soldiers, while table 6 examines this same data *within and across* classifications.

The occupations of these men represented a broad spectrum encompassing more than 450 separate vocational pursuits. On a purely alphabetical scale, they ranged from accountants to wood sellers. Between these extremes, attorneys and pail makers shared the dubious status of being held to service with shoemakers and sleigh makers, druggists and wheelwrights, boat pilots and tinkers, sextons and saloon keepers, laborers and publishers, railroaders and balloonists, necromancers and physicians, jewelers and stonecutters, bird fanciers and veterinary surgeons.[23]

TABLE 5

OCCUPATIONAL COMPOSITE OF DRAFTED MEN HELD TO SERVICE, 1863–1865

Occupational Category	Paid Commutation		Furnished Substitutes		Conscripted	
	N	%	N	%	N	%
Farmers & farm workers	1,813	53.3	3,191	43.1	2,214	62.8
Skilled workers	556	16.3	1,386	18.7	419	11.9
Unskilled workers	437	12.8	754	10.2	636	18.1
White-collar & commercial	308	9.0	733	9.9	61	1.7
Professional	77	2.3	152	2.0	30	0.8
Miscellaneous	61	1.8	76	1.0	13	0.4
Unknown	152	4.5	1,116	15.1	151	4.3
TOTAL	3,404	100	7,408	100	3,524	100

Social lines became blurred as the draft reached out and tapped men from all occupations, ages, and backgrounds. Walter Curry, a 30-year-old Iowa miller who had been born in Pennsylvania, and George Waite, a 25-year-old New Hampshire–born jeweler, found themselves among the class of conscripts with Garrett Moore, a 40-year-old Iowa farmer who had been born in Tennessee. Thirty-year-old Michael McDermott, an Iowa farmer who had been born in Ireland, and New Hampshire–born Nicholas Varney, a 31-year-old carpenter, furnished substitutes. Two New Hampshire–born men, a 36-year-old lumberman and a 39-year-old merchant, decided to pay the three-hundred-dollar fee, as did 37-year-old C. Herschler, an Iowa distiller who had come from Germany.

Drafted Union men who were not fortunate enough to receive an exemption were held to service and had ten days in which to pay commutation, find a substitute, or enter the army. A survey of the 14,336 drafted men who faced these choices and how they compared to other men across their occupational group requires a different approach to the data. Although the vertical format used in table 5 and elsewhere in this study is the most valuable for comparing smaller groups to larger populations and for determining whether conscription fell disproportionately on any group, a horizontal display as used in table 6

TABLE 6

DISTRIBUTION OF DRAFTED MEN ACROSS OCCUPATIONS, 1863–1865

Occupational Category	Total Number	Paid Commutation		Furnished Substitutes		Conscripted	
		N	%	N	%	N	%
Farmers & farm workers	7,218	1,813	25.1	3,191	44.2	2,214	30.7
Skilled workers	2,361	556	23.5	1,386	58.7	419	17.8
Unskilled workers	1,827	437	23.9	754	41.3	636	34.8
White-collar & commercial	1,102	308	28.0	733	66.5	61	5.5
Professional	259	77	29.7	152	58.7	30	11.6
Miscellaneous	150	61	40.7	76	50.7	13	8.6
Unknown	1,419	152	10.7	1,116	78.7	151	10.6
TOTAL	14,336	3,404	23.7	7,408	51.7	3,524	24.6

can sometimes help to elucidate certain trends, such as how men fared within their occupational group when drafted.

As shown in table 6, unskilled workers were, within their group, the least likely to escape conscription, but a surprising 11.6 percent of professionals experienced difficulty, as did 30.7 percent of the farmers and 17.8 percent of the skilled workers. With 5.5 percent, members of the commercial classes enjoyed the greatest advantage for escaping personal service. Professional men and skilled workers, with 58.7 percent, hired substitutes in the same proportion, while those in the white-collar occupations led all groups with 66.5 percent. Unskilled workers and farmers with 41.3 and 44.2 percent, respectively, furnished the fewest; nevertheless, over two-fifths of them found replacements. With a range of 23.5 to 29.7 percent, approximately one-fourth of all drafted men managed to pay commutation regardless of their status. This suggests that widespread access to the three-hundred-dollar exemption fee was available to all groups. To a lesser extent, a similar pattern emerges in the hiring of substitutes.

When viewed solely on the basis of table 6, unskilled workers, with 34.8 percent, were the most likely to be conscripted within their occupational category. This figure can be misleading, however, because only 1,827 of the 14,336 men held to service were from this group. This represents only 12.7 percent of the total pool and is lower than their proportion in the Union army and in the Northern male population at large (see table 4). Considering that skilled workers comprised a quarter of these same populations and that only 2,361 were held, the proportion drafted from their group also was significantly lower, with 16.5 percent. Conversely, 7,218 farmers made up more than half of the men held. At 50.4 percent, a farmer's chance of being liable to the draft was higher.

Tables 4 and 5 are the most useful for assessing how federal conscription fell on Union men. According to the 1860 population survey, and Wiley's and McPherson's samples, a higher proportion of farmers entered the army than their numbers warranted. They also made up almost 63 percent of the conscript pool (see table 5). Another 18.1 percent of the pool consisted of unskilled workers, but since they represented 16.7 percent of the population and approximately 15 percent of all Union troops, the draft did not fall disproportionately on this group to a significant extent. Whether compared to the 1860 census or to Bell Wiley's sample, men in the commercial and professional classes, and skilled workers, were less likely to enter the army. When held to service they were more likely than not to pay three hundred dollars or provide a substitute.

As already illustrated, conscription fell heaviest on farmers and to a much lesser extent on unskilled workers. Also, farmers received only 33.7 percent of the exemptions for humanitarian causes. As reflected in table 7, only 10.3

percent of farmers were excused for being aliens, which indicates that most farmers were native-born. They fared much better in obtaining exemptions for physical disability, and of the 4,853 men in this sample, farmers received 41 percent of them. Unskilled workers received a higher proportion of exemptions for hardship and for alien status than their numbers warranted, but they were released less often for physical disability.

The greatest beneficiaries of the hardship and alien exemptions were skilled and unskilled workers and members of the white-collar classes. Skilled workers also claimed almost one-fourth of all disability exemptions. This percentage paralleled their proportional representation both in the general population and in the army. In the area of medical exemptions, the white-collar and commercial classes (14.9 percent) fared best of all whether compared to their proportional representation in the Union army or the general population. They received more disability exemptions than their numbers warranted.

The age of Union soldiers ranged from 12 to 70, with 98 percent of the concentration falling between 18 and 45. Compared to the average Union soldier, drafted men tended to be older. This trend is not surprising, since the age of liability was limited to a span of 20-to-45 years of age. The median

TABLE 7

Occupational Composite of Men Exempted for Disability,
Alienage, and Hardship Reasons, 1863–1865

Occupational Category	Physical Disability		Alienage		Hardship	
	N	%	N	%	N	%
Farmers & farm workers	1,991	41.0	103	10.3	196	32.7
Skilled workers	1,208	24.9	322	32.2	176	29.4
Unskilled workers	635	13.1	349	34.9	116	19.3
White-collar & commercial	727	14.9	104	10.4	89	14.8
Professional	145	3.0	24	2.4	9	1.5
Miscellaneous	37	0.8	8	0.8	2	0.3
Unknown	110	2.3	90	9.0	12	2.0
TOTAL	4,853	100	1,000	100	600	100

age for all Union soldiers was 23.5, but it increased significantly to 29.4 years for those held to service.[24] Drafted men who paid commutation tended to be the youngest, with a median of 28.7. Over half of them (56.5 percent) were under 30 years old. Those who furnished substitutes had a median age of 29.5, and less than half (45.6 percent) were under 30. Conscripts comprised the oldest class with a median age of 30.1. Less than half of them (46.6 percent) also were under 30.

Conscription tended to force older men into the army or at least required them to furnish a substitute or pay commutation. The system was less successful in encouraging the foreign-born either to serve or to provide some form of alternate service. They comprised approximately one-fourth of the army but provided only 16.8 percent of the conscripts and 12.4 percent of the substitutes. Only 9.4 percent contributed to the commutation fund. In the aggregate, the 1,830 foreign-born represented 12.7 percent of the men held. With 865, those born in Germany were the largest contingent, followed by Ireland with 360 and England with 226 men. Among the other countries represented were Austria, Belgium, France, Holland, Switzerland, and Russia.

The absence of widespread liability to the actual draft among the foreign-born can be attributed mainly to the policy that exempted aliens who had neither voted nor declared their intention to become United States citizens. Those who had inadvertently violated this policy, thereby forfeiting their special exemption status, sometimes chose another path of evasion.

The American military tradition is multidimensional, but where the threat of compulsory service exists or where the conflict has been a divisive one, men of military age (and in some cases their families) have responded predictably. For a variety of reasons, many volunteered. As others faced the prospect of being called into service, some grudgingly went, whereas others relied on a variety of legal deferments to escape or to postpone service in an unpopular war. Those who could not qualify for a special exemption, or for reasons of conscience, sometimes skedaddled.

In the American Revolution, 50,000 to 100,000 Loyalists and their families are estimated to have left the colonies rather than side with their neighbors in the fight against the British Crown.[25] They were motivated to leave mainly for ideological reasons. Although they did not have to face the specter of national conscription, they would have been expected to contribute to their local militias in one form or another had they remained in their communities.

Protest against a conscription system or a particular conflict in the twentieth century has assumed numerous forms but generally has involved a decision not to register for the draft or to leave for another country. Despite the improved efficiency of drafting, conflicting figures nevertheless make it difficult to gauge the extent to which these activities have occurred in modern times. In part this is due to various provisions for liberal deferments, particularly for married men, students, and those in certain occupations. The availability of these deferments, as well as allowances for conscientious objectors, helped mitigate hard personal choices concerning the draft.[26] In any case, the best estimate of draft evasion in World War I appears to be 12 percent. For later conflicts, the figures are even more elusive. In World War II, estimates range from 500,000 delinquents, or approximately 5 percent of the 10 million inductees, to a low of 0.5 percent. For the Vietnam War, one student suggests a figure of 100,000 deserters and evaders but excludes those men who received questionable deferments or who failed to register. Also, this calculation is very conservative given the delinquency rate of over 20 percent early in the Vietnam War.[27]

Illegal evasion also occurred in the North during the Civil War. There were 161,244 men who, in the words of Robert Sterling, chose "the other less honorable avenues of escape." By later standards this is a precise figure, but it applies only to the two-year period of federal conscription. In addition to this group, an estimated 40,000 to 50,000 other Union men evidently "skedaddled" in 1861 and 1862 rather than face their respective state drafts.[28] These 161,244 men represented 20.8 percent of the names drawn under the four federal calls, or 12.8 percent of the number of troops that are estimated to have been raised between 1863 and 1865.

The Union men who failed to appear for the federal draft have been discussed in a thought-provoking study. Peter Levine believes that the draft discriminated against the "unpropertied," and he is critical of historians for ignoring illegal draft evasion because of their "preoccupation with commutation as a measure of the impact of conscription on particular kinds of people." Instead of basing interpretations on economic determinism, Levine, referring to earlier findings of Richard D. Brown and Eric Foner, contends that the draft not only "outlined class distinctions in terms of property, but also . . . in terms of culture and values." Although illegal draft evasion occurred in all types of constituencies later in the war, areas that experienced the highest incidence of this activity tended to be Democratic, Catholic, and foreign-born. Levine's belief is in accord with Robert Sterling's tentative conclusion that overt draft resistance emerged among populations that were predominantly Democratic, foreign-born, Catholic, and poor. Levine admits that his findings too are speculative because of "the need to identify more precisely the people who became illegal draft evaders."[29]

Levine's conclusions raise some interesting questions and issues that deserve further consideration. Foremost among these is the absence of extensive data, which may very well limit, if not preclude, further studies on the characteristics of Civil War men who failed to appear. This dearth of information is understandable since drafting officials in most instances recorded only a man's name, and not other vital data, if a man did not report. Thus, a researcher examining the presumed social status of illegal evaders through an occupational analysis would encounter difficulty because of incomplete or nonexistent source material. Also, to increase the validity of a study on illegal evasion, the researcher should select an area that will permit comparison with those men who chose to escape the draft through commutation or substitution. However, only seven states, primarily in the East and New England, were subject to all four drafts, and the data for most of these areas are scanty.[30]

These factors necessarily impose limitations on studies that compare illegal evasion in the various regions. For example, the response of citizens in Indiana toward the draft would be extremely difficult to gauge. Traditionally viewed as a Copperhead stronghold, the Hoosier State was exempt from the first two national drafts. As such, its citizens did not have to choose between commutation or illegal evasion. Delaware was among the few states to be liable under all four federal drafts, and in February 1864 it approved a law that paid two-thirds of the three-hundred-dollar commutation fee for every one of its drafted white citizens. If illegal evaders had no choice other than to flee to avoid the draft, why did 389 (18.7 percent) of the 2,081 men drawn in the March 1864 draft fail to appear?[31] Perhaps these particular border state men refused to fight against the South; but in the absence of evidence, historians will never know their motivations, let alone who they were.

One of the greatest difficulties in dealing with illegal evasion is identifying exactly who chose not to appear before the examining board. Not all of these men deliberately failed to report. As described in chapter 6, the enrollment process was at times sporadic and was not subject to systematic verification. As such, men were ordered to report who had died, who had moved, or who already had entered the army. In the first draft sailors posed a special problem, since they were not exempt from the draft until February 1864. Some were ordered to report but could not appear because they were in active service with the Union navy.[32]

The only relatively complete information uncovered on the failure to report in the seven geographical areas examined here comes from the thirtieth district of New York. Unfortunately, it is limited solely to the last draft call, which was conducted in this district from March 17 to April 6, 1865. The area under discussion encompassed Erie County, New York, which includes Buffalo and is adjacent to the Canadian border. Its proximity to Canada is important because the city was a haven for draft dodgers during the Civil War. Widespread crimping occurred as unscrupulous agents crossed into Fort Erie, drugged British soldiers, and put the sedated men into the Union army. The vast extent of this activity contributed greatly to the strained relations between the United States and Great Britain.[33] Politically, the district was heavily Democratic, and for both the Thirty-eighth and Thirty-ninth Congresses, a Democratic representative was elected. In the 1864 presidential election, only 49.4 percent of the votes cast in Buffalo went to Abraham Lincoln, which was below the national average of 53 percent.[34] Although the thirtieth district is not the ideal sample for drawing firm conclusions about the typical person who failed to report, it does reveal some information on Northern delinquents. For comparative purposes and to provide as broad a framework as possible, additional categories of liable men who were drawn in this district for the December 1864 draft are included in table 8.

Of those men classified as draft evaders in the thirtieth district, 44.3 percent were unskilled workers. A significant proportion of men in the skilled and white-collar classes were also among the skedaddlers. Class lines, however, are not necessarily that clear. Compared to the occupational distribution of Union troops, proportionally more skilled and unskilled workers furnished substitutes or were conscripted in this draft. Furthermore, 1,708 men were drawn in this district, and the 497 evaders represented 29.1 percent of this total. The high number of men who failed to report is curious, since there was a reasonable expectation that the war would be over soon. With a median age of 31.3 years, these 497 delinquents were older than the average man who was held to service.

TABLE 8

FAILED TO REPORT

Occupational Category	Failed to Report		Alien Exemptions		Disability Exemptions		Furnished Substitutes		Conscripted	
	N	%	N	%	N	%	N	%	N	%
Farmers & farm workers	17	3.4	3	4.8	25	10.1	9	6.1	9	15.2
Skilled workers	149	30.0	21	33.9	107	43.3	58	39.2	23	39.0
Unskilled workers	220	44.3	21	33.9	60	24.3	34	22.0	17	28.8
White-collar & commercial	58	11.7	7	11.3	35	14.2	41	27.7	5	8.5
Professional	4	0.8	—	—	6	2.4	2	1.3	—	—
Miscellaneous	2	0.4	—	—	—	—	1	0.7	—	—
Unknown	47	9.4	10	16.1	14	5.7	3	2.0	5	8.5
TOTAL	497	100	62	100	247	100	148	100	59	100

Even more significant, over two-thirds of them, 68 percent, were foreign-born. Of the 341 foreign delinquents in this category, 193 were German, and another 93 were Irish. This finding helps to confirm Levine's suspicion that the foreign-born comprised many of the "illegal evaders."[35]

Until more is known about these evaders, the rest of Levine's tentative conclusions remain open to debate. Delinquency was not a phenomenon peculiar to the Civil War; it has appeared in one form or another whenever compulsory service has been instituted in America. For some wars, the incidence of draft evasion is comparable to that of the Civil War North. When factors such as institutionalized deferments, exemptions, and the failure to register are taken into account, these Union draft evaders may have composed less of a problem.[36] Another important variable is the fact that no residency requirement existed for Union volunteers. Those who enlisted were credited to the localities that recruited them, not to the ones in which they lived. When a man enlisted without notifying the authorities in his home district, he would be listed as a delinquent if his name was drawn in the draft.

Within this broader perspective, further postulations can be made about who Union illegal evaders were. Aside from those who were not notified by virtue of already being in service or for other reasons, some men may have been influenced to flee by ideological considerations. Certainly family ties and strong commitments to a belief persuaded a few men not to fight in the Union army, especially if they lived in the border states. As McPherson and Wiley have shown, the foreign-born were underrepresented in the Union army. Many of them felt no great affinity or patriotic call for fighting in a foreign army for a foreign cause, and this attitude certainly did not change with the advent of federal conscription. Other would-be soldiers undoubtedly refused to lay their lives on the line to eliminate slavery. However, illegal evasion occurred in the North before emancipation became an issue. No doubt, too, there existed other reasons that transcend all civilizations and wars. In September 1861, one Iowa citizen in a letter to a friend revealed that he felt both of them were really "*runts*" who were physically incapable of serving; but, just in case they were taken in the state draft, they should be ready to move to Canada. He told of a mutual acquaintance who had been notified to report and who was preparing to leave "*instanter* for parts unknown."[37] As reflected in this letter, some men were cowards, and cultural and ideological considerations notwithstanding, they would not serve under any circumstances.

Despite the limited evidence on illegal evaders in the North, Levine adds to the knowledge on Civil War conscription. His work marks the first scholarly effort to consider those who failed to report, and to view the draft in the context of reactions to the currents of modernization that were occurring throughout the Civil War North. As cultures, values, and attitudes were undergoing change, citizens were faced with "conflicting claims of allegiance between familiar, local-community ties and the demands of an intruding national authority."[38] Within this context, and in spite of certain reservations with the applicability of the modernization thesis for mid-nineteenth-century studies, he has done more than merely taken an abstraction and given it reality.[39] His supposition of a relationship between illegal draft evaders and modernization, however, may be more appropriate for the drafting system that emerged in World War I, during the more modern "*Nation-State*" phase of American military history, than for the Civil War North.[40]

Until further evidence on illegal evaders becomes available, historians must rely on variables such as commutation and substitution for assessing how the draft affected Union males. Men in all occupational settings took advantage of these privileges, and the extant evidence indicates that the draft fell most disproportionately on farmers when compared to their representation in the Union army and the total male population. Nevertheless, the draft was not that burdensome on most farmers, given that only 46,347 Union men became conscripts. Why then was there so much antagonism toward conscription? This question can only be answered by examining the draft within a larger context of Northern attitudes and perceptions toward Provost Marshal General James B. Fry, his bureau, and other factors that emerged in the last two years of the war.

"$300 OR YOUR LIFE"

The Draft Hits Home

As Provost Marshal General Fry prepared to send his army of enrollment officers to the doorstep of every home, understandably few Union men welcomed the approach of the federal draft. Military men, on the other hand, applauded the program, as revealed in General William T. Sherman's comment that the "conscript Bill is all even I could ask, it is the first real step toward war."[1] Republican editors also endorsed the draft, as did some writers and other intellectuals who defended it as a necessary war measure.[2] Rather than greeting it with anticipation, however, most citizens that spring and summer dreaded the prospect of federal conscription.

Those affected by the draft responded to it in different ways. Some communities attempted to avoid it altogether by filling quotas with men other than their own. Individuals, too, sought escape. Some simply complained and had their grievances resolved satisfactorily. Others overtly challenged the system, with varying degrees of success. Most men complied with the law because they discovered it was not so stringent after all. Although the draft imposed on them, the liberal exemption policies made it more of an inconvenience than a serious threat. Even though three hundred dollars represented approximately three-fourths of a workingman's yearly earnings in 1863, which seemed to place commutation beyond the reach of most men, the exemption fee came to be viewed more as friend than foe by the end of 1863. During the course of this subtle change in attitude, most Northerners realized that their initial notions about the draft, which had originated in the Democratic press, differed greatly from reality.

*T*he partisan mood that permeated the last session of the Thirty-seventh Congress had carried over to the press. Gone was the tenuous spirit of cooperation that had existed the previous summer. In its stead was a sharply divided view of administration policy, including the conscription act. Predictably, Republican journals supported the draft; Democratic newspapers condemned it and helped create an impression in the minds of many Northerners that the Enrollment Act was inherently unfair.[3]

As a partisan issue, commutation naturally attracted the attention of opposition editors, such as the ultraconservative editor of the *Crisis*, Samuel Medary. In his continuing effort to discredit the Lincoln administration and the draft, Medary referred to the provision as "$300 or Your Life" when he charged that conscription fell most heavily on the working class. To keep the issue before the public mind, he often reprinted letters from subscribers who opposed the exemption fee.[4] Other Democratic journals expressed similar views. After the New York riots of July 1863, the *Detroit Free Press* accused the wealthier classes of having influenced Congress to authorize such "insidious distinctions between rich and poor."[5] The *Cleveland Plain Dealer* erroneously asserted that every man served in the Confederacy, while the Union encouraged "certain social distinctions."[6] Commutation favored the manufacturing districts of New England, argued the *Chicago Times*.[7] From Portland, Maine, the *Eastern Argus* contended that the fee placed an excessive burden on the poor.[8] Ironically, one Democratic journal, the *New York Herald*, supported commutation because it would force abolitionist Quakers either to fight or pay three hundred dollars.[9]

Republican journals generally defended commutation as an equitable policy. The *Boston Daily Journal* emphasized its impartiality, and the *Washington, D.C. Daily Morning Chronicle* and the *New York Times* echoed this opinion.[10] Poor men benefited, argued the *Cleveland Leader*, because the clause placed a ceiling on the price of substitutes.[11] Although the *New York Tribune* favored the fee, it supported the draft with or without the inclusion of this clause.[12] That demagogues could easily exploit the class issue provoked the ire of Murat Halstead, editor of the *Cincinnati Daily Commercial*.[13]

Unlike Samuel Medary and other Democratic journalists who charged that the Enrollment Act discriminated against the poor, Democratic congressmen—with a few exceptions, such as Chilton A. White and William S. Holman—objected to the high cost of commutation, not to the principle of the exemption fee itself. Indeed, many Democratic congressmen probably found the Enrollment Act to be a fair and humane law, particularly given the liberal exemptions contained in the second section. But the general public did not read the congressional debates. They read newspapers or listened to spokesmen like Clement L. Vallandigham. Within days of the law's passage, he described it as "THREE

HUNDRED DOLLARS OR YOUR LIFE." As a leading Peace Democrat, he reversed his cooperative tone from the summer before and now urged municipalities to remedy any unfairness by paying the fee for each of their drafted citizens.[14]

Several communities implemented versions of Vallandigham's suggestion by the summer of 1863. Some saw this as a convenient way to meet quotas with money instead of men. Others wanted to avoid disturbances that had occurred elsewhere. Much of their concern stemmed from the New York draft riots of July 1863, some of the worst riots in American history. Other violent challenges to the federal draft also arose, particularly during the enrollment process that spring. Almost one hundred agents were injured as they went from door to door to compile their information, and at least two died while executing their duty. This resistance was a prelude to the violence that erupted when the actual draft went into operation.[15]

Violent reactions to federal conscription took place in all sections of the North but tended to be isolated to certain areas and confined largely to the late spring and summer of 1863. In the Midwest, resistance occurred in Minnesota, Wisconsin, Michigan, and Illinois but was concentrated mainly in Ohio, Indiana, and Iowa. Based on an analysis of the counties where the disorders were prevalent, Robert Sterling finds that draft resisters were principally poor, foreign-born Democrats who were influenced by party spokesmen.[16] This pattern was repeated elsewhere. In New England, disruptions took place mainly in Vermont and New Hampshire. Most of the disorders in New Hampshire occurred in Democratic areas and can be attributed to discontent over the commutation clause and how it was misinterpreted by party leaders. In Vermont, much of the resistance stemmed from Irish workers in the marble quarries at Rutland. Similar to the disturbances they created in the Pennsylvania coalfields in 1862, Irish-born miners once again challenged the system when federal conscription was implemented.[17]

The most famous of these disturbances occurred when violence erupted in New York City in the summer of 1863. On Saturday, July 11, the draft commenced in New York's predominantly Irish ninth district. As names were drawn and announced, rumblings of discontent over being forced to fight for black freedom in "a rich man's war and a poor man's fight" could be heard in the crowd. The timing of the draft was unfortunate because this resentment simmered over the weekend and was reinforced in the grogshops on Sunday. Five days of disorder commenced on Monday. As angry men and their women-folk roamed the streets and ravaged the city, they directed most of their animosity toward blacks and those who represented authority. A black orphanage was burned, and the rioters lynched at least one black male who happened to cross their path. In the course of these rampages, John A. Kennedy, the police superintendent, was beaten so badly that he nearly died. Horace Greeley, the abolitionist editor of the *New York Tribune*, was among prominent Republicans whose offices or homes were sacked. Local policemen were no match for the mob. Only the arrival of army troops from Gettysburg, in conjunction with the local police, managed to restore order by July 17, 1863. The days of turmoil had exacted a high toll. In addition to an untold amount of property damage, over one hundred people perished, including eleven blacks, eight soldiers, and two policemen.[18]

No subject has dominated the literature on the Civil War draft more than resistance and the related issue of class discrimination. Historians strongly disagree on the causes of this opposition. Despite the significant alterations that Congress later made to the commutation clause, scholars tend to concentrate mainly on section thirteen in the original Enrollment Act because it is the provision that bore directly on the disorders that erupted in 1863. John Hay and John G. Nicolay, Lincoln's private secretaries, for example, traced the New York troubles to the exemption fee. James Ford Rhodes also supports this view, although he tempers his assessment with a discussion of economic considerations that caused commutation to become "the main grievance" among the poor.[19]

Some twentieth-century historians also stress economic reasons when they discuss the draft riots in New York City and in other urban areas. They conclude that the disruptions can be traced directly to the animosity that had long existed between black and white workers, particularly Irish longshoremen. The exemption fee, as this thesis goes, acted as a catalyst in bringing labor and racial tensions to the surface. The Irish in particular detested the thought that they would be forced to fight in a war that would free the slaves and inundate the North with more of their economic competitors. According to this interpretation, class discrimination represented only one link in a series of long-standing complaints that culminated in the riots.[20]

This argument challenges the view that the commutation clause served as the sole irritant in the New York City disorders. Despite the deemphasis on the relative importance of the exemption fee, however, other twentieth-century writers continue to argue that the Civil War was "a rich man's war and a poor man's fight." James McCague's 1968 study, *The Second Rebellion: The Story of the New York City Draft Riots of 1863*, for example, perpetuates the nineteenth-century viewpoint "that rich men had three hundred dollars and poor men did not. The draft was class discrimination on the face of it." In *Armies of the Streets: The New York City Draft Riots of 1863*, Adrian Cook echoes this theme. Since three hundred dollars represented approximately a laborer's annual wage and the exact price of commutation, the exemption fee "brought charges that the Lincoln administration was waging a rich man's war and poor man's fight all too convincing, and it was bitterly resented." Despite

Cook's belief that the exemption fee discriminated against the poor, *Armies of the Streets* comes closest to being the definitive work on the actual riots. Among his several contributions, Cook scrutinizes the thesis that deep-seated economic causes accounted for the riots and concludes that the "intense racial prejudice of white New Yorkers in [the] 1860s," not fear of competition, caused them.[21]

Although the New York City disturbances tend to attract the most attention, studies of opposition elsewhere tend to question whether resisters really objected to the idea of mandatory military service. Instead, they were motivated by other reasons to challenge the system that the draft represented. Some of these works place antidraft sentiment within a larger framework of Copperheadism and general Democratic opposition to emancipation and other Republican policies. Foremost among these monographs are Arnold Shankman's *The Pennsylvania Antiwar Movement* and Hubert Wubben's *Civil War Iowa and the Copperhead Movement*. Their primary analyses focus on antiwar and political movements, of which the draft is one small facet.[22]

Robert Sterling in his "Civil War Draft Resistance in the Middle West" argues that opposition to the draft cannot be traced solely to discrimination, and that it was not simply another form of dissent toward the Northern war effort. Consistent with this view, he believes that midwestern dissenters cannot be placed under the "umbrella of copperheadism" because they had a variety of motives for circumventing, if not challenging, the draft. Their reasons included racism, political partisanship, a distaste for military service, and a rejection of the centralizing nature of the conscription laws. All of these factors "were intensified by patent inequities in the law and partiality and fraud in the administration of the law."[23] Grace Palladino in her study of resistance in the Pennsylvania coalfields argues convincingly that historians have placed too much emphasis on the violence that occurred and discusses the "broad range" of reactions that cut across party lines. Even the miners who resisted were not necessarily opposed to military service. What they found objectionable was the evolving relationship between the mine owners and the provost marshal, who helped suppress unionizing efforts.[24]

Common to all of these studies is that overt resistance to the federal draft occurred principally in Democratic areas among the foreign-born and working classes. In urban areas, the Pennsylvania coalfields, and the marble quarries of Vermont, the culprits were mainly Irish. On the surface, their opposition stemmed partly from the commutation clause, which they perceived as being discriminatory. The three-hundred-dollar fee was less a cause than a catalyst, however, and brought other grievances into the open. As Cook, Palladino, and Sterling have shown, draft resisters did not necessarily oppose the principle of obligatory military service. Depending on the area, the basis for their objections emanated mainly from racial animosity, general dissatisfaction with the Lincoln administration, and discontent with employers who sought to employ federal authority against their interests.

Many contemporaries nevertheless believed these outbreaks stemmed primarily from federal conscription. Overt resistance on the streets, in the coalfields, and in the cornfields, however, was only one of the threats that President Lincoln faced in enforcing the federal draft. Equally as important, he had to contend with challenges of a more official nature. Although governors complained about quotas, one in particular, Governor Horatio Seymour of New York, questioned the appropriateness and validity of federal conscription. In a lengthy letter of August 3, 1863, he not only charged that New York's quota was excessive but also criticized the federal government for failing to notify him of forthcoming drafts so he could take preventive measures to avoid future disturbances in New York City. In response, Lincoln ordered Edwin Stanton to telegraph Seymour in advance of any draft calls. He also promised to create a commission to investigate the claims of inflated levies.[25]

Seymour further objected to the draft on constitutional grounds. He urged that the draft be suspended so the law could be reviewed. Volunteering also deserved another chance, he argued. Four days later, on August 7, Lincoln responded personally to the governor's suggestions in a strongly worded letter that revealed his attitude toward the Union volunteer and Confederate conscription systems. The president did not oppose a judicial review by the Supreme Court, but he was unwilling "to lose the '*time*' while it is being obtained." Nor would he "re-experiment with the volunteer system, already deemed by congress . . . to be inadequate" because it would be unfair to soldiers who were already in the field. In his defense of the Union draft, Lincoln implied that the Confederacy had a worse system because it forced men into the service "very much as a butcher drives bullocks into a slaughter-pen. No time is wasted, no argument is used . . . [and it] produces an army with a rapidity not to be matched on our side." As the chief executive, he would adhere to constitutional safeguards, but he also had a responsibility to be "practical" in sustaining the "free principles of our common country."[26]

Seymour did not press the issue of the draft's constitutionality to its logical conclusion because this issue already was being raised in various Northern courts. In addition to hearing cases on the law's constitutionality, many judges, especially at the state level, granted writs of habeas corpus to conscripts, thereby forcing their release from the military. By late summer, Lincoln became so irritated with these diverse challenges that he decided to suspend the writ in all draft-related cases. On September 15, 1863, he issued a proclamation to this effect citing as his authority the Habeas Corpus Act of March 3, 1863.[27]

Fortunately for the Lincoln administration, the question of the law's constitutionality never reached the Supreme Court. Although a majority of the justices probably would have sustained the validity of the Enrollment Act, there is strong reason to believe that Chief Justice Roger B. Taney would have dissented. Taney was a fervent states' rights Democrat who believed that congressional power "to raise and support armies" did not extend to conscripting citizens under a national draft law. In his view, the states had neither conferred nor delegated this authority to the national government. Perhaps in anticipation of a ruling, he expounded at length on the independence of the sovereign states in an unpublished opinion.[28]

Had a negative Supreme Court decision been rendered, it would have dealt a devastating blow to the draft's enforcement. Nevertheless, Lincoln still had to contend with legal threats at the state level. In all but one instance, the courts upheld the federal government. Only in *Kneedler v. Lane* did it experience a temporary setback. By a narrow margin of three Democrats to two Republican jurists, the Pennsylvania Supreme Court ruled that Congress had exceeded its power in bypassing state sovereignty. On November 9, 1863, the court decided that only the states, through the militia system, possessed the power to furnish soldiers on a large scale. Within months, the Pennsylvania tribunal reversed this decision when the political composition of the court changed in favor of the Republicans following the defeat at the polls of C. J. Lowrie, the Democratic chief justice, who had presided over the *Kneedler v. Lane* decision.[29] The new court upheld Congress's power to "raise and support armies" through conscription. Its decision echoed a similar view that Lincoln had articulated just a few months earlier in an unpublished essay.[30]

Complaints came from other quarters as well. As during the militia drafts of the previous fall, Edwin Stanton received sundry requests for special group exemptions from the draft. None were included in the Enrollment Act, and Stanton may have earlier interceded to limit the number of special exemption categories. One of his biographers, for example, argues that he opposed the insertion of commutation and substitution from the outset.[31] This assessment is undoubtedly correct, but Stanton probably had to acquiesce in these provisions because of the support they enjoyed in Congress. Within the context of universal liability, the provisions for commutation and substitution not only were designed to soften the impact of national conscription on a war-weary public, but also had to serve as surrogates for occupational exemptions to minimize the effect on industrial and manufacturing pursuits. They further allowed men to avoid service for any reason, including religious scruples.

Based on experiences in the fall of 1862, Stanton understood that commutation would be an unacceptable alternative to the Quakers. Many could not contribute to the war in any form. One Vermont Quaker in particular attracted national attention in 1863, and his activities ultimately led to the sect being effectively released from the draft. The case involved Cyrus G. Pringle, who had been drafted in July. Pringle's devout faith prevented him from obeying military orders and performing basic functions, including the maintenance of his weapon. Individuals offered to pay his three-hundred-dollar fee to obtain his release from active service, but he refused all such overtures. In the course of his service, he proved to be a constant source of irritation to the military authorities. On one occasion, a few of his fellow soldiers restrained him while others placed military equipment on the reluctant warrior. Pringle suffered jeers from many of his superiors, as well as imprisonment among deserters and bounty jumpers, but his conscience would not permit any compromise. When Lincoln learned of Pringle's dilemma, and of others who were equally devoted to their faith, he ordered their immediate release.[32] To avoid further complications with the Quakers, the provost marshal general issued a directive on December 15 ordering the parole of all such individuals, who would not have to report until "called for."[33]

This benevolent policy nonetheless failed to satisfy the Quakers. By December 1863 they were besieging their officials with memorials and visits to gain an unequivocal exemption from the draft, because they were being forced "to disregard the well known obligations of their religion."[34] Most religious groups, however, were satisfied with commutation. Only when Congress began considering commutation's recall did this vocal segment of the population begin protesting on a large scale. Remonstrances came from Episcopalians, Lutherans, the Amana Society in Iowa, the Ebenezer Society near Buffalo, New York, and other ministers of the gospel.[35] One Protestant bishop expressed the views of many when he requested that ministers of the gospel at least be specifically excused from the draft if commutation was repealed.[36] One citizen, however, demanded the abolition of all exemptions, including those that professed a "religious doctrine."[37]

Congress granted some religious groups a special dispensation in the Amendatory Act of February 24, 1864, but limited the privilege of commutation for most other men. During most of 1863, however, those with conscientious scruples, or in religious vocations, were subject to the draft along with locomotive engineers, physicians, and other groups whom the War Department had exempted during the fall of 1862.[38] So vast was the law's net that, similar to Union sailors, acting assistant surgeons—who were performing military duty without commissions—remained liable to conscription in 1863. Before the year ended, they and other groups requested occupational exemptions from the draft.[39]

Other individuals also demanded special consideration. Section one of the law effectively made many aliens among those liable to the draft. Where the 1862 policy held to service only those who had voted in an election, the Enrollment Act included all foreigners who had simply declared their intention to become United States citizens. To reinforce the law, Lincoln, on May 8, 1863, issued a proclamation specifying that liable aliens had 65 days to decide whether to comply with the law or to leave the country.[40] Foreigners petitioned the government and asked that all unnaturalized citizens be excused from liability to military service, particularly those who had declared their intention to acquire citizenship prior to the passage of the federal draft law. The foreign-born were not of one mind on this issue, however, and some insisted that all aliens be held accountable under the draft.[41]

Despite the unhappiness with certain features of the Enrollment Act in some quarters, the initial fear of many Northerners toward conscription in 1863 began to dissipate as the year wore on. The dread of conscription was still present, but it came to be viewed more as a nuisance than as a threat to a person's well-being. As towns and individuals became knowledgeable on ways to circumvent the draft, challenges to the system declined. A draft could be avoided altogether if a community had excess credits from earlier calls, or officials could try to fill quotas with men from other areas. Another alternative was raising necessary funds to cover the cost of the exemption fee for any of a community's drafted citizens. Those who lived in more frugal localities had to fend for themselves, but they could be very resourceful.

In 1863 the Lincoln administration made it clear that the draft would be enforced. Part of the public's acquiescence that year also can be attributed to several important factors that effectively reduced quotas. Excess credits put off the draft in some instances. Ten of the twenty-two states that were potentially liable escaped conscription in 1863 through a combination of abundant credits and the success that some experienced in filling their quotas with recruits. In those areas that had to conscript, the widespread availability of the commutation privilege helped to lessen the impact of personal service.

Government officials also initiated various programs that significantly reduced the number of new troops required. Among the most important of these was the enlistment of black troops. Faced with the prospect of personal service, whites gladly let blacks go in their place. Shortly after the passage of the Enrollment Act, the War Department issued guidelines for the recruiting of blacks. Although the men were classified as United States Colored Troops, the areas in which they enlisted received troop credits against their quotas, which in 1863 tended to benefit the border states. To further offset criticism, a loyal slave master received compensation or the federal bounty for each of his slaves so recruited. Largely through the efforts of General Lorenzo Thomas, at least 76,000 black troops were in uniform by the end of 1863.[42]

Another program that helped to ease the strain on Northern quotas was the creation of the Invalid Corps, or as it later came to be known, the Veteran Reserve Corps. Fry proposed its establishment on April 28, 1863. Its central purpose was to allow men who were no longer fit for field duty to remain

in active service, and to permit the reenlistment of those who had been discharged because of wounds or serious illness. These soldiers had an important
role because they relieved able-bodied men from light assignments, such as
garrison and hospital duties. Fry also made extensive use of them throughout
his bureau as guards and clerks. By November 1, 1863, 18,255 disabled men
had cast their lot with the Invalid Corps; 60,508 enlisted men and 1,096 officers
ultimately made this choice. In a sense these men were the true patriots in
the Union army because they were prohibited from receiving any government
bounties. Had they accepted a discharge they would have been entitled to
an eight-dollar monthly pension. By remaining in the service, they were paid
according to rank and consequently received as little as $13 a month.[43]

In terms of the total number of men acquired, a more significant program
occurred when the War Department authorized white recruits to receive large
bounties from some twelve million dollars of commutation money that it had
collected. The government paid $302 for first-time enlistees. A soldier with
at least two years of service received $402 for reenlisting. If most of his unit
remained in service, the government also authorized a 30-day furlough for
all men, conferred the title of "veteran" on the unit, and allowed its members
to wear a service chevron on their sleeves.[44]

These symbols of manhood and battlefield service were not the only motivating factors that prompted many veterans to remain in the field. The prospect
of a furlough was paramount in many of their minds because by the winter
of 1864, "a spirit of disillusionment and desperation rather than hopefulness
and resolution" had begun to affect the attitudes of many experienced soldiers.
In anticipation of the battles that lay ahead, many hoped to see home one
last time before they took to the field again that spring. Other forces were
at work as well. Veterans came under enormous pressure from their officers
and fellow soldiers to reenlist and thereby retain the integrity of the regiment
and to qualify for the 30-day leave.[45] Sometimes these decisions had an ironic
quality. Thomas Crowl of the 87th Pennsylvania refused to be cajoled into
extending his term and preferred counting the days until his discharge. Within
three months of his expected release he was captured. He died in Danville
Prison on September 18, 1864, the same day that his original three-year enlistment was due to expire.[46]

Sometimes those on the home front also pressured their men to remain
in the service. Even before the Veteran Volunteer program was authorized,
the wife of one soldier strongly encouraged him to accept a discharge and
then immediately reenlist for a combined federal and local bounty of $502.
Like Crowl, George Edwards had no desire to stay in the army, but he was
tempted by this large amount of money.[47] Still others were unable to take advantage of the generous monetary inducements being offered because more than
a year remained on their original three-year enlistment. This exclusion

prompted one irritated soldier to remark that Major General James Birdseye McPherson could kiss his posterior since McPherson, as the federal government's agent, refused to accept the services of all soldiers who wanted to reenlist.[48]

For those who qualified, the diverse pressures combined with the dual stimulus of generous bounties and a 30-day furlough to tempt many of them to reenlist. Moreover, those who did so could choose where they wanted to be credited. This policy led to complaints from various areas because a veteran would understandably select a community that offered a high bounty.[49] Also, he could reenlist for the federal bounty and then enlist as a substitute if he so chose. An embarrassed Henry Wilson attempted to explain the rationale behind this peculiar practice, which in reality denied the government additional men.[50] Despite this quirk the program was relatively successful, and by the winter of 1863–64 over 136,000 veterans had decided to remain in the field.[51] Since these men would have been exempt from the draft upon discharge, their decision reflected the temptation of the federal bounty—among other important influences—in stimulating enlistments. This sum, combined with local money, not only retained experienced troops but assisted many communities in filling at least part of their quotas with men.

Despite an estimated 231,000 men who either joined or remained in the army as a direct result of the United States Colored Troops, the Veteran Reserve Corps, and the Veteran Volunteer program, more soldiers were still needed. Many communities not fortunate enough to escape the draft increasingly came to rely on initiative and ingenuity in filling their assigned quotas. Some areas saw the draft as a convenient way to remove undesirable elements from their midst and meet federal requisitions at the same time. Recruiting on foreign soil was another strategy, and one community favored recruiting Indians for state service.[52] Others recommended the enlistment of rebel deserters and prisoners of war, and in October 1863 at least 150 of these individuals enlisted in the Union army at one camp in Indiana.[53]

Many localities chose adding to their financial burdens as the most expedient way to bypass the 1863 draft. In the wake of the July riots, New York City passed an ordinance authorizing a three-hundred-dollar payment to any of its drafted citizens. An individual could use the money to pay the exemption fee, to furnish a substitute, or to retain it as a bounty if he chose to enter the army.[54] A few other communities relied on a version of New York City's program. Many New Hampshire towns, for example, contributed three hundred dollars toward the purchase of a substitute, preferably a foreigner, for each of their drafted men.[55] This policy was so successful that 75 percent of the drafted men in the Granite State, the highest proportion of any state, furnished substitutes.[56]

Most areas circumvented the law by simply paying the commutation fee.[57]

Not every citizen, however, consented to this blatant practice. One irate constituent wrote Governor William A. Buckingham that several neighboring towns were securing appropriations for this purpose. He predicted that most of this local legislation would pass easily, even in communities without "Copperhead Selectmen." The governor was urged to follow the example of the "Supreme Judicial Court of Maine," which had decided that towns acted illegally in levying any form of a commutation tax.[58] Neither the Maine judiciary nor Buckingham, however, had any power over the Delaware legislature. In February 1864 it passed a law authorizing payment of two hundred dollars to all of its drafted white citizens. This money was to be applied toward the three-hundred-dollar commutation fee.[59] Lincoln inadvertently encouraged this practice when he ruled that districts would receive troop credits for any conscripts who paid commutation. In this order of November 1, 1863, Lincoln also placed these individuals on a parity with those who furnished substitutes by granting them a draft exemption for a full three years.[60]

Drafted men residing in areas that were either financially unable or morally unwilling to pay the fee resorted to other means to obtain the money. Although three hundred dollars represented approximately three-fourths of a laborer's annual wage by 1863, soldiers thought this sum was reasonable.[61] One referred to it as a "cheap sale."[62] Another, in the 117th New York Volunteer Infantry, thought that "the men are few who won't pay $300 before they will come."[63] If necessary, farms and property could be mortgaged. Among its more disruptive effects on the family, the war gave women greater opportunities to work outside the home. Even though women received significantly lower wages than men, every dollar helped toward purchasing exemption for a loved one who would otherwise have to go to war.[64] Wages lagged behind inflation, but spiraling costs contributed toward exemption in this instance because the government had to accept its steadily depreciating greenbacks as legal tender in the payment of commutation.

Most of these individuals did not have to resort to mortgaging property, draining a family's limited resources, or taking other drastic measures to pay the full three hundred dollars. Within days after approval of the Enrollment Act, Indiana's governor informed Stanton of his belief that Democrats, in their secret societies, would contribute to a special fund to pay the fee of any of their drafted members.[65] Oliver Morton never had the opportunity to prove his hypothesis because his state escaped conscription under the first two calls, when all drafted men were eligible for the commutation privilege. The idea of organizations paying the fee, however, became quite popular in the draft-liable areas of the North during 1863 and the first half of 1864. Some church congregations experimented with a plan to assess all of their members with a fee to pay the three hundred dollars for any of their young men who were drafted.[66] In the absence of a sponsoring organization, individuals formed com-mutation clubs or insurance societies. In return for a membership fee, a man would be assured of receiving three hundred dollars in the event he was drafted. Although this fee ranged from fifty to one hundred dollars, draft-liable men in certain wards in Cleveland, Ohio, paid as little as ten dollars into such associations.[67]

This practice became so pervasive by mid-December 1863 that Fry found it necessary to write a letter in which he criticized these "corporations or clubs." He predicted that they, combined with the men who furnished substitutes, would prevent the government from acquiring needed men under future drafts. Based on his experience under the first call, he estimated that two-thirds of the three million men his bureau enrolled that year would be exempt for one reason or another. Of the remaining one-third, substitution and especially commutation would effectively relieve 86 percent of them from duty for a three-year period.[68]

*E*ighteen sixty-three was a year of transition in the North for mobilizing manpower. The principle of national conscription had been established, and although the system was not very efficient in directly raising men through con-scription, it more than any other factor that year brought the war home to countless Union citizens as the enrollment process got under way. The year also marked a new point of departure for the Lincoln administration in raising an army. No longer did it have to depend on state governors to comply with quotas and enforce the draft; but political realities dictated that troops still be raised through volunteering whenever possible.

Although a few federal officials abused their authority in implementing the law, the Lincoln administration on the whole handled its newly acquired power relatively well and generally remained conscious of the need to make a distaste-ful law as palatable as possible to the public. When necessary, however, the president flexed his muscles to sustain this new national authority. He effectively met most direct challenges to conscription, including overt resistance and ad-verse judicial actions; but, if the Union army was to be replenished, it could not survive more subtle threats such as commutation. By granting a three-year exemption to 52,288 able-bodied men who paid three hundred dollars each in 1863, the exemption fee privilege had already cost the army the equivalent of over 50 new full-strength infantry regiments. This predicament and others called for a definite response from officials in the Lincoln administration, which included asking Congress to make certain alterations in the Enrollment Act.

"MEN NOT MONEY"

December 1863–July 1864

The North was in a much stronger position as 1863 gave way to 1864. Significant military victories at Gettysburg, Vicksburg, and Chattanooga had given a much-needed boost to morale at home. Moreover, the Lincoln administration had survived court challenges while demonstrating its resolve to enforce the draft. If the federal government was to continue prosecuting the war, however, it would need to strengthen existing methods for raising troops and to develop new approaches in tapping available Northern manpower.

From the winter to the early summer of 1864, the Lincoln administration tried various tactics in sustaining the army. In addition to the draft, it continued to rely on the costly federal bounty system until early April. After this program ended, it tried two new volunteer programs that officials referred to as the One Hundred Days Men and the Representative Recruits. Although highly publicized, these expedient plans produced limited results in acquiring a significant number of new troops.

Changes in the federal conscription system had the greatest potential for furnishing more men, but achieving substantive revisions in existing policy proved to be difficult. The Thirty-eighth Congress opened its first day with a demand for modifications to the Enrollment Act, and it closed on March 3, 1865, with a vote on changes to the draft law. Although other major issues and measures occupied the attention of the Thirty-eighth Congress during its 15-month tenure, its members nevertheless consumed an inordinate amount of time on three substantial revisions to the Enrollment Act. All three revisions culminated in compromise legislation, partly because of an absence of rapport between Henry Wilson and Robert C. Schenck, the new leader of the House Military Committee. They not only differed with each other but also encountered intraparty dissension within their respective chambers and strong disagreements within their committees on many an occasion. The protracted discussions on the draft also paralleled a subtle change in direction. Where the focus in the Thirty-seventh Congress was more on framing a humane law than an effective one, members of the Thirty-eighth Congress slowly and painfully were forced into reversing this equation. Although their activities still produced politically acceptable alternatives, they reluctantly had to place greater emphasis on personal service rather than on humanitarian concerns, particularly when it came to sensitive areas such as the future of commutation.

The Amendatory Act of February 24 was the first step in a long process that ended with the withdrawal of the commutation privilege for most Northern men.[1] Even before the Thirty-eighth Congress convened on December 7, 1863, pressures against the popular clause began mounting. As early as November 14, Senator John Sherman revealed privately that he thought his colleagues would remove the exemption fee. The War Department certainly favored its repeal, as evident in a letter from Provost Marshal General Fry in which he urged its revocation except for certain religious groups.[2]

This attitude received grass roots support from several areas after Congress assembled. Indiana senator Henry S. Lane, who served on Wilson's military committee, received letters from various constituents in support of his anticommutation position.[3] From the neighboring state of Illinois, which like the Hoosier State had escaped conscription under the first two draft calls, came petitions from groups such as the " CHICAGO WORKING MEN'S ASSOCIATION," which claimed to have over one thousand members. This organization, which also might have served as a fraternal order for German radicals, supported the abolition of all special exemptions except for hardship reasons.[4] Congressman James A. Garfield received a similar remonstrance from a German radical group in Newark, New Jersey, another nonliable state in 1863. Its members demanded the repeal of all exemptions.[5] From Bucks County, Pennsylvania, an area where a large percentage of men had paid commutation, came a petition signed by 221 men that protested against any tampering with this privilege.[6]

Regardless of a state's draft liability in 1863, Union men disagreed over what should be done about the exemption fee. Two men in nonliable Ohio, for example, proposed a sliding scale of commutation based on one's ability to pay.[7] From Cass County, Michigan, which was part of a district where over two-thirds of the drafted men had paid the fee in 1863, the Board of Supervisors demanded the immediate repeal of the fee in spite of its obvious popularity.[8]

The split in these petitioners' attitudes was reflected among members of the Thirty-eighth Congress. At noon on December 7, 1863, most of the 34

Republicans, 12 Democrats, and 3 Unionists in the Senate assembled to open the proceedings of the second Civil War Congress.[9] Within minutes after the roll was called, Henry S. Lane announced his intent to introduce a bill repealing the commutation clause. A few days later, he explained that the draft law had been "passed as a military measure to raise men, and not as a financial measure . . . if we could print soldiers as fast as we can print greenbacks," only then should the fee be retained.[10]

With this action, the Indiana Republican set the wheels in motion on an issue that would consume much of Congress's time in the next two-and-a-half months. Lane and the other members of the Senate Military Committee were at odds with their chairman. Henry Wilson insisted on retaining some form of the fee, and since he had disregarded this strong group recommendation, he was challenged openly in the Committee of the Whole. When Wilson proved reluctant to consider repeal, one senator took the drastic step of presenting an alternate bill on the Senate floor. In an effort to resolve this impasse and regain his role as the principal director of conscription legislation, Wilson reported a measure on December 18 with several amendments. During his introductory remarks, he noted his committee's unanimity on all provisions except the one pertaining to commutation. The others favored its repeal, but he had "serious doubts" about the wisdom of tampering with the popular measure.[11] In the days before the Christmas recess, this nascent split in attitudes dominated the Senate whenever commutation was discussed. So sensitive was this issue that it fragmented the upper house into groups that, with the exception of the draft-free Far West, transcended party and sectional lines. In voting on amendments that concerned the exemption fee, even senators from the same state and same party consistently voted on opposite sides of the question.[12]

The House of Representatives with its membership of 103 Republicans, 74 Democrats, and 6 Unionists was quite active in considering various conscription proposals prior to the Christmas recess. Exclusive of tangential issues relating to the draft, such as increasing soldiers' pay, fourteen different congressmen from both parties either offered resolutions or announced their intention to recommend amendatory bills to the Enrollment Act during December. Appropriately, Isaac N. Arnold, who had introduced a resolution calling for commutation's repeal in the last minutes of the Thirty-seventh Congress, became the first representative in the Thirty-eighth to recommend a similar proposal. On December 8 he renewed his plea to have the exemption fee repealed, and six days later he formalized his intent with a bill that was referred to the House Military Committee.[13]

Six of the nine members of the military committee had been recently elected to the House. Of these newcomers, the two most important were Robert C. Schenck and James A. Garfield. Both were Ohioans who, until just a few weeks before, had been Union generals in active service. Schenck was appointed chair,

Henry Wilson (circa 1865), as the chair of the Senate Committee on Military Affairs and the Militia, was the person most responsible for developing the legislation that established conscription in the North. (*Harper's Pictorial History of the Civil War*. Chicago: Star Publishing Company, 1866, p. 187)

James Barnet Fry (circa 1865) was the architect of the federal conscription system in his capacity as the provost marshal general. (*Battles and Leaders of the Civil War*. New York: Century Company, 1888, vol. 3, p. 33)

New York City draft riots. There are several dozen extant sketches of the New York disorders. This one, which is not widely known, shows rioters in the process of sacking residences on Lexington Avenue on July 13. (Benjamin LaBree, *The Pictorial Battles of the Civil War.* New York: Sherman Publishing Company, 1885, vol. 2, p. 224)

Union soldiers and the draft riots. Thomas Nast sketched this particular scene that depicts the reactions of Union soldiers when they learned of the turbulence in New York City. (Benjamin LaBree, *The Pictorial Battles of the Civil War.* New York: Sherman Publishing Company, 1885, vol. 2, p. 238)

MEN WANTED
FOR THE
NAVY!

All able-bodied men not in the employment of the Army, will be enlisted into the Navy upon application at the Naval Rendezvous, on Craven Street, next door to the Printing Office.

H. K. DAVENPORT,
Com'r. & Senior Naval Officer.

New Berne, N. C.,
Nov. 2d, 1863.

Recruiting for the Union navy. As reflected in this poster, volunteering was relied on exclusively in attracting prospective sailors. As a result of this activity, an additional 105,963 men would enter the naval service by the end of the war. (National Archives, Record Group 45, Office of Naval Records and Library, Subject File 1775–1910)

PEACE COMMISSIONERS.

LIKELY YOUNG MAN. "Plaze, Sir, have ye any employment for a boy as a Pace Commissioner?"

RECRUITING OFFICER. "As Peace Commissioner? I guess so. We want about 300,000 just like you. Step round!"

"We Need Men." Implicit in this humorous illustration from a popular Northern magazine is the heavy emphasis that continued to be placed on volunteering and bounties near the end of the war. (*Harper's Weekly*, Feb. 25, 1865)

THE RECRUITING BUSINESS.

VOLUNTEER-BROKER (*to Barber*) "Look a-here — I want you to trim up this old chap with a flaxen wig and a light mustache, so as to make him look like twenty; and as I shall probably clear three hundred dollars on him, I sha'n't mind giving you fifty for the job."

Unsavory substitutes. In placing unfit men into military service, unethical substitute and bounty brokers resorted to deceptive practices such as the scene depicted in this illustration. (*Harper's Weekly,* Jan. 23, 1864)

The drafting process. General Fry required that a blindfolded man select the names of enrolled men from a large enclosed wheel. This particular scene occurred in the ninth district of New York in the early fall of 1863. (Benjamin LaBree, *The Pictorial Battles of the Civil War.* New York: Sherman Publishing Company, 1885, vol. 2, p. 231)

Recruiting and bounties. Although based on a recruiting station in City Hall Park, New York, this illustration was typical of similar activities in many other Northern communities. The absence of foliage and the federal bounty advertisement for new recruits and Veteran Volunteers indicates that this particular scene was probably prepared sometime in the late fall of 1863. (*The American Soldier in the Civil War.* New York: Bryan, Taylor & Co., 1895, p. 239)

"*Come quick and get your greenbacks*" appears in the first entry among this selection of 19 notices for recruits and substitutes. These are fairly typical of the advertisements that were published in many Northern newspapers during the last few months of the war. As indicated in this particular example, men in New York City could expect to command anywhere from $800 for home service to $1,526 if they enlisted for three years. Of course, part of their stipend went to the recruiting or substitute broker who retained them. (*New York Herald*, Feb. 14, 1865)

"Without delay or annoyance" symbolized the relative ease with which men in some areas were able to hire substitutes after the repeal of the commutation privilege. Qualified replacements were not as abundant in others, and men who were held to service had no other choice except to become federal conscripts after July 1864. (*Cincinnati Daily Commercial*, Oct. 22, 1864)

DRAFTED MEN,

—IN—

Ohio, Indiana or Kentucky,

WANTING

SUBSTITUTES,

CAN OBTAIN THEM,

ON REASONABLE TERMS,

—WITHOUT—

DELAY OR ANNOYANCE,

ON APPLICATION AT

No. 15 West Third street.

The *"Grand Review"* of the Union army after the war ended. This Mathew Brady photograph of Major General Horatio G. Wright's 6th Corps marching down Pennsylvania Avenue was probably taken on May 23, 1865. (Library of Congress)

Black soldiers in Union blue. Approximately 179,000 black men became Union soldiers during the war and somewhere between another 9,000 and 25,000 joined the Union navy. The men in this particular detachment were part of the 4th United States Colored Infantry and were stationed at Fort Lincoln in the District of Columbia when this undated photograph was taken. (Library of Congress)

and with the able assistance of the energetic Garfield, this committee emerged as one of the more important and forceful in the Thirty-eighth Congress. After only two meetings before the Christmas recess, they had prepared their first piece of military legislation. The measure concerned a minor amendment to the Enrollment Act, but the House was in no mood to tamper with the draft act and refused to approve the legislation.[14] Undeterred by this action, Schenck convened his committee during the Christmas recess to consider a proposal from Secretary of War Edwin Stanton regarding a review of what caused men to be exempt from the draft for reasons of physical disability.[15]

Within minutes after the Senate reconvened following the Christmas recess, Wilson introduced his new amendatory bill, S. 36. During the first full day of debate on January 7, 1864, his colleagues agreed to all proposed amendments except for the section that concerned the exemption fee and additional changes that other senators had proposed. By the end of the day it became apparent that these modifications hinged on the fate of commutation.[16] Once Congress resumed its consideration of the draft bill, most senators quickly aligned themselves with either the procommutation Wilson or the anticommutation Lane faction. Over much of the next two weeks, Republican senators became embroiled in heated arguments over retaining this policy. Although senators directed their attention to other draft issues, especially exemption for religious reasons and the authorization of new troop credits, they returned time after time to the status of the three-hundred-dollar fee.

Throughout the proceedings, Lane remained very critical of Henry Wilson. On one occasion the persistent Hoosier alluded to Massachusetts as he charged that "you require the personal service, the blood . . . of the brave volunteers of my State, and you tell the people of other States, whose patriotism has not been so ardent . . . that they discharge their full duty by paying $300."[17] Others were equally outspoken. James Nesmith, an Oregon Democrat, warned his colleagues that the epithet "DIED OF COMMUTATION" would appear on the nation's tombstone if Congress refused to repeal commutation.[18]

The defenders of the controversial fee usually relied on the argument that it benefited poor men by imposing a ceiling on substitute prices. Edgar Cowan of Pennsylvania, a state in which 63 percent of the conscripts had paid commutation during 1863, asserted that all the men in his community had managed to pay the three hundred dollars. Therefore reasoned the senator, its widespread availability demonstrated the law's fairness.[19] Daniel Clark of New Hampshire contended that the clause, in its present form, helped poor men beyond any doubt. Although he appreciated Lane's concern that the draft yielded few men, he believed that the draft in conjunction with volunteering would raise all the troops needed. Jacob Collamer, from the neighboring state of Vermont, revealed that he was less disposed toward the welfare of poor men. He opposed any tampering with the fee because he wanted to protect the man of "moderate circumstances" most of all from being conscripted. If any sections defeated the law's purpose, they were those exempting men for reasons of hardship or physical disability.[20]

In an effort to maintain a broad appeal for commutation and to prevent it from being voted on directly, Wilson and his like-minded colleagues moved from one expedient to another. Among other tactics, they relied on sundry amendments to consume time and cloud the issue. After more than a week the main question was still unresolved. Indeed, as a result of Wilson's efforts to protect commutation, he sacrificed complete control over the course of the legislation. His frequent assurances that the Senate could finally dispense with S. 36 by the end of a day's debate came to naught. After the Senate made its almost daily modification of the clause, other members offered new suggestions that led in turn to additional arguments and roll calls.

As early as the second full day of debate, Wilson's inability to keep the bill on a direct course became apparent. Under normal circumstances, a chairman could rely on fellow committee members for assistance in retrieving a measure from potential disaster. Five of the other six members of the military committee, however, were still firmly opposed to Wilson's position on the commutation clause. They were upset because he had violated their wishes by not recommending repeal. Consequently, he had to assume sole responsibility for moving and protecting the bill.

On January 14, 1864, Wilson finally conceded "to embarrass a direct vote" on commutation. This sudden change in attitude undoubtedly resulted from a meeting the day before when his committee conferred with the House Military Committee on the pending conscription law. Although the minutes of the House Military Committee do not reveal the actual topics discussed during this session, one individual (who evidently was privy to such meetings) recorded the gist for his readers. In a January 13 dispatch, "PERLEY" noted that "Senator Wilson favored commutation, but other members of the Senate committee opposed it. The House committee unanimously recommended commutation."[21] Hence the Senate could reject the money privilege because Wilson could depend on the House to retain it in some form.

The fragmentary nature of the Senate debates was reflected in voting behavior. A total of 28 votes occurred in the Senate, and half of these pertained to some aspect of commutation. By comparison, the House recorded only 17, and 6 of these were taken on draft-related resolutions. On the Senate votes, party discipline was extremely weak, but party loyalty dominated in the House. This pattern suggests that House members generally supported Schenck and his military committee at this time. Senators, however, were dissatisfied both with Wilson's insistence on protecting commutation and his handling of the entire bill.[22]

Unlike the chaotic situation Wilson created in the Senate, Schenck and his committee managed to keep a tight rein over the direction of the measure in the House on February 1–3 and 8–12, 1864. House members considered numerous draft-related issues, but they focused their attention on six general areas. Among the more important of these were the disposition of commutation, religious exemptions, conscription of blacks, and compensation for loyal masters whose slaves were taken by the government for the army.

Commutation was not as volatile an issue in the House because Schenck's committee decided not to force repeal at this time. Rather it chose to retain the price at three hundred dollars, but to reduce the exemption period to one year. Some congressmen attempted unsuccessfully to restore the full three-year period. After eight days of discussion, voting took place February 12 on the commutation bill and various proposals, including one to draft blacks. If a slave, the conscript would be freed and his master would receive the federal bounty. In an 83-to-67 vote, the House passed an amendment that revealed strong party unity. A similar level of discipline was demonstrated on a roll call to require the publication of enrollment lists. After the House rejected this proposal, it passed the bill in a 94-to-60 vote. The Republicans were unanimous in their support of the revised bill, and the Democrats maintained a high degree of unity. Two of the five members of the minority party who voted in its favor were Archibald McAllister and Moses F. Odell, both members of the military committee.[23] This vote terminated further House consideration of the draft bill until one week later, when members had to decide whether to accept a Conference Committee report.

Henry Wilson's problems resurfaced once the report was ready. When he tried to obtain approval without having the bill printed, various members insisted on a published version before taking any vote. After it was printed, however, senators initially refused to accept it, and many expressed displeasure over the two sections that Wilson had explained the previous night. On one of two roll calls taken, seven Republicans voted to reject the change that left the commutation fee at three hundred dollars rather than raising it to a higher figure. With this matter out of the way, senators turned their attention to the sensitive issues of conscripting slaves and emancipating those who were drafted. After a few partisan speeches, the Senate proceeded to accept the report in a 26-to-16 vote. Of the 26 members voting in favor, 3 were Democrats, while 9 of the 16 opposed were Republicans.[24]

Schenck enjoyed more creditability among his colleagues in the House. After general remarks and some limited discussion, the House proceeded to vote. With party lines drawn, it concurred in the report of the Conference Committee by a 71-to-23 vote.[25]

With this vote and President Lincoln's approval of the bill on February 24, the long weeks of pettiness, delays, and redundant roll calls finally drew to a close. At least initially, the struggle to approve this measure seemed worthwhile. Among its several provisions, it authorized the president to call for an unlimited number of soldiers and reduced the exemption period to one year for those who paid commutation. In a further effort to secure as many men as possible, Congress withdrew all of the humanitarian exemptions in the second section of the Enrollment Act, permitted the conscription of slaves, increased the penalties on officials who issued fraudulent statements in accepting recruits, and reaffirmed the policy of drafting liable aliens who had either voted or indicated that they would become citizens. Congress also significantly limited a substitute's qualifications. Henceforth, if a drafted man furnished a replacement who was subsequently conscripted, the principal would either have to provide another man or enter the military himself. This change induced men to find substitutes who were either an eligible alien, under twenty years of age, or a veteran volunteer who was willing to reenlist. The law further allowed enrolled men to furnish a substitute before a draft was ordered, instead of waiting to be drafted when the supply of available candidates was more limited.[26]

In addition to strengthening the existing conscription system, the measure was fair inasmuch as it tried to rectify past wrongs. Minors who had enlisted without parental consent, for example, would be released upon the restitution of all bounty money. Communities would now be permitted to claim troop credits for local men who enlisted in the navy. Also, these men would have the option of selecting bounty money in lieu of prize money.

Congress demonstrated as well that it could respond to pressures from most petitioners who wanted changes in the system. Drafted men who were conscientiously opposed to war now would have the option of either serving as "noncombatants" or paying commutation. Their money was to be set aside for "the benefit of sick and wounded soldiers." Although Quakers had sought an unequivocal exemption from military service, Congress had nevertheless mollified its hard position in deference to this group.[27] For the greater convenience of individuals who lived far away from the headquarters of their district provost marshals, Congress called upon the secretary of war to have local enrollment boards meet throughout their districts "at such points as are best calculated to accommodate the people thereof."[28] Another petitioner recommended making aliens liable to the draft. He also proposed a system of supplemental drafts, whereby conscription would continue in a community until it filled its quota. Congress incorporated versions of both of these suggestions.[29] It also responded favorably to those who wanted quotas determined according to a local rather than a subdistrict formula. In an effort to be as just as possible toward communities that had filled their quotas, provost marshals were ordered to implement this change "as far as practicable."[30]

Six days before the February act was signed into law, a relieved Henry Wilson referred to it as an "efficient" measure.[31] He did not have to wait long to test the accuracy of his opinion. On March 14, Lincoln called for another two hundred thousand troops. Under the provisions of the call, localities had until April 15 to fill their quotas with volunteers before a draft commenced.[32] To the relief of those communities that had to fill quotas, the federal bounty was still available for a few weeks. Although it had been due to expire the previous January, Congress had passed a resolution to continue it until April 1, 1864. It was not renewed again until Congress passed the Amendatory Act of July 4.[33]

The bounty extension enabled many communities to fill, and even exceed, their assigned quotas. Once the final returns were tabulated under this call, and after the men who paid commutation were deducted, over 95 percent of those who entered the military did so as volunteers.[34] Bounties were the critical factor because they comprised the only economic incentive to enlist in the spring of 1864. Wages were high and certain old problems persisted. A private's monthly pay not only remained at $13, but he continued to receive it at irregular intervals.[35] Further, the government still seemed to demonstrate a lack of compassion toward its prisoners of war because of its reluctance to effect a general prisoner exchange. Letters from these unfortunate men, in which they described their deplorable living conditions, understandably dampened any rekindling of a volunteering spirit based mainly on patriotic appeals.[36]

The press reinforced the notion of insensitivity in the public mind as it continued to criticize the government's position on the prisoner exchange issue, the ineffective pay policy, and the general competence of the Lincoln administration.[37] It also reported on recruiting frauds perpetrated by government officials, which added to the continuing complaints over excessive quotas.[38] This perennial sore point was made worse as some states and communities intensified their efforts in searching for recruits to reduce quotas at home.[39] To compound the problem, the supply of available men was being steadily reduced because of a severe dearth of labor in the North.[40] By the spring of 1864, the need for more manpower reached such a critical stage that constituents everywhere began pressuring their congressmen to promote a more active immigration program as a partial solution.[41]

In an effort to meet some of these complaints and to raise some troops without a draft, the Lincoln administration experimented with two programs before commutation was finally repealed. On April 21, 1864, five midwestern governors offered to raise one hundred thousand men for a period of a hundred days to free experienced troops from garrison duty. Two days later, Lincoln accepted their offer with the provisos that these special troops would not receive bounties, nor would states and localities be granted any credit toward quotas.[42] In July, Lincoln encouraged other states to participate in this program.[43]

Of the five original states, only Ohio exceeded its quota of thirty thousand men. It did so by almost 21 percent, but the other four states had deficiencies that ranged from 43 percent to a high of 64 percent for Indiana.[44] The Hoosier State experienced difficulty in meeting its commitment because of the approaching harvest season. There persisted as well a general attitude that the western states had already supplied more than their share of men, while the eastern states had shirked their obligations.[45]

These considerations did not deter Ohio men from going to war for this brief period. Unlike Indiana men, they faced the possibility of being drafted under the March call. Many were serving already in the Ohio Militia and were influential members in their communities. Men from Cleveland apparently welcomed this interruption from their business affairs and looked forward to this short sojourn to the field, so long as they could go with their social peers.[46] In Warren, however, some of these new soldiers disliked the prospect of leaving the comforts of home.[47] Their uneasiness was compounded when they and others in at least five Ohio Hundred Days Regiments felt they had been deceived. Instead of being assigned to more comfortable garrison duty, they were ordered to relieve veteran soldiers from digging trenches and other mundane chores. In the sweltering June climate of Virginia, many of them, who weeks before had been practicing law or pursuing mercantile interests, fell ill. In angry despair, they accused the government of misusing them.[48]

Despite these problems, the program furnished over 83,000 men of the 113,000 requested from the twelve states that ultimately participated.[49] Although the service of the Hundred Days Men had limited short-term value, it allowed at least some veteran units to be sent temporarily to the front and relieved others from the drudgeries of soldiering.

An effort that was accompanied by much more fanfare, but which yielded relatively few men, was a program for Representative Recruits. On June 26, Provost Marshal General Fry announced that individuals who were not liable to drafting would now be allowed to place a recruit into service. In return for bearing the expense of enlisting a soldier, these public-spirited citizens would receive a certificate from the government, and the donor's name would be inscribed in the recruit's official records.[50] Lincoln furnished a recruit, and the program was widely publicized. But it fizzled! Fry, who seldom conceded any shortcomings in his bureau, acknowledged that the result hardly justified the effort because the government obtained less than 1,300 new soldiers. He later revealed why the government had even sponsored such a dubious undertaking. In his postwar *Final Report*, he noted that commutation's repeal was anticipated, and with "the consequent rise in the price of substitutes it was determined to make an effort to procure some recruits without a formal call."[51]

That Lincoln would support such questionable programs is understandable because he was acutely sensitive that spring to public attitudes toward the draft. On May 1, for example, Stanton urged him to raise more troops, but Lincoln demurred. Under no circumstances did he want to order another draft so soon after the March call.[52] As casualty reports continued arriving from the campaigns in the Wilderness and Spotsylvania, he came to the realization that he had no other choice. He began making preparations to order another call for three hundred thousand men on May 17, but never issued it. That same day the New York *World* and the New York *Journal of Commerce* published a false draft order calling for another four hundred thousand men. Lincoln's reaction was immediate. He notified Major General John Dix, who commanded the New York district to "arrest and imprison" the perpetrators of this hoax.[53] In the wake of the adverse public response toward still another draft call that stemmed from the bogus proclamation, Lincoln decided to hold his plans in abeyance despite the pressing needs of the army.[54]

Lincoln could not defer action on the draft for too long. Casualties from the spring campaigns were mounting, and despite the major modification to the commutation privilege earlier that winter, it continued to frustrate the acquisition of replacements for Union ranks. On June 6, Fry informed Stanton of his opposition to the exemption fee because the government was not procuring enough substitutes with the commutation money that it had. In support of his argument, he cited the figures from a recent supplementary draft that had been ordered in certain districts. Of the 14,741 drawn, 7,016 (or almost half) received exemptions for physical reasons or other causes. Of the remaining 7,725 men, 5,050 paid the fee and 1,416 furnished substitutes. Only 1,259 were actually held to "personal service." He emphasized that the army could not "be materially strengthened so long as the $300.00 clause is in force."[55]

Stanton strongly endorsed Fry's appeal. To broaden the base of support for this unpopular move, he alluded to the possibility that, if commutation was repealed, the period of service might be reduced. At Stanton's request, Lincoln, in his only public support of a pending conscription bill, referred Fry's report and Stanton's endorsement to Congress with his "concurrence in the recommendation therein made." In a related action, the president also met privately with the House Military Committee either shortly before or after this written request to press for a stronger draft law.[56]

The Senate had already begun moving toward commutation's repeal a few weeks earlier. On May 23, Edwin D. Morgan, a member of the military committee, introduced S. 286. It remained on the table for over two weeks until the administration's recommendation arrived. After that point, the proposed modification to the conscription bill dominated business in the upper house from June 8 to the end of the first session on July 4. The House of Representatives was also preoccupied with the proposal, but for a lesser period from June 21 to July 2.

Similar to the experience of a few months before, a seesaw battle ensued between the Senate and the House, and within these two chambers, over the ultimate content of the final bill. Although both military committees ultimately recommended commutation's repeal, each house reported a different proposal, S. 286 and H.R. 549. Neither of these bills received congressional approval. Instead, a nonmember of the House Military Committee, Nathaniel B. Smithers of Delaware, introduced a compromise measure. His proposal generated enough of a consensus that a bill, after a conference committee reviewed and modified it, passed both houses by narrow margins.[57] Also, the influence of the men from Massachusetts once again proved to be a dominating factor in determining the bill's content.

Even though both military committees recommended recalling commutation altogether, it continued to be the crux of the controversy because its repeal depended solely on the approval of other policies. In varying degrees, many of these tangential proposals offended other congressmen. As before, opinion was divided over the desirability of the three-hundred-dollar exemption fee both among congressmen and their constituents.[58] Even within the higher echelons of the government there was disagreement. While Stanton urged commutation's recall, Salmon P. Chase supported its retention, no doubt because it would continue to help his hard put Treasury Department.[59]

Representatives also experienced mixed feelings over commutation. They were aware of the need to replace the tremendous casualties that the Union army was suffering as it continued to hammer away at the Confederacy in places such as Spotsylvania, Cold Harbor, and Petersburg.[60] But they were also conscious of another equally pressing need, namely their political futures. With elections looming for all within a few months, various members shuddered at the thought of removing commutation without providing some compensating programs.[61] The major ones included provisions for retaining substitution; restoring the federal bounty; reducing a drafted man's period of service from three years to one; and, ever conscious over public sensitivity to reducing quotas, devising new methods for obtaining credits. In addition to commutation, each of these questions fostered intense debate in both chambers and in most instances led to roll calls. Indeed, four Senate votes alone occurred on whether to reduce the service requirement to one year.[62]

The most volatile of these issues was Southern recruitment. This policy essentially would authorize a state to go into conquered areas to recruit men who would then be credited against a loyal state's quota.[63] Although the program ultimately yielded meager results—1,405 agents managed to recruit only 5,052 Southern blacks—an impression emerged that New England in general, and Massachusetts in particular, would benefit greatly, which provoked the ire of congressmen from other areas.

As before, the divisiveness over commutation and the amendments that it fostered was reflected in Republican voting behavior. During the course of the House debates, 22 roll calls were taken. On many of these votes, party discipline fell sharply for the House Republicans when compared to the previous winter. So sensitive was this issue that some members refused to attend one House caucus meeting that had been called specifically to determine the fate of the exemption fee. Despite Schenck's efforts to present a unified front through a series of caucus meetings with his party, and despite his attempts to build a coalition with enough members to pass a bill, members of his committee and other Republicans, including Thaddeus Stevens, openly challenged him on the floor of the House.[64]

The commutation issue and other proposals that depended on its future status were responsible for splintering House Republican ranks. In one vote, in which exactly two-thirds of the House members present voted to retain the fee, a perturbed James A. Garfield was finally led to remark that "this Congress must sooner or later meet the issue face to face, and I believe the time will soon come . . . when we must give up the war or give up the commutation."[65] In the last vote on the bill before it went to the Conference Committee, Schenck, after days of effort, finally managed to persuade just enough aberrant Republicans to vote with him so that the measure could pass by 82 to 77.[66]

Senate Republicans too remained divided over the proposed draft bill. Of the 21 votes taken on this legislation, 9 of which were procedural, the majority party increased its unity only slightly from the previous winter. Party discipline among the Democrats, however, rose sharply on most of the roll calls.[67] The absence of strong Republican unity in voting concealed the change that marked Senate Republican attitudes toward the July legislation. Instead of a Senate chamber laden with intraparty disputes, reasonable decorum prevailed. This metamorphosis was due to Henry Wilson, who wisely refrained from pushing his desire to retain the fee too ardently so long as substitution was retained and a provision was made for Southern recruitment.[68]

Wilson would support commutation's repeal only if Southern recruitment was authorized. Otherwise, he would oppose any tampering with the fee, because he feared that manufacturing interests would suffer if the draft drained away too many skilled workers. His explanations were to no avail. Initially, most senators would favor the provision only if Southern black recruits were classified as United States Volunteers, thereby indirectly benefiting the quotas of all states. Republican and Democratic senators alike called upon each state to fill quotas from its own population and charged that too many white men remained at home in certain states. Lazarus Powell of Kentucky, for example, proposed a residence clause for all new recruits. In that way Kentucky and the Midwest would not have to compete with the East and its liberal bounties. In the end, Wilson lost in his bid to have the Senate endorse such a policy before it approved its version of the draft bill. He was not that concerned, however, because Bay State representatives, with the assistance of a few from other states, would insist on its inclusion before they would support any bill.[69]

Antipathy toward the Bay State's efforts to protect its citizens at the expense of all others was most bitter in the House. In a way, Schenck was partly responsible for this volatile atmosphere because he ultimately reported an amended bill that included a provision for Southern recruitment. He had no other choice if he was to woo the Massachusetts representatives to resolve an impasse that had developed over the conscription bill. By so doing, he had to risk alienating other Republicans, especially from the Midwest and the border states, who disliked the proposal.

Midwestern and border state representatives were outraged at the prospect of Southern recruitment. To them, it had the trappings of just another Massachusetts scheme to avoid meeting troop obligations. On June 25, various congressmen addressed this issue. Foremost among the critics was Robert Mallory of Kentucky. He predicted that western men would "never consent to the blood of their free white men [being] mingled on your battle fields with that of the negro [*sic*] of the South, brought by New England money." Samuel S. Cox, an Ohio Democrat, reflected midwestern attitudes when he asked, "How many [blacks are being enlisted] in this city where there now is an agency for the purpose of recruiting men for Massachusetts?"[70]

House approval of its version of the draft bill remained uncertain until the very moment of its passage on June 28. With adjournment nearing and other business pending, some members who disliked Southern recruitment refrained from comment. On June 29, the Senate rejected the House bill. Given the opportunity to discuss the measure once again on June 30 and July 1, the dormant opposition burst into the open. As in the Senate, party lines were transcended as congressmen voiced their displeasure with the proposed program. James F. Wilson, an Iowa Republican, insisted that a state's draft quota be drawn only from among its own residents. Aaron Harding of Kentucky criticized Massachusetts's men for evading service by sending blacks in their place. The most revealing remarks of all came from Frank C. LeBlond, an Ohio Democrat, who indicated that "there has been a bargain and sale made, and the bill shaped to suit the needs of Massachusetts and enable her to go into my State and others to purchase negroes [*sic*]."[71]

LeBlond was partially correct. The acceptance of Southern recruitment as part of this latest bill remained certain only if prodraft House Republicans could avoid alienating the Massachusetts contingent with its crucial ten votes. The Bay State group insisted on other concessions, as well. Equally as much, they wanted provisions that would restore bounties, reduce the period of service to one year, and retain the substitute clause. They had their way on all points of contention, and their ten votes proved to be the deciding factor behind House approval of the Conference Committee report.[72]

When the report reached the Senate, controversy over Southern recruitment resurfaced, and the report consequently was rejected. In the course of the discussion, Garrett Davis of Kentucky accused Massachusetts of trying to reopen the slave trade in its quest to recruit Southern blacks. Thomas A. Hendricks best reflected the attitudes of many senators, however, when he stated that the program "is commutation in negroes [*sic*]. The Senate says, 'No commutation in money,' and the House says, 'We will agree to that, but we will have commutation in negroes [*sic*].'" After these remarks, and with the earlier public support of Wilson's old antagonist, Henry S. Lane, the Senate finally agreed to reconsider the conference report. In the closing hours of the first session, the Senate accepted it by 18 votes to 17.[73]

The time and energy that Schenck, Wilson, and other congressmen expended was reflected in the final version of the bill. The principal purpose of the Enrollment Act had been to acquire men, not money, in the least objectionable way possible. This primary goal had not been attained, and the onus for strengthening the law fell on the Thirty-eighth Congress. Consistent with the trend that had begun to emerge in December 1863, and which culminated in February 24 legislation, the July 4 measure placed greater emphasis on obtaining men rather than excusing them. Within this framework the July Act gave the president more flexibility in calling for volunteers, because now he could call for an unlimited number to serve for periods ranging from one to three years. Among the other major provisions was the repeal of commutation, except for those who "were conscientiously opposed to the bearing of arms."[74]

With elections on the horizon, congressmen wanted to offset any negative public reaction by compensating for commutation's removal with other policies. Accordingly, they required the discharging of minors, allowed drafted men to select their own units, and abolished supplementary drafts. Most significant, the act retained substitution; reduced the period of a drafted man's service from three years to one; authorized credits for all men who enlisted in the Union navy; provided for Southern recruitment; and reinstituted the federal bounty in amounts from one hundred to three hundred dollars, with one-third payable in advance and the rest in installments.[75]

Except for Southern recruitment, a version of all of these policies probably would have been incorporated into the bill even in the absence of strong pressure from the Massachusetts delegation. Congress saw the draft as its "most politically sensitive issue" that spring and had no desire to alienate any constituent unnecessarily.[76] Indeed, as reflected in the strong support for bounties in the House, federal officials preferred "trying the old way" rather than instituting some long-term policy for manpower mobilization.[77] Aside from political pressure, there was another pragmatic reason for placing a renewed emphasis on the bounty system. With wages high and employment plentiful at this point in the war, men had little incentive to enter the army as a recruit or substitute without generous pecuniary inducements. As noted earlier, the Lincoln administration had abandoned federal bounties from April 1 to July 4, and instead experimented with a program of short-term enlistments. But the failure of these programs in meeting the long-term needs of the Union army quickly had become apparent.

The February and July amendatory acts were part of the evolutionary process that placed more emphasis on personal service. These measures were also important in that no mention was made of expanding the age range for draft liability. Under the Militia Act, men between the ages of 18 and 45 were subject to the draft. This span was narrowed to between 20 and 45 in the Enrollment Act and remained unchanged throughout the war. This modification proved to be important, because 18- and 19-year-olds could still enter the military as recruits and as substitutes.[78] The government could therefore maintain the threat of drafting, without tampering with a major source of manpower that draft-liable men drew on for replacements.

COMMUTATION'S REPEAL
AND CLASS DISCRIMINATION

I n an unpublished letter written a few months after the New York City riots, Abraham Lincoln recorded his opinion on whether the Northern draft discriminated against the workingman. From his vantage point, the president believed that the commutation fee held down substitute prices and therefore enabled men to avoid "service who are too poor to escape it but for it." In his view the substitute clause clearly favored the wealthier classes because they could afford to hire replacements. He further noted that true impartiality in the federal draft system could be attained only with the revocation of both the commutation and substitute clauses, but to remove the substitute privilege would make the draft "more distasteful than it now is."[1]

According to Lincoln's personal secretaries, John G. Nicolay and John Hay, the president refrained from publishing this letter because he doubted the "propriety" of appealing to loyal Northern Democrats over the heads of their leaders.[2] In the wake of the New York disorders, when many local governments undermined the law's intent by paying the fee for their citizens, he might have believed that the three-hundred-dollar privilege ultimately would be repealed. Rather than take a public position that might prove awkward to defend at a later date, he wisely left well enough alone. Despite the letter's limited circulation, it is important because it reveals Lincoln's attitude toward commutation. Also, it indicates that he was sensitive to class differences that existed in the Civil War North. These differences could be exacerbated if the commutation privilege was eliminated while substitution was retained.

Lincoln was very perceptive in anticipating this concern, because commutation's repeal brought renewed charges that the Union draft discriminated against the poor. As congressmen vacillated over the fate of the popular clause in June and July 1864, newspaper editors watched their actions closely and commented accordingly. In a complete reversal of opinion from the spring of 1863, Democratic journalists criticized any tampering with the $300 fee.[3] The *Chicago Times* called on Congress to retain it so that the average man could excuse himself from fighting for a "despised and inferior race." On one occasion, it even praised the Republican *New York Times* for its rare "attack of common sense" in recognizing that the draft would now become "absolute . . . in the case of all but the wealthy class of the community."[4] The *Detroit Free Press* severely chastised Michigan Republican congressmen, who by voting for repeal deprived "the poor man of every chance to commute."[5]

Lest Democrats now open themselves to charges of "*inconsistency*" for defending commutation, Samuel Medary of the *Crisis* explained that his party had opposed it originally only to discover that its unfairness could be avoided. Rather than accept the inherent social inequality implied in the system, the Democrats "true to their principles of justice, clubbed together and where a man was too poor to raise the money himself, they helped him raise it."[6] From the capital, the *Daily National Intelligencer* labeled "repeal . . . the most oppressive act that Congress could do."[7] The *Cleveland Plain Dealer* implied that an organization of brokers favored repeal to enhance their own fortunes. In the following days, it urged the community to place a greater emphasis on volunteering because repeal would "draw the line still more strongly . . . between rich and poor."[8] The *New York Herald* also stressed the discriminatory nature of the proposed new law as it diplomatically called upon Congress to make the new law "as little oppressive as possible."[9]

Before Lincoln signed H.R. 549 into law, many Republican newspapers shared the sentiments of the Democratic press. The *Cincinnati Daily Commercial* contended that given the law of supply and demand, only "the wealthiest classes" could now provide substitutes. It further recommended that instead of relying on the dubious success of drafting, a greater emphasis should be placed on recruiting.[10] The *New York Tribune* thought repeal would definitely place the military burden of the war on the working classes. When the House voted initially to retain the fee, the *Cleveland Leader* praised it for this wise decision. Both it and the *Boston Daily Journal* warned Congress to proceed cautiously in amending the clause because of the hardship it would place on the poor.[11]

The *Boston Daily Journal* mirrored the attitudes of Henry Wilson and the Massachusetts delegation. It wanted commutation retained in addition to a program that authorized Southern recruitment. Consistent with these goals, it dismissed sectional critics who opposed Massachusetts's efforts to enlist men from other states because each section needed to concentrate on its own form of wealth. The West, with its surplus of young men, could easily fill its quotas; other states had to look elsewhere for manpower. It warned that adverse effects on the material production of the North could be anticipated unless blacks and immigrants were encouraged to join the Union army in larger numbers.[12]

Republican newspapers in the capital generally favored the recall of commutation so long as Congress retained substitution. A negative ballot "to exempt any drafted man capable of serving efficiently without furnishing an exempt substitute, simply votes to insure the eventual success of the rebellion," argued the editor of the *Washington, D.C. Evening Star*.[13] Similarly, the editor of the *Washington, D.C. Daily Morning Chronicle* believed that "if men of means are to be exempted from actual service by paying a fine, it should be the full value of a substitute," not three hundred dollars.[14] On occasion, the *New York Times* echoed this opinion and urged the wealthy to hire representative recruits. Such a course was only proper, since they gained material advantages from the war. While the paper lamented the passing of commutation, it defended substitution because it provided "the only means of sparing that class . . . who work with their brains—who do the planning and directing of the national industry."[15]

The seeming unfairness of the draft initially divided opinion when commutation and substitution were introduced in the spring of 1863, but months before the end of the war these issues largely disappeared. Historians have reached no such accord. The class issue continues to attract their attention because it is usually considered the principal cause behind draft resistance. The range of opinion on this issue is so broad that some believe the draft discriminated against the working poor throughout the war, a few contend that the recall of the three-hundred-dollar exemption fee was discriminatory, and another argues that the conscription laws did not intend to place the draft's burden on any particular group.[16] Still another criticizes all past works for focusing on the men who paid commutation and substitution fees, rather than on those who failed to report.[17]

Among the more important works that reflect the traditional viewpoint is the two-volume study by Fred A. Shannon. He argues that the draft discriminated against the working classes because the cost of exemption was financially beyond their reach.[18] This view is echoed in Robert Sterling's "Civil War Draft Resistance in the Middle West." Like Shannon, he believes that commutation favored the well-to-do and disagrees strongly with Eugene Murdock's suggestion that the exemption fee did not hurt the poor. In full accord with Shannon's position, Sterling argues that the Enrollment Act provided "protection for the moderately well-to-do and the rich . . . [and] represents one of the worst pieces of class legislation ever passed by the United States Congress." To substantiate his case, he relies on the timeworn assumption that "a poor laborer or a poor farmer earning approximately $1 a day could [not] raise $300 to avoid personal service."[19]

Consistent with this emphasis, Sterling takes issue with Murdock and Hugh

G. Earnhart, who believe that most workingmen were able to escape the draft through commutation. Using per capita valuation for districts in New York State, Murdock argues there "was just as much paying of commutation to avoid the draft in poor districts as there was in wealthy districts." Although Murdock identifies reservations that he has with this approach, his words of caution have not precluded others from criticizing his methodology. Sterling, for example, finds a "questionable use of data in calculating percentages." Such censure notwithstanding, Murdock's analysis represents the first study to raise doubts as to whether the Civil War "was a rich man's war and a poor man's fight" because of the draft.[20]

In a later study, Hugh Earnhart computed percentages for various occupational groups and compared them before and after the repeal of commutation in July 1864. Based on an examination of four Ohio districts, he concludes that the recall of the fee privilege "was *unfair* class legislation because it took from the poor man his only chance to escape service and left only the wealthy an avenue of escape in the substitute clause."[21] The accuracy of Earnhart's raw data is not disputed, but his findings are only partially correct because he relies on the number of men drawn as the basis for his calculations, not those who were held to service.

In considering how the draft affected men in certain occupational classes, the analysis must be confined to those men who were held to service, not to the number of men drawn. Rather than deduct the number of men who either were exempted, discharged, or who failed to report, Earnhart includes them in his statistical computations and understandably reaches the conclusion that commutation's repeal marked the beginning of discrimination against the workingman. Unlike those held to service, all others drawn in a draft did not have to exercise an option of either paying commutation, providing a substitute, or going to war.

According to Earnhart's figures, 23.7 percent of the drafted laborers in Ohio's fifth district paid commutation, 1.7 percent hired substitutes, and 13.6 percent were conscripted under the March 1864 call. After commutation was repealed, only 8.6 percent were able to furnish substitutes, although none were drafted. Using his tabular format and confining the calculations to the total held to service, the revised figures indicate that 60.9 percent of the drafted laborers paid commutation, 4.3 percent furnished substitutes, and 34.8 percent were conscripted under the March 1864 call. After July 1864, all of the drafted laborers furnished substitutes. The number of laborers who provided substitutes dramatically increased in the fifth district when the three-hundred-dollar exemption fee was no longer available. Also, merchants, ministers, bankers, and brokers managed to avoid conscription before July 1864 in this district but were not as fortunate in the last two drafts of the war.[22]

Similar patterns emerge in the other Ohio districts. In the eighteenth, for example, Earnhart reports that 17.3 percent of drafted laborers paid the fee, another 20.6 percent furnished substitutes, and 4 percent were conscripts under the March 1864 call. Later, only 28 percent hired substitutes and 2.1 percent became conscripts. For the March 1864 call, the revised figures are 41.3 percent who paid commutation, 49.2 percent who provided substitutes, and 9.5 percent who became conscripts. Commutation's repeal did not adversely affect the 115 drafted laborers in this district in a significant way, because 93 percent found substitutes. Based on these revised calculations, the demise of the exemption fee did not harm Ohio workingmen because substantial numbers managed to furnish physical replacements.[23]

The value of Earnhart's work lies in essentially confirming Murdock's suggestion that commutation did not discriminate against the working classes. The combined contribution of these studies rests in challenging the validity of the class discrimination thesis, and methodological difficulties notwithstanding, it appears relatively certain that the working classes generally could take advantage of the three-hundred-dollar fee. As discussed earlier (chapter 8, table 6), approximately one-fourth of all drafted men paid commutation regardless of their occupational status. Admittedly, some men lived in communities that paid it for them, but others managed to raise the money needed in other ways, such as banding together in clubs.

Both Earnhart and Murdock doubt whether workingmen were able to raise enough money to hire substitutes. Their reservations stem in part from Lincoln's belief that commutation helped to hold down the cost; once the three-hundred-dollar exemption privilege was no longer available, prices skyrocketed.[24] Their assumption is partially correct because prices increased significantly in some geographical areas but not in others. An even more important factor than cost was the availability of a sufficient number of men who were willing to offer their services as substitutes.

From Cincinnati, an Irish immigrant wrote his brother that he anticipated no difficulty in finding a replacement, since he planned to borrow the money from friends who were not drafted. He further predicted that the recall of the $300 fee would prevent many poor men from acquiring substitutes because the price would undoubtedly rise to $2,000.[25] Time proved him wrong, however. In the March 14 draft in Ohio's first district, which included Cincinnati, only 19 percent of the laborers in this city provided substitutes. An average of 38 percent managed to find replacements for the drafts ordered on July 18 and December 19, 1864.[26] Also, the price of substitutes did not rise as high as predicted because an ample supply of Union men were willing to go as replacements. Substitute brokers were quite active in this city, and one promised to obtain replacements with no "DELAY OR ANNOYANCE" for any drafted man who lived in Ohio, Indiana, or Kentucky.[27] Prices also varied and tended to increase as a draft approached. In July 1864, one Cincinnati man paid $475 for a black replacement. Two months later, another had to pay $900.[28]

Rates varied in other areas as well. The price of a substitute in the District of Columbia typically cost $800 to $1,000, but in Maine a willing replacement could command only $650.[29] Some 28 percent of the farmers in south-central Ohio managed to avoid the draft by paying an average of $474.25 for each substitute.[30] Less than three hundred miles away in Oil City, Pennsylvania, however, a man noted that he anticipated paying an even $1,000 for a man to go in his place.[31] Prospective substitutes in Detroit could expect no more than $500.[32] By early January 1865, a substitute could garner as much as $1,800 in New York City, but principals were paying as little as $220 for a one-year man, $430 for a two-year man, and $650 for a three-year man.[33] Men who desired substitutes evidently had to pay only these small amounts, while the city and county governments contributed the balance.[34]

Financial support from local and state governments in some areas helped significantly in enabling men to furnish a substitute. All a Massachusetts resident had to pay was $125 to the state toward the purchase of a Southern recruit.[35] In Cleveland, substitutes received between $300 and $500, and the city reimbursed $100 to each principal who provided one.[36] Partially as a result, laborers in Ohio's eighteenth district, which included Cleveland, could avoid conscription with relatively little difficulty. In the last nine months of the war, 93 percent of them furnished replacements.[37] By mid-February, New York State had passed a law that gave $300, $400, or $600, respectively, to any drafted citizen who furnished a substitute for one, two, or three years.[38] According to one estimate in the *New York Herald*, this rebate effectively reduced the price to $200 for a one-year, $300 for a two-year, and $400 for a three-year substitute.[39] In New Jersey, the Newark City Council had enacted a similar law the previous spring. All that one of its drafted citizens had to contribute toward a substitute was $50 plus "$2 for expenses," and the city bore the remaining cost of $400.[40]

In the absence of governmental subsidies, or as a supplement to these grants, draft-liable men resorted to many of the same techniques they had used when commutation was available. They especially favored banding together in clubs and local associations. In return for a fee, a member was eligible to draw on a common fund to help defray the cost of a substitute in the event he was drafted. More often than not the cost of this privilege was nominal. For $25, Detroit men could join one of several such organizations, and in Chicago, fees varied from $25 to $40.[41] In the District of Columbia, the price of membership ranged from a low $25 in one ward protection club to a high of $240 in another.[42] Ten Indianapolis men formed an organization that required an initial $200 deposit from each person and a legal commitment to contribute to the group all money that the city might pay toward an individual's substitute.[43] In addition to local and state grants, a New York City resident had other avenues to help him escape the draft. He could join one of several ward or local associations, or he could simply pay $150 to one organization that guaranteed his exemption from the draft.[44]

Without external support or the availability of an insurance society, a prospective conscript could always hope for assistance from other quarters. On January 13, 1865, Thomas A. Scott, vice-president of the Pennsylvania Railroad Company, requested permission from the War Department to furnish three-year replacements for any of the company's skilled workers who were drafted and to credit them in one of three localities. Others had to rely on the goodwill of their friends and neighbors by soliciting contributions. One brazen constituent, for example, asked his congressman for a $60 loan to help defray the cost of a substitute. The government granted Scott's request, but the congressman evidently ignored the plea of his desperate constituent.[45]

The approach of a draft induced anxiety among Northern men, but in the war's last nine months this apprehension became even more acute because of the increased competition for substitutes.[46] The demands of the last two troop calls compounded the problem because they were the most burdensome in terms of sheer numbers. The July call required 500,000 one-year men, and the December 1864 call demanded the equivalent of 300,000 three-year men. The 1863 and March 1864 calls in the aggregate had called for 700,000 men. After enlistment credits had been taken into account under the first two calls, a total of 34,913 men furnished substitutes, and only 13,297 went as conscripts. Under the July 1864 call alone, 28,502 drafted men furnished substitutes and 26,205 entered the army as conscripts.[47]

Logically, the last two drafts should have fallen heaviest on workingmen. Although they had been able to take advantage of commutation, they presumably could not compete economically with their social betters in hiring qualified substitutes, particularly given the increasing scarcity of replacements after July 1864. To test the validity of this assumption, three tables are presented here (tables 9, 10, and 11) that are designed to gauge the impact of the fee's repeal on various occupational categories. For comparative purposes, four districts in Ohio, two in Michigan, and one in New York have been selected, because all three experienced federal conscription both when commutation was available and after it was repealed. Also, these areas reflected the national trend of more men being forced into the army after July 1864. Whereas 377 men from these districts had gone as conscripts prior to July 1864, 1,492 did so in the last two drafts. These districts further represent a mixture of urban and rural areas, and also of Republicans and Democrats. Finally, they reveal certain variations of the way in which the federal draft affected various occupational groups in the North.[48] In New York's thirtieth district, for example, proportionately fewer farmers had to render personal service after July 1864.

As shown in table 9, professional men in western New York remained unaffected by commutation's removal. None were conscripted either before or after its repeal because all who had been drafted managed to pay three hundred dollars or to find a substitute. Skilled and unskilled workers represented a larger percentage of the conscript pool in this New York district after July 1864, but proportionately fewer men in white-collar occupations in this district became actual conscripts. Among the white-collar and commercial classes for all areas, the fee's recall had the most adverse effect on Ohio's public servants, manufacturers, and bankers, as reflected in table 10.

Not only did more white-collar Ohio men enter the army after July 1864, but proportionately more Ohio farmers and professional men also were represented in the total conscript pool. Conversely, the likelihood of entering the service was reduced for the skilled and unskilled workers in this state. As shown in table 11, Michigan followed a similar pattern.

In the aggregate, tables 9–11 reveal that the draft tended to distribute its burdens more equitably on men in all occupational classes after July 1864

TABLE 9

New York

Occupational Category	Before July 1864						After July 1864			
	Commutation		Substitutes		Conscripted		Substitutes		Conscripted	
	N	%	N	%	N	%	N	%	N	%
Farmers & farm workers	120	43.2	126	23.9	10	29.4	9	6.2	9	15.2
Skilled workers	79	28.4	165	31.3	12	35.3	58	39.0	23	39.0
Unskilled workers	44	15.8	67	12.7	5	14.7	34	23.0	17	28.8
White-collar & commercial	23	8.3	140	26.6	5	14.7	41	27.6	5	8.5
Professional	6	2.2	15	2.9	—	—	2	1.4	—	—
Miscellaneous	2	0.7	6	1.1	—	—	1	0.7	—	—
Unknown	4	1.4	8	1.5	2	5.9	3	2.1	5	8.5
TOTAL	278	100	527	100	34	100	149	100	59	100

TABLE 10

Oнıo

Occupational Category	Before July 1864						After July 1864			
	Commutation		Substitutes		Conscripted		Substitutes		Conscripted	
	N	%	N	%	N	%	N	%	N	%
Farmers & farm workers	591	40.2	68	16.6	91	47.4	526	50.9	638	71.7
Skilled workers	307	20.9	77	18.7	48	25.0	154	14.9	141	15.8
Unskilled workers	299	20.3	136	33.1	50	26.0	156	15.1	59	6.6
White-collar & commercial	241	16.4	125	30.4	3	1.6	143	13.8	38	4.3
Professional	30	2.0	5	1.2	—	—	17	1.7	13	1.5
Miscellaneous	3	0.2	—	—	—	—	1	0.1	1	0.1
Unknown	—	—	—	—	—	—	36	3.5	—	—
TOTAL	1,471	100	411	100	192	100	1,033	100	890	100

in most districts. A more implicit trend suggests that the ability of a drafted man to escape personal service had less to do with his occupational status than with the availability of an ample supply of potential substitutes in his area. Michigan serves as a good example of this pattern. In various manuscript collections that reflect popular opinion in this state during the last nine months of the war, apprehension over finding substitutes appears repeatedly. For example, an army doctor urged his brother to acquire a replacement as soon as possible before the draft, since the number of eligible men would become scarcer after that point.[49] Another Michigan man, who had encountered difficulty in finding a substitute at home, apparently expressed his frustration to his officer brother in the field. Much to his relief, he learned that a replacement could be obtained in Tennessee for three hundred dollars. The officer promised to simply delay the formal mustering of a new recruit who, in return for the money, would willingly change his status to that of a substitute.[50] No source better captures the popular feeling of these draft-liable men than the observation of a young Michigan soldier who was assigned to the Provost Marshal General's Bureau. He heard frequently from home and, on one occasion, noted

TABLE 11

MICHIGAN

Occupational Category	Before July 1864						After July 1864			
	Commutation		Substitutes		Conscripted		Substitutes		Conscripted	
	N	%	N	%	N	%	N	%	N	%
Farmers & farm workers	348	59.5	108	61.0	102	67.5	252	71.2	418	77.0
Skilled workers	97	16.6	24	13.6	25	16.6	27	7.6	64	11.8
Unskilled workers	44	7.5	12	6.8	15	9.9	7	2.0	35	6.4
White-collar & commercial	49	8.4	22	12.4	3	2.0	2	0.6	7	1.3
Professional	23	3.9	5	2.8	—	—	7	2.0	8	1.5
Miscellaneous	9	1.5	—	—	1	0.7	—	—	2	0.4
Unknown	15	2.6	6	3.4	5	3.3	59	16.6	9	1.6
TOTAL	585	100	177	100	151	100	354	100	543	100

in his diary "that the Plymouth folks were very much scared about the coming draft. They have the money but cant [*sic*] find the men."[51]

Class antagonisms exist in all societies, and the Civil War North was no exception. Writing in March 1864, Henry C. Lea defended the exemption clauses as absolutely necessary to spare society's contributors from the burdens of military service. A few months earlier, an opposing view of who contributed most to the Northern war effort had appeared in *Fincher's Trade Review*. In this anonymous 1863 article, the author contended that laborers were the real "producers" and that they should remain home until all the "non-producers" were drafted.[52]

Without a doubt, class tensions existed in Northern society and occasionally found expression in strikes and publications such as these two essays. To some extent the Union draft may have echoed these distinctions, but it contributed little to their substance. Certainly the perception of discrimination existed in the early days of the federal draft and found an outlet in disturbances such as the New York riots. Once communities began paying all or part of the fee for their citizens, while drafted men in other areas found ways to circumvent the draft, discrimination became a dormant issue insofar as conscription was concerned. It did not reemerge until after Congress recalled the three-hundred-dollar privilege in July 1864. Lincoln thought workingmen could not pay for a substitute, and various newspaper editors and congressmen, among others, shared his view. Once again, however, prices did not rise as dramatically as predicted in many areas. Further, states and communities contributed significant sums toward bounties and the purchase of substitutes, and most drafted men managed to find ways to make up the difference in cost.

Men from all social stations were able to take advantage of commutation, and this nondiscriminatory pattern did not change after the fee's repeal. Without question, the purchase price of a substitute placed more of an economic hardship on carpenters and laborers than on lawyers and physicians. Nevertheless, a high proportion of workingmen had paid commutation, and after its demise many furnished substitutes. Theodore Roosevelt, Sr., father of the future president; Grover Cleveland, who became president in 1884; James G. Blaine, Cleveland's opponent in that bitterly fought contest; Oliver Moore, a 33-year-old Iowa trapper; and Nathan Carter, a 43-year-old New Hampshire laborer, had one thing in common. Each had hired a replacement during the Civil War. This privilege was not restricted to the rich and influential; it was accessible to any man who could raise the money, and even more important, find a surrogate. Depending on the geographical area, Northern men sometimes encountered difficulty in finding a substitute, and where the supply was limited, some were held to service in the last nine months of the war. Laborers, wheelwrights, and tinkers continued to enter the army; but proportionately more bankers, manufacturers, and in some districts, farmers and professional men, became conscripts too.

Arguments that the draft discriminated against the workingman began disappearing from editorial columns by midsummer 1864. This waning interest further indicates that the class issue had become unimportant where conscription was involved. Nevertheless, in the immediate wake of commutation's repeal, Northern men were understandably nervous over how this latest change would affect them personally. Once they began responding to the last two calls of the war, it became apparent that legal evasion was still possible through community and private resources. Consequently, much of their concern toward the draft dissipated by September 1864. They could relax, but there was little respite for community leaders who had to continue grappling with ways to fill quotas from their diminishing pools of resident manpower. Nor did worries subside among Republican politicians, who feared the ramifications of the draft as they made preparations for the upcoming fall elections.

ALIENATION AND THE DRAFT

July 1864–April 1865

Discontent toward the Lincoln administration existed during much of the war, nurtured in particular by issues such as emancipation and the peaks and valleys that Union military successes and failures brought to the home front. The summer of 1864 was no exception. When congressmen returned to their districts that summer, they encountered constituents who were angry and disheartened with the war's progress. Northern citizens everywhere were tired of the seemingly endless troop calls, bounty drives, and special assessments for local bounties, which taxed their purses as well as their patience. This annoyance combined with depression over the state of the Union army. Most citizens were saddened over the tremendous number of casualties taken in the Wilderness. To add to their woes was the Union defeat at Kennesaw Mountain and the evident stalemate that had developed at Petersburg. In the meantime, Confederate General Jubal Early continued to roam the Shenandoah Valley and once appeared on the outskirts of Washington. He continued to befuddle Union strategists until September, when General Phillip Sheridan finally brought him to heel at Winchester, and then at Fisher's Hill.

A revived peace movement took hold during most of the summer. As Democrats seemingly moved toward greater unity, Republicans became increasingly nervous over the strife within their ranks. Some raised the possibility of holding another convention to nominate a different presidential candidate.[1] In late August, President Lincoln even penned a private memorandum that he had others sign and seal. Not until after the elections were over did he order its contents revealed. So serious were the splits in his party and the lack of progress on the battlefield in late August that he doubted the likelihood of his reelection that fall.[2]

In addition to Union military reverses and the split within party ranks, a major reason for Republican woes that summer stemmed from the draft. Secretary of State William Seward reflected the sentiments of many when he confided to his wife on August 22 that "the approach of a draft . . . is creating much uneasiness, and the uneasiness speaks out through the press." Seward nevertheless tried to maintain a balanced perspective, however, and commented on how well recruiting seemed to be progressing.[3]

Many of Seward's fellow Republicans were not as sanguine and saw only doom awaiting them. Sometimes their concerns bordered on paranoia. As they heard and absorbed more and more of their angry constituents' complaints with the Lincoln administration and the draft, they began to reveal their fears that Copperheads and other Democrats would defeat loyal candidates at the polls. In the throes of their depression, some echoed the opinion that the ranks of their party were being depleted because only Democrats skedaddled before a draft. Consequently, a greater burden was placed on Republicans to enter the army.[4] Evidently, it did not occur to these Republicans that draft evaders certainly would not return to vote at the risk of being apprehended. At the opposite end of the political spectrum, Democrats viewed the Republicans as the principal culprits when it came to shirking one's duty. They especially criticized the Loyal Leagues, which made "strenuous efforts" to avoid conscription at the expense of the Democrats.[5]

In the Midwest, Republicans were nervous too over activities of Copperhead organizations that were plotting against them. The "secret society scarecrow" made its appearance just before the election in groups such as the Knights of the Golden Circle and the Sons of Liberty. One view holds that these organizations were created through the fertile imaginations of Republican politicians, that their purpose was to discredit the Democrats, and that no real conspiracy existed. Recent scholarship questions the validity of this thesis by demonstrating that certain treasonable groups were active in the Midwest, and that their agendas included various plots against the federal government.[6]

Regardless of these Republican activities, there was no quarreling over two realities that summer. Commutation was gone, and on July 18, Lincoln issued a call for five hundred thousand more men. The order further scheduled a draft for September 5 in those areas that had not filled their quotas with volunteers.[7] Lincoln came under enormous pressure both to proceed with the draft as scheduled and to postpone it for a few months until the elections were over. Soldiers understandably tended to favor the July call.[8] The military, which had grown extremely disillusioned with the home front by 1864, pressed the government for conscription to proceed on schedule. Following Seward's unauthorized Auburn speech in late August, when he indicated that no further drafts would be necessary, generals Ulysses Grant and William Sherman interceded with strong letters of rebuttal.[9] On September 13, Grant alluded to

Seward's speech before he emphatically stated that conscription "is soon over, and ceases to hurt after it is made."[10] That same day, Wisconsin senator James R. Doolittle echoed this opinion in a telegram to Lincoln, Stanton, and Fry: "Do not postpone. . . . The fear of a draft is greater than the reality, and is more depressing. . . . While pending, all fear it."[11]

Republicans disagreed on the wisdom of concluding the draft quickly. One influential Republican leader had mixed reactions over whether to complete the draft in his district. Although clearly anxious over the possible adverse effects of another draft, Schuyler Colfax, Speaker of the House in the Thirty-eighth Congress, considered capitalizing on this otherwise dismal situation. In a July 25 letter to the president, he suggested that Lincoln arrange to furlough certain Indiana regiments so they could vote. To enhance his party's chances for success at the polls even further, he also recommended that the draft remain "*pending*" at election time. Such a strategy might dissuade some potential Democrats from voting because of the danger of having their names transferred from the poll to the enrollment list.[12]

Lincoln vacillated briefly, then ordered the draft to proceed on September 19, two weeks after the originally scheduled date. Once the decision was made, most Republicans came to share Doolittle's opinion. James G. Blaine, who ultimately provided a substitute, wanted the draft drawn to a close as soon as possible because otherwise a "district is kept in a ferment for weeks." Blaine contacted his Republican colleague Elihu B. Washburne, who was still in Washington, and urged him to visit Stanton. He was to convey the necessity of completing the draft quickly to minimize its effect on the upcoming elections in Ohio and Pennsylvania. More than any other Republican that fall, Blaine epitomized his party's attitude toward conscription when he stated that "the dreaded draft is now going on all over the country. . . . Like the old ladies' tea party, 'It will be good to have it over with.'"[13]

By the time elections were held in October and November, the Republicans had reversed their downhill slide and reunited, whereas the Democrats had splintered. Further, Republicans benefited from Union successes on the battlefield. Leaving nothing to chance, they also granted requests to have soldiers sent home on furlough in those states that did not allow them to vote by absentee ballot. Lincoln was particularly concerned over Indiana and asked General Sherman to send home as many Hoosier troops as he could spare. Sherman complied by issuing furloughs to several thousand troops. Abuse of the soldier vote led to Democratic charges of fraud and intimidation at the polling booth. Approximately 150,000 soldiers completed ballots, and they proved to be a deciding factor in some state and local elections. Connecticut and New York soldiers definitely contributed to the margin of Lincoln's electoral vote. Except to convey the point that 78 percent of the soldiers preferred Abraham Lincoln over the Democratic candidate, General George B. McClellan, the military vote did not decide the outcome of the presidential race. Among civilians, Lincoln garnered 53 percent of the popular vote and secured victory in enough states to win the presidency in the electoral college. In the end, Republicans carried numerous contests at the state and local levels. They suffered significant defeats only in Kentucky, Delaware, and New Jersey.[14]

Blaine's worries over the draft as a factor in the elections proved for naught when voters went to the polls. Aside from the fact that over half of the drafted men had been able to hire substitutes, conscription was not as onerous as it had been previously. The term of service was now limited to one year only for those who were unable to find replacements. By election time the draft had been completed in most areas, and many others had been successful in filling their quotas with volunteers. This resulted mainly from the reappearance of high, competitive bounties, which when combined with excess credits, helped to reduce potential draft quotas significantly. Of the 500,000 men who were called for, less than half (231,918) were drawn. Of these, only 26,205 were conscripted, and another 28,502 furnished substitutes. Almost a fourth of those held were in Indiana, which along with Illinois, Iowa, Missouri, and West Virginia experienced the federal draft for the first time.[15] These states also tended to complain the loudest over quotas.[16]

Conscription was not a factor in the Indiana election but may have been in Pennsylvania.[17] In other states, Democrats unsuccessfully sought to make the draft a potent issue. In New York, for example, the press reminded voters that Republican congressmen Orlando Kellogg and Reuben Fenton had voted to repeal commutation.[18] Kellogg nonetheless was returned to his seat in the Thirty-ninth Congress, and Fenton was successful in his bid for the governor's seat.[19] Ironically, his opponent was Horatio Seymour, the most important public official of all to question and object to federal drafting. No other example better represents how weak an issue conscription had become by the 1864 autumn elections.

Numbers and factors such as the one-year draft policy alone cannot explain why the draft was a moot issue in the election. After a series of Union military disasters, victories that September at Atlanta and Sheridan's success in securing the Shenandoah Valley helped to restore Northern morale. News of these events was followed by a statement on September 24 that the secretary of the navy had ordered the suspension of further transfers from the land forces because the navy now had sufficient sailors.[20] More good news emerged in early October when Solicitor General William Whiting, who was administratively part of the Provost Marshal General's Bureau, allegedly stated that the success of recruiting would probably eliminate the need for further drafts. Regardless of the questionable origin and use of this opinion, Whiting's view was aired in the press before the presidential election.[21] The combination of these announcements lent credence to the belief that the end of the war was fast approaching.

Financially pressed and war-weary citizens seemingly would no longer need to worry about future draft calls once they met the requisitions that had been assigned under the July order.

Despite Republican anxieties over the draft that summer, the potency of the conscription issue had been successfully defused. Although they healed their internal divisions in time for the elections and conducted a well-orchestrated campaign, they took nothing for granted and remained nervous over the possible effect of the draft. Democrats were aware of this sensitivity. Never one to miss a target of opportunity, Samuel Medary, editor of the *Crisis*, tapped this raw Republican nerve when he observed in early October that "FRY says that the overplus of the present draft will be credited to *the next*. Ask your Republican neighbors, just before they go to the polls, how they like the sound of '*the next*.'"[22] Just a few weeks before his death, Medary had become an oracle.

*A*s the holiday season approached in late 1864, the draft and other unpleasant thoughts had begun to evaporate in many Northern communities. Although sons and husbands were still far away, the progress of the Union army that fall suggested that families might be reunited before another Christmas passed.

The North had been lulled into a false sense of hope. On December 19, communities were jolted from this fleeting euphoria when Lincoln ordered a troop call for three hundred thousand men. As part of the order, another draft was scheduled to commence on February 15 in those districts that failed to fill their quotas with volunteers. The suddenness of this announcement and the poor timing were compounded when Fry changed the policy for determining credits under earlier calls. With the election no longer at risk and with the need to make up a deficiency of men furnished under the July call, he decided that all localities would furnish a full three hundred thousand men, instead of permitting them to reduce their respective levies on the basis of previous credits. From an official standpoint, all excess credits had been taken into account before the quotas were assigned. But the disallowance of credits was the lesser of two evils. When citizens learned that they would be required to furnish the equivalents of three-year men, the distrust of Fry's bureau that had been simmering beneath the surface boiled into outrage. A district with a 500-man quota would have to furnish either 1,500 one-year men, 500 three-year men, or some combination of both.[23] As localities across the North learned of this mandate, they saw only the largest figure, which they interpreted as just another of Fry's arbitrary decisions. His competency was questioned, and throughout the North citizens called for his removal.

The antagonism that had emerged toward Fry's agency in 1863 was directed primarily at quotas and local provost marshals. It had been building intermittently throughout 1864, and it reached a crescendo by 1865. Whereas before only individuals had protested sporadically over allegedly unjust quotas, now whole communities and several state governors acted in unison to challenge this latest mandate for more troops.[24] In an effort to defuse this disenchantment, both Lincoln and Fry wrote several explanatory letters.[25] Fry's nebulousness only added to the confusion. Indeed, the more he wrote, the more incompetent he appeared. As complaints mounted in the winter of 1864–65 and as critics focused increasingly on the hapless provost marshal general, the prestige of his bureau fell to its lowest level of the war. Nor did the anger subside. In a parody of Fry's instructions, Murat Halstead, a highly respected Republican editor, published a lengthy list of fictitious orders that read in part:

> 1) Jan. 1, G.O. 7,843—'The last call for 300,000 is independent of all former calls, and excesses on former calls will not be allowed.'
> 2) Jan. 1, G.O. 7,844—'The last call for 300,000 is not independent of former calls, and excesses will be counted.'
> 3) Jan. 1, 2 P.M., G.O. 7,845—'General order no. 7,844 of this series, issued from this office, is hereby revoked.'
>
> . . . .
>
> 10) Jan. 3, 1865, 4 P.M., G.O. 7,852—'A former order from this bureau having been so constructed as to mean that red hair is a sufficient cause for exemption, is hereby explained so as to apply only in cases where the claimant for exemption shall have been dead for two weeks.'[26]

This ridicule undermined the credibility of the Provost Marshal General's Bureau and lent support to the belief that Fry was both incompetent and capricious. This latter belief stemmed mainly from Fry's policy of denying any further credits for men enlisted prior to December 19. Also at issue was his decision to increase New York City's quota by approximately 14,000 troops in January 1865. Some editors believed he was using the power of his office to punish this predominantly Democratic city.[27] Opposition toward him continued to mount and transcended party and sectional lines. Some people demanded his removal, and only a few defended him against his critics.[28]

To add to Fry's woes, a major scandal surfaced that January involving the crediting of seamen for the Union navy. According to the law, seamen could be accepted only at a naval rendezvous. To facilitate such enlistments, government regulations allowed communities and principals who hired naval substitutes to present a certificate to their district provost marshal noting that the future sailor had enlisted at the rendezvous. This method was ripe for fraud and abuse. Sailors already in active service and hence credited elsewhere signed blank forms for bounty brokers. They, in turn, sold them to districts that needed to fill quotas. Sometimes naval officers, both knowingly and unwittingly, assisted these agents in carrying out these deceptions.[29]

Taken together, these actions almost caused Fry's downfall. Lincoln managed to deflect some of the criticism from Fry when he created a special quota commission on February 6. This action spared him the distasteful task of removing Fry and simultaneously reduced the number of complaints against Fry's bureau.[30] No such action, however, could remove the distrust toward the government and the alienation that had come to permeate Northern society.

The outburst against Fry cannot be viewed as a partisan issue because he upset Republicans and Democrats alike. Neither can it be viewed in isolation from a general state of unrest among Northerners, who had become disenchanted with the methods used in raising troops. For those on the home front, Fry was merely a convenient target. Those in the field, however, believed that those on the home front were the principal villains. In the army, a general state of disillusionment had begun to take hold by 1864 as veterans increasingly came to view the home front with contempt. Soldiers were not only upset with the general caliber of conscripts and recruits, including bounty men and physically unqualified substitutes, but also with practically everything civilian. Their disdain even extended to members of the Christian Commission, who were there to comfort and assist them. Many of these emissaries were of draft age, seemed physically fit, but remained behind the lines.

Soldiers reserved their greatest displeasure for those who remained at home. Especially critical of those who paid commutation or provided substitutes, they did not realize that these practices no longer carried a "stigma" and instead had become "commercial processes complete with advertising, agents, brokerages, complex financial negotiations, and exchanges of large sums" of money. Legal evasion also divided families. One soldier in the 11th Pennsylvania was outraged when he learned that his brothers had joined a draft insurance society rather than join him in the field. As soldiers became more and more distant from their communities, some became disenchanted with their neighbors and families, including their women, who had encouraged them to enlist in the first place. Any remaining respect they had after years in the field was reserved for those who exhibited courage, particularly the enemies they faced in battle.[31]

Veteran soldiers were unaware of the transformation that had occurred at home during the two or three years they had been away. Nor did they comprehend the financial and emotional difficulties that many of their communities were facing by the late spring and early summer of 1864. Rather, their disillusionment paralleled a nascent wave of disaffection toward the war that was beginning to take hold on the home front. Although some individuals welcomed the high bounties and substitute fees they could command for relatively short periods of service, the majority of the civilian sector was experiencing the strains of three years of war.[32] Communities were tired and simply had no more men to give. Their resident manpower resources had been depleted, often because many of their young men had been tempted away by high bounties offered by other towns or states. As casualties kept mounting so did the number of widows and orphans, which added still further to the burden of local relief.[33]

Dwindling pools of resident manpower and escalating costs alone cannot account for the malaise that characterized local recruiting efforts. Although high bounties tempted men, many of those with families were still reluctant to enlist. Citizens continued to view the government as callous, especially toward those who were bearing the greatest cost. Irregular pay periods continued to be a major problem in some units. Soldiers heard constantly from loved ones who were "suffering for want of money; some are [being] turned out of doors," noted one sergeant in the 117th New York Volunteers. To compound matters, the government had also failed to develop a system of speedy payment of balances due from bounties, back pay, and pensions to the heirs of deceased veterans.[34]

As always, the administration's reluctance to effect a general prisoner-of-war exchange remained a source of despair. In the absence of an established program, government officials received numerous letters from constituents pleading with them to use their influence to arrange special exchanges for their loved ones. Among the letters that General Grant received was one from a disabled soldier who urged him to reach an accord with the Southern authorities so that his fellow soldiers would no longer have to suffer.[35] Few Northerners understood Grant's reasons for not pursuing a formal exchange program during most of the war and ignored the various strategical and political considerations, including the Confederacy's unwillingness to release its black prisoners of war. After numerous delays over this particular issue, the South finally relented in January 1865. Not only was it desperate for men, but the Confederacy found it increasingly difficult to provide for its Union prisoners. Faced with these circumstances, it agreed to resume exchanges on a regular basis for all of its captives, including blacks.[36]

The resumption of exchanges helped to soften the impact of the war in its final months, but nothing short of its end could remove the hard realities that the conflict brought home with depressing regularity. The human cost of the war was staggering for both the North and South. Disease and battlefield casualties ultimately took the lives of approximately 618,000 Northern and Southern men. More American soldiers and sailors died in those four short years than in all the conflicts combined up to the beginning of the Vietnam War, including the Second World War, when 405,399 Americans lost their lives. These raw numbers reveal only part of the reality, and at least one other comparison invites attention. In a recent analysis, Maris Vinovskis calculates that the ratio of military deaths per 10,000 population in the Civil War was 182. In World War II it declined to 30, and for Vietnam it decreased even more dramatically to 3 deaths for every 10,000 persons in the American population at that time. Measured by any standard, the Civil War was "the bloodiest event in our history."[37]

In varying degrees, every Northern community felt the war's impact. Although the demands for manpower were greater in the South, the numerous troop calls and the emotional drain of the war had sapped the energy of the Northern people. Before the carnage ended, almost one in six Union soldiers died while in the army. Another 275,000 survived with wounds, many of them handicapped for the remainder of their lives. Citizens "did not live the war on a national scale; they lived it from the perspective of their communities"; the town of Auburn, Massachusetts, serves as a good example of the emotional and physical toll that the war was taking. It sent 10 percent of its total male population to war, and of the 97 neighbors who became Union soldiers, 15 did not return.[38]

Filling quotas in the last two years of the war has been viewed within the "context of local patriotism" because local rallies continued to be held to raise money for bounties, while organizations in other localities continued to collect monies for the relief of soldiers' families.[39] Most communities, however, had to resort to special assessments on property and to social pressure to raise funds, because the effectiveness of the old methods had diminished greatly with the appearance of the federal draft and the prolongation of the war.[40] A major factor too was apportioning credits on a subdistrict rather than a local basis. This policy continued to create "very bitter feelings" toward Fry's bureau, as Wisconsin's governor James T. Lewis noted in a letter to Fry on January 10, 1865.[41] It contributed as well to the increasing tendency to fill quotas with men from other areas and, if necessary, to resort to paper credits.[42]

A callousness had taken hold, and in many areas efforts to encourage enlistments were "directed to self-interest as much as to patriotism."[43] Competitive bounties from other areas were draining away residents who understandably enlisted elsewhere for a higher sum of money. This factor more than any other created a perception of unfairness. As these practices became more widely known, bitter resentment began to surface against Massachusetts.

Despite the war's toll on towns such as Auburn, the Bay State, especially from the late spring of 1864, was viewed as a villain by many Northerners. Although Massachusetts finished the war with an excess of credits, it also gained "a tarnished reputation for patriotism."[44] This harsh view was not unjustified, due largely to the efforts of Governor John A. Andrew and John M. Forbes. As early as April 1864, Forbes suggested ways to circumvent quotas. A few months later, a Major Ware informed Andrew that some enlistment papers were being altered to increase the state's credits. By July 2, 1864, on the same day that the House approved Southern recruitment, Forbes advised his governor to establish two separate recruiting organizations, one official and the other consisting of private citizens. He reasoned that it would not be to Massachusetts's advantage to "combine with *other states*" because "they would cheat us."[45]

Forbes's concern that others would try to deny Massachusetts its share of troop credits under the Southern recruitment policy was without foundation. In the final tally, it managed to corner almost a quarter of the 5,052 new troops gained through the activities of 1,045 state-appointed agents.[46] The small return scarcely justified the acrimony that the 10 Bay State representatives had encountered when they forced Congress to accept the program in the July 4 Amendatory Act. Instead of supplying a significant number of men to deduct from the state's quota, all that it had created was the extreme displeasure of military commanders in the South, a new source of fraud in filling quotas, and more resentment toward the Bay State in its attempt to evade its obligations.[47]

In addition to the active recruitment of blacks, the Bay State concentrated on the recruitment of foreigners. Samuel Medary, no friend of Massachusetts (or any Republican for that matter), reported a story under the heading "OLD MASSACHUSETTS FOREVER—HOW SHE GETS OUT OF THE DRAFT—SENDS GREETINGS TO OHIO!!!" State residents allegedly were being allowed to enlist in coastal defense units for a $632 bounty. Their purpose, according to Medary, was to defend the ports through which foreign recruits entered to fill the state's quotas.[48]

Whether or not this particular episode had any substance, John Andrew endorsed a request from Springfield's mayor on August 20, 1864, to postpone the draft because he anticipated filling the local quotas with three hundred foreigners within a month.[49] Some of these men may have been assigned to one of Massachusetts's light artillery batteries stationed at Harper's Ferry, where in early October an officer in another Massachusetts battery encouraged them to desert for the purpose of joining his unit. When Stanton learned of this activity, his response was immediate: "Stop the evil at all hazards. If need be, try the guilty parties by drum-head court-martial, and execute the sentence." On occasion, new troops recruited in one Massachusetts town did not even arrive in a forward area before they were enticed to renege on their enlistment so they could be credited to another Massachusetts locality for a higher bounty. When Fry learned that Boston recruiting agents were obtaining bona fide recruits from the city of Worcester who had not yet been mustered into service, he ordered the state's provost marshal "to forbid and prevent this practice."[50]

Where troop credits were concerned, Massachusetts exhibited a zeal unrivaled by any other area. The tactics used and the tempo for the race in obtaining men from other areas were set by its chief executive. No potential credits got past the watchful eyes of John Andrew. The number of sailors ultimately credited to Massachusetts attested not only to his ability but also to his attentiveness in the matters of quotas and credits. Of the 105,963 sailors and marines enlisted during the war, the Bay State received credit for 19,983 of them.[51]

Most of these naval credits came from other states. Leaving nothing to chance, Andrew had taken steps to ensure that as many of these men as possible were credited to Massachusetts. In February 1865, he proposed to stop all naval enlistments in his state except for those credited to Massachusetts. For all other recruits, he recommended the establishment of a special commission to determine residency before accepting them into the Union navy. This suggestion provoked the ire of a high-level naval official, A. N. Smith, because it "would cause delay in enlistments, if not stop them altogether." He also feared the reaction of other states. In the end, the commission was formed and it consisted of two members, John Andrew and John Clifford, an ex-governor of Massachusetts. They compiled a list of names, credited approximately 16,000 to their state, and convinced the War Department to accept their findings.[52]

A. N. Smith was correct that the creation of this commission would only engender more ill will toward the Bay State. One irate Hoosier asked Governor Oliver P. Morton whether there was any truth to the allegation that he had sold Indiana's naval credits to Massachusetts. Fellow New Englanders James G. Blaine and Frederick A. Pike, whose state lacked a naval rendezvous, were extremely irritated. During the consideration of the final conscription bill that winter, these Maine Republicans successfully convinced the House to agree to a residency requirement for all future naval credits. With the war's end less than two months away, this restriction hardly affected Massachusetts at all. Andrew had already cornered a significant portion of the credits allowed under the amendatory acts of February 24 and July 4, 1864.[53]

Despite the envy and resentment toward the Bay State and its resourceful governor, many other Northern communities mirrored the activities of Massachusetts in the last nine months of the war. Crimping—the illegal enlistment of men from other areas—returned, to the anger and vexation of local officials.[54] With the cooperation of local authorities, agents recruited rebel prisoners of war, boys in reformatory schools, convicts and ordinary prisoners. Such practices had become so pervasive in the District of Columbia by the winter of 1864–65 that Congress passed legislation to curb the abuses that had arisen from the enlistment of men who were in jail or prison.[55] As men became scarcer, some debated the merits of making 18- and 19-year-olds liable to service. Others proposed increasing the maximum draft age from 45 to 55.[56]

Expanding the age base for drafted men would not correct the defects in a system that had gone awry. There was simply no accountability, which added to the number of men required and contributed to the atmosphere of alienation surrounding the government and the draft in 1864–65. The interest of a principal in the qualifications of his replacement ended once the provost marshal handed him a certificate releasing him from the draft. On a larger scale, concern disappeared as soon as recruiting committees filled local quotas. Concomitant with this malaise, the period from July 1864 onward witnessed a revival of bounty jumping and an increase in desertions.[57]

Regardless of party affiliation, the press lambasted not only Fry and the draft's administration but also focused attention on bounty jumpers, who plagued recruiting efforts. Equally detestable to these editors was the class of substitute brokers who cheated new recruits out of their bounty money or who enlisted unfit men. Even before the Senate and House military committees reported the proposed amendments to the conscription bill on the open floor, the *New York Times* reflected the current press mood when it urged Congress to make "each principal liable for the physical or moral defects of his substitute, and forcing everybody who sends a cripple, or an idiot, or a diseased man, or a drunkard, or a blackguard of a pronounced type to the army . . . to take his place."[58]

*E*ditors were not alone in their condemnation of the abuses that had arisen from the bounty system. On February 9, 1865, Ohio governor John Brough laid the blame squarely on the general government, which had begun the system and now had to "assume the initiative in restraining it." He suggested three reforms for consideration: the abolition of all local bounties, the establishment of a set price for substitutes, and the imposition of a residency requirement for all new recruits. Brough was on a roll. Three days earlier he had voiced his opinion on the prohibitive cost of bounties and the "red tape" that was being generated from Washington in assigning quotas. To reduce alienation and regain "the confidence of the people," he urged that Congress return the responsibility for recruiting and drafting to the control of the several states.[59]

Brough's letters and editorial opinions were symptomatic of the widespread dissatisfaction with various aspects of the federal draft. Officials and editors were most unhappy with the Provost Marshal General's Bureau and bounties, which yielded few good recruits for the vast sums expended. Other Northern groups were perturbed with the existing system for different reasons. From the religious sector came petitions insisting on exemptions for "all ministers of the gospel in actual pastoral duty." This ground swell was not limited to one or two sects but reflected the attitudes of Baptists, Presbyterians, Episcopalians, Methodists, Lutherans, the Second Dutch Reformed church, and others.[60]

Interestingly, Quakers that winter were relatively quiet. They had achieved everything possible under the clause in the February 1864 act, which allowed those "conscientiously opposed to the bearing of arms" either to pay commutation or to serve in a "non-combatant" capacity. Congress had already accommodated the Friends as far as possible and further protest seemed futile.[61] General complaints were absent too from the Roman Catholic church, but some of its clergy were unhappy. In the opinion of one district provost marshal, the provision in the February 1864 act did not extend to Catholics. He refused to accept commutation money from one priest on the ground that historically his church hardly qualified as a messenger of peace.[62] Members of the Holy Cross Order in South Bend, Indiana, also felt victimized by the system. Based on a recommendation from generals Grant and Sherman in the fall of 1863 to exempt these Catholics from conscription, the Lincoln administration decided to parole those members who had been drafted. This special dispensation was withdrawn in December 1864 because it was alleged that several of its members had voted the anti-Unionist ticket in the November elections. On learning of this reversal, Mrs. Ellen Sherman, an ardent Roman Catholic and wife of General Sherman, interceded on the order's behalf in an effort to have the privilege restored.[63]

Special pleas and demands surfaced from nonclerical sectors of the population as well. From across the North came requests that ranged from reactivating the state militias and exempting their members from the draft to granting a three-year exemption to men who had paid commutation under the March 1864 call.[64] One idea that enjoyed widespread popularity was a recruiting program that resembled proportional representation. Under this scheme a group of draft-liable men would band together to raise volunteers, who in turn would be credited as substitutes for any members who were drafted.[65] Although a version of this idea ultimately was approved, General Fry and various government officials frowned on this proposal. Robert C. Schenck, for example, believed it would deplete the government's supply of qualified recruits by accepting one man while exempting another. He also found the plan impractical; "Who shall designate the members of the association who are to be exempted?"[66]

Other individuals wanted reforms that would place more men into the military rather than broaden exemptions. Proposals for repealing Southern recruitment, requiring subdistricts to compensate the government for any of their men rejected as physically unfit, and instituting periodic bounty payments headed the list. The pervasive abuses arising from the bounty system caused other individuals to recommend that Congress consider adopting a policy that would hold subdistricts and principals accountable for any of their recruits or substitutes who subsequently deserted.[67] In the wake of the revelations of fraud in recruiting seamen, high-ranking naval personnel asked Congress to approve punitive measures as one way of counteracting the popularity of paper credits.[68] The Union navy also wanted deserters to make up lost time. Rather than wait for congressional action in this area, the army simply implemented this policy on February 8, 1865.[69] Congress reacted positively to many of these suggestions for raising and retaining soldiers when it turned its attention once again to correcting deficiencies in the national conscription system it had created almost two years earlier.

In considering the Amendatory Act of March 3, 1865, the Thirty-eighth Congress continued to react to circumstances rather than to initiate policy and guide the North with an overall plan for mobilization. They focused on correcting many of the abuses that had arisen in the system and, consistent with a pattern that had begun to emerge during the first session, emphasized the need to acquire men, but not at the expense of making the system totally unacceptable to those whom it affected. The threat of drafting was maintained, but the emphasis remained on raising soldiers in the "old way."

Although the end of the war was drawing near, the latest proposals to amend the conscription bill experienced much difficulty in gaining quick congressional approval when the bill was introduced in late January 1865. Conscription was still a volatile and divisive issue. Some of the revisions to the law that had been approved the year before had created new quirks and abuses in the system while some old difficulties remained. Henry Wilson and Robert Schenck were still at odds. Jealous of each other's powers they reported separate bills, and each essentially derailed the other's proposal when it reached his respective chamber. In the end, both had to compromise by having certain features embodied in a bill, H.R. 170, that pertained to officers' servants.[70]

Wilson was now in a better position than in previous sessions. Reelected to the Senate in January 1865, Wilson was under less pressure and could be more accommodating toward his colleagues. They needed stroking because they were in a feisty mood and wanted to see certain changes. Much of their attention focused on three issues: the repeal of Southern recruitment, whether to subject bounty and substitute brokers to punishment, and whether to discharge men who had enlisted into the old regiments in 1862. Many of these soldiers had volunteered with the understanding that they would be released when their units were mustered out of service.[71] The most bitter debate revolved around the status of Southern recruitment. Senators expressed their displeasure because they had been forced into accepting the program the previous summer in return for a bill that repealed commutation. When the vote finally came on its future, sectionalism dominated. Nine New England senators joined one from New York and two from the draft-free Far West in favor of retaining Southern recruitment. These 12 votes were insufficient for reversing the overwhelming mandate of 28 others from the Middle Atlantic, Midwest, and border states. The Democrats were unanimous for repeal, but as before, the issue shattered Republican ranks.[72]

Senate Democrats were much more cohesive on the seven roll calls taken on this conscription bill than were their Republican colleagues. Voting behavior on eighteen roll calls in the House exhibited a similar pattern, but compared to Senate Republicans, the majority party was not as fragmented.[73] This relative unity does not suggest that Robert Schenck enjoyed broad-based Republican support for his new draft bill. From the first day, he encountered difficulty in having the measure placed on the agenda. At times Schenck let his temper flare as he became increasingly impatient with delays and dissent from within his own party. Despite these occasional lapses in judgment, his persistence and effective use of the other members of the House Military Committee in channeling debate prevailed in the end.

Although tired and irritable, Schenck managed to keep debate focused on five main issues that concerned House members. Of broadest interest were a proposed residency requirement for new recruits and the liability of principals and communities who furnished unacceptable recruits and substitutes. Also, certain groups and members expressed particular interest in the distribution of naval credits, the status of deserters, and the release of soldiers who had enlisted into three-year regiments in 1862 on the assumption that they would be discharged in 1864. Southern recruitment received comparatively little attention because the Senate had already voted against it and the House bill contained a provision for its repeal. After several days of protracted debate, the House passed a bill. The Senate rejected it and demanded a conference committee. Further discussion ensued, and the North's last conscription law finally cleared the Thirty-eighth Congress in its closing hours.[74]

In final form, the Amendatory Act of March 3, 1865, was a hodgepodge of new policy on such diverse areas as the distribution of officer rations, dismissal, engineer regiments, restrictions on officer servants, and bounty payments to the heirs of soldiers. Of the law's twenty-seven sections, only fifteen pertained directly to drafting and recruiting. Despite Fry's and Schenck's objections, the bill contained a provision that allowed draft-liable men to organize into groups and to use recruits as substitutes for members who were conscripted. In an act of delayed justice, Congress further required the War Department to honor any promises that an official had made to any black recruit that he would "receive the same pay and allowances" as a white soldier.

Among other important provisions was the repeal of Southern recruitment. Both houses also insisted on a requirement that the president issue a proclamation in which deserters who returned to their units within two months would be pardoned. Those who accepted this offer would have to make up their absence by serving an additional period of time beyond their original discharge date. Deserters who failed to return would lose all "rights of citizenship." Other major sections dealt mainly with quotas and the regulation of substitute brokers and recruiting agents. In an effort to remove the temptation of men to enlist in another locality for a higher bounty, Congress finally imposed a residency requirement. It further called for the punishment of agents, brokers, and military officers who enlisted minors, felons, intoxicated persons, or deserters. Men who furnished substitutes without the assistance of an agent would now be held accountable if the government subsequently found a substitute unacceptable. In such cases, a principal would have to provide another one. For knowingly recruiting a substitute who planned to desert, a principal would find himself in the army in place of the person he hired.[75]

Within six weeks after Lincoln approved this final conscription act, the Union armies converged on the remnants of the Confederate forces, and the name "Appomattox" made its way into the history books. Although the war continued to linger in the memory of many, especially veterans, other significant events such as reconstruction came to overshadow, and eventually replace, the war's presence. Issues of the moment, which had seemed so important at the time, were the first to disappear from the collective consciousness. As the memory of the war grew dimmer so too did the election of 1864, which the Republicans had fretted over because of their concerns that the draft would hurt them at the polls. Lincoln's pre-Christmas call for three hundred thousand troops on December 19, the seething resentment toward Massachusetts, and the anger toward Provost Marshal General Fry also began to fade. Before the effectiveness of the March 1865 measure even could be tested through another troop call, Secretary Stanton decided to "discontinue the business of recruiting and drafting" on April 13, 1865.[76] Unlike his order three years earlier, there was no misunderstanding this one. The war had ended, and with it the Union draft for the Civil War generation.

CONCLUSION

Each era in American history has encountered its own special set
of circumstances for responding to the country's military needs.
At times, pure voluntarism has been relied on; at other times, conscription
has been emphasized. Whatever the prevailing method, each period has mirrored the attitudes of its parent society.[1] These differences notwithstanding,
the Union draft and twentieth-century conscription systems share certain features. Judicial reviews, requests by vocal groups to expand exemption or deferment categories, constant changes in the draft laws, skedaddling and other
forms of illegal evasion, and overt and covert resistance are timeless challenges
that have surfaced whenever a draft system has been imposed.[2] "Hell, no,
we won't go," pervaded the streets during the Vietnam War. "Over the hill
in October" became the rallying cry for the antidraft forces in 1941 as Congress
was preparing to extend the term of service for American men who had been
drafted less than a year earlier. These slogans are in the tradition of the Civil
War's "$300 or Your Life."

With the possible exception of the New York draft riots, "a rich man's
war and a poor man's fight" is the one theme most often associated with Northern conscription.[3] Given the importance attached to class discrimination and
its relationship to the federal draft, this emotional issue needs to be examined
through as many avenues as possible to assess its validity. These include the
attitudes and actions of Civil War contemporaries, the draft's effect on Northern
men, the extent to which the Union army was representative of the larger society,
and appropriate comparisons to other eras.

Within this multidimensional approach, the Civil War was not "a rich man's
war and a poor man's fight" as a result of federal conscription. Henry Wilson
certainly watched over his state's industrial interests, but his efforts did not
stem from any desire to protect the interests of the rich as a general class.
He was concerned that the law, which embodied the revolutionary concept
of true national conscription, would serve as a stimulus to recruitment, that
it would be made as agreeable as possible to the public, and that it would
not fall disproportionately on any occupational or social class. Wilson rose

from the working classes and he understood their needs. Had he sought solely to shelter the rich from the draft, or more broadly the middle class entrepreneurs in his state and elsewhere, he would have confined the exemptions in section thirteen to substitution alone, because well-to-do citizens could afford to hire replacements. Instead, Wilson included a provision for a three-hundred-dollar commutation fee, which was intended to hold down the price of substitutes. Further, he deliberately included various hardship exemptions in the second section so that the draft would not fall harshly on certain families. Although skilled workers and those engaged in commercial pursuits tended to be the greatest beneficiaries of these humanitarian exemptions, unskilled workers qualified for them in a higher proportion than their numbers warranted.[4] Wilson might be accused of developing an ineffective law in the winter of 1863, but he cannot be charged with recommending a conscription bill that favored one class or group over another.

Such an assessment cannot be limited exclusively to Wilson's attitudes. On a broader scale most congressmen agreed with his position on the exemption fee. When the question of retaining the clause surfaced in the House in February 1863, the vote split Democrats and Republicans alike. Within a week a similar pattern emerged among senators in both parties when a proposal was made to repeal commutation before Lincoln signed the Enrollment Act into law. Later in the Thirty-eighth Congress, most Democrats supported commutation, but the issue inflicted deep divisions in Republican ranks.

Accusations of class discrimination and its relationship to the draft originated largely in the Democratic press and among some opposition leaders who raised the issue in the spring of 1863. It was embraced by Democratic editors in search of a potent issue that could be used to discredit the Republicans. They admitted as much a year later by reversing their position when Congress began tampering with the fee's status.

Rhetoric aside, workingmen were able to take advantage of commutation and substitution. Through the use of private resources, community contributions, insurance societies, and clubs, most drafted men could escape military service if they wished. Indeed, only 46,347 men became federal conscripts, which represented less than one percent of the military-age population in the North in 1860. Measured by any standard, the federal draft was not a tremendous burden on individual Northern males. After commutation's repeal, substitute prices were expected to skyrocket beyond the reach of workingmen. In certain areas, however, a reverse trend occurred. After July 1864, the draft's burdens were dispersed more widely among all occupational classes in Michigan and Ohio, although the change was not as abrupt in western New York. In Michigan and Ohio proportionally fewer laborers were taken, while more of their social betters—bankers and lawyers—found it increasingly difficult to escape the draft's net. All prospective conscripts were affected by general policy changes. Following the fee's recall, an attorney or a physician was just as likely as a wheelwright or a laborer to experience more difficulty in finding a qualified replacement than in raising the money.

The class discrimination charge has emerged during all mobilization and military recruitment phases in America's history, and its application has more validity for certain periods in the twentieth century than for the Civil War North. Under the Selective Service System, for example, the public found educational deferments to be patently unfair. In the era before access to higher education was available to a broader social base in the population, this policy not only facilitated the postponement of military service for middle-class and upper-class men, but increased the likelihood that they could avoid the draft altogether. Those who did not ultimately escape usually could rely on their educational attainments to obtain safer assignments, such as clerks or technicians.

Student deferments vexed twentieth-century draft officials for a variety of reasons. Before, during, and after the Korean War, the educational establishment constantly pressed General Lewis B. Hershey to remain conscious of the need for generous deferments. A generation later at the height of the Vietnam War, these institutionalized postponements added to feelings of class favoritism as student deferments came to be seen as inequitable havens. Hershey nevertheless resisted any changes in the basic structure of the draft, including the use of deferments. His refusal to reform the system in any significant way and a tendency on the part of some draft administrators to punish campus protesters by removing their deferment privileges exacerbated the draft's unpopularity in the 1960s. As opposition to the draft increased, Hershey became the main target of the discontent and was finally removed as the head of the Selective Service System. With his departure, the way was paved for the elimination of the selective draft and its replacement with the All Volunteer Force. After experimenting with selective service for more than half a century, the nation had returned to pure voluntarism.[5]

Charges of class favoritism were the most salient and pervasive during the Vietnam War era, and the view is generally held that the young men who entered the army as draftees or volunteers were not representative of society at large. Instead, they consisted mainly of poor whites, blacks, and Hispanics. They were assigned to line units in disproportionate numbers and, as "grunts," suffered the greatest number of battlefield casualties.[6] Nor have charges of class discrimination disappeared following the appearance of the All Volunteer Force, as reflected in the observation that "market forces have replaced state coercion . . . it is now a mercenary military of poor 'volunteers,' rather than a conscripted military of poor draftees."[7]

Taking this statement at face value, the substitute privilege has returned in a more indirect and insidious form, but opinions vary over whether this phenomenon is entirely negative. One proponent of the present system argues, from a historical perspective, that economically and socially disadvantaged citizens have always had to serve, but many have been able to use military service as a vehicle for social mobility. An opposite view holds that the All Volunteer Force is discriminatory and that, with the exception of the Vietnam War, the Selective Service System made the military more representative of the population at large.[8]

Some of these contemporary views rest more on opinion than on strong evidence, but regardless of their relative merits, the Union army was more representative of the population than many of its counterparts in the twentieth century. If any class was underrepresented in Northern ranks, it was unskilled workers.[9] Both as a result of voluntary enlistments and the draft, laborers, bankers, ministers, farmers, and men in some 450 other occupational pursuits entered the Union army and were exposed to the same risks as rank-and-file replacements in infantry regiments.

Despite initial perceptions of the Civil War generation, and the historical opinion that adheres to the view that the Union draft represented "a rich man's war and a poor man's fight," Northern conscription was fairer than most of the methods used in raising America's armies in the twentieth century. Commutation and substitution were accessible to virtually all Northern men regardless of occupational status. Only the lottery system based on birthdates that was instituted in the early 1970s even approaches the impartiality of the Northern draft. Both methods were fair, but they were not very efficient in allocating manpower between the military and the home front. Although America has experimented with a variety of methods in raising an army, it has never reached a consensus on a citizen's service obligation. Until it does, future generations will continue wrestling with the issue of class favoritism.[10]

The Union draft offered little in the way of guidance to later draft officials for addressing issues of class discrimination, but the experiences of Provost Marshal General Fry and his subordinates in other areas provided ample information. Within weeks after the Civil War ended, Fry ordered his state and district provost marshals to prepare historical reports. Some of the more thoughtful of these documents reveal the several and diverse difficulties that these officials faced on a daily basis. Indeed, a few were studied in detail when America was preparing to institute the draft system in World War I. One in particular that was prepared by Brevet Brigadier General James Oakes, who served as the assistant provost marshal general in Illinois, stands out for a series of recommendations that he made. In one form or another, many of them appeared later in the Selective Service System.[11]

Among Oakes's several major suggestions was the need to have liable men report for enrollment, rather than use enrolling officers to canvass the countryside. This policy was especially critical in determining accurate quotas because "if the enrollment is right, all is right; if wrong, all is wrong." He also opposed the use of substitute brokers but felt less strongly about bounties. He believed that higher military pay was preferable, but if bounties were to be used again, under no circumstances should advance payments be allowed. Concomitant with this suggestion was his firm belief that a residency requirement was essential to eliminate problems stemming from quotas, bounty jumping, and the antagonism that poorer communities felt toward richer localities who enticed their men away. Oakes further advocated that all short-term enlistments be avoided because of the difficulties they created in determining proper credits. On a related issue, he recommended that quotas never again be levied on a subdistrict basis. Instead, they should be allocated to the individual states, who would then assign local quotas.[12] Beginning in the First World War, and continuing to 1973 when the All Volunteer Force replaced the Selective Service System, the importance of local determination had a pivotal role. Community boards received quotas based on the enrolled population, and within the parameters of general guidelines they determined who could best be spared from their residential military-age population.

Other of Oakes's recommendations that crept into later draft systems included avoiding provisions for substitution. Mustering-out pay at the conclusion of a soldier's term of service came to replace bounty payments. To compensate for the loss of immediate cash in hand, soldiers were paid in a regular and timely manner, and supplementary allotments were made available to those with families. Except for those who enlisted in National Guard units, where a six-month period of active duty was generally followed by some multiyear period of active reserve duty, the service term for conscripts and regular recruits was at least two years and in some instances for the duration of the conflict. Nor would local boards have to beat the bushes to enroll the male residents of military age in their areas. Following an extensive publicity campaign, National Registration Days were proclaimed on some occasions, and men had to report in person at designated sites. As time passed, men were expected to register automatically when they reached their eighteenth birthday.

Federal officials also went beyond Oakes's report by instituting new directions for America's draft system. Three changes in particular resulted directly from perceived difficulties with the Union draft. At various times, conscription was emphasized over recruiting as the principal means for raising an army. In World War I, for example, 72 percent of the soldiers placed in America's wartime army were conscripts. This high percentage rose from a belief that the Civil War draft had failed because it raised so few men. Twentieth-century officials attributed this low return to the poor image of the Union conscript, which ran counter to the historic notion of the citizen-soldier. To eliminate this ostracism, conscription was henceforth presented as a patriotic duty.[13]

The second difference was equally as profound. Convinced that much of the antagonism with the Union draft came from the appointment of military officers in civilian districts, Congress insisted that the drafting mechanism remain in the hands of local civilian boards rather than under the control of military-appointed district provost marshals. This fundamental change was more in keeping with American attitudes toward "localism, individualism, [and] civilian control of the military."[14] Third was an overriding concern with conscription's potential effect on the civilian economy. To rectify this deficiency with the Union draft, the federal government through local civilian boards and general guidelines, and not the individual, decided who could best be spared for military service and who should be exempted or deferred. While a citizen's military obligation would still entail a universal liability, it would be "implemented on a *selective* basis."[15]

Despite the advantage of previous experience, and the seemingly greater efficiency implied in the later conscription and mobilization systems, each version has encountered problems peculiar to its place in time. Although the original Selective Service System developed in a climate of Progressivism with its emphases on efficiency and rationality, there was no consensus over what model would best serve the military needs of the nation. Enormous pressure came from groups who wanted to implement Universal Military Training instead of Selective Service. The original Selective Service System also developed within a context of preparing to send young American men overseas to fight in a foreign war. Preparedness was at odds with isolationism, and this same split reappeared two decades later. Indeed, the country was so divided on the eve of World War II that when Congress voted on extending the one-year service term of the men who had been drafted in 1940 under America's first peacetime conscription system, the bill passed in the House of Representatives by only one vote.

With the combination of recruiting, bounties, drafting, and all of the attendant difficulties that resulted in obtaining men for the Union army, the methods employed in the Civil War North were indeed curious. Certainly this fragmented approach lacked the rationality of later systems and reflected Congress's attitude of responding more to pressures and personal preferences than anticipating long-term needs. Nevertheless, the system was the most appropriate for the Civil War generation, it worked despite its flaws, and it had far-reaching ramifications for the future.

More than two decades after the end of the Civil War, the author of *Peck's Bad Boy* recalled why he volunteered for the 4th Wisconsin Cavalry. George Peck was not afraid of being drafted; nor did he reveal any strains of patriotic sentiment. Absent too was even a sense of adventure and excitement, which is surprising, because he later entertained generations of Americans with his tales of a misspent youth. Enlisting in 1864, Peck thought the war would soon be over and was motivated to volunteer solely to collect a three-hundred-dollar bounty. Within a day, he came to regret his decision. Had he waited to enlist he learned that he could have commanded twelve hundred dollars from another town. Through the years, this hasty decision lingered in his memory: "I have met with many reverses of fortune . . . but I never suffered more than I did when I found that I had to go to war for a beggarly three hundred dollars bounty, when I could have had twelve hundred dollars." Even more important than this painful recollection was the immediate effect that this action had on him after he enlisted. Although he ultimately achieved officer rank, he dwelled on "the loss of that nine hundred dollar bounty." It dampened his "ardor" and affected any enthusiasm he might otherwise have had for soldiering.[16]

Bounties undoubtedly were often a curse to Northern recruiting activities and the Union army. Nevertheless, both the Union and the Confederacy had to work within a culture that preferred voluntarism over compulsory service. Consequently, each had to rely on a parallel system of recruiting and drafting in raising and sustaining its armies, but the North was in a far better position for attracting recruits through bounties.[17] These generous financial incentives served as a mitigating influence and helped Union men to tolerate conscription. The draft was a nuisance, but it was not necessarily a threat to them. Some even welcomed its approach because they could command high amounts of cash as recruits or substitutes.

Men who volunteered in the last two years of the war generally did so of their own volition. As General Oakes observed in concluding his extensive report, the war had "demonstrated to the world the invincible power of citizen soldiery in a just cause."[18] Any method that understated the importance of voluntarism in raising Union armies would have failed, and the creators of the federal draft system recognized the preeminence of this attitude. Although the drafting mechanism was inefficient, it was indirectly effective in mobilizing manpower.[19] The fact that only 3.67 percent of the troops were federal conscripts does not fully reveal the extent to which the draft sustained the Union army, despite bounty jumpers, substitute brokers, paper credits, and deserters. In conjunction with bounties, it stimulated—some might say forced—communities to fill quotas when patriotism began to wane in the last two years of the war. Further, it encouraged another 118,010 Union men to furnish substitutes. When these men are added to the number of conscripts, the federal draft was directly responsible for 13.02 percent of the troops raised from March 1863 through April 1865.

Some of these substitutes were black, but many more of their race entered the army as recruits. White resistance to blacks in uniform diminished greatly after the federal draft, and approximately 168,000 more black men became Union soldiers as a result. They represented another 13.31 percent of the estimated 1,261,567 troops raised in the last two years of the war.[20] More than any other factor, the federal draft gave them the opportunity to demonstrate their devotion to the Union through their prowess on the battlefield. Their numbers not only hastened Union victory, but their exploits laid the foundation for advancing their civil rights. Although indirectly, the draft contributed substantially to these later gains.

On a more direct and noticeable level, the federal draft demonstrated the North's resolve to continue prosecuting the war. It contributed to the centralization of federal authority and established the principle that the state has a right to take its citizens in a time of need. The application of this newfound authority was held in limbo after the Civil War, but it reemerged time and time again in the twentieth century as America confronted new dangers but old questions. On the continuum of American military history, the Union draft was more than an isolated phenomenon or tangential aberration, because it contributed significantly to later periods of military mobilization. It, and its Southern counterpart, left the legacy that the Constitution did indeed empower the federal government "to raise and support armies" through national conscription whenever necessary.

A P P E N D I X

NATIONAL ARCHIVES AND RECORDS ADMINISTRATION
RECORDS OF THE PROVOST MARSHAL GENERAL
(RECORD GROUP 110)

A Note on Methodology

In the course of manuscript research for my doctoral dissertation, I slowly developed the impression that the Northern draft did not impose an undue hardship on most men who were summoned to report for examination. Supported only by tangential and impressionistic evidence, I began questioning the extent to which the Civil War may have been "a rich man's war and a poor man's fight" in the North. Since the class issue went well beyond the central purpose of my work, I narrowed my examination only to how it related to the Enrollment Act and the subsequent pieces of amendatory legislation. At the same time, I hoped to return one day to the class issue.

In 1980 and 1981, I was finally able to revisit the National Archives to locate and examine the Descriptive Books and their equivalents among some fifteen hundred feet of materials that constitute the Records of the Provost Marshal General (Record Group 110). As true in so many research endeavors into original sources, this search proved to be far more involved and protracted than I had anticipated. Before my experiences in dealing with these nineteenth-century materials fade from memory, I want to chronicle the major difficulties I encountered to help save time and effort for those who dare to venture forth into Record Group 110 and other archival materials from the middle period of American history.

Prior to visiting the National Archives, I completed some preliminary research on the states that seemed the most appropriate to examine. I was interested mainly in surveying those areas that were liable to all four federal drafts because I planned to generate enough data to determine how commutation's repeal affected men according to occupation. Simultaneously, I requested a copy of any inventories and other research aids that were available. Based on this information, I planned to examine materials from seven states. I was also aware that, as with personal manuscript collections, some major gaps in data undoubtedly would surface that would preclude further research into an area. What I did not realize was the extent to which this would happen.

After I completed a cursory examination of the Descriptive Books and their equivalents for the original seven states, I realized that in most cases the data were either nonexistent or so sparse that I had to alter my original plan. For example, Vermont and most of the congressional districts in Michigan had so little data that further work would have been futile. Of the seven states, only two—Delaware and New Hampshire—had sufficient evidence to warrant further research, and even here some difficulties occurred. In the case of Delaware, occupational data existed on only 4 of the 435 men who paid commutation in the draft of 1863. In the instance of New Hampshire, only 11 men throughout the entire state were held to service under the last draft call. Fortunately, the second and third districts in Michigan, both of which had been liable to all four drafts, contained relatively extensive information.

Although disappointed with the results of this preliminary survey, I decided that I could generate enough data to draw some generalizations on how the draft affected Union men in Delaware, Michigan, and New Hampshire. I also realized that I would require more information from other geographical areas if I wanted to draw broader conclusions on the nature of men who were conscripted, who paid commutation, who provided substitutes, and who were exempted for various causes such as physical disability.

Accordingly, I examined select areas that had been liable to only one, two, or three of the federal drafts. Ohio was excluded altogether because Hugh G. Earnhart already had covered the draft to some extent in that state in "Commutation: Democratic or Undemocratic?" *Civil War History* 12 (1966): 132–42. After completing this additional survey, I determined that the records for Kansas, which conducted a draft in 1865; Iowa, which held a draft in July 1864; and Rhode Island, which was liable to the 1863 draft, had sufficient data, were geographically diverse enough, and were manageable in size to warrant further examination. During this phase I decided to include the thirtieth district in New York State as well. It was liable to all drafts except the one in July 1864. More important, I had uncovered information on some 497 men who had failed to report for the December 1864 draft. This was a real find because personal data usually were not recorded beyond a delinquent's name. Some diligent clerk evidently decided to complete this record by generating the information from some other source.

These principal surveys also uncovered some problems I had not expected. In many cases the sources were not paginated which made it difficult to pinpoint the exact pages to be filmed. Very often this required the time-consuming task of noting the name of the first person on the first page, counting the pages, and then noting the name of the last person on the last page. Through no fault of the archives' staff, the absence of precise information increased the likelihood of errors, which became evident once the film arrived and was checked. In turn, supplemental microfilm orders had to be placed. Further, the manuscript title of a source often differed from the name assigned to it in the official register. Fortunately, the use of assigned entry numbers in the inventories eliminated some of the confusion in locating particular sources, and these numbers are included whenever these sources are cited in this study.

Another problematic aspect of this research arose when manuscript pages for a certain area were bound into another, seemingly unrelated, source. For instance, the information on the men held to service in Iowa's sixth district was not contained in the Descriptive Books. Rather, the data appeared at the end of a source pertaining to Fort Dodge and Marshalltown, both of which were located in Iowa's sixth district. In other instances, data on drafted men were interspersed in sources such as "Medical Registers." This experience merely reaffirms the maxim that a researcher in nineteenth-century records can never assume that a source does not exist simply because it is not where it is supposed to be located.

After I left the National Archives, I reviewed my notes and ordered the materials that I needed on microfilm. Over the past several years, the data were extracted from the film with the assistance of several qualified students. After the raw data were verified, the general content was reviewed and decisions were made about the tabular format before these 20,789 men were classified by occupation. As noted in chapter 8, the work done by Theodore Hershberg and Robert Dockhorn, "Occupational Classification," *Historical Methods Newsletter* 9 (1976): 59–98, was especially helpful because their work pertained directly to America in the 1860s. After considering and experimenting with a variety of formats, I adapted a version for most of the tables in my study that follows the one used by James M. McPherson in *Ordeal by Fire: The Civil War and Reconstruction* (New York: Alfred A. Knopf, 1982), p. 359.

There remains much to be gleaned about American society in the 1860s from the data in Record Group 110. Despite my work in these sources, I have only scratched the surface and, despite the difficulties I encountered, others should not be deterred from pursuing research projects based on these materials. Above all, it is imperative to have a general research plan in place and to do as much preliminary research as possible before visiting the National Archives. At least initially, any new study should have a much narrower focus than what I began with, because the frustrations of this long, drawn out endeavor often led me to wonder whether it was worth doing. Only now can I say that it was.

NOTES

NIHS	Northern Indiana Historical Society
NYPL	New York Public Library
NYSL	New York State Library
OHS	Ohio Historical Society
ORHS	Oregon Historical Society
PSUL	Pennsylvania State University Library, Pennsylvania Historical Collections
RBHL	Rutherford B. Hayes Library
SHSW-AD	State Historical Society of Wisconsin, Archives Division
SHSW-LD	State Historical Society of Wisconsin, Library Division
UPL	University of Pennsylvania Library, Special Collections
WRHS	Western Reserve Historical Society
WVAH	West Virginia Department of Archives and History
WVUL	West Virginia University Library

National Archives Manuscript Sources

HCMAM	House Committee on Military Affairs and the Militia
HCNA	House Committee on Naval Affairs
NA	National Archives and Records Administration
RG 24, NA	Records of the Bureau of Naval Personnel
RG 46, NA	Records of the United States Senate
RG 94, NA	Records of the Adjutant General's Office
RG 107, NA	Records of the Office of the Secretary of War
RG 108, NA	Records of the Headquarters of the Army
RG 110, NA	Records of the Provost Marshal General's Bureau
RG 233, NA	Records of the United States House of Representatives
SCMAM	Senate Committee on Military Affairs and the Militia

Select Published Federal Government Sources

CG   United States, Congress. *Congressional Globe.* 46 vols.
                  Washington, 1834–73.

OR   ———. War Department. *The War of the Rebellion: A
                  Compilation of the Official Records of the Union and
                  Confederate Armies.* 128 vols. Washington, D.C.:
                  Government Printing Office, 1880–1901.

U.S. Stats.   *United States Statutes at Large.*

PREFACE

1. Allan G. Bogue, *The Congressman's Civil War* (Cambridge: Cambridge University Press, 1989), p. xvi, identifies the essence of this imbalance but does not share the opinion that enough Civil War studies have been done in certain areas. For a discussion of the trend that began in the late 1960s "to read the Civil War out of American history," see Eric Foner, *Politics and Ideology in the Age of the Civil War* (New York: Oxford University Press, 1980), pp. 3–12. See also Maris A. Vinovskis, "Have Social Historians Lost the Civil War? Some Preliminary Demographic Speculations," *Journal of American History* 76 (1989): 34–58.

2. James M. McPherson, *Battle Cry of Freedom: The Civil War Era* (New York: Ballantine Books, 1988), p. 865.

3. In this recent work, McPherson finds that studies on Civil War conscription are inadequate (p. 876). Unfortunately, he is on the mark in assessing the literature on Southern conscription. The only general study on the Southern draft is Albert B. Moore's very dated but yet to be superseded *Conscription and Conflict in the Confederacy* (New York: Macmillan Co., 1924). There are a few studies with a more limited focus that discuss some aspect of the Southern draft, and they are mentioned in the notes of chapter 1. By contrast, various good secondary accounts are available on some aspects of the Northern draft and related areas, such as the bounty system and recruiting activities. For the more important of these, see James W. Geary, "Manpower Mobilization," in Eugene C. Murdock, *The Civil War in the North: A Selective Annotated Bibliography* (New York: Garland, 1987), pp. 164–84.

4. An abundance of source material does not always answer all questions. For example, Confederate president Jefferson Davis formally requested a conscription law, but there is no extant evidence to indicate that Abraham Lincoln assumed the initiative in this area. Otherwise, ample source material on the Union draft has, in turn, contributed to conflicting opinions on several major issues. For a discussion of the most important interpretations, see James W. Geary, "Civil War Conscription in the North: A Historiographical Review," *Civil War History* 32 (1986): 208–28.

INTRODUCTION

1. John Whiteclay Chambers II, *To Raise an Army: The Draft Comes to Modern America* (New York: Free Press, 1987), pp. 4–12, 261–76. A multitude of studies are devoted to some aspect of the various mobilization systems that have been used in twentieth-century America. Some of the better studies are cited in this book, especially Chambers's work, which is destined to become a classic. Not only is it the most comprehensive work on the World War I draft, but it also presents broad and well-founded conclusions on the difficulties of mobilizing military manpower in America.

2. Ibid., pp. 5–7, 29, 39.

3. Ibid., pp. 5–6, 13–25; Russell F. Weigley, *History of the United States Army* (New York: Macmillan Co., 1967), pp. 3–5, 9–12, 14–20, 40–42; and Don Higginbotham, *The War of American Independence: Military Attitudes, Policies, and Practice, 1763–1789* (New York: Macmillan Co., 1971), pp. 391–93.

4. Some states continued to allow commutation until the federal draft began in March 1863. After that date, Congress set the amount at three hundred dollars, which exempted a man for three years. In February 1864, it retained this figure but reduced the exemption period to a single draft only. Later that year Congress repealed commutation for most Northern men. After that point, only men who could demonstrate that they were "conscientiously opposed to the bearing of arms" continued to enjoy the privilege. The policy of substitution, in which a drafted man was allowed to furnish a physical replacement, was allowed during the entire period of the federal draft.

5. James W. Geary, "A Lesson in Trial and Error: The United States Congress and the Civil War Draft, 1862–1865" (Ph.D. diss., Kent State University, 1976), pp. 462–65; and Albert Burton Moore, *Conscription and Conflict in the Confederacy* (New York: Macmillan Co., 1924), pp. 191–227.

6. *U.S. Stats.* 1:271–74, 424–25.

7. Weigley, *United States Army*, pp. 126, 189; and Chambers, *To Raise an Army*, pp. 36–39.

8. The basis for the quantitative data in my dissertation was derived from the roll call information compiled by the Inter-University Consortium for Political Research at the University of Michigan. For detailed information on the application of the statistical methodology in the dissertation, see pp. 475–81 for the Thirty-seventh Congress, and pp. 482–502 for the Thirty-eighth Congress. The party identification of each congressman was derived from the information in *The Tribune Almanac for the Years 1838 to 1868 Inclusive: Comprehending the Politicians Register and the Whig Almanac . . .* (New York: *New York Tribune*, 1868); and United States Congress, *The Biographical Directory of the American Congress* (Washington, D.C.: Government Printing Office, 1971).

9. For Fry's full and unabridged report, see *Final Report to the Secretary of War by the Provost Marshal General* in *Journal of the House of Representatives*, 39th Cong., 1st sess., 1866, H. Exec. Doc. 1, vol. 4 (Serials 1251–52). For the abridged version, see *OR*, ser. 3, 5:599–933.

10. James W. Geary, "Civil War Conscription in the North: A Historiographical Review," *Civil War History* 32 (1986): 208–28.

11. Ibid., p. 228.

CHAPTER ONE. VOLUNTARISM

1. *Chicago Times,* July 7, 1862.

2. The only general work on the Southern draft is Albert Burton Moore's *Conscription and Conflict in the Confederacy* (New York: Macmillan Co., 1924). A few other works discuss some limited aspect of the system and its operations. See, for example, William T. Auman, "Neighbor against Neighbor: The Inner Civil War in the Randolph Country Area of Confederate North Carolina," *North Carolina Historical Review* 61 (January 1984): 59–92; Memory F. Mitchell, *Legal Aspects of Conscription and Exemption in North Carolina, 1861–1865* (Chapel Hill: University of North Carolina Press, 1965); Douglas Clare Purcell, "Military Conscription in Alabama during the Civil War," *Alabama Review* 34 (1981): 94–106; and William L. Shaw, "The Confederate Conscription and Exemption Acts," *American Journal of Legal History* 6 (1962): 368–405.

3. The Confederacy authorized a $50 bounty in December 1861 and increased it to $100 in February 1864. Moore, *Conscription and Conflict,* pp. 7, 308, offers no real explanation for the relatively low bounties; but Eugene C. Murdock, *One Million Men: The Civil War Draft in the North* (Madison: State Historical Society of Wisconsin, 1971), p. 24, speculates that since "there was little money to begin with, it could not be squandered in bribing men to volunteer."

4. Moore, *Conscription and Conflict,* pp. 13–16. For the original text of Davis's special message of March 28, 1862, to Congress, see James D. Richardson, comp., *The Messages and Papers of Jefferson Davis and the Confederacy, Including Diplomatic Correspondence, 1861–1865,* rev. ed. (New York: Chelsea House–Robert Hector, 1966), 1:205–6.

5. Moore, *Conscription and Conflict,* pp. 53–59, 63–70, 105. In the form of a five-hundred-dollar tax, the law also extended commutation to members of certain religious sects.

6. On the resentment of Confederate soldiers toward men who hired substitutes or benefited from other exemptions, see Reid Mitchell, *Civil War Soldiers* (New York: Viking, 1988), pp. 160–62.

7. Moore, *Conscription and Conflict,* pp. 27–51, 191–227, 295–96.

8. Ibid., pp. 162–90. These rulings not only met the immediate needs of the Confederacy but also stood the test of time. More than a half century later in *Arver v. United States,* the U.S. Supreme Court would refer to them when it upheld the constitutionality of the Selective Service Act of May 18, 1917. For a succinct overview of these legal decisions, and their long-term significance, see Shaw, "Confederate Conscription and Exemption Acts," 368–405.

9. On the enrollment and use of slaves, see Moore, *Conscription and Conflict,* pp. 399, 343–49, 404–5. For Lee's letter of January 11, 1865, to Andrew Hunter, see

OR, ser. 4, 3:1012–13. As early as May 1861, Southern citizens implored Jefferson Davis to begin using blacks in the army. See a series of letters from citizens and soldiers in Ira Berlin et al, eds., *Freedom: A Documentary History of Emancipation, 1861–1867* (Cambridge: Cambridge University Press, 1982), pp. 282–99.

10. For a general overview of the "shared culture" and motivations behind volunteering in the North and South in 1861, see Mitchell, *Civil War Soldiers*, pp. 1–23.

11. For some of the more colorful descriptions on the martial atmosphere in the Union in the spring of 1861, see Bell Irvin Wiley, *The Life of Billy Yank: The Common Soldier of the Union* (Baton Rouge: Louisiana State University Press, 1971), pp. 28–32.

12. For ethnic motivations, competition between groups, and the appeals that were used to encourage ethnic volunteering throughout the war, see William L. Burton, *Melting Pot Soldiers: The Union's Ethnic Regiments* (Ames: Iowa State University Press, 1988), pp. 33–71.

13. Roy P. Basler, ed., *The Collected Works of Abraham Lincoln* (New Brunswick: Rutgers University Press, 1953), 4:353–54; *U.S. Stats.* 12:287–91; and John Quinn Imholte, "The Legality of Civil War Recruiting: U.S. versus Gorman," *Civil War History* 9 (1963): 422–29. For the view that the "long-lasting impact of Bull Run on the North was not defeatism, but renewed determination," see James M. McPherson, *Battle Cry of Freedom: The Civil War Era* (New York: Ballantine Books, 1988), p. 348.

14. The difficulties the North experienced in logistics, military organization, and general mobilization in the first year of the war are covered in several good accounts. Even more works chronicle topics that have more of a human dimension, such as recruiting efforts, rates of disease, camp life, and the effect of military successes and reverses on the home front and enlistments. See, for example, Herman Hattaway and Archer Jones, *How the North Won: A Military History of the Civil War* (Urbana: University of Illinois Press, 1983), pp. 101–52; McPherson, *Battle Cry of Freedom*, pp. 308–453; and J. G. Randall and David Donald, *The Civil War and Reconstruction*, 2d ed. (Lexington: D. C. Heath & Co., 1969), pp. 190–219. McPherson's discussion is especially good on comparing events that occurred in both the North and South at particular times.

15. Dr. William Clenden (Camp Union, W.Va.) to Gen. Schenck, Nov. 18, 1861; and Robert C. Schenck (Camp Ewing, [W.Va.?]) to Sally, Oct. 21, 1861, Robert Cummings Schenck Papers, RBHL; and George H. Covode (Harrison's Landing) to Father, July 17, 1862, John Covode Papers, HSWP.

16. James F. Wade (Camp near Richmond) to Mother, June 7, 1862, Benjamin F. Wade Papers, LC.

17. McPherson, *Battle Cry of Freedom*, p. 367, finds that "Northern morale was at its lowest ebb since the days after Bull Run." For a discussion of the economic hard times in the Midwest, see Frank L. Klement, *The Copperheads in the Middle West* (1960; reprint, Gloucester, Mass.: Peter Smith, 1972), pp. 3–6. Of the New England states, only Vermont and Rhode Island exceeded their assigned quotas under Lincoln's call of May 3, 1861. Rhode Island had an excess of almost 27 percent, which was undoubtedly due in part to its enlightened program for the care of soldiers' families.

The Middle Atlantic states, when they filled their quotas at all, managed to exceed their levies by no more than 10 percent. All of the Midwest states exceeded their quotas by as much as 10 percent. Illinois had almost 72 percent more, and Indiana oversubscribed its levy by 58 percent. For the original quotas assigned and troops furnished, see *OR*, ser. 3, 4:1264.

18. Albert G. Riddle (Wash.) to S. Williamson, Dec. 10, [1861], Samuel Williamson, Jr., Papers, WRHS.

19. Simeon Rush (Gallipolis, [Ohio]) to B. F. Wade, Jan. 1, 1861 [1862], Wade Papers. In this same collection, see also L. V. [Bireaux?] (Akron, Ohio) to B. F. Wade, Nov. 1, 1861; Mother [Mrs. B. F. Wade] (Jefferson, [Ohio]) to Jim [Wade], Nov. 5, 1861; and Silas Potter (Jefferson Co., Ohio) to B. F. Wade, Jan. 3, 1862.

20. W. W. Dawson (Cincinnati) to A. Boys, Feb. 6, 7, 1862, Alexander St. Clair Boys Papers, OHS.

21. *OR*, ser. 3, 1:722–23.

22. See, for example, Timothy C. Day (Cincinnati) to B. F. Wade, Feb. 2, 1862; Sherman Blocker (Wadsworth, Ohio) to B. F. Wade, Feb. 5, 1862; and N. H. Dunlevy, (Lebanon, Ohio) to B. Wade, Feb. 7, 1862, Wade Papers.

23. *OR*, ser. 3, 2:2–3.

24. Benjamin P. Thomas and Harold M. Hyman, *Stanton: The Life and Times of Lincoln's Secretary of War* (New York: Alfred A. Knopf, 1962), pp. 201–2, 206; Allan Nevins, *The War for the Union* (New York: Charles Scribner's Sons, 1960), 2:63; and Fred A. Shannon, *The Organization and Administration of the Union Army, 1861–1865* (1928; reprint, Gloucester, Mass.: Peter Smith, 1965), 1:266–68.

25. *OR*, ser. 3, 2:2–3, 29, 44, 109.

26. General William T. Sherman referred to Stanton's decision as a great mistake. W. T. Sherman (Camp before Cornith) to Brother, May 12, 1862, in Rachel Sherman Thorndike, ed., *The Sherman Letters: Correspondence between General Sherman and Senator Sherman from 1837 to 1891* (1894; reprint, New York: DaCapo Press, 1969), pp. 148–50. By mid-April 1862, sickness and other causes had reduced the strength of one unit from one thousand men to "less than two hundred and fifty . . . fit for duty," observed one officer. R. K. Scott (Crumps Landing) to P. Chance, Apr. 15, 1862, Robert Kingston Scott Papers, OHS. For other letters concerning the depleted state of the army, see Lt. Benjamin F. Perry (Camp near [Birney?], Va.) to B. F. Wade, June 14, 1862, Wade Papers; Lt. Col. James C. Rice (near New Bridge, Va.) to E. Corning, June 9, 1862, Erastus Corning Papers, AIHA; and Col. R. H. Rurk (near Richmond) to H. B. Wright, June 17, [1862], Hendrick Bradley Wright Papers, HSP.

27. Thomas and Hyman, *Stanton*, p. 206. For the dampening effect of the April 3 order on enlistments, see, for example, Hal [H. E. Parsons] (Ashtabula, Ohio) to Sister, July 7, 1862, Wade Papers; and George H. Chester (New London, Conn.) to Wm. A. Buckingham, June 5, 1862, William A. Buckingham Papers, CSL.

28. William Best Hesseltine, *Civil War Prisons: A Study in War Psychology* (1930; reprint, New York: Frederick Ungar Co., 1964), pp. 7, 10–12, 15. One individual praised a congressman who supported this resolution because volunteers expected to receive

the same treatment and privileges accorded soldiers in previous wars. W. W. Johnson (Ironton, Ohio) to S. S. Cox, Dec. 1861, Samuel Sullivan Cox Papers, BUL.

29. For an excellent survey of the issues involved on prisoner-of-war exchanges during the Civil War, see McPherson, *Battle Cry of Freedom*, pp. 791–802.

30. E. Mathers (New Creek, Va.) to W. T. Willey, Feb. 11, 1862, Waitman T. Willey Papers, WVUL. Shannon, *Organization and Administration* 1:245–47, briefly discusses the impact that irregular pay periods and inflation had on Union soldiers, particularly in the later war years.

31. There is conflicting evidence on wages in the North during the Civil War. Assuming that a laborer worked 52 weeks a year, and not deducting for living expenses such as housing, a conservative estimate for a laborer's annual wage in 1861 would be $336.91. This figure is derived from the average daily wage for a laborer multiplied by six days and then by 52 weeks. Economists differ in the figures for wages and rate of inflation during the Civil War. See, for example, Reuben Kessel and Arman Alchian, "Real Wages in the North during the Civil War: [Wesley Frank] Mitchell's Data Reinterpreted," *Journal of Law and Economics*, 1959:95–113; Clarence D. Long, *Wages and Earnings in the United States, 1860–1890*, a study by the National Bureau of Economic Research, New York (Princeton: Princeton University Press, 1960), pp. 129–55; and Harold Underwood Faulkner, *American Economic History*, 7th ed. (New York: Harper & Row, 1954), pp. 332–34.

32. McPherson, *Battle Cry of Freedom*, pp. 437–50, provides a good survey on the economic problems that plagued both sections and finds that inflation caused "an average decline of 20 percent in real wages of Northern workers by 1863 or 1864."

33. *OR*, ser. 1, 46:561–62.

34. For the gloominess that pervaded the army, see, for example, Dan (Harrison Landing, Va.) to Cal, July 11, 1862, Edwin J. March Papers, MHC-UM; and Henry L. Doolittle (Jacinto, Miss.) to Father, July 9, 1862, James Rood Doolittle Papers, SHSW-LD. In a second letter of the same date to a brother, young Doolittle asserted that the North would have to adopt conscription if it hoped to defeat the South.

35. Basler, *Collected Works* 5:293–94, 296–97; Thomas and Hyman, *Stanton*, p. 206.

36. Basler, *Collected Works* 5:304.

37. See, for example, *OR*, ser. 3, 2:198–99, 202–5, 212–13, 221–23.

38. Letter to Thurlow Weed in Frederick W. Seward, *William Henry Seward* (New York: Derby & Miller, 1891), 3:115.

39. Two summers later at a speech in Auburn, New York, Seward created a problem for the Lincoln administration when he asserted that further drafting was unnecessary. Among the steps that were used to negate the unintentional effect that Seward's "unauthorized" speech had on recruiting was a request that Stanton made to General Ulysses S. Grant. On September 11, 1864, he telegraphed Grant and asked him to prepare something he could use "for publication." Two days later, Grant responded. He referred to Seward's Auburn speech, indicated that new troops were badly needed, and observed that "a draft is soon over, and ceases to hurt after it is made. . . . [Its] enforcement . . . will save the shedding of blood to an immense degree" because it would have an adverse effect on Confederate morale. General William T.

Sherman sent a similar telegram two days later. See *OR*, ser. 1, vol. 42, pt. 2, pp. 783–84; and ser. 3, 4:712–13.

40. John Whiteclay Chambers II, *To Raise an Army: The Draft Comes to Modern America* (New York: Free Press, 1987), pp. 47–48, reaches a similar conclusion that the North was making plans to rely on "voluntarism augmented by state drafts," but he overstates the importance of the relatively small number of enlistments that were due to expire in the summer of 1862.

41. On the early sentiment for conscription, see, for example, George S. Boutwell (Boston) to J. Andrew, Aug. 17, 1861, John Andrew Papers, MHS; John Pitcher (Mt. Vernon, [Ind.]) to O. Morton, Sept. 26, 1861, Oliver P. Morton Papers, ISL-AD; A. H. Brainwell, Military Secretary to Governor Samuel J. Kirkwood (Iowa City) to O. Brooke, Sept. 18, 1861, Samuel J. Kirkwood Papers, Letterbook, vol. 1, ISHS; John Sherman (Mansfield, Ohio) to Brother, Sept. 12, 1861, in Thorndike, *Sherman Letters*, pp. 129–30; and speech of John Sherman at Mt. Gilead, Ohio, Sept. 27, 1861, quoted in *Toledo Blade*, Oct. 5, 1861. See also directive from Adjutant General of Ohio, Sept. 27, 1861, copy in Samuel Medary Papers, OHS. This order established local committees for recruiting purposes. It also threatened drafting in those communities that did not fill their quotas with volunteers.

42. *OR*, ser. 3, 4:421; and, for Lincoln's June 1864 endorsement, see *CG*, 38th Cong., 1st sess., p. 2804. For some of Lincoln's thoughts on the federal conscription law, see an August 7, 1863, letter to Gov. Horatio Seymour of New York, and his unpublished "Opinion of the Draft," which he authored in September 1863. Basler, *Collected Works* 6:369–70, 444–49. Refer to chapter 10 of this study for further information on this meeting between Lincoln and the House Military Committee.

43. Carl Sandburg, "Lincoln and Conscription," *Illinois State Historical Society Journal* 32 (1939):7.

44. *OR*, ser. 3, 2:212–13, 223.

45. Bell Irvin Wiley, *The Road to Appomattox* (New York: Atheneum, 1968), p. 120. Historians sometimes differ over the major turning points of the war. McPherson, *Battle Cry of Freedom*, pp. 857–58, for example, identifies four. In addition to McClellan's defeat in the early summer of 1862, other significant events included Union victories at Antietam in 1862; consecutive victories in Gettysburg, Vicksburg, and Chattanooga in 1863; and the capture of Atlanta and defeat of Jubal Early's army in the Shenandoah Valley in September 1864.

CHAPTER TWO. THE SUMMER OF 1862

1. See, for example, various items from 1861 in the Joel Brigham Papers, OHS; and A. Henry (Philadelphia) to Gen. M. C. Meigs, Nov. 27, 1861, Alexander Henry Papers, HSP.

2. See remarks of John Hale in *CG*, 37th Cong., 2d sess., pp. 3321–22; and *OR*, ser. 3, 2:111, 202–3. See also E. L. Hayes (Camp Burton, St. Louis) to Joel Brigham, Sept. 18, 1861, Brigham Papers.

3. Entry of Dec. 23, 1864, in diary of Michael Frash, IHS. For a detailed account of the Indianapolis execution, see James Barnett, "The Bounty Jumpers of Indiana,"

Civil War History 4 (1958): 429–36. Such executions had similar chilling and somber effects on other soldiers who witnessed them. See, for example, Will (Camp on the Rapidan) to Father, Sept. 18, 1863, William Houghton Papers, IHS; J. W. Nichoson (Camp Blair, Mich.) to Mary, Joe, and Mother, Mar. 8, [1865], John W. Nichoson Papers, MHC-UM; and Aug. 2, 1863, entry in James Houghton Journal, MHC-UM.

4. "Veteran" ([n.p.]) to Gov. Buckingham, Mar. 11, 1865, William A. Buckingham Papers, CSL; A. Willert, Hq., (Cincinnati, Ohio) to [John] Sherman, Feb. 10, 1865, Benjamin F. Wade Papers, LC; and Fred A. Shannon, *The Organization and Administration of the Union Army, 1861– 1865* (1928; reprint, Gloucester, Mass.: Peter Smith, 1965), 2:79–80.

5. For Sherman's September 4 letter see *OR*, ser. 1, 38:791–94; for Grant's September 10 letter, see *OR*, ser. 3, 4:706.

6. For the most thorough account of bounty jumpers and brokers, see chapters 9–12 in Eugene C. Murdock, *One Million Men: The Civil War Draft in the North* (Madison: State Historical Society of Wisconsin, 1971), pp. 218–304.

7. John Brough (Columbus, Ohio) to R. C. Schenck, Feb. 9, 1865, Robert Cummings Schenck Papers, RBHL.

8. Emory Upton, *The Military Policy of the United States* (Washington, D.C., Government Printing Office, 1904), p. 7; Ella Lonn, *Desertion during the Civil War* (1928; reprint, Gloucester, Mass.: Peter Smith, 1966), pp. 127–42, 226–27; Shannon, *Organization and Administration* 2:49–99; Eugene C. Murdock, *Ohio's Bounty System in the Civil War* (Columbus: Ohio State University Press, 1963); Eugene C. Murdock, *Patriotism Limited, 1862–1865: The Civil War Draft and the Bounty System* (Kent: Kent State University Press, 1967); and Murdock, *One Million Men*. Murdock's quote is from *Patriotism Limited*, p. 84. Reid Mitchell, *Civil War Soldiers* (New York: Viking, 1988), pp. 182–83, covers Southern desertion but virtually ignores Northern bounty jumping and desertion because he believes that desertion "did not cripple the Union war effort . . . [and] did not demoralize Northern society."

9. George W. Peck, *How Private Geo. W. Peck Put Down the Rebellion . . .* (Chicago: Belford, Clarke, & Co., 1887), pp. 13–14; Frank R. Judd (Guardhouse, 3d Div., 24 A.C.) to Maj. Gen. B. F. Butler, Jan. 6, 1864; and N. B. Judd (Berlin) to L. Trumbull, Nov. 16, 1864, Lyman Trumbull Papers, ISHL.

10. Admittedly, some substitutes skedaddled at the earliest opportunity even as late as March 1865. One such episode is described in John Nichoson's March 8 letter to his family (see n. 3 above). At the other extreme were those such as Hiram Saxton, who after service with the 70th New York Volunteers where he was wounded both at Williamsburg and Gettysburg, received a discharge. In the fall of 1864, he reentered the army as a substitute and was assigned to the 9th Michigan Infantry. Shortly thereafter, he penned a letter in which he not only revealed his high spirits, but his intense support for Lincoln and deep commitment to the Union cause. See H. G. Saxton (Chattanooga) to Charlie, Dec. 8, 1864, Charles Butler Papers, MHC-UM.

11. Murdock, *One Million Men*, p. 342.

12. These calculations are based on information that appears in Lonn, *Desertion during the Civil War*, pp. 153–54, 233.

13. *U.S. Stats.* 12:731–37; and 13:6–11.

14. For financial conditions during this period, see Bray Hammond, *Sovereignty and an Empty Purse: Banks and Politics in the Civil War* (Princeton: Princeton University Press, 1970), pp. 251–52. In this otherwise fine study, Hammond unfortunately does not really consider the relationship between economic conditions in the North and the bounty system. This area is definitely in need of further study.

15. David Donald, ed., *Inside Lincoln's Cabinet: The Civil War Diaries of Salmon P. Chase* (New York: Longmans, Green and Co., 1954), p. 98.

16. Murdock, *One Million Men*, p. 5; and Murdock, *Ohio's Bounty System*, p. 9.

17. Shannon, *Organization and Administration*, 2:80.

18. Seamen were effectively precluded from receiving other bounties until February 1864, when communities began receiving credits against their quotas for naval enlistments.

19. Shannon, *Organization and Administration* 2:54. The short-term effect of advance bounty payments definitely helped to stimulate enlistments for longer periods. In a July 3 dispatch to Stanton from Israel Washburn, for example, the Maine governor expressed doubt whether he could recruit men for more than six months. See *OR*, ser. 3, 2:201. Twelve days later he informed Vice-president Hannibal Hamlin that enlistments would probably improve, especially for the old regiments. He attributed this change in attitude to a new policy that allowed volunteers to receive at least a $70 bounty before departing for the field. See Israel Washburn (Augusta, Maine) to H. Hamlin, July 15, 1862, Israel Washburn Papers, LC.

20. The absence of timely pay was a particularly critical issue for soldiers with families. In a very poignant letter, one soldier in the 50th Ohio Volunteer Infantry wrote Governor John Brough to explain that he had deserted because he had received no pay, and his wife and three children were starving as a consequence. Jacob Dennis ([n.p.]) to John Brough, Mar. 20, 1864, John Brough Papers, OHS.

21. *OR*, ser. 3, 2:44, 76–77, 84–85, 100; Richard H. Abbott, *Cobbler in Congress: The Life of Henry Wilson, 1812–1875* (Lexington: University Press of Kentucky, 1972), pp. 128–29; and *U.S. Stats.* 12:605.

22. *OR*, ser. 3, 2:186. See also Abbott, *Cobbler in Congress*, pp. 128–29; and *U.S. Stats.* 12:597–600.

23. *OR*, ser. 3, 2:936–41; quote from p. 939).

24. Shannon, *Organization and Administration* 2:57.

25. William B. Hesseltine, *Lincoln and the War Governors* (1948; reprint, Gloucester, Mass.: Peter Smith, 1972), pp. 201–2, 274; and Frank L. Klement, *The Copperheads in the Middle West* (1960; reprint, Gloucester, Mass.: Peter Smith, 1972), pp. 75–76.

26. *OR*, ser. 3, 2:319.

27. Abbott, *Cobbler in Congress*, pp. 128–29, 133–41. For a detailed analysis of the Bay State's economic motives behind Southern recruitment, see Abbott's excellent study, "Massachusetts and the Recruitment of Southern Negroes, 1863–1865," *Civil War History* 14 (1968): 197–211.

28. For general biographical information, see George Henry Haynes, "Henry Wilson," in *Dictionary of American Biography* (New York: Scribner's and Sons, 1936), 20:322–25.

29. Abbott, *Cobbler in Congress*, 122–23.

30. Ibid., pp. 127, 129, 141.

31. Ibid., p. 131. Refer either to chapter 5 of this study for a discussion of the attitudes and actions of Senate Democrats on S. 493 that occurred on February 4 and 5, 1863; or my "The Enrollment Act in the Thirty-seventh Congress," *Historian* 46 (1984): 566–68.

32. Abbott, *Cobbler in Congress*, pp. 127–41.

33. *CG*, 38th Cong., lst sess., pp. 63–67, 235, 245, 3206, 3487, 3489–91.

34. Shannon, *Organization and Administration* 2:60.

35. *New York Herald*, Aug. 6, 7, 1862; *Cleveland Plain Dealer*, Aug. 27, 1862.

36. *Detroit Free Press*, June 24, 1864; and *Washington, D.C. Daily National Intelligencer*, June 20, 1864. For further information on this shift in editorial opinion, see chapter 11 of this study.

37. Haynes, "Henry Wilson," p. 323.

CHAPTER THREE. THE MILITIA ACT AND THE SUMMER OF LOST OPPORTUNITY

1. L. S. Foster (Wash.) to William A. Buckingham, July 8, 1862, Special Folder—Lot D, William A. Buckingham Papers, CSL. See also Erastus Corning (Wash.) to Daughter, July 4, 1862, Erastus Corning Papers, AIHA; J. A. Gurley (Wash.) to [William H.] Smith, July 5, 1862, Alphabetical Folders, Box 15, William Henry Smith Papers, OHS; and T. O. Howe (Wash.) to Grace, July 2, 1862, Timothy Otis Howe Papers, SHSW-LD.

2. *Cincinnati Daily Commercial*, July 9, 1862; and *Chicago Times*, July 7, 1862. In June 1863, Maj. Gen. Ambrose Burnside ordered the *Times* to suspend publication because of its alleged treasonous assertions. Lincoln acted quickly and rescinded Burnside's order. For a discussion of this episode, see J. G. Randall and David Donald, *The Civil War and Reconstruction*, 2d ed. (Lexington: D. C. Heath & Co., 1969), p. 307.

3. This chapter is a vastly condensed version of the one that appeared in my earlier study, "A Lesson in Trial and Error: The United States Congress and the Civil War Draft, 1862–1865," (Ph.D. diss., Kent State University, 1976), pp. 31–59, 475–80.

4. The radical Republicans included several New England senators and others, such as James H. Lane of Kansas and Lyman Trumbull of Illinois. They comprised a bloc of fourteen senators who agreed on at least 80 percent of the roll calls taken.

5. For a discussion of the Second Confiscation Act in Congress, see Leonard P. Curry, *Blueprint for Modern America: Nonmilitary Legislation of the First Civil War Congress* (Nashville: Vanderbilt University Press, 1968), pp. 78–100.

6. *CG*, 37th Cong., 2d sess., p. 3198.

7. See, for example, D. S. Phillips (Springfield, Ill.) to Sen. Trumbull, July 5, 1862, Lyman Trumbull Papers, LC. Phillips told of the dissatisfaction among white troops in the field because of their having to perform menial details. In their letters home, they repeatedly made this complaint, which in turn discouraged other white men from volunteering.

8. *CG*, 37th Cong., 2d sess., pp. 3198–3200, 3232, 3234, 3337–38.

9. Ibid., pp. 3203–6, 3227–28, 3231–37, 3342, 3249–53. For Browning's account of the conversation between him and Lincoln, see Theodore Calvin Pease and James G. Randall, eds., *The Diary of Orville Hickman Browning* (Springfield: Illinois State Historical Library, 1927), 1:555.

10. Geary, "Lesson in Trial and Error," pp. 43–45; and *CG*, 37th Cong., 2d sess., pp. 3220–21, 3231–37, 3249.

11. *CG*, 37th Cong., 2d sess., p. 3289.

12. Ibid., p. 3322.

13. Ibid., pp. 3337–39; and Geary, "Lesson in Trial and Error," pp. 47–48.

14. *CG*, 37th Cong., 2d sess., pp. 3321–22.

15. Ibid., pp. 3343–46.

16. Ibid., p. 3351; and Geary, "Lesson in Trial and Error," pp. 51–52.

17. My earlier conclusions on Republican voting on the Militia Act were subsequently confirmed by Allan G. Bogue in *The Earnest Men: Republicans of the Civil War Senate* (Ithaca: Cornell University Press, 1981). On the basis of his research on Senate Republicans, he finds that Wilson's two bills, which culminated in the Militia Act, "produced more examples of extremely strong disagreement along the radical-moderate continuum than any other measure discussed in the second session of the Thirty-seventh Congress" (p. 160). For a detailed description of the radical and moderate factions in the Republican party, see pp. 88–124 of Bogue's study.

18. *CG*, 37th Cong., 2d sess., pp. 3397–98.

19. James G. Randall, *Constitutional Problems under Lincoln*, rev. ed. (Urbana: University of Illinois Press, 1964), pp. 254–55.

20. William B. Hesseltine, *Lincoln and the War Governors* (1948; reprint, Gloucester, Mass.: Peter Smith, 1972), pp. 290–91.

21. *U.S. Stats.* 12:597–600. The lack of equal pay had a demoralizing effect on black troops and led to mutiny in one unit. This discriminatory practice was not corrected until June 1864. For one of the better accounts on this issue, see Herman Belz, "Law, Politics, and Race in the Struggle for Equal Pay during the Civil War," *Civil War History* 22 (1976): 197–213.

22. For the text of the Second Confiscation Act, see *U.S. Stats.* 12:589–92.

23. Geary, "Lesson in Trial and Error," p. 55.

24. For a particularly good account on white soldiers' attitudes toward the use of black soldiers, see Randall C. Jimerson, *The Private Civil War: Popular Thought during the Sectional Conflict* (Baton Rouge: Louisiana State University Press, 1988), pp. 72–74, 76–78, 86–111.

25. Pease and Randall, *Browning* 1:555. In a July 22 "Memorandum on Recruiting Negroes," Lincoln clarified his position on the use of black troops. He expressed

no reservations toward enlisting slaves of disloyal owners, but imposed restrictions on taking those of loyal owners. He may have prepared this memorandum at a cabinet meeting that day. See Roy P. Basler, ed., *The Collected Works of Abraham Lincoln* (New Brunswick: Rutgers University Press, 1953), 5:338. This position did not necessarily mean that Lincoln was ready to use blacks in a combatant role because, at a July 22 cabinet meeting, he indicated that he "was unwilling" to arm blacks. See David Donald, ed., *Inside Lincoln's Cabinet: The Civil War Diaries of Salmon P. Chase* (New York: Longmans, Green and Co., 1954), p. 99.

26. For an analysis of the two proclamations, especially what the January document meant to recruiting black troops, see John Hope Franklin, *The Emancipation Proclamation* (New York: Doubleday & Co., 1963), pp. 55–88, 129–46.

27. J. M. Forbes (Boston) to Mr. Sedgwick, June 7, 1862, in Sarah Forbes Hughes, ed., *Letters and Recollections of John Murray Forbes* (Boston: Houghton, Mifflin Co., 1899), 1:316–17.

28. Mary Frances Berry, *Military Necessity and Civil Rights Policy: Black Citizenship and the Constitution, 1861–1868* (Port Washington, N.Y.: Kennikat Press, 1977), p. 43.

29. *Douglass' Monthly* (Aug. 2, 1863): 852, quoted in James M. McPherson, ed., *The Negro's Civil War: How American Negroes Felt and Acted during the War for the Union* (New York: Vintage Books, 1964), p. 161.

30. Berry, *Military Necessity and Civil Rights Policy*, p. 103; and Geary, "Lesson in Trial and Error," pp. 196–97, 464. In addition to the 179,000 black soldiers, some 7,000 white officers served in the black regiments. Curiously, Dudley Taylor Cornish, *The Sable Arm: Negro Troops in the Union Army, 1861–1865* (New York: W. W. Norton & Co., 1966); and Joseph T. Glatthaar, *Forged in Battle: The Civil War Alliance of Black Soldiers and White Officers* (New York: Free Press, 1990), are silent on the importance of the Militia and Enrollment acts in encouraging black recruitment. For other significant secondary sources on black troops, see my "Blacks in Northern Blue: A Select Annotated Bibliography of Afro-Americans in the Union Army and Navy during the Civil War," *Bulletin of Bibliography* 45 (1988): 183–93. It should be supplemented with Glatthaar's *Forged in Battle*, which provides new information on the attitudes of black troops and how they interacted with their white officers. See in particular pp. 28 and 61–80. For the most thorough study on black sailors, see David Lawrence Valuska, "The Negro in the Union Navy," (Ph.D. diss., Lehigh University, 1973).

31. *CG*, 37th Cong., 3d sess., pp. 282, 695, 924.

32. It is difficult to determine the exact number of blacks recruited prior to 1863. Even the leading authorities on black troops do not address these figures directly, but they provide pieces of information that suggest that probably 10,000 were raised. This includes almost 3,000 who enlisted in the Louisiana Guards, and regiments that were recruited in Kansas and the Sea Islands. In any case, at least 168,000 blacks were recruited in the last two years of the war out of the total 179,000 who served in the Union army. Cornish, *Sable Arm*, pp. 287–89, estimates that they comprised "between 9 and 10 per cent of the total number of Union soldiers" and explains some of the difficulties in determining precise numbers. Ira Berlin et al, eds., *Freedom: A Documentary History of Emancipation, 1861–1867* (Cambridge: Cambridge University Press,

1982), pp. 12–14, further calculates that roughly 33,000 Northern blacks were recruited for the army while at least 141,000 came from the Border and Confederate states.

33. Frederick W. Seward, *William Henry Seward,* (New York: Derby & Miller, 1891), 3:115–16.

CHAPTER FOUR. "BREATH ALONE KILLS NO REBELS"

1. For example, William Best Hesseltine, *Lincoln and the War Governors* (1948; reprint, Gloucester, Mass.: Peter Smith, 1972), p. 277, believes that recruiting was moving steadily when Stanton acted "without warning"; while James M. McPherson, *Battle Cry of Freedom: The Civil War Era* (New York: Ballantine Books, 1988), p. 491, finds that new recruits were coming "forward with painful slowness." Evidence exists to support both points of view.

2. David Donald, ed., *Inside Lincoln's Cabinet: The Civil War Diaries of Salmon P. Chase* (New York: Longmans, Green & Co., 1954), p. 100; and Roy P. Basler, ed., *The Collected Works of Abraham Lincoln* (New Brunswick: Rutgers University Press, 1953), 4:338.

3. *OR,* ser. 3, 2:212–13, 223.

4. Samuel Shellabarger (Springfield, Ohio) to A. Lincoln, July 21, 1862, Records of the Office of the Secretary of War, "Letters Received," Irregular Book 5, 99, RG 107, NA; and Samuel Shellabarger (Springfield, Ohio) to A. Lincoln, July 26, 1862, Robert Todd Lincoln Collection of the Abraham Lincoln Papers, ser. 1, LC.

5. W. N. Barnes (Wmson. Co., Tenn.) to Gideon Welles, July 23, 1862, Gideon Welles Papers, CHS.

6. Caleb B. Smith (Bedford Springs) to Edwin Stanton, July 29, 1862; and Maj. Gen. Henry Halleck, ([n.p.]) to Edwin Stanton, Aug. 3, 1862, Edwin M. Stanton Papers, LC.

7. *Cincinnati Daily Commercial,* July 11, 15, 1862. See also issues for July 19, 28, 31 and Aug. 5, 26, 1862.

8. *Daily Ohio State Journal,* Aug. 1, 11, 1862. See also editions for July 30 and Aug. 5, 1862.

9. See, for example, *Canton Ohio Repository,* July 30 and Aug. 13, 1862. The radical Republican *Ashtabula Sentinel* linked its editorials on the draft to the necessity for using black troops. See the editions for July 16, 23, 1862. See also *Cleveland Leader,* July 31 and Aug. 5, 7, 14, 1862.

10. *Boston Daily Journal,* Aug. 5, 6, 1862. See also editions for July 17 and Aug. 8, 9, 12, 13, 1862.

11. *Washington, D.C. Evening Star,* Aug. 6, 1862. See also *Washington, D.C. Daily National Intelligencer,* Aug. 5, 1862.

12. *New York Times,* July 10, 17, 18, and Aug. 4, 1862. See also editions for July 11, 28, 31, 1862.

13. *New York Tribune,* Aug. 15, 1862. See also July 9, 10, 11, 16, 17, 1862, for Greeley's comments on the Militia Act, especially for provisions that authorized the employment of blacks in the Union army. For his views in support of strong war measures, particularly drafting, see editions for July 9 and Aug. 5, 9, 1862.

14. *Chicago Times*, July 7, 1862. For further editorial comments on the draft, see the editions for July 17, 23, and Aug. 5, 1862. For the *Times*'s hostile attitude toward the use of black troops, see also editions for July 10, 12, 14, 16, 1862.

15. *Cincinnati Enquirer*, Aug. 3, 1862. See also issues for Aug. 6, 14, 15, 16, 1862.

16. *Cleveland Plain Dealer*, July 21, 1862. See also July 30, 31, 1862. Despite its support of the draft, this paper hoped that quotas could be filled through volunteering. See also editions for Aug. 12, 13, 18, 26, 27, 28, 1862.

17. *Detroit Free Press*, July 13, 15, 16, and Aug. 10, 1862. See also July 12, 15, 27, and Aug. 2, 1862.

18. *Portland* (Maine) *Eastern Argus*, July 22 and Aug. 9, 1862; and *New York Herald*, Aug. 6, 1862. See also *Herald* editions for July 13, 18 and Aug. 4, 5, 7, 1862.

19. *Columbus Crisis*, July 30, 1862. See also editions for Aug. 6, 13, 20, 1862.

20. *OR*, ser. 3, 2:291–92, 333–35. Within days after Stanton issued the August 4 order, his office received numerous requests from businessmen to broaden the category of occupational and special exemptions. C. P. Buckingham, his assistant adjutant general, responded to most of these requests. In reply to one individual who wished to exempt many railroad employees, Buckingham tersely responded that "locomotive engineers will be exempt on the same principle with telegraph operators; no others." See *OR*, ser. 3, 2:322. For examples of other requests, see pp. 319, 331, 346, 348.

21. Quote from McPherson, *Battle Cry of Freedom*, pp. 492–93. McPherson uses the 300,000 figure, and Fred A. Shannon, *The Organization and Administration of the Union Army, 1861–1865* (1928; reprint, Gloucester, Mass.: Peter Smith, 1965), 1:290–91, uses the higher 334,835 figure. For the most accurate source of information on the 1862 quotas, see *OR*, ser. 3, 4:1264–65.

22. *OR*, ser. 3, 2:188, 291; and 4:1294–95.

23. Alex [Alexander] Ramsey (Saint Paul, Minn.) to Edward Salomon, Oct. 31, 1862, Records of the Office of the Executive, Incoming Letters from Individuals Representing Governmental Departments, SHSW-AD. Salomon's November 4 reply is located in the Records of the Office of the Executive, General Letterbooks, SHSW-AD.

24. *OR*, ser. 3, 2:369, 672–73, 674, 960.

25. Quote from Benjamin P. Thomas and Harold M. Hyman, *Stanton: The Life and Times of Lincoln's Secretary of War* (New York: Alfred A. Knopf, 1962), pp. 279–80. For the best survey of the governors' responses toward the militia draft, see Hesseltine, *Lincoln and the War Governors*, pp. 201–2, 273–88.

26. *Detroit Free Press*, July 15, 1862. Michigan did permit the payment of a one-hundred-dollar commutation fee in lieu of personal service. See issue of *Free Press* for July 19.

27. The War Department telegraphed this order to governors David Tod of Ohio and Oliver P. Morton of Indiana on September 4, 1862. *OR*, ser. 3, 2:512; and unpublished journal of John Butler, "A little collection or Condensed Accounts Began; not finished," Sept. 7, 8, 15, 16, and Oct. 4, 6, 7, 1862, pp. 27–41. A true copy of Buckingham's telegram is between pages 41–42, John Butler Papers, WRHS. Other Quakers pleaded with their governors to exempt their sect from military duty. See, for example, George Bradley (New Town, [Conn.]) to Wm. A. Buckingham, Aug. 11,

1862, William A. Buckingham Papers, CSL; and David Marshall (Carthage, Rush Co., Ind.) to O. P. Morton, Aug. 13, 1862, Oliver P. Morton Papers, ISL-AD.

28. *Detroit Free Press*, July 13, 1862.

29. Timothy Dwight (New Haven) to William A. Buckingham, Aug. 5, 1862; Theodore D. Woolsey (New Haven) to Gov. Buckingham, Aug. 5, 1862; and Anonymous ([n.p.]) to Gov. Buckingham, Aug. 1862, Buckingham Papers.

30. Eli Whitney (Whitneyville, Conn.) to W. A. Buckingham, Aug. 8, 1862; H. R. Bigelow (New Haven) to W. A. Buckingham, Aug. 6, 1862, Buckingham Papers. The War Department provided little guidance in this matter. Although "all artificers and workmen employed in any public arsenal or armory" were exempted, it acted on individual requests to excuse "skilled gun-makers" who were employed in the private sector. The War Department evidently chose not to disseminate its decision to discharge these workers as a matter of general policy. See *OR*, ser. 3, 2:334, 341, 346, 348.

31. A. H. Bymington (Norwalk) to Governor, Aug. 6, 1862, Buckingham Papers.

32. *Boston Daily Journal*, Aug. 4, 13, 1862.

33. W. M. Dickson (Cincinnati) to S. P. Chase, Aug. 28, 1862, Stanton Papers.

34. One Ohio man was offered $300 to go as a substitute. Mary [Smith] ([Hillgrove, OH]) to Brother, Oct. 13, 1862, William James Smith Papers, OHS. A Michigan man was willing to pay $200. W. H. Faxon (Ovid [Mich.]) to Albert, Aug. 7, 1862, Henry Albert Potter Papers, MHC-UM. In Pennsylvania, the prices ranged from $300 to $1,500. James McCormick (Danville, [Pa.]) to H. B. Wright, Nov. 10, 1862, Hendrick Bradley Wright Papers, HSP; and comment of Thaddeus Stevens on Feb. 24, 1863, in *CG*, 37th Cong., 3d sess., p. 1261.

35. N. C. Perry (Chester, Conn.) to Wm. A. Buckingham, Aug. 27, 1862, Buckingham Papers; Susan M. Pond (Brattleboro, Vt.) to J. Gilmore, Aug. 12, 1862, Joseph Gilmore Papers, NHHS; and C. E. Hawley (Scranton, Pa.) to H. B. Wright, Oct. 17, 1862, Wright Papers.

36. Deposition of William G. Tuttle (Woodbury, Conn.) Aug. 23, 1862, Buckingham Papers. See also petition of A. Giddings et al (Plymouth, [Conn.]) to W. A. Buckingham, Aug. 6, 1862; Lerman W. Cutler (Watertown, Conn.) to Gov. Buckingham, Aug. 8, 1862; petition of William Cothren et al (Woodbury, Conn.) to the Governor, Aug. 30, 1862, Buckingham Papers; Thomas W. Ellis (Hadley Falls, Mass.) to Gov. Andrew, July 22, 1862, John Andrew Papers, MHS; and Mollie McCord (McCordsville, [Ind.]) to Brother Will, Sept. 4, 1862, William Steele Papers, IHS.

37. J. H. Lucas (Edgartown, Mass.) to John A. Andrew, Oct. 5, 1862, Andrew Papers.

38. *Portland* (Maine) *Eastern Argus*, July 16, 1862. See also editions for Aug. 8, 14, 1862; and *Chicago Times*, Aug. 7, 1862.

39. N. C. Perry (Chester, Conn.) to W. A. Buckingham, Aug. 27, 1862, Buckingham Papers; and W. H. Faxon (Ovid, [Mich.]) to Albert, Aug. 7, 1862, Potter Papers.

40. See, for example, S. L. [DeBruder?] (Rockport, Ind.) to Gov. Morton, Aug. 7, 1862; J. H. Cravens (Osgood, Ind.) to O. P. Morton, Aug. 7, 1862, Morton Papers; and A. H. Thrasher (Chardon, Ohio) to Albert G. Riddle, July 13, 1862, Albert Gallatin Riddle Papers, WRHS. Historians who have discussed the social ostracism attached

to drafting assume that it continued throughout the war. See, for example, Shannon, *Organization and Administration* 2:57–58; and Eugene C. Murdock, *Ohio's Bounty System in the Civil War* (Columbus: Ohio State University Press, 1963), p. 4. Little evidence exists to support this assumption. Once quotas were assigned on a district basis with the Enrollment Act of March 3, local pride started to diminish and drafting came to be no longer viewed as a social disgrace in many areas.

41. Judith Lee Hallock, "The Role of the Community in Civil War Desertion," *Civil War History* 29 (1983): 123–34.

42. For complaints over quotas, see for example, Jonathon [Skinner?] (Eastford, [Conn.]) to W. Buckingham, Aug. 6, 1862; Henry W. Peck (Bethlehem, Conn.) to Gov. Buckingham, Aug. 8, 1862; Ira Morse (Danbury, Conn.) to Gov. Buckingham, Aug. 9, 1862, Buckingham Papers; and M. Wheeler Sargeant (Winona, Minn.) to Gov. Ramsey, Aug. 19, 1862, Alexander Ramsey Papers, MIHS.

43. Osmer C. Hills (Easthampton, Conn.) to Brother, Aug. 12, 1862, letter reprinted in *Lincoln Lore*, no. 1564 (1968): 4 (original at Lincoln National Life Foundation).

44. For the view that these 161,244 "illegal evaders" disappeared before a draft for reasons that included cultural and political reasons, see Peter Levine, "Draft Evasion in the North during the Civil War, 1863–1865," *Journal of American History* 67 (March 1981): 831–33. Refer to chapter 8 of this study for a discussion of Union skedaddlers under federal conscription.

45. *OR*, ser. 3, 5:730–39. The War Department did not compile any records on the number of skedaddlers in 1862, but Shannon, *Organization and Administration*, 1:184–85, estimates that the figure was in the range of forty to fifty thousand individuals.

46. Hubert H. Wubben, *Civil War Iowa and the Copperhead Movement* (Ames: Iowa State University Press, 1980), p. 44.

47. *OR*, ser. 3, 2:321–22, 329, 370.

48. Ibid., pp. 525–26. For the bipartisan editorial opinion in support of restricting skedaddlers, see *Chicago Times*, Aug. 9, 1862; *Washington, D.C. Daily National Intelligencer*, Aug. 12, 1862; *Washington, D.C. Evening Star*, Aug. 12, 1862; *Baltimore Sun* quoted in *Washington, D.C. Evening Star*, Aug. 12, 1862; *Detroit Free Press*, Aug. 9, 10, 12, 13, 1862; *New York Herald*, Aug. 9, 10, 1862; *Cincinnati Gazette* quoted in the *Columbus Crisis*, Aug. 13, 1862; *Cleveland Leader*, Aug. 8, 9, 11, 12, 1862; and *New York Times*, Aug. 9, 10, 12, 1862. On August 9 the *New York Tribune* favored the order, although it feared that it would interfere with the business pursuits of the country.

49. R. H. Stephenson (Newark, Ohio) to W. H. Smith, Aug. 13, 1862, William Henry Smith Papers, OHS. Governor Tod in his demand for a one-thousand-dollar bond was merely complying with his instructions from the War Department. In a memorandum of August 11, L. C. Turner, the judge advocate, stipulated that a draft-eligible man had to provide either this sum or a substitute (see *OR*, ser. 3, 2:348–49).

50. R. H. Stephenson (Altoona, Pa.) to Wm. Henry [Smith], Aug. 22, 25, 1862, William Henry Smith Papers. Another individual, who claimed to know Governor Edwin Morgan personally, requested a pass for the purpose of taking a few ladies to Montreal. He, too, disavowed any intention of avoiding conscription. Charles A.

Mann, (Saratoga, N.Y.) to John O. Cole, Aug. 17, 1862, John O. Cole Papers, AIHA. Across the state, a clerk in the Mayor's Office at Buffalo complained that the pass system led to a significantly increased work load. Elias O. Salisbury (Buffalo) to Sister, Aug. 15, 1862, Civil War Papers, BHS.

51. Levi P. Norton (Plantville, Conn.) to Governor W. A. Buckingham, Mar. 19, 1863, Buckingham Papers.

52. David Ross Locke, *The Struggles (Social, Financial, and Political) of Petroleum V. Nasby* (Boston: I. N. Richardson & Co., 1872), pp. 50–53. For the propaganda value of the Nasby letters during the Civil War, see James W. Geary, "Examining Societal Attitudes through Satire: Petroleum Vesuvius Nasby Fights the Civil War," *Illinois Quarterly* 44 (1982): 29–37.

53. Basler, *Collected Works* 5:433–36, 444. For one of the better discussions of the divided attitudes of Union soldiers toward the Emancipation Proclamations, see Reid Mitchell, *Civil War Soldiers* (New York: Viking, 1988), pp. 126–31. For a succinct summary of civilian attitudes and some of the political consequences resulting from the issuance of the two documents, see John Hope Franklin, *The Emancipation Proclamation* (New York: Doubleday & Co., 1963), pp. 78–84, 129–38. For one of the better overviews of the reactions to the proclamations in the Midwest, see V. Jacque Voegeli, *Free but Not Equal: The Midwest and the Negro during the Civil War* (Chicago: University of Chicago Press, 1967), pp. 73–90.

54. Basler, *Collected Works*, 5:436–37.

55. For a discussion of the political events that culminated in the 1862 fall elections, see Hesseltine, *Lincoln and the War Governors*, pp. 249–72.

56. For an excellent summary of these legal actions, see James G. Randall, *Constitutional Problems under Lincoln*, rev. ed. (Urbana: University of Illinois Press, 1964), pp. 252–56.

57. Neither of the two major works on Pennsylvania draft resistance discuss the 1862 episodes in great detail. See Grace Palladino, "The Poor Man's Fight: Draft Resistance and Labor Organization in Schuylkill County, Pennsylvania, 1860–1865" (Ph.D. diss., University of Pittsburgh, 1983), 23–31, passim; and Arnold M. Shankman, *The Pennsylvania Antiwar Movement, 1861–1865* (Rutherford: Fairleigh Dickinson University Press, 1980), pp. 141–60. Of the two, Palladino's study is the more analytical. Robert E. Sterling, "Civil War Draft Resistance in the Middle West" (Ph.D. diss., Northern Illinois University, 1974), pp. 96–131, is the most thorough and comprehensive treatment of the 1862 disorders in that region. Of numerous articles that focus on more specific geographical areas, Lawrence H. Larsen, "Draft Riot in Wisconsin, 1862," *Civil War History* 7 (1961): 421–27, is among the better ones for its discussion of the importance that whiskey may have had in encouraging the 1862 disorders in Wisconsin.

58. See, for example, Francis P. Griffith (LaGrange, Ind.) to Gov. Morton, Aug. 6, 1862, Morton Papers; and S. Lervis (Southington, [Conn.]) to W. A. Buckingham, Aug. 7, 1862, Buckingham Papers. One constituent advised a recently defeated Republican congressman to insist on another election to be held concurrently with a pending draft. This would discourage most aliens from voting against him again, because of the fear of nullifying their statements that they had never exercised the franchise. Peter Yates (Milwaukee) to [J. F.] Potter, Dec. 6, 1862, John Fox Potter Papers, SHSW-LD.

59. Labor shortages, with resulting higher wages and increased inflation, occurred in areas with a high rate of enlistments and drafting. This scarcity, in turn, retarded volunteering. See, for example, Sgt. Walter Warner ([n.p., Mich.]) to Capt. J. [James] Sligh, Jan. 3, 1863, Sligh Family Papers, MHC-UM; Maj. Gen. John A. McClernand (Springfield, Ill.) to E. M. Stanton, Nov. 10, 1862, Stanton Papers; and John F. Seymour (Utica, [N.Y.]) to E. Corning, Dec. 22, 1862, Lindsey Folder, Erastus Corning Papers, AIHA.

60. J. W. McCrath (Monroe, [Mich.]) to Capt. [James W.] Sligh, Nov. 21, 1862, Sligh Family Papers.

61. Cornelius M. Sisten (Camp Abercrombie, Va.) to Erastus Corning, Jan. 17, 1863, Corning Papers. One high-ranking officer asserted that his troops had not been paid in six months, and this was affecting the morale of married soldiers in particular. Brig. Gen. C. P. Hamilton (Hq., Left Wing, Army of the Tennessee) to Sir [J. F. Potter], Jan. 7, 1863, Potter Papers, SHSW. See also Thomas Jones et al (Camp Convalescent) to John C. Covode, Jan. 29, 1863, John C. Covode Papers, LC.

62. A. G. [Hartshorn?] (Racine, Wis.) to J. R. Doolittle, Dec. 19, 1862, Doolittle Papers, SHSW-LD.

63. Jane E. Waldron (De Soto, Vernon County, Wis.) to A. Gibbs, Dec. 21, 1862, Addison C. Gibbs Papers, ORHS.

64. For a copy of this petition, see Oliver P. Morton (Indianapolis) to A. Ramsey, Nov. 29, 1862, Ramsey Papers. High wages and inflation even hindered volunteering for state service in the Far West. See, for example, John Darragh (Dallas City, Oreg.) to Gov. Gibbs, [Feb. 1, 1863]; and Samuel May (Salem, [Oreg.]) to Gov. A. Gibbs, Feb. 2, 1863, Gibbs Papers. Despite the pervasiveness of this problem, Congress would not act on Morton's recommendation for another year and a half. When it finally decided to increase the pay of the Union private, it amounted to a trifling sum of three dollars per month. In large part, this policy of too little, too late, had its origins in the heavy reliance that Congress placed on the bounty system.

65. Frank [?] (Camp Pitchin) to Sister, Dec. 28, 1862, Ramsey Papers; C. H. Corning (Camp near Rockville, Md.) to Uncle, Sept. 8, 1862, Corning Papers; and Daniel Kent (Harpers Ferry) to Father and Mother, Oct. 22, 1862, Daniel Kent Papers, MHC-UM. One overly candid officer sent home on recruiting duty inadvertently deterred volunteering with his accounts of the harsh life in the field. M. D. Hubbard (North White Creek, [N.Y.]) to E. Morgan, Sept. 17, 1862, Cole Papers.

66. *New York Times*, July 13, 1862. See also edition for July 24, 1862. For a discussion of the cartel and the camps of instruction, see William Best Hesseltine, *Civil War Prisons: A Study in War Psychology* (1930; reprint, New York: Frederick Ungar Co., 1964), pp. 68–76.

67. See, for example, S. J. Maynard (Factoryville, Pa.) to H. B. Wright, Jan. 16, 1863, Wright Papers.

68. Edward Salomon (Madison, Wis.) to E. M. Stanton, Oct. 20, 1862, General Letterbooks, SHSW-AD; and W. Hoffman ([n.p.]) to Edward Salomon, Nov. 10, 1862, Incoming Letters, SHSW-AD.

69. G. O. Steele (Wilkes Barre, [Pa.) to H. B. Wright, Dec. 23, 1862, Wright Papers; Jane E. Waldron (De Soto, Vernon County, Wis.) to A. Gibbs, Dec. 21, 1862,

to Gibbs Papers; Tom [Prickett] (camp near Nashville, Tenn.) to Matilda, Dec. 21, 1862, Thomas Prickett Papers, IHS; Lew Wallace (Nashville, Tenn.) to Wife, Dec. 22, 1862, Lew Wallace Papers, IHS; E. A. Hitchcock (Washington City) to Mrs. Mann, Dec. 16, 1862; and E. A. Hitchcock (Washington City, D.C.) to Niece Mary, Dec. 18, 1862, Ethan Allan Hitchcock Papers, LC.

70. Even before the August draft order, congressmen were active in encouraging enlistments. See, for example, speech of William P. Cutler in Julia Cutler's *Life and Times of Ephraim Cutler Prepared from His Journals and Correspondence, with Biographical Sketches of Jervis Cutler and William Parker Cutler* (Cincinnati: Robert Clarke & Co., 1890), pp. 326–33. See also Preston King (Ogdensburg, [N.Y.]) to J. R. Doolittle, Sept. 9, 1862, James Rood Doolittle Papers, NYPL; and speeches of John Sherman, John A. Bingham, and Waitman T. Willey, at Wheeling, West Virginia, on August 12, 1862, quoted in *Wheeling Daily Intelligencer*, Aug. 13, 1862. Governor Ramsey apparently did not speak but did give one hundred dollars to a bounty fund. Diary of Gov. Alexander Ramsey, entry for Sept. 10, 1862, Ramsey Papers.

71. Clement L. Vallandigham, *Speeches, Arguments, Addresses, and Letters of Clement L. Vallandigham* (New York: J. Walter & Co., 1864), pp. 397–417.

72. Margery Greenleaf, ed., *Letters to Eliza from a Union Soldier, 1862–1865* (Chicago: Follett, 1970), pp. 5–6; K. Jack Bauer, ed., *Soldiering: The Civil War Diary of Rice C. Bull* (San Rafael: Presidio Press, 1977), pp. viii–ix, 2–3; and Frank L. Byrne, ed., *The View from Headquarters: Civil War Letters of Harvey Reid* (Madison: State Historical Society of Wisconsin, 1965), pp. x–xi.

73. Greenleaf, *Letters to Eliza*, p. 8; and Bauer, *Soldiering*, p. 8.

74. For a particularly good account of how mercenary recruiting had become in one locality between August and December 1862, see Michael H. Frisch, *Town into City: Springfield Massachusetts, and the Meaning of Community, 1840–1860* (Cambridge: Harvard University Press, 1972), pp. 60–63.

75. Historians usually assert that the draft stimulated recruiting. See, for example, Shannon, *Organization and Administration* 1:291, 308; and Allan Nevins, *The War for the Union* (New York: Charles Scribner's Sons, 1960), 2:465. There is no doubt that it served as an incentive during the 1862 drafts. See, for example, H. Burr Crandall (South Adams [Mass.]) to Gov. Andrew, Aug. 8, 1862, Andrew Papers; George W. Vedden (Troy, [N.Y.]) to Uncle William, Aug. 17, 1862, Civil War Papers, BHS; H. W. Patrick (Athens, Minn.) to A. Ramsey, Aug. 11, 1862, Ramsey Papers; and A. H. Bymington (Norwalk, [Conn.]) to Governor, Aug. 6, 1862, Buckingham Papers.

76. Figures vary for the number of men furnished under the 1862 calls. For a detailed discussion of these and other figures, refer to chapter 7 of this study.

77. *Report of the Secretary of War*, December 2, 1862, in *CG*, 37th Cong., 3d sess., appendix, pp. 28–32.

CHAPTER FIVE. MAJORITY STRENGTH VERSUS MINORITY POWER

1. Leonard P. Curry, *Blueprint for Modern America: Nonmilitary Legislation of the First Civil War Congress* (Nashville: Vanderbilt University Press, 1968), pp. 244–53.

2. This chapter is a condensed version of the one that appeared in my "A Lesson in Trial and Error: The United States Congress and the Civil War Draft, 1862–1865," (Ph.D. diss., Kent State University, 1976), and it is an expanded and updated version of my article "The Enrollment Act in the Thirty-seventh Congress," *Historian* 46 (1984): 562–82 (reprinted with permission of Gerald Thompson, editor of the *Historian*). For detailed information on the individual roll call votes and a full chronicle of the journey of the Enrollment Act through Congress, see "Lesson in Trial and Error," pp. 94–168, 475–80.

3. For the argument that the draft discriminated against the poor, see, for example, James McCague, *The Second Rebellion: The Story of the New York City Draft Riots* (New York: Dial Press, 1968), p. 18; Jack Franklin Leach, *Conscription in the United States: Historical Background* (Tokyo: Charles B. Tuttle Co., 1952); p. 250; Fred A. Shannon, *The Organization and Administration of the Union Army, 1861–1865* (1928; reprint, Gloucester, Mass.: Peter Smith, 1965), 1:298–99, 308; 2:11–14, 21–22, 33–34; and James M. McPherson, *Ordeal by Fire: The Civil War and Reconstruction* (New York: Alfred A. Knopf, 1982), pp. 356–57. McPherson, in his later work, *Battle Cry of Freedom: The Civil War Era* (New York: Ballantine Books, 1988), pp. 602–8, modifies his position by finding that class discrimination and the draft, at least in the North, "lacked objective reality." Shannon, *Organization and Administration* 1:298, 300–2, also argues that the Enrollment Act sheltered states' rights. Leach, *Conscription*, pp. 168, 453; and William B. Hesseltine, *Lincoln and the War Governors* (1948; reprint, Gloucester, Mass.: Peter Smith, 1972), pp. 291–92, believe that the measure had an adverse impact on the doctrine.

4. Shannon, *Organization and Administration* 1:302–3, 310–13, 319–22, contends that the Republican leadership controlled the measure throughout the proceedings and that only insignificant modifications were made to the bill. Leach, *Conscription*, pp. 170–71, 188–89, 198, 201–2, 204, 207–9, makes a similar argument although he mentions that the House experienced more difficulty in passing the bill. Leonard P. Curry, "Congressional Democrats: 1861–1863," *Civil War History* 12 (1966): 225, notes briefly, however, that the House Democrats filibustered until they succeeded in their attempts to discuss the measure.

5. On the various difficulties that faced the Lincoln administration in the fall and winter of 1862, see, for example, Bray Hammond, *Sovereignty and an Empty Purse: Banks and Politics in the Civil War* (Princeton: Princeton University Press, 1970), pp. 251–52, 296; Benjamin P. Thomas and Harold M. Hyman, *Stanton: The Life and Times of Lincoln's Secretary of War* (New York: Alfred A. Knopf, 1962), pp. 245–53; and V. Jacque Voegeli, *Free but Not Equal: The Midwest and the Negro during the Civil War* (Chicago: University of Chicago Press, 1967), pp. 73–90, 95–108.

6. Howard K. Beale, ed., *Diary of Gideon Welles*, 3 vols. (New York: W. W. Norton & Co., 1960), 1:397. Unfortunately, the records from the Senate Committee on Military Affairs and the Militia have not been preserved in the National Archives, RG 46. Those for the House Military Committee exist only for a brief period before July 1862, and for certain periods during the tenure of the Thirty-eighth Congress.

On February 16, 1863, Henry Wilson noted, however, that several provisions of the proposed bill were "incorporated . . . after much examination and reflection, and with the approbation of several of our most experienced military men." The chairman of the House Military Committee made similar remarks on February 23, 1863. See *CG*, 37th Cong., 3d sess., pp. 978, 1213–14. Mary Frances Berry, *Military Necessity and Civil Rights Policy: Black Citizenship and the Constitution, 1861–1868* (Port Washington, N.Y.: Kennikat Press, 1977), p. 50, also notes in her study on raising black troops that she was unable to find any record of a formal administration proposal for the federal draft bill.

7. Frank L. Klement, *The Copperheads in the Middle West* (1960; reprint, Gloucester, Mass.: Peter Smith, 1972), p. 76.

8. W. T. Sherman (Camp near Vicksburg) to Brother, Jan. 25, 1863, in Rachel Sherman Thorndike, ed., *The Sherman Letters: Correspondence between General Sherman and Senator Sherman from 1837 to 1891* (1894; reprint, New York: DaCapo Press, 1969), p. 184.

9. [Lieber, Francis], "Conscription and Volunteering as Methods of Recruiting National Armies," *Brownson's Quarterly Review* 25 (1863): 55–77 (quotes from pp. 61, 73). For other intellectual support for a strong draft law prior to the Enrollment Act, see Lorraine Anderson Williams, "The Civil War and Intellectuals of the North" (Ph.D. diss., American University, 1953), pp. 181, 187.

10. *OR*, ser. 3, 2:936–41.

11. Ella Lonn, *Desertion during the Civil War* (1928; reprint, Gloucester, Mass.: Peter Smith, 1966), pp. 145, 151.

12. Hammond, *Sovereignty and an Empty Purse*, pp. 251–52.

13. The purchasing power of real wages for Northern workers declined approximately 20 percent in value "by 1863 or 1864." McPherson, *Battle Cry of Freedom*, p. 448.

14. See Reid Mitchell, *Civil War Soldiers* (New York: Viking, 1988), pp. 126–27; and Bell Irvin Wiley, *The Life of Billy Yank: The Common Soldier of the Union* (Baton Rouge: Louisiana State University Press, 1952), pp. 40–44.

15. Charles Sumner (Washington) to J. M. Forbes, Dec. 28, 1862, in Sarah Forbes Hughes, ed., *Letters and Recollections of John Murray Forbes* (Boston: Houghton, Mifflin Co., 1899), 1:352–53. See also Voegeli, *Free but Not Equal*, p. 110.

16. Roy P. Basler, ed., *The Collected Works of Abraham Lincoln* (New Brunswick: Rutgers University Press, 1953), 6:28–30; and *U.S. Stats.* 12:731–37. Berry, *Military Necessity and Civil Rights Policy*, p. 103, finds that the Enrollment Act was the "greatest single force" in promoting black recruitment. See also Geary, "Lesson in Trial and Error," pp. 196–97, 464.

17. See, for example, Hesseltine, *War Governors*, pp. 291–302; McCague, *Second Rebellion*, p. 17; and Leach, *Conscription*, pp. 162, 171, 188, 209, for the argument that the Enrollment Act was considered and approved during the "last minutes" of the Thirty-seventh Congress.

18. Allan G. Bogue, *The Earnest Men: Republicans of the Civil War Senate* (Ithaca: Cornell University Press, 1981), pp. 90–101, 118–19, 160–65, 231, emphasizes the

disagreement within the Republican party. For a view that stresses the "ideological unity" and general cohesiveness of the Republican party, see Herman Belz, *Emancipation and Equal Rights: Politics and Constitutionalism in the Civil War Era* (New York: W. W. Norton & Co., 1978), pp. 23–31.

19. Bogue, *Earnest Men*, pp. 118–19, 141–42, 151–75, 266–68, 292–93, 298, 306–7. Since a principal focus of Bogue's work concerns emancipation and some judicial and Southern issues, he does not consider the Enrollment Act. He examines the Militia Act in more detail, and discusses Senate activity on certain sections in the three pieces of amendatory legislation to the Enrollment Act that were considered in the Thirty-eighth Congress. In a later work, *The Congressman's Civil War* (Cambridge: Cambridge University Press, 1989), Bogue also neglects representatives' attitudes toward the Enrollment Act's passage. Nevertheless, this work is useful for his discussion of the important roles of patronage and the caucuses. He finds that Republicans used the caucus to advance radical policies rather than to rely on them as "a harmonizing agency." Partially as a result of this direction, these meetings did not serve "to win [advance] approval of legislation." See in particular pages 31–40 and 121–32.

20. Curry, "Congressional Democrats," p. 215. For the best discussion of some of the problems that the quorum principle created before May 4, 1864, when the Senate redefined it as "a majority of 'the Senators duly chosen,'" see Bogue, *Earnest Men*, pp. 69–71, 79.

21. For an excellent overall description of the impact of the Senate Democrats throughout the tenure of the Thirty-seventh Congress, particularly in the area of nonmilitary legislation, see Curry, "Congressional Democrats," pp. 214–15.

22. For a similar treatment of House Democrats, see ibid., pp. 224–25; and, for a succinct discussion of congressional action on the Negro Troop Bill, see Curry, *Blueprint for Modern America*, pp. 64–67.

23. *CG*, 37th Cong., 3d sess., pp. 558, 639, 705.

24. The weather report was taken from the *Washington, D.C., Evening Star*, Feb. 5, 1863.

25. *CG*, 37th Cong., 3d sess., pp. 706–12, 714–16, 728–30, 732–39. For the voting scores on individual roll calls, and the arguments presented during the Senate debates, see Geary, "Lesson in Trial and Error," pp. 102–20, 151–60.

26. *CG*, 37th Cong., 3d sess., pp. 714, 737, 816, 860, 976–78.

27. For a discussion of this special legislation, see Bogue, *Earnest Men*, pp. 274–75.

28. Basler, *Collected Works* 6:277–78; Shannon, *Organization and Administration* 2:208, 217.

29. Deals and pressures brought to bear on individual senators were not unusual in the Civil War Senate. Such activity occurred, for example, in voting on the Wade-Davis bill in July 1864. See Herman Belz, *Reconstructing the Union: Theory and Policy during the Civil War* (Ithaca: Cornell University Press, 1969), p. 222.

30. The three far western members were Milton S. Latham and James A. McDougall of California, and James W. Nesmith of Oregon. Henry M. Rice of Minnesota

left office in March 1863. See Curry, "Congressional Democrats," p. 221, for an analysis of John B. Henderson's voting behavior on nonmilitary measures.

31. *CG*, 37th Cong., 3d sess., pp. 977, 978, 980–84, 988–90, 996, 1000. This recommendation probably came as no surprise to Wilson's colleagues. The previous day, the Washington correspondent for the *New York Tribune* noted that the Senate would probably propose a change that would permit commutation. See Special Dispatch, Wash., Feb. 15, 1863, in *New York Tribune*, Feb. 16, 1863.

32. *CG*, 37th Cong., 3d sess., pp. 977–78, 981–83, 996, 1444. Although the Senate did not record a roll call on the question of retaining the exemption fee on February 16, it did so on March 2, 1863. On that day, two Democrats, seven Republicans, and a Unionist voted in favor of recalling commutation against twenty Republicans, three Democrats, and two Unionists.

33. The defeat of this amendment would have affected at least one congressman had he been reelected; Galusha Grow, Speaker of the House, received his notice to report within months after the Thirty-seventh Congress had ended. Although the local enrollment board released him because of physical unfitness, he nevertheless provided a substitute. See Emily C. Blackman, *History of Susquehanna County, Pennsylvania: From a Period Preceding Its Settlement to Recent Times . . .* (Philadelphia: Claxton, Remsen & Haffelfinger, 1873), p. 247. When historians comment on the attempt to make the draft law palatable to the public, they usually support their arguments with references to commutation, not to the hardship exemptions contained in the second section. See, for example, Murdock, *One Million Men*, pp. 197, 340; Leach, *Conscription*, pp. 454–55; and Shannon, *Organization and Administration* 1:304–6.

34. *CG*, 37th Cong., 3d sess., pp. 979, 999–1000.

35. Ibid., pp. 985–88, 994–97, 999–1002. Only on the proposal authorizing naval credits did a tendency toward regional unity emerge. The eleven votes in favor of this particular amendment all came from New England senators who hoped to reap reduced troop levies for their states, since seamen would be credited to the area where they enlisted, not where they resided.

36. In a letter to his niece, Senator Timothy O. Howe told of his increasing weariness as a result of the rigorous session. See Timothy O. Howe (Washington, D.C.) to Grace Howe, Feb. 13, [1863], Timothy Otis Howe Papers, SHSW-LD. Other senators commented on the excessive work load. See, for example, Preston King (Washington, D.C.) to E. D. Morgan, Feb. 14, 1863, Edwin D. Morgan Papers, NYSL; and H. Wilson (Washington, D.C.) to J. Schouler, Feb. 1, 1863, James Schouler Papers, MHS.

37. Republican journalists gave a different interpretation of the absence of the opposition. AGATE (pseudonym of Whitelaw Reid, the Washington correspondent for the *Cincinnati Gazette*) attributed it to inebriation. He quoted one of the absentees as allegedly saying that "four of our men were so drunk they couldn't leave their rooms, others had gone off to a party." *Cincinnati Gazette* quoted in *Cleveland Leader*, Mar. 7, 1863. Reid failed, however, to explain the continued presence of James A. McDougall, who had perhaps the most notorious reputation as a drunkard among his colleagues. A more accurate account was given by a Washington Republican newspaper. It noted

that opposition members simply left the Senate chamber that evening before the voting began. See *Washington, D.C. Daily Morning Chronicle*, Feb. 18, 1863. See also issues for Feb. 17, 20, 25, 1863.

38. See, for example, M. J. Paine (Milwaukee) to J. F. Potter, Feb. 18, 1863, John Fox Potter Papers, SHSW-LD; and Alfred Phelps (Chardon, Ohio) to A. G. Riddle, Feb. 1, 1863, Albert Gallatin Riddle Papers, WRHS.

39. W. Bell, Jr., (Newark, Ohio) to S. S. Cox, Feb. 18, 1863, Samuel Sullivan Cox Papers, BUL. See also R. George Dun ([n.p.]) to S. S. Cox, Feb. 18, 1863; A. L. Olmstead (Columbus) to S. S. Cox, Jan. 10, 1863, Cox Papers; and Lou P. [Ruerr?] (Reading, Pa.) to H. B. Wright, Feb. 1, 1863, Hendrick Bradley Wright Papers, HSP.

40. *CG*, 37th Cong., 3d sess., pp. 1149, 1175.

41. For comments on this storm, see *Washington, D.C. Evening Star*, Feb. 23, 1863.

42. *CG*, 37th Cong., 3d sess., pp. 1213–14. For an eyewitness, though pro-Republican, account of the bill's progress through Congress, see Noah Brooks, *Washington, D. C. in Lincoln's Time*, ed. Herbert Mitgang (1896; reprint, Chicago: Quadrangle Books, 1971), pp. 294–95. For the individual debates and roll calls in the House on the Enrollment Act, see Geary, "Lesson in Trial and Error," pp. 129–43.

43. *CG*, 37th Cong., 3d sess., pp. 1214–35, appendix, pp. 172–77.

44. Ibid., pp. 1248–49.

45. Ibid., pp. 1249–53. Republican party cohesion was particularly strong on February 24. Conversely, the Democrats were noticeably weak on the call for adjournment and the motion to clear the galleries. However, they had supported Vallandigham's call of the House and opposed the suspension of the rules with a high degree of unanimity.

46. *CG*, 37th Cong., 3d sess., pp. 1255–60, 1263–65, 1267–70, 1273–75; and John B. Steele (Washington, D.C.) to Erastus Corning, Mar. 6, 1863, Erastus Corning Papers, AIHA.

47. *CG*, 37th Cong., 3d sess., pp. 1253–55, 1260–63, 1265–67, 1270–73.

48. *CG*, 37th Cong., 3d sess., pp. 1260–61.

49. Ibid., pp. 1288–92. Other proposed modifications consented to without a division included authorizing military commanders to grant furloughs to enlisted men. The House also rejected several changes without a roll call. Among the more important of these were proposals regulating substitute brokers, limiting the enrollment to whites, exempting individuals with conscientious scruples, and reducing the commutation fee to two hundred dollars.

50. *CG*, 37th Cong., 3d sess., pp. 1225, 1261–62, 1291–93; appendix, p. 163.

51. For a discussion of the division between the "Legitimatist" and "Purist" factions within the Democratic party, see Joel H. Silbey, *A Respectable Minority: The Democratic Party in the Civil War Era, 1860–1868* (New York: W. W. Norton & Co., 1977), pp. 49–61, 90–92, 110–14. Although this split was most conspicuous until late 1862, it continued throughout the war. As an opposition party, Silbey also sees congressional Democrats as being in a weak position to influence legislation because Republicans enjoyed numerical dominance. For an opposing view that relies on a roll call

analysis of Democratic voting behavior, see Jean H. Baker, "A Loyal Opposition: Northern Democrats in the Thirty-seventh Congress," *Civil War History* 25 (1979): 139–55. Baker further argues that the Democrats were unified as a party on issues that pertained directly to the war and others such as civil liberties, but experienced less cohesiveness in economic areas.

52. According to Bogue, *Earnest Men*, p. 102; and Curry, "Congressional Democrats," pp. 220–21, Democrats generally were more unified than Republicans in the Thirty-seventh Congress. That House Republicans demonstrated more unity in voting on the Enrollment Act than did the Democrats can undoubtedly be attributed partly to the close of the Thirty-seventh Congress, when many Republicans would lose their seats. Unlike the Democrats who could only offer disenchantment with the war as a unifying base, the Republicans had the far more tangible asset of patronage to wield their preponderantly lame-duck party into line. Through either choice or defeat, 65 of them did not return to Congress the following December. Through the system of rewards and punishments for favorable votes on this measure as well as other legislation, the Lincoln administration managed to dispel any notions it might have entertained of voting against the conscription bill. The defeated Ohio Republicans—Albert G. Riddle, John A. Gurley, and Sidney Edgerton—for example, received appointments as the envoy to Matanzas and Cuba, the territorial governor of Arizona, and a federal judgeship, respectively. Another member, Alexander Diven, became an army colonel and later the acting provost marshal general for the western division of New York State. Nor did the administration overlook a minority party member who had crossed party lines consistently to vote with the Republican majority. On 11 of the 12 roll calls, including the passage of S. 511, William E. Lehman of Pennsylvania voted with the Republicans. This maverick Democrat, who had failed to secure renomination to Congress, returned to his district as the local provost marshal. Conversely, the erratic Martin F. Conway, who aligned himself with the Democrats, received no public appointment from the Lincoln administration. The information on Conway and Diven can be found in Dumas Malone, ed., *The Dictionary of American Biography* (New York: Charles Scribner's Sons, 1936). For the other individuals, see the respective entries in United States Congress, *The Biographical Directory of the American Congress* (Washington, D.C.: Government Printing Office, 1971).

53. *CG*, 37th Cong., 3d sess., pp. 1292, 1404–5, 1426; appendix, pp. 161–63.

54. Ibid., pp. 1328–29; and Memorial of Samuel Hilles et al to the Meeting for Sufferings of Philadelphia (Orthodox) Yearly Meeting, Mar. 20, 1863, in Edward Needles Wright, *Conscientious Objectors in the Civil War* (1931; reprint, New York: A. S. Barnes & Co., 1961), p. 66.

55. For the several speeches, see *CG*, 37th Cong., 3d sess., pp. 1363–89.

56. Ibid., pp. 1389–91.

57. Ibid., pp. 1389–90. Henry Wilson was one of the eight who favored the exemption. With S. 511 safely past the scrutiny of Congress, Wilson could now be more responsive to the petitions he had received from Quakers that told of their dilemma. See petition of William Wood, clerk for the Religious Society of Friends in the State of New York, Feb. 24, 1863; petition of Joseph Snowden, clerk for Quakers

in Pennsylvania, New Jersey and Delaware, Feb. 24, 1863; and petition of Francis T. King, clerk for the Baltimore Yearly Meeting, Feb. 25, 1863, all addressed to Senate and House of Representatives of the United States. Series 37A–J6, "Petitions of Various Subjects . . . Jan. 10, 1862 . . . to . . . Feb. 25, 1863," SCMAM, RG 46, NA. Wilson noted these petitions on February 26, 1863, all of which were ordered to "lie on the table." See *Journal of the Senate*, 37th Cong., 3d sess., Serial 1148, p. 340. Quakers also petitioned the president for relief. See Snowden petition above in Robert Todd Lincoln Collection of the Papers of Abraham Lincoln, ser. 1, LC; and petition of Jonathon DeVol and George B. Eddy (Saratoga, N.Y.), to the President of the United States, Mar. 12, 1863, in *OR*, ser. 3, 3:64. At least during 1863, the Catholic clergy tended to appeal to their governors in the hope of receiving exemptions from the draft. See, for example, Robert E. V. Rice (Suspension Bridge, N.Y.) to Gov. Seymour, July 31, 1863, Horatio Seymour Papers, NYSL; and P. T. O'Reilley (Boston, Mass.) to J. A. Andrew, Aug. 3, 1863, John Andrew Papers, MHS.

58. Geary, "Lesson in Trial and Error," pp. 154–55.

59. Ibid., p. 1391. From February 20 to March 2, 1863, Senator John Sherman received at least fifteen letters from Ohioans recommending individuals for appointment to district provost-marshalships, enrollment boards, and as examining surgeons, John Sherman Papers, LC. His Ohio colleague, Benjamin F. Wade, received at least ten such requests in the week of March 4 to 11, 1863, Benjamin F. Wade Papers, LC. See also John Tapley, (Racine, Wis.) to J. R. Doolittle, Feb. 19, 1863, James Rood Doolittle Papers, SHSW-LD. A newly elected Republican congressman came to Washington for the express purpose of seeing Lincoln before making his recommendation. See Thomas T. Davis (Washington, D.C.) to the President, April [13 or 15?], 1863, Lincoln Papers, ser. 2. Governors also received letters that requested their influence in procuring a district provost-marshalship. See, for example, George H. Belden (Eugene City, Oreg.) to Gov. A. Gibbs, Mar. 2, 1863, Addison C. Gibbs Papers, ORHS; and James H. Morton (Springfield, Mass.) to J. A. Andrew, Mar. 6, 1863; and George N. Uston (Dunbury, Mass.) to Gov. Andrew, Mar. 7, 1863, Andrew Papers. A former governor, who was a successful candidate for a seat in the Thirty-eighth Senate, was very much interested in this area of patronage. Diary of Alexander Ramsey, entries for May 2, 3, and 5, 1863, Alexander Ramsey Papers, MIHS.

60. *CG*, 37th Cong., 3d sess., pp. 1438–40.

61. Ibid., pp. 1441–46.

62. Ibid., pp. 1444–48.

63. Based on a cluster bloc, the eight Republican senators who agreed on at least 80 percent of the twenty-five roll calls taken were Henry Wilson and Charles Sumner of Massachusetts, William Fessenden and Lot Morrill of Maine, Daniel Clark of New Hampshire, Lafayette Foster of Connecticut, Solomon Foot of Vermont, and Samuel Pomeroy of Kansas.

64. Curry, "Congressional Democrats," pp. 213–29, also believes that the Senate Democrats served as a loyal opposition in their actions toward nonmilitary legislation. Baker, "Northern Democrats," pp. 139–55, expands this interpretation to include Democrats in both the House and Senate.

CHAPTER SIX. CREDITS, QUOTAS, AND CONFUSION

1. James M. McPherson, *Battle Cry of Freedom: The Civil War Era* (New York: Ballantine Books, 1988), p. 421. For the view that the draft was a "failure," but that the threat of being conscripted served as a stimulus or "spur to volunteering," see Allan Nevins, *The War for the Union* (New York: Charles Scribner's Sons, 1960), 2:465.

2. For the full text of the Enrollment Act, see *U.S. Stats.* 12:731–37.

3. Ibid. 13:380. The percentages are derived from figures in *OR*, ser. 3, 5:730.

4. Entries for Aug. 11, 19, 1863, in Howard K. Beale, ed., *Diary of Gideon Welles* (New York: W. W. Norton & Co., 1960), 1:397, 407. In December 1863, Stanton finally decided to grant a blanket exemption to seamen, although clerks in all governmental departments would remain liable to service. See *OR*, ser. 3, 3:1166–67.

5. In early 1864, the *ad interim* chief of the Naval Bureau of Equipment and Recruiting informed the House Committee on Naval Affairs that the navy needed at least 3,500 more men. Only 190 new sailors enlisted weekly, which was hardly enough to fill the numerous vacancies that resulted from deaths and other causes. See A. N. Smith (Washington, D.C.) to A. H. Rice, Jan. 19, 1864, HR 38A–E13.11, "Recruiting Problems and Frauds," HCNA, RG 233, NA.

6. For these grievances and others, see, for example, letters of Issac N. Brevoort (US *Potomac*, Western Gulf Blockading Squadron) to [George P. Nutting?], Dec. 30, 1863; and J. M. Day ([Bauistoble?]) to [Gorde?], Jan. 7, 1864, HCNA, RG 233, NA.

7. *U.S. Stats.* 13:6–8. At this time Congress neither corrected the deplorable living conditions in the Union navy, nor did it require the government to discharge seamen on schedule. Consequently, sailors persisted with their grievances as reflected in their letters to the chairman of the Senate Committee on Naval Affairs. See petition of Benjamin F. Dudley et al (US *Ossipee*, off Galveston) to J. P. Hale, Mar. 1864; Issac B. Brevoort (US *Potomac*, Pensacola Bay) to [J. P. Hale], Apr. 15, 1864; and Samuel P. Crafts (USS [*Shockikin?*], James River) to [J. P. Hale], Feb. 22, 1864, John P. Hale Papers, NHHS.

8. W. T. Sherman (Camp before Vicksburg) to Brother, Apr. 23, 1863, in Rachel Sherman Thorndike, ed., *The Sherman Letters: Correspondence between General Sherman and Senator Sherman from 1837 to 1891* (1894; reprint, New York: DaCapo Press, 1969), p. 193. See also W. Zackman (Bonet Carrie) to Nancy, Feb. 23, 1863, William Zackman Papers, RBHL.

9. See letters from Sgt. T. Kellogg (Maumee City and East Toledo) to Col. Scott, Dec. 3, 24, 1863; Capt. J. H. Long (Bryan, Ohio) to Col. R. K. Scott, Dec. 3, 8, 10, 11, 19, 24, 29, 1863; and Lt. R. Masters (Franklin, Ohio) to Col. R. K. Scott, Dec. 4, 12, 1863, Robert Kingston Scott Papers, OHS. In one Indiana locality, the regimental recruiting program proved to be a complete failure. A. T. Rose (Spencer, Ind.) to O. Morton, Dec. 21, 1863, Oliver P. Morton Papers, ISL-AD. An individual in one Michigan county, which offered a two-hundred-dollar local bounty, noted optimistically that its quota would be filled with little difficulty. J. Seymour (Flushing, Mich.) to J. W. Longyear, Dec. 15, 1863, John Wesley Longyear Papers, MHC-UM.

10. Robert Robinson (Philadelphia) to S. Randall, Feb. 24, 1864, Samuel J. Randall Papers, UPL.

11. Eugene C. Murdock, *One Million Men: The Civil War Draft in the North* (Madison: State Historical Society of Wisconsin, 1971), pp. 15–17; and Ezra J. Warner, *Generals in Blue: Lives of the Union Commanders* (Baton Rouge: Louisiana State University Press, 1964), pp. 162–63.

12. Edward Salomon (Madison, Wis.) to James B. Fry, Aug. 10, 1863, General Letterbooks; and James B. Fry (Washington, D.C.) to Edward Salomon, Aug. 20, 1863, Incoming Letters from Individuals Representing Governmental Departments, both sources in Records of the Office of the Executive, SHSW-AD. See also James B. Fry (Washington, D.C.) to Edwin Morgan, Aug. 14, 1863, Edwin D. Morgan Papers, NYSL.

13. In one instance, Illinois and Missouri claimed credit for the same 3,129 men. See *OR*, ser. 3, 3:1098.

14. Ibid. 5:632–33, 642–43, 650–51, 662–64, and *U.S. Stats.* 13:7, 379, 380.

15. *U.S. Stats.* 12:732; and C. W. Cathcart, (Westerville, Ind.) to H. Lane, Dec. 17, 1863, Henry S. Lane Papers, IHS.

16. See, for example, S. S. (Portsmouth, N.H.) to J. P. Hale, July 2, 1863, Hale Papers; D. D. Perkins (Hartford, Conn.) to James B. Fry, Oct. 24, 1863, William A. Buckingham Papers, CSL; petitions of A. W. Longley et al (Berlin, Mass.) to W. B. Washburn, Jan. 11, 1864; and H. N. Bigelow et al (Clinton, Mass.) to W. B. Washburn, Jan. 9, 1864, HR38A–H1.1, HCMAM, RG 233, NA.

17. *U.S. Stats.* 13:6; and *OR*, ser. 3, 3:1195.

18. For Lincoln's original draft order and his three later proclamations, see Roy P. Basler, *The Collected Works of Abraham Lincoln* (New Brunswick: Rutgers University Press, 1953), 6:239–40, 523–24, 7:164, 245. Compare the differences in Fry's methods of computation in *OR*, ser. 3, 5:633–37, 730–34. For an analysis of Fry's figures, see chapter 7 of this study.

19. Editorial criticism of Fry became particularly virulent in January and February 1865. For the bipartisan press charges of incompetency, see, for example, *New York Tribune*, Jan. 31 and Feb. 4, 1865; *Cincinnati Daily Commercial*, Feb. 4, 1865; *Cleveland Plain Dealer*, Jan. 18, 25, and Feb. 17, 1865; *Detroit Free Press*, Jan. 6 and Feb. 1, 1865; *New York Times*, Jan. 2, 1865; and *Cleveland Leader*, Feb. 8 and Apr. 4–8, 10, 1865.

20. For the most thorough discussion on the Conkling-Fry controversy, see Eugene C. Murdock, *Patriotism Limited, 1862–1865: The Civil War Draft and the Bounty System* (Kent: Kent State University Press, 1967), pp. 216–28.

21. Grace Palladino, "The Poor Man's Fight: Draft Resistance and Labor Organization in Schuylkill County, Pennsylvania, 1860–1865" (Ph.D. diss., University of Pittsburgh, 1983), pp. 15–18, 234, 244; Robert E. Sterling, "Civil War Draft Resistance in the Middle West," (Ph.D. diss., Northern Illinois University, 1974), pp. 138, 150–53, 160–65, 455, 481–85, 656–68; and Phillip Shaw Paludan, *"A People's Contest:" The Union and Civil War, 1861–1865* (New York: Harper & Row, 1988), p. 236.

22. Harold M. Hyman, *A More Perfect Union: The Impact of the Civil War and Reconstruction on the Constitution* (New York: Alfred A. Knopf, 1973), pp. 219–21;

and Murdock, *One Million Men*, pp. 346–47. For a discussion of the general activities and some of the difficulties that district provost marshals encountered, see Murdock, *One Million Men*, pp. 92–117.

23. W. S. Schenck (Dayton, Ohio) to Cousin [R. C. Schenck], Feb. 10, 1865, Robert Cummings Schenck Papers, RBHL.

24. C. S. Medary, Actg. Prov. Mar., 11th District, (Goshen, N.Y.) to [former] Provost Marshal of 11th District, May 7, 1864, Samuel Medary Papers, OHS.

25. See, for example, Cadwell's letters of Feb. 20 and Mar. 4, 1862, to B. F. Wade, Benjamin F. Wade Papers, LC.

26. The information on Diven can be found in Dumas Malone, ed., *The Dictionary of American Biography* (New York: Charles Scribner's Sons, 1936), 5:322; for Lehman, see United States Congress *The Biographical Directory of the American Congress* (Washington, D.C.: Government Printing Office, 1971).

27. After only a few months as the local provost marshal in Philadelphia, Lehman expressed his annoyance at the constant accusations of corruption directed at his office. In a letter to the city's Mayor, Lehman indicated that any abuses occurring in his area of responsibility would be dealt with quickly. The charges of malfeasance evidently were without foundation, and Lehman executed the duties of his office very well during the remainder of the war. W. E. Lehman (Philadelphia) to A. Henry, Aug. 17, 1863, Alexander Henry Papers, HSP.

28. This episode is recounted in Richard H. Abbott, *Cobbler in Congress: The Life of Henry Wilson, 1812–1875* (Lexington: University Press of Kentucky, 1972), p. 134.

29. *OR*, ser. 3, 4:1149–50.

30. Letter in support of Dr. T. F. Murdock from G. E. Morgan (Baltimore, Md.) to R. Schenck, Jan. 4, 1865, Schenck Papers; and W. H. Mussey (Cincinnati) to W. H. Smith, Dec. 12, 21, 1864, William Henry Smith Papers, OHS. For an excellent discussion of the numerous problems that these surgeons faced, see Murdock, *One Million Men*, pp. 121–53.

31. Asst. Adjutant General (Washington, D.C.) to Commanding Officer (Draft Rendezvous, Pittsburgh, Pa.), June 10, 1864, in entry 398, "Drafted Bureau, Letters Sent," vol. 1, RG 94, NA. At least in one instance men continued to pay commutation after the privilege was repealed because they believed that they had been conscripted under the March 1864 draft. Because of the increasing complexity of the system, the local provost marshal inadvertently accepted their money. When their request for exemption was ultimately denied, they applied for the return of their commutation money and, as late as the spring of 1865, had not received a refund from the government. Col. A. L. Jefferies (Washington, D.C.) to Warren Noble, Mar. 4, 1865; and Statement of Board of Enrollment (Sandusky, Ohio) to James B. Fry, Apr. 13, 1865, Warren P. Noble Papers, RBHL.

32. Darius Cadwell (Jefferson, Ohio) to Col. J. H. Potter, July 21, 1864; Darius Cadwell (Jefferson) to Col. J. H. Potter and Gen. J. B. Fry, June 15, 1864; and Lt. Charles H. Brown (Washington, D.C.) to Capt. Cadwell, June 21, 1864, Darius Cadwell Papers, WRHS.

33. William B. Pratt (Prattsburgh, N.Y.) to Gov. Seymour, Nov. 29, 1864, Horatio

Seymour Papers, NYSL; Jen [O. A. Jennison] (Lansing) to J. Longyear, Jan. 23, 1865, Longyear Papers; and John Butler (Goshen) to James A. Garfield, Aug. 2, 1864, John Butler Papers, WRHS.

34. For Fry's instructions of April 21, 1863, see *OR*, ser. 3, 3:125–46.

35. The difficulties with the enrollment process have been covered very well in various works. See, for example, Hugh G. Earnhart, "The Administrative Organization of the Provost Marshal General's Bureau in Ohio, 1863–1865," *Northwest Ohio Quarterly* 37 (1966): 87–99; Jack Franklin Leach, *Conscription in the United States: Historical Background* (Tokyo: Charles B. Tuttle Co., 1952), pp. 251–75; and Murdock, *One Million Men*, pp. 26–61.

36. Darius Cadwell (Jefferson, Ohio) to J. B. Fry through J. H. Potter, May 24, 1864, Cadwell Papers. For a similar incident, see James C. Lucas (Pike County, Ohio) to M. Curnant, Aug. 12, 1864, Patrick Keran Collection, OHS.

37. For Fry's initial set of regulations, see *OR*, ser. 3, 3:125–46.

38. For soldiers' attitudes toward conscripts, substitutes, and bounty men, see, for example, Gerald F. Linderman, *Embattled Courage: The Experience of Combat in the American Civil War* (New York: Free Press, 1987), pp. 227, 263; and Sept. 4, 1864, letter of William T. Sherman to Henry Halleck, *OR*, ser. 1, 38:791–94.

39. David M. Kennedy, *Over Here: The First World War and American Society* (New York: Oxford University Press, 1980), pp. 152–53; and John Whiteclay Chambers II, *To Raise an Army: The Draft Comes to Modern America* (New York: Free Press, 1987), pp. 61–62.

40. Many excellent studies cover the draft systems in twentieth-century America. For the most succinct account of Crowder's difficulties and conscription in World War I, see Kennedy, *Over Here*, pp. 144–90; for a more detailed account, see Chambers, *To Raise an Army*, pp. 131–35, 180–84, 189–202. George Q. Flynn, *Lewis B. Hershey: Mr. Selective Service* (Chapel Hill: University of North Carolina Press, 1985) is unsurpassed on the life and influence of General Hershey. All of these studies draw heavily on manuscript and archival material. Unfortunately, James B. Fry's personal papers were destroyed in a fire in 1885, which necessarily limits a more thorough understanding of the architect of the Provost Marshal General's Bureau.

41. For a detailed description of Union recruiting activities in the last two years of the war, see Murdock, *One Million Men*, pp. 5, 154–69. For the opinion that troops were raised after 1863 in one locality "within the context of constant local patriotism," see Emily J. Harris, "Sons and Soldiers: Deerfield, Massachusetts and the Civil War," *Civil War History* 30 (1984): 157–71.

42. Harris, "Sons and Soldiers," p. 170.

43. For the complete story of William Graham, see Murdock, *One Million Men*, pp. 3–5.

44. Ibid., p. 7.

45. Austin Blair (Jackson) to D. M. Fox, Oct. 21, 1863, Edwin J. March Papers, MHC-UM; and *OR*, ser. 3, 5:730.

46. Mary A. Grant (Lebanon) to C. B. Grant, Nov. 21, 1863, Claudius Buchanan Grant Papers, MHC-UM.

47. Henry L. Stone (Windsor, Canada) to Azariah Gordon, Dec. 24, 1863, Special Subject Folder of Henry S. Lane Papers, IHS. See also Fred A. Shannon, *The Organization and Administration of the Union Army, 1861–1865* (1928; reprint, Gloucester, Mass.: Peter Smith, 1965), 2:70–71.

48. William F. Raney, "Recruiting and Crimping in Canada for the Northern Forces, 1861–1865," *Mississippi Valley Historical Review* 10 (1923): 21–33; Marguerite B. Hamer, "Luring Canadian Soldiers into Union Lines during the War Between the States," *Canadian Historical Review* 27 (1946): 150–62; and Robin W. Winks, *Canada and the United States: The Civil War Years* (Baltimore: Johns Hopkins University Press, 1960), pp. 178–205. Winks's account is particularly good for its scrutiny of the view that Canada was pro-Northern because of the large number of its citizens who served in the Union army. Although some enlisted out of an affinity for the Union cause, many more were either enticed by bounties or were the targets of questionable enlistments. If anything, widespread crimping and the presence of skedaddlers may have soured Canadian attitudes toward the North.

49. In one instance, for example, some German immigrants were irate over losing some of their bounty money but were not that upset over finding themselves as new Union recruits in the 20th Massachusetts Infantry. Mack Walker, "The Mercenaries," *New England Quarterly* 39 (1966): 390–98. For the view that the government did not overtly sanction the recruitment of foreigners, but did encourage immigration for this purpose, see Robert L. Peterson and John A. Hudson, "Foreign Recruitment for Union Forces," *Civil War History* 7 (1961): 176–89. On the opposition of British manufacturers, particularly toward the efforts of the American Emigrant Company in enticing their skilled workers to the United States, see Charlotte Erickson, *American Industry and the European Immigrant, 1860–1865* (1957; reprint, New York: Russell & Russell, 1967), pp. 20–22.

50. Numerous studies identify the harsh methods that were used in placing former slaves into service. See especially John W. Blassingame, "The Recruitment of Colored Troops in Kentucky, Maryland, and Missouri, 1863–1865," *Historian* 29 (1967): 633–45; C. Peter Ripley, "The Black Family in Transition: Louisiana, 1860–1865," *Journal of Southern History* 41 (1975): 369–80; and John David Smith, "The Recruitment of Negro Soldiers in Kentucky, 1863–1865," *Kentucky Historical Society Register* 72 (1974): 364–90.

51. *OR*, ser. 3, 5:601.

CHAPTER SEVEN. QUOTAS AND OTHER NUMBERS

1. Eugene C. Murdock, *One Million Men: The Civil War Draft in the North* (Madison: State Historical Society of Wisconsin, 1971), pp. 154–77, provides the most thorough discussion of the frantic efforts that many communities made to fill quotas but does not fully analyze Fry's figures. For an excellent local study that discusses the effect that the misunderstanding of quotas and credits has had on conclusions drawn about one state, see William C. Wright, "New Jersey's Military Role in the Civil War Reconsidered," *New Jersey History* 92 (1974): 197–210. Based on his detailed analysis,

Wright finds that "the two statements that New Jersey supplied more men than it was required to and that there was no draft in New Jersey are both false."

2. James M. McPherson, *Battle Cry of Freedom: The Civil War Era* (New York: Ballantine Books, 1988), p. 492.

3. For the view that the North was unsuccessful in raising men in 1862 under one or both calls see, for example, Benjamin P. Thomas and Harold M. Hyman, *Stanton: The Life and Times of Lincoln's Secretary of War* (New York: Alfred A. Knopf, 1962), p. 245; and Herman Hattaway and Archer Jones, *How the North Won: A Military History of the Civil War* (Urbana: University of Illinois Press, 1983), p. 275. Fred A. Shannon, *The Organization and Administration of the Union Army* (1928; reprint, Gloucester, Mass.: Peter Smith, 1965), 1:290–91, calls the 1862 draft a "failure" because it only secured 87,588 men out of the 334,835 required. He discusses the 1862 quotas in somewhat more detail than most historians, and in a convoluted way reaches the conclusion that "time credits" equaled out in the end.

4. Compare *OR*, ser. 3, 5:1264–65; and Fry's full *Final Report to the Secretary of War by the Provost Marshal General* in Journal of the House of Representatives, 39th Cong., 1st sess., 1866, H. Exec. Doc. 1, vol. 4, (Serials 1251–52), p. 160.

5. Based on calculations in Fry's abridged *Report* in *OR*, ser. 3, 5:636–39, 730–39. Most historians use the 46,347 figure. See, for example, McPherson, *Battle Cry of Freedom*, p. 601; and E. B. Long, *The Civil War Day by Day: An Almanac, 1861–1865* (Garden City, N.Y.: Doubleday & Co., 1971), p. 707; Peter J. Parish, *The American Civil War* (New York: Holmes & Meier, 1975), p. 143. Shannon, *Organization and Administration* 2:160, relies on the figure of 52,000.

6. Ibid., and Peter Levine, "Draft Evasion in the North during the Civil War, 1863–1865," *Journal of American History* 67 (Mar. 1981): 821. Another good example of how these 44,403 substitutes for enrolled men created confusion occurs in James McPherson's two general histories. In *Ordeal by Fire: The Civil War and Reconstruction* (New York: Alfred A. Knopf, 1982), p. 357, he includes these men and finds that conscripts and substitutes made up less than 10 percent of the Union army. In his later work, *Battle Cry of Freedom*, p. 605, he excludes these men and finds that conscripts and substitutes comprised only 7 percent of the Union forces.

7. The leading expert on the Northern bounty system finds that it is impossible to determine the number of bounty jumpers. See Murdock, *One Million Men*, p. 342. On the history of Thomas Ryan, who jumped bounty at least thirty times, see James Barnett, "The Bounty Jumpers of Indiana," *Civil War History* 4 (1958): 429–36. For the most reliable composite on total Union desertions, see Ella Lonn, *Desertion during the Civil War* (1928; reprint, Gloucester, Mass.: Peter Smith, 1966), pp. 153–54, 233.

8. Long, *Civil War Day by Day*, pp. 705–6.

9. Fry's complete *Final Report*, p. 160; and *OR*, ser. 3, 4:1269–70; 5:640.

10. For a discussion on this special legislation, see Allan G. Bogue, *The Earnest Men: Republicans of the Civil War Senate* (Ithaca: Cornell University Press, 1981), pp. 274–75.

11. Fry's *Final Report*, pp. 160, 165–68, 176–79, 186–91, 200–205.

12. Ibid., p. 160.

13. For a discussion of the use of commutation money in the payment of bounties in the fall of 1863 and winter of 1864, and for the trouble that Fry encountered with Congress for disbursing these funds, see Shannon, *Organization and Administration* 2:81–82.

14. *OR*, ser. 3, 5:729.

15. McPherson, *Ordeal by Fire*, p. 181. Hattaway and Jones, *How the North Won*, p. 721, estimate that up to 87 percent of Southern white males served in the Confederate military.

16. The information in tables 2 and 3 is derived from *OR*, ser. 3, 5:730–39. It follows a format similar to one that appears in Murdock, *One Million Men*, pp. 350–56. He includes information for each of the states, but neither identifies the number of men discharged nor the respective numbers of men who were exempted for disability and for other causes.

17. The extant source material on substitutes for drafted men and enrolled men is sporadic and is scattered throughout the "Descriptive Books" and their equivalents in RG 110, NA. For an example of information on one consolidated group of substitutes for enrolled men in the first district of New Hampshire, see the last eighteen unnumbered pages in "Descriptive Books of Drafted Men and Substitutes Exempted from Service, 1863–65," vol. 15, entry 645, RG 110, NA.

18. See, for example, Long, *Civil War Day by Day*, pp. 707–8; Hattaway and Jones, *How the North Won*, pp. 439–40; and Elden E. Billings, "The Civil War and Conscription," *Current History* 54 (1968): 336. For an estimate that places the number of Union conscripts at a low 2 percent, see John Whiteclay Chambers II, *To Raise an Army: The Draft Comes to Modern America* (New York: Free Press, 1987), p. 62.

19. Hugh G. Earnhart, "Commutation: Democratic or Undemocratic?" *Civil War History* 12 (1966): 132–42. For an analysis of Earnhart's figures, see chapter 11 of this study.

20. *OR*, ser. 3, 4:1264–65.

21. Figures also vary on Confederate conscription. McPherson, *Ordeal by Fire*, p. 182, estimates that 120,000 Southerners were drafted and another 70,000 served as substitutes. E. B. Long, *Civil War Day by Day*, believes that there were 81,993 conscripts, but his figure is based solely on states east of the Mississippi. The most detailed discussion of figures can be found in Albert Burton Moore's *Conscription and Conflict in the Confederacy* (New York: Macmillan, 1924), pp. 355–61, but he concludes that "it is impossible to say how many men passed through the channels of conscription." Using Moore's raw data and other sources, Hattaway and Jones, *How the North Won*, pp. 116, 125, venture a guess that the Confederate army was comprised of 10.9 percent drafted men, and that conscription encouraged another 10.2 percent to volunteer.

22. This estimate is based on figures derived from the United States *Census* that were compiled by E. B. Long, *Civil War Day by Day*, pp. 700–704.

23. Under the March 1864 call in Delaware, for example, at least 28 blacks commuted, 3 provided substitutes, and 74 were conscripted. "Descriptive Books of Drafted Men, Aug. 1863–Mar. 1865," 3 vols., nos. 19–21, entry 3782, RG 110, NA.

CHAPTER EIGHT. YANKEE RECRUITS, CONSCRIPTS, AND ILLEGAL EVADERS

1. Marvin R. Cain, "A 'Face of Battle' Needed: An Assessment of Motives and Men in Civil War Historiography," *Civil War History* 28 (1982): 5–27. This survey should be supplemented by recent studies, especially Randall C. Jimerson, *The Private Civil War: Popular Thought during the Sectional Conflict* (Baton Rouge: Louisiana State University Press, 1988), pp. 27–49, 76–78, 86–111, 198; Gerald F. Linderman, *Embattled Courage: The Experience of Combat in the American Civil War* (New York: Free Press, 1987), pp. 216–39, 261–64; and Reid Mitchell, *Civil War Soldiers* (New York: Viking, 1988), pp. 18–23; 56–59, 65–75, 82–89, 126–31, 195–96.

2. For soldiers' negative comments toward conscripts, see, for example, Linderman, *Embattled Courage*, pp. 227, 232.

3. Refer to the appendix of this study for further information on the sources from which these data were derived. For citations to specific states and draft districts, see notes 20 and 21 of this chapter.

4. John S. Haller, "Civil War Anthropometry: The Making of a Racial Ideology," *Civil War History* 16 (1970): 309–24.

5. For an abridged version, see *OR*, ser. 3, 5:758–80. For the 158 tables on physical characteristics and medical disabilities of Union men who were examined under the auspices of General Fry's bureau, see the full *Final Report to the Secretary of War by the Provost Marshal General* in *Journal of the House of Representatives*, 39th Cong., 1st sess., 1866, H. Exec. Doc. No. 1, vol. 4 (Serials 1251–52), appendix, Doc. 8, pp. 258–699.

6. Benjamin Apthorp Gould, comp., *Investigations in the Military and Anthropological Statistics of American Soldiers* (Cambridge: U.S. Sanitary Commission, 1869), pp. 186–205, 208–17, 626–27. Robin W. Winks, *Canada and the United States: The Civil War Years* (Baltimore: Johns Hopkins University Press, 1960), pp. 182–83, finds Gould's figures to be of little value for his study because nativity data were not recorded in early enlistment records. Further, Gould relied heavily on surveys that asked former officers "to estimate nativities of their respective regiments." On this questionable basis, he projected that 2.65 percent of Union soldiers came from Canada.

7. Bell Irvin Wiley, *The Life of Billy Yank: The Common Soldier of the Union* (Baton Rouge: Louisiana State University Press, 1971), pp. 296–312.

8. James M. McPherson, *Ordeal by Fire: The Civil War and Reconstruction* (New York: Alfred A. Knopf, 1982), p. 359. Copyright 1982 by Alfred A. Knopf, Inc. Table reprinted by permission of the publisher.

9. Ibid., p. 357; James M. McPherson, *Battle Cry of Freedom: The Civil War Era* (New York: Ballantine Books, 1988), p. 608; and Wiley, *Billy Yank*, p. 303.

10. McPherson, *Ordeal by Fire*, p. 357.

11. Ibid., p. 358. There may have been legitimate reasons in accounting for the reluctance of ethnic groups to enlist. For a recent study that uses promotion of the foreign-born as the principal variable in arriving at the conclusion that they were discriminated against in the Union army, see Kevin J. Weddle, "Ethnic Discrimination in Minnesota Volunteer Regiments during the Civil War," *Civil War History* 35 (1989): 238–

59. For a study that traces a greater tendency among the foreign-born to desert because of the absence of strong community ties, see Judith Lee Hallock, "The Role of the Community in Civil War Desertion," *Civil War History* 29 (1983): 123–34.

12. Earl J. Hess, "The 12th Missouri Infantry: A Socio-Military Profile of a Union Regiment," *Missouri Historical Review* 76 (1981): 53–77; and David F. Riggs, "Sailors of the U.S.S. *Cairo*: Anatomy of a Gunboat Crew," *Civil War History* 28 (1982): 266–73.

13. W. J. Rorabaugh, "Who Fought for the North in the Civil War? Concord, Massachusetts, Enlistments," *Journal of American History* 73 (1986): 695–701.

14. Emily J. Harris, "Sons and Soldiers: Deerfield, Massachusetts and the Civil War," *Civil War History* 30 (1984): 157–71.

15. Ibid., pp. 157, 165.

16. Maris A. Vinovskis, "Have Social Historians Lost the Civil War? Some Preliminary Demographic Speculations," *Journal of American History* 76 (1989): 34–58.

17. Ibid., pp. 43–45. Of the numerous local studies on Massachusetts, only one mentions the state and federal conscription systems. Unfortunately, it is limited to a discussion on the number of men furnished and not to the character of residents who either entered the army or remained at home. Michael H. Frisch, *Town into City: Springfield, Massachusetts, and the Meaning of Community, 1840–1880* (Cambridge: Harvard University Press, 1972), pp. 56–66.

18. On the importance of bounties as a motivating influence, see Eugene C. Murdock, *One Million Men: The Civil War Draft in the North* (Madison: State Historical Society of Wisconsin, 1971), especially pages 154–69.

19. James Bamon ([Oil City, Pa.]) to H. Stroman, Apr. 5, 1865, Henry Stroman Papers, OHS.

20. For Delaware, Michigan, and Rhode Island, see Delaware—"Descriptive Books of Drafted Men, Aug. 1863–Mar. 1865," 3 vols., entry 3782; Michigan, Second District—"Descriptive Books of Drafted Men, 1863–1865," 3 vols., entry 5992; Michigan, Third District—"Descriptive Book of Drafted Men, 1863–1864 [1865?]," 1 vol., entry 6014; Rhode Island, First District—"Register of Drafted Men, 1863," 1 vol., entry 1331; and Rhode Island, Second District—"Descriptive Book of Drafted Men, 1863," 1 vol., entry 1348. All sources part of RG 110, NA.

21. Iowa, First District—"Descriptive Book of Drafted Men, Oct.–Dec., 1864," 1 vol., entry 6397; Iowa, Second District—[source is not designated, the manuscript title says "Medical Register of Examinations of Drafted Men, Nov. 1864–May 1865"], 1 vol., entry 6413; Iowa, Third District—"Descriptive Book of Drafted Men, Sept. 1864–Feb. 1865," 1 vol., entry 6429, and "Medical Register of Examinations of Enrolled Men, 1864–65," 1 vol., entry 6428; Iowa, Fourth District—"Medical Register of Drafted Men, Sept. 1864–Feb. 1865," 1 vol., entry 6450; Iowa, Fifth District—"Descriptive Book of Drafted Men [undated]," 1 vol., entry 6470; and Iowa, sixth District—[very peculiar untitled source, part of records for Fort Dodge and Marshalltown], 1 vol., entry 6495. The records for Kansas and New Hampshire are more accessible and are clearly identified as "Descriptive Books." For Kansas's northern district see entry 6551, and for the southern district see entry 6552. For New Hampshire's first district see

entry 645, for the second district see entry 667, and for the third district see entry 681. For New York's thirtieth district, see "Descriptive Book of Drafted Men, Aug. 1863–June 1864," 1 vol., entry 2291, for the calls of 1863 and March 1864; and for the December 1864 call, see "Register of Drafted Men, Mar.–Apr. 1865," 1 vol., entry 2292. All sources are part of RG 110, NA.

22. Numerous sources, including Benjamin Gould's 1869 general categories, were used in constructing a matrix for the purpose of assigning an individual to a particular occupational group. The most beneficial and helpful was Theodore Hershberg and Robert Dockhorn's "Occupational Classification," *Historical Methods Newsletter* 9 (1976): 59–98. This important work, which relies on vertical categories, stems in part from earlier studies that examined occupations in North America in 1860. Among the more important of these is Theodore Hershberg et al, "Occupation and Ethnicity in Five Nineteenth-Century Cities: A Collaborative Inquiry," *Historical Methods Newsletter* 7 (1973): 174–216, a study in which five independent researchers attempted to establish comparable occupational scales in the five cities of Philadelphia, Hamilton, Ontario, Kingston, Buffalo, and Poughkeepsie, New York. While these works did not answer all questions, they helped immensely in facilitating my work. After experimenting with a variety of general formats, the most appropriate was a version of the one that James McPherson developed for his table on Union soldiers.

23. Compare this range of occupations for drafted men to those for all recruits as described in Wiley, *Billy Yank*, pp. 303–4.

24. McPherson, *Battle Cry of Freedom*, p. 608.

25. G. N. D. Evans, ed., *Allegiance in America: The Case of the Loyalists* (Reading, Mass.: Addison-Wesley Co., 1969), pp. 189–93.

26. Deferments created a multitude of administrative and political difficulties for twentieth-century draft officials. Three excellent studies cover this area in detail. For World War I, see John Whiteclay Chambers II, *To Raise an Army: The Draft Comes to Modern America* (New York: Free Press, 1987), pp. 153–63, 188–96. For the post–World War I era, see George Q. Flynn, "The Draft and College Deferments during the Korean War," *Historian* 50 (1988): 369–85; and his *Lewis B. Hershey: Mr. Selective Service* (Chapel Hill: University of North Carolina Press, 1985), especially pp. 81–82, 91–94, 105–16, 151, 193–215, 218–19, 234–35.

27. Chambers, *To Raise an Army*, p. 213; Flynn, *Hershey*, p. 79; and Myra McPherson, *Long Time Passing: Vietnam and the Haunted Generation* (Garden City; N.Y.: Doubleday & Co., 1984), pp. 402–3. For the most accurate calculations on Vietnam, see Chambers, p. 343, n. 34.

28. Robert E. Sterling, "Civil War Draft Resistance in the Middle West" (Ph.D. diss., Northern Illinois University, 1974), p. 163. For other comments on pre–1863 skedaddlers, refer to chapter 4 of this book.

29. Peter Levine, "Draft Evasion in the North during the Civil War, 1863–1865," *Journal of American History* 67 (Mar. 1981): 816–34.

30. *OR*, ser. 3, 5:730–39.

31. Ibid., p. 733. For a brief discussion of this law, see Harold Bell Hancock, *Delaware during the Civil War* (Wilmington: Historical Society of Delaware, 1961), p.139.

32. *U.S. Stats.* 13:6–8.

33. Marguerite B. Hamer, "Luring Canadian Soldiers into Union Lines during the War Between the States," *Canadian Historical Review* 27 (1946): 155–56, 159–60; and William F. Raney, "Recruiting and Crimping in Canada for the Northern Forces, 1861–1865," *Mississippi Valley Historical Review* 10 (1923): 25–26, 28–30.

34. *The Tribune Almanac for the Years 1838 to 1868 Inclusive: Comprehending the Politicians Register and the Whig Almanac . . .* (New York: New York Tribune, 1868); and William Frank Zornow, *Lincoln and the Party Divided* (Norman: University of Oklahoma Press, 1954), p. 209.

35. Levine, "Draft Evasion," p. 828.

36. Conscription in America has been in limbo since 1973 when it was replaced with the All Volunteer Force. Even without the prospect of actually being drafted, some American men continue to ignore the highly publicized legal requirement that they must register with the Selective Service System after their eighteenth birthday. The extent of this noncompliance has been estimated at between "7 and 25 percent." Michael Useem, "Conscription and Class," *Society* 18 (1981): 28.

37. Henry [n.p.], Sept. 23, 1861, to Lal [Laurel Summers], quoted in Hubert H. Wubben, *Civil War Iowa and the Copperhead Movement* (Ames: Iowa State University Press, 1980), p. 44.

38. Levine, "Draft Evasion," pp. 833–34.

39. For concerns with the modernization thesis, see Eric Foner, *Politics and Ideology in the Age of the Civil War* (New York: Oxford University Press, 1980), pp. 21, 33.

40. For the operations of the draft during America's *"Nation-State"* phase, see Chambers, *To Raise an Army*, especially pp. 6, 174–204, 266–67.

CHAPTER NINE. "$300 OR YOUR LIFE"

1. W. T. Sherman (Camp before Vicksburg) to Brother, Mar. 14, 1863, in Rachel Sherman Thorndike, ed., *The Sherman Letters: Correspondence between General Sherman and Senator Sherman from 1837 to 1891* (1894; reprint, New York: DaCapo Press, 1969), p. 193. For the Enrollment Act's welcome reception among the rank-and-file, see, for example, Daniel Habaker (Murfreesboro, Tenn.) to Brother, Mar. 30, 1863, W. W. Carey Papers, ISL-ID; Horace Hobart (Camp near Murfreesboro) to Brother, Mar. 2, 1863, Horace Hobart Papers, IHS; James (Camp near Murfreesboro) to Sister, Mar. 11, 1863, James S. Thomas Papers, IHS; Tom (Readyville, Tenn.) to Matilda, Mar. 16, 1863, Thomas Prickett Papers, IHS. See also [John C. Love] (Murfreesboro) to Parents, Mar. 15, 1863, John C. Love Papers, MHC-UM.

2. For the most thorough discussion of intellectual reaction toward Northern conscription, see Lorraine Anderson Williams, "The Civil War and Intellectuals of the North" (Ph.D. diss., American University, 1953), pp. 178–90. Williams does not consider the draft in her article, "Northern Intellectual Reaction to Military Rule during the Civil War," *Historian* 27 (1965): 334–49; but she does discuss how intellectuals disagreed over the appropriateness of subordinating civilian to military authority even in wartime. George M. Fredrickson, *The Inner Civil War: Northern Intellectuals and the Crisis of the Union* (New York: Harper & Row, 1965), pp. 72–78, 148–50, discusses

the enthusiasm of intellectuals toward the war in 1861 but does not address their views on conscription except in a broad context of individual attitudes in the later war years. These views included that of Walt Whitman, who was disturbed by the increasing prevalence of military discipline in American society.

3. James M. McPherson, *Battle Cry of Freedom: The Civil War Era* (New York: Ballantine Books, 1988), p. 608, reaches a somewhat similar conclusion that perception was important. He argues that actual discrimination against workingmen may have lacked "objective reality," but Democrats managed to use the draft as a symbolic means to illustrate "class" differences.

4. *Columbus Crisis*, Mar. 4 and Apr. 1, 1863. See also Feb. 25, Mar. 4, Apr. 8, 27, and June 24, 1863.

5. *Detroit Free Press*, July 18, 1863. See also Mar. 3, 4, 6, 7, 1863.

6. *Cleveland Plain Dealer*, Mar. 17, 1863. See also Feb. 6, 11, 14, 17–20, 25, 26, and Mar. 7, 13, 27, 1863.

7. *Chicago Times*, Mar. 3, 5, 1863. See also Feb. 23, 27, and Mar. 3, 4, 1863.

8. *Portland* (Maine) *Eastern Argus*, Mar. 3, 1863. See also Mar. 4, 12, and July 15, 1863.

9. *New York Herald*, Feb. 26, 27, and Mar. 2, 1863. The Republican *Washington, D.C. Evening Star* shared the *Herald's* sentiment with respect to religious men being drafted. See Feb. 17, 1863, edition.

10. *Boston Daily Journal*, Feb. 20, 24, 27, 1863; *Washington, D.C. Daily Morning Chronicle*, Feb. 17, 18, 20, 25, 26, and Mar. 2, 1863; and *New York Times*, May 26, 1863. See also Feb. 20, 21, and Apr. 18, 1863.

11. *Cleveland Leader*, Apr. 21 and Feb. 26, 1863.

12. *New York Tribune*, Feb. 23, 1863. See also Mar. 23, 1863.

13. *Cincinnati Daily Commercial*, Mar. 19, 1863. See also Apr. 4, 15, 23, June 25, and July 14, 16, 1863.

14. For a copy of this March 13, 1863, speech at Dayton, Ohio, see Clement L. Vallandigham, *The Record of Hon. C. L. Vallandigham on Abolition, the Union, and the Civil War* (Cincinnati: J. Walter & Co., 1863), p. 246.

15. For a general discussion of enrollment and draft resistance in areas other than New York City, see Fred A. Shannon, *The Organization and Administration of the Union Army, 1861–1865* (1928; reprint, Gloucester, Mass.: Peter Smith, 1965), 2:192–95; and Eugene C. Murdock, *One Million Men: The Civil War Draft in the North* (Madison: State Historical Society of Wisconsin, 1971), pp. 40–61.

16. Robert E. Sterling, "Civil War Draft Resistance in the Middle West" (Ph.D. diss., Northern Illinois University, 1974), pp. x–xv, 659–60, 667–68. For questions that Sterling did not address in his study, see James W. Geary, "Civil War Conscription in the North: A Historiographical Review," *Civil War History* 32 (1986): 219–20.

17. William Marvel, "New Hampshire and the Draft, 1863," *Historical New Hampshire* 36 (1981): 58–72; Arnold M. Shankman, *The Pennsylvania Antiwar Movement, 1861–1865* (Rutherford: Fairleigh Dickinson University Press, 1980), pp. 141–60, 217–19; and Grace Palladino, "The Poor Man's Fight: Draft Resistance and Labor Organization in Schuylkill County, Pennsylvania, 1860–1865" (Ph.D. diss., University

of Pittsburgh, 1983), pp. 1–37, 160–230. On resistance in Vermont, see Phillip Shaw Paludan, *"A People's Contest": The Union and Civil War, 1861–1865* (New York: Harper & Row, 1988), p. 191.

18. Numerous studies discuss the four days of rioting in detail. For one of the more scholarly treatments, see Adrian Cook, *The Armies of the Streets: The New York City Draft Riots of 1863* (Lexington: University Press of Kentucky, 1974). For a good popular account, see James McCague, *The Second Rebellion: The Story of the New York City Draft Riots* (New York: Dial Press, 1968). For a contemporary account, see David M. Barnes, *The Draft Riots in New York, July 1863* (New York: Baker & Godwin, 1863). Although this work is little more than an extremely biased account of the valorous actions of the New York Police Department, it is useful for reconstructing certain events.

19. John G. Nicolay and John Hay, *Abraham Lincoln: A History* (New York: Century Co., 1886), 7:26–27; and James Ford Rhodes, *History of the United States from the Compromise of 1850 . . .* (New York: Macmillan Co., 1899), 4:321–22.

20. The economic reasons behind the draft riots in New York City and elsewhere have attracted the attention of some twentieth-century historians. They conclude that the disruptions can be traced directly to the labor conflict that existed between blacks and the white working classes, especially Irish longshoremen. In particular, see Emerson D. Fite, *Social and Industrial Conditions in the North during the Civil War* (New York: Macmillan Co., 1910), pp. 189–90; Williston H. Lofton, "Northern Labor and the Negro during the Civil War," *Journal of Negro History* 34 (1949): 251–73; and Albon P. Man, Jr., "Labor Competition and the New York Draft Riots of 1863," *Journal of Negro History* 36 (1951), pp. 375–405. Although the Irish were the main participants in the New York City disorders and in the other draft disturbances during 1863, they were not necessarily representative of their ethnic group. For the estimate that 140,000 Irish-born men served in the Union army, see John Whiteclay Chambers II, *To Raise an Army: The Draft Comes to Modern America* (New York: Free Press, 1987), pp. 54–55.

21. McCague, *Second Rebellion*, p. 18; and Cook, *Armies of the Streets*, pp. 52, 205–6. For a recent study that examines the long-range ramifications of the riots on political, social, and labor relations in New York City, see Iver Bernstein, *The New York City Draft Riots: Their Significance for American Society and Politics in the Age of the Civil War* (New York: Oxford University Press, 1990). For other works on the New York disorders and resistance elsewhere, see James W. Geary, "Manpower Mobilization," in Eugene C. Murdock, *The Civil War in the North: A Selective Annotated Bibliography* (New York: Garland, 1987), pp. 164–84.

22. Shankman, *Pennsylvania Antiwar Movement*, pp. 141–60, 217–19; and Hubert H. Wubben, *Civil War Iowa and the Copperhead Movement* (Ames: Iowa State University Press, 1980), pp. 62–63, 125–29, 158–62, 222–28.

23. Sterling, "Civil War Draft Resistance," pp. v–xi, 481–85, 659–60, 667–68.

24. Palladino, "Poor Man's Fight," pp. 14, 165–67, 234, 242, 244.

25. *OR*, ser. 3, 3:612–19. For one of the better discussions of Seymour's relations with the federal government, see Eugene C. Murdock, *Patriotism Limited, 1862–1865: The Civil War Draft and the Bounty System* (Kent: Kent State University Press, 1967), pp. 63–80.

26. Roy P. Basler, ed., *The Collected Works of Abraham Lincoln* (New Brunswick: Rutgers University Press, 1953), 6:369–70.

27. The habeas corpus issue was of such profound importance that at least three of Lincoln's cabinet members commented extensively on it in their diary entries for September 14, 1863. Two of them, Welles and Bates, also noted Lincoln's ill temper toward the judges who issued the writs. Bates even remarked that the president was "more angry than I ever saw him." See Howard K. Beale, ed., *Diary of Gideon Welles* (New York: W. W. Norton & Co., 1960), 1:431–33; Howard K. Beale, ed., *The Diary of Edward Bates, 1859–1866,* volume 4 of *Annual Report of the American Historical Association for the Year 1930* (Washington, D.C.: Government Printing Office, 1933), pp. 306–7; and David Donald, ed., *Inside Lincoln's Cabinet: The Civil War Diaries of Salmon P. Chase* (New York: Longmans, Green & Co., 1954), pp. 192–94. For a copy of Lincoln's proclamation suspending the writ, see Basler, *Collected Works,* 6:451–52.

28. For the original text of Taney's uncirculated opinion, see John O'Sullivan and Alan M. Meckler, eds., *The Draft and Its Enemies: A Documentary History* (Urbana: University of Illinois Press, 1974), pp. 79–92. This reprinted version is especially useful for the many fine editorial notes and related sources of documentation. For a detailed account of the litigation resulting from the Enrollment Act, see Jack Franklin Leach, *Conscription in the United States: Historical Background* (Tokyo: Charles B. Tuttle Co., 1952), 353–85.

29. For a succinct discussion of this case, see J. L. Bernstein, "Conscription and the Constitution: The Amazing Case of Kneedler *v.* Lane," *American Bar Association Journal* 53 (1967): 708–12.

30. On or about September 14, 1863, Lincoln recorded his opinions on the draft's constitutionality and whether the commutation clause discriminated against the poor. For this unpublished essay, see Basler, *Collected Works* 6:444–49.

31. Benjamin P. Thomas and Harold M. Hyman, *Stanton: The Life and Times of Lincoln's Secretary of War* (New York: Alfred A. Knopf, 1962), p. 281.

32. For the best account of Pringle's experiences and those of other Friends, see Peter Brock, *Pacifism in the United States from the Colonial Era to the First World War* (Princeton: Princeton University Press, 1968), pp. 751–55. In addition to the Quakers, Brock also discusses Mennonites, Shakers, and other groups in both the North and South (pp. 780–866).

33. *OR,* ser. 3, 3:1173.

34. William Wood, Clerk, Religious Society of the State of New York, Jan. 4, 1864; Levi Jessup, Clerk for Eastern Indiana and Western Ohio, Dec. 22, 1863; Samuel Boyce, Clerk, Yearly Meeting of the Society of Friends for New England, Jan. 1, 1864; and John Scott, Clerk for the Baltimore Yearly Meeting, embracing Maryland, Virginia, and parts of Pennsylvania, Dec. 31, 1863. All were addressed to the Senate and House of Representatives and are located in series number Sen. 38A–H10.2, "Petitions and Memorials Relative to the Amendment of the Conscription Law, Dec. 8, 1863 . . . to . . . Feb. 1865," SCMAM, RG 46, NA. One Quaker elder, in early January 1864, made a special visit to Washington for the express purpose of presenting his sect's views before the military committees of both houses. See entries for Jan. 4, 6–8, 1864, in "John Butler [Memo Book]," John Butler Papers, WRHS. Although based mainly

on published sources and limited largely to the Society of Friends, a leading authority in the area of religious grievances with the Civil War draft contends that the Quakers were the only group to insist on an unequivocal exemption from liability to conscription. See Edward Needles Wright, *Conscientious Objectors in the Civil War* (1931; reprint, New York: A. S. Barnes & Co., 1961), pp. 4–5.

35. For the Episcopalians, see ten printed petitions in three groups, sent mainly to Senator James Dixon of Connecticut between December 15, 1863, and January 7, 1864. See also Alonzo Potter, bishop of the Protestant Episcopal Church in Pennsylvania, and William Bacon Stevens, asst. bishop, Diocese of Pennsylvania, Dec. [18–20], 1863. For the Lutherans, see two petitions from Heinrich [Hahn?] et al (Buffalo, N.Y.), Dec. 19, 1863; and six others in the same group dated between Dec. 24, 1863, and Jan. 4, 1864. For the Amana and Ebenezer societies, see Charles W. Winzenriee et al [late Dec. 1863 or early Jan. 1864]. For ministers of the gospel, see Rev. John Pleasanton Duhannel, rector of St. Thomas Church (Newark, Del.), Dec. 10, 1863. With the exception of those sent to Dixon, all petitions were sent to the Senate and House of Representatives and are in ser. 38A–H10.2, SCMAM, RG 46, NA.

36. Bishop Thomas L. Grace (St. Paul, Minn.) to A. Ramsey, Dec. 18, 1863, Alexander Ramsey Papers, MIHS. See also James Bittner et al (Pine Hill, [Pa.]), to Senate and House of Representatives, [Jan. 4, 1864], ser. 38A–G12.8, "Exemption of Ministers of the Gospel from Military Duty," HCMAM, RG 233, NA. Eighteen religious leaders wrote their congressman in an effort to have him secure special exemptions for them. See H. Penfield et al (Niles, Mich.) to C. Upson, Dec. 1, 1863, ser. HR38A–H1.7, HCMAM, RG 233, NA.

37. Fred [Dittenana?] et al (Philadelphia) to Senate and House of Representatives, Feb. 12, 1864, ser. 38A–H1.1, "Tabled Petitions and Memorials Relative to Amendment of the Conscription Law, Dec.7, 1863 . . . to . . . Mar. 3, 1865," HCMAM, RG 233, NA.

38. *OR*, ser. 3, 2:333–34, 358.

39. See printed petitions of John Bell (Philadelphia), Dec. 28, 1863; and petition with sixty-eight signatures from fourteen other Philadelphia hospitals beginning with William V. [Slattery?] et al, Gen. Hosp. (Philadelphia), Dec. 28, 1863. For boat pilots, see Wm. Bennett et al ([n.p.]), [late Dec. 1863 or early Jan. 1864]. All petitions sent to Senate and House of Representatives, ser. 38A–H10.2, SCMAM, RG 46, NA.

40. For a copy of this proclamation, see Basler, *Collected Works* 6:203–4.

41. One group of alien petitioners referred to the Enrollment Act as "undemocratic legislation" because "they declared [their] intent *before* & not *after* [the] draft act." See Henry Holmitz et al (New York) to Congress, Dec. 21, 1863, ser. 38A–H10.2, SCMAM, RG 46, NA. See also Foreign Citizens of New York to R. C. Schenck, Jan. 5, 1864, ser. HR 38A–H1.7, HCMAM, RG 233, NA. Other foreigners were disturbed over the actions of their fellow aliens in attempting to evade service. They demanded that all unnaturalized citizens be held to service. See C. Bartell et al, German Union Association (Baltimore), to House of Representatives, Dec. 1863, ser. HR 38A–H1.7, HCMAM, RG 233, NA. One ardent Unionist protested that all aliens, except temporary residents, should be drafted. Henry P. Scholte ([Pella?], Iowa) to Senate and House of Representatives, Dec. 15, 1863, ser. 38A–H10.2, SCMAM, RG 46, NA.

42. For the War Department's efforts in recruiting blacks during 1863, see Dudley Taylor Cornish, *The Sable Arm: Negro Troops in the Union Army, 1861–1865* (New York: W. W. Norton & Co., 1966), pp. 112–31. See also *OR*, ser. 3, 3:1178–79.

43. *OR*, ser. 3, 3:1052–53, 5:679–82, 560–67.

44. For a detailed discussion of the origins, nature, and abuses of the Veteran Volunteer Program, as well as the legal problems that arose from the distribution of commutation money as bounties, see Shannon, *Organization and Administration* 2:62–69.

45. Gerald F. Linderman, *Embattled Courage: The Experience of Combat in the American Civil War* (New York: Free Press, 1987), pp. 261–64.

46. Thomas Crowl (Cold Harbor, Va.) to Mary Crowl, June 10, 1864, Thomas O. Crowl Papers, PSUL. Leon J. Stout of the Pennsylvania State University Library —Archives kindly verified the dates of Crowl's enlistment, death, and prisoner-of-war status.

47. George Edwards (New York City) to Sister, Aug. 26, 1863; and George Edwards (New York City) to Wife, Aug. 30, 1863, George Edwards Papers, IHS.

48. Will (Camp Hebrew) to ID [Israel D. Roberts], Jan. 14, 1864, William and Jesse M. Roberts Papers, SHSW-LD.

49. Shannon, *Organization and Administration* 2:69.

50. *CG*, 38th Cong., 1st sess., pp. 122–23.

51. *OR*, ser. 3, 5:650–51.

52. Alexander Ramsey's subordinates thought this proposal was extremely impractical. See Henry Swift (Minneapolis) to A. Ramsey, Sept. 11, 1863; and Gen. H. H. Silbey (St. Paul) to Alexander Ramsey, Sept. 12, 1863, Ramsey Papers.

53. [?] Stansifer (Indianapolis) to O. P. Morton, Oct. 19, 1863, Oliver P. Morton Papers, ISL-AD. Ultimately, six thousand Confederate prisoners-of-war would join Union ranks. They were formed into six regiments and assigned to the West, where they served from late 1864 to September 1866. D. Alexander Brown, *Galvanized Yankees* (Urbana: University of Illinois Press, 1963), is the standard account on this subject. Conversely, Southern refugees, many of whom had fled to avoid the draft, had no desire to enter the Union army. On this basis, one group even petitioned Congress with a request to be relieved from liability under federal conscription. See Issac N. Niswander et al (Preble County, Ohio) to Robert Schenck, [Jan. 1864], ser. HR38A–H1.7, HCMAM, RG 233, NA.

54. Murdock, *Patriotism Limited*, pp. 21–24; and Leach, *Conscription*, pp. 311–13.

55. On January 8, 1864, Senator Daniel Clark referred to the pervasiveness of this practice in his state. See *CG*, 38th Cong., 1st sess., p. 140.

56. Based on percentages computed from figures given in *OR*, ser. 3, 5:730.

57. For a discussion of local ordinances in some other areas, see Leach, *Conscription*, pp. 313–18.

58. Solon B. Johnson (Cornwall, Conn.) to W. Buckingham, July 20, 1863, William A. Buckingham Papers, CSL.

59. For a discussion of this law, see Harold Bell Hancock, *Delaware during the Civil War* (Wilmington: Historical Society of Delaware, 1961), p. 139.

60. For a copy of this order, see Basler, *Collected Works* 6:553–54.

61. Opinions vary on the extent to which wages lagged behind prices in the North. Most historians agree that wages increased by 50 to 60 percent. McPherson, *Battle Cry of Freedom*, pp. 448–49, finds that inflation outpaced wages by 20 percent. Paludan, *"People's Contest,"* p. 182, believes that purchasing power decreased significantly because prices rose by almost 100 percent. For other sources on wages and prices, refer to chapter 1 of this study.

62. Henry A. Potter (Maysville, Ala.) to Father, Nov. 8, 1863, Diaries and Letters of Henry Albert Potter, MHC-UM.

63. Hermon (Fort Baker, Washington., D.C.) to Father, Mar. 27, 1863, in Harry F. Jackson and Thomas F. O'Donnell, eds., *Back Home in Oneida: Hermon Clarke and His Letters* (Syracuse: Syracuse University Press, 1965), p. 65.

64. Women's role in the work force increased from a prewar level of 25 percent to almost a third by the war's end. McPherson, *Battle Cry of Freedom*, p. 449. For a comparison of wages between men and women in some occupations, see Fite, *Social and Industrial Conditions*, pp. 186–87; and Paludan, *"People's Contest,"* p. 182–83.

65. O. P. Morton (Indianapolis) to Edwin Stanton, Mar. 6, 1863, Edwin M. Stanton Papers, LC.

66. Brock, *Pacifism in the United States*, pp. 803–4.

67. One individual in Massachusetts paid $50. Sophie (Belchertown) to Sara, June 26, 1864, Charles and Sara T. D. Robinson Papers, KSHS. For an example of a contract used in the creation of a commutation club that had a $100 membership fee, see Thomas J. Mendenhall et al (Circleville, Ohio), May 26, 1864, Thomas J. Mendenhall Papers, OHS. For the sums paid into such organizations in various Ohio localities, see Eugene C. Murdock, *Ohio's Bounty System in the Civil War* (Columbus: Ohio State University Press, 1963), pp. 15–17.

68. *OR*, ser. 3, 3:1176.

CHAPTER TEN. "MEN NOT MONEY"

1. Portions of this chapter are a condensed version of two chapters that appeared in my "A Lesson in Trial and Error: The United States Congress and the Civil War Draft, 1862–1865" (Ph.D. diss., Kent State University, 1976). For information on the individual roll call votes and a full chronicle of the journey of the February 24, 1864, Amendatory Act through Congress, see "Lesson in Trial and Error," pp. 207–82; and for the July 4, 1864, Amendatory Act, see pp. 306–49. For information on the statistical methodology used for the Thirty-eighth Congress, see pp. 482–502.

2. John Sherman (Mansfield, Ohio) W. T. Sherman, Nov. 14, 1863, William T. Sherman Papers, LC; and *OR*, ser. 3, 3:1051.

3. Thomas Smith (Versailles, [Ind.]) to H. S. Lane, Jan. 1, 1863, [1864], Henry S. Lane Papers, IHS; and Officer (Hq., 3d Div., Stevensburgh) to Senator Lane, Dec. 12, 1863; and C. W. Cathcart (Westerville, Ind.) to H. S. Lane, Feb. 5, 1864, Henry S. Lane Papers, IU-LL.

4. W. Hasse, President, "CHICAGO WORKING MEN'S ASSOCIATION," to Senate and House of Representatives, Dec. 30, 1863, ser. HR38A–G12.7, "Petitions and Memorials Relative to the Conscription Law," HCMAM, RG 233, NA.

5. Louis Greiner et al (Newark, N.J.) to Senate and House of Representatives, Jan. 12, 1864, ser. HR38A–H1.1, HCMAM, RG 233, NA.

6. Jacob Leatherman et al and Rev. Jacob Overholtzer et al (Bucks County, Pa.) to Senate and House of Representatives, [Jan. 1864], ser. HR38A–H1.l, HCMAM, RG 233, NA.

7. A. W. Eckert and A. B. King (Seven Mile, Butler County, Ohio) to House of Representatives, Jan. 6, 1864, ser. HR38A–H1.1, HCMAM, RG 233, NA.

8. Ira Brownell, Clerk, copy of Resolutions passed unanimously by the Board of Supervisors of Cass County, Mich. to C. Upson, Dec. 8, 1863, ser. HR38A–H1.1, HCMAM, RG 233, NA; and copy to Sen. Z. Chandler, ser. 38A–H10.2, SCMAM, RG 46, NA. Based on the figures in James Fry's full *Final Report to the Secretary of War by the Provost Marshal General in Journal of the House of Representatives*, 39th Cong., 1st sess., 1866, H. Exec. Doc. 1, vol. 4 (Serials 1251–52), p. 69, 67 percent of the drafted men in Michigan's second district paid commutation in 1863.

9. *CG*, 38th Cong., 1st sess., pp. 3–4, 17.

10. Ibid., pp. 61–62.

11. Ibid., pp. 37, 48.

12. Ibid., pp. 63–67, 85–86; and Geary, "Lesson in Trial and Error," pp. 482–94.

13. *CG*, 37th Cong., 3d sess., p. 1552. Not all of these proposals appear in *CG*, 38th Cong., 1st sess., pp. 12–95, passim, for the period December 8 to 23, 1863. This source needs to be supplemented with the United States House of Representatives, *Journal of the House of Representatives of the United States, being the First Session of the Thirty-eighth Congress*, 38th Cong., 1st sess., 1863 (serial 1179), pp. 20–100, passim.

14. The House Military Committee held only three meetings before the Christmas recess. See entries for December 15, 21, and 23, 1863, in HR38A–E8, "Minutes of the Committee on Military Affairs," HCMAM, RG 233, NA. No record of the minutes of the Senate Military Committee could be found in Record Group 46 at the National Archives. *CG*, 38th Cong., 1st sess., pp. 94–95. Garfield and Schenck worked closely with each other and subsequently shared a house in the capital, which they turned into a "'second army headquarters'" during the Thirty-eighth Congress. For the best treatment on their close relationship, see Allan Peskin, *Garfield* (Kent: Kent State University Press, 1978), pp. 228–30 (quote from Peskin, p. 229).

15. *OR*, ser. 3, 3:1197–98.

16. *CG*, 38th Cong., 1st sess., pp. 95, 100, 119–27.

17. Ibid., pp. 142–43, 229, 257.

18. Ibid., pp. 201, 224, 226–27.

19. This percentage is based on information recorded in Fry's *Final Report*, pp. 177–78.

20. *CG*, 38th Cong., 1st sess., pp. 140–44.

21. Ibid., pp. 200, 202. Quoted from "PERLEY," Washington, D.C. Jan. 13, 1864, in *Boston Daily Journal*, Jan. 14, 1864; and entry for Jan. 13, 1864, in the "Minutes of the Committee on Military Affairs," HR 38A–E8, HCMAM, RG 233, NA.

22. Geary, "Lesson in Trial and Error," pp. 229–31.

23. *CG*, 38th Cong., 1st sess., pp. 579–80, 597–606, 626–30. Six months before, John Murray Forbes suggested to Edwin Stanton that bounties be given to any owners whose slaves entered the army. Stanton replied that this proposal was already under consideration, but he was hoping that the loyal owners in Maryland and Missouri would initiate this proposal. For the government to move unilaterally in this direction would pose an "insurmountable difficulty" in the minds of some, but Stanton did not regard it "as any obstacle whatever." Edwin Stanton (Washington, D.C.) to J. M. Forbes, Aug. 11, 1863, in Sarah Forbes Hughes, ed., *Letters and Recollections of John Murray Forbes* (Boston: Houghton, Mifflin Co., 1899), 2:69–70. Clauses for paying bounties to slave owners and conscripting slaves would appear in Section 24 of the February 24 Amendatory Act.

24. *CG*, 38th Cong., 1st sess., pp. 723–24, 746–56. Wilson's efforts to emancipate slaves who served the Union on this particular vote drew praise from people who were not even his constituents. See, for example, George Lansing Taylor (Seymour, Conn.) to H. Wilson, Feb. 27, 1864, Henry Wilson Papers, LC.

25. *CG*, 38th Cong., 1st sess., pp. 733, 766–68.

26. *U.S. Stats.* 13:6–11. Historians sometimes overlook this group of substitutes, which can have a bearing on their conclusions. Refer to chapter 7 of this study for further information on these 44,403 substitutes for enrolled men.

27. *U.S. Stats.* 13:9. Refer to chapter 9 of this study for petitions from Quakers and other religious groups.

28. *U.S. Stats.* 13:8–9; and Joint Resolution of the Michigan Legislature to Michigan's Senators and Representatives in Congress, Feb. 5, 1864, ser. 38A–H10.2, "Petitions and Memorials Relative to the Amendment of the Conscription Law . . . Dec. 8, 1863 . . . to . . . Feb. 1865," SCMAM, RG 46, NA.

29. *U.S. Stats.* 13:6, 7, 9; and Henry P. Scholte ([Pella?], Iowa) to Senate and House, Dec. 15, 1863, ser. 38A–H10.2, SCMAM, RG 46, NA.

30. *U.S. Stats.* 13:6.

31. *CG*, 38th Cong., 1st sess., p. 747.

32. *OR*, ser. 3, 4:181.

33. Ibid., pp. 137–38, 140–42, 148. For a copy of this congressional resolution, see p. 154.

34. This percentage excluded the 32,678 men who paid commutation, which left a balance of 259,515 men who entered the service. Of this number, 3,416 were actually drafted and 8,911 were substitutes. This percentage was computed on the basis of information contained in *OR*, ser. 3, 4:1266; 5:734.

35. An officer commanding a black regiment reported that the lack of pay was demoralizing many of his men, especially since local charities were refusing to provide for their families. Col. A. S. Hartwell (Hq., 55th Mass. Vols., [Palatka?], Fla.) to Edward W. Kinsley, Apr. 9, 1864, John Andrew Papers, MHS. One soldier with a wife and five children apparently had not been paid for six months. See Sarah Lewis (New Lisbon, Ind.) to O. P. Morton, July 1, 1864, Oliver P. Morton Papers, ISL-AD. See also John O'Connor (Folly Island, S.C.) to Captain Cole, Apr. 6, 1864, John O. Cole Papers, AIHA.

36. In testifying before a congressional committee in March 1864, recently

released Col. A. D. Streight of Indiana elaborated on a theme that Southern authorities consciously followed harsh policies toward their captives. The *New York Times*, in turn, argued that such revelations seriously hampered Northern recruiting. See William Best Hesseltine, *Civil War Prisons: A Study in War Psychology* (1930; reprint, New York: Frederick Ungar Co., 1964), pp. 193–94. See also Capt. E. C. Parker (Libby Prison) to Wife, Nov. 12, 15, 1863, Civil War Papers, BHS; Lucius Fairchild (Madison, Wis.) to J. R. Doolittle, Mar. 18, 1864, James Rood Doolittle Papers, SHSW-LD; and Jesse W. Parker (Camp Parole) to John W. Longyear, Feb. 21, 1864, John Wesley Longyear Papers, MHC-UM.

37. See, for example, *Detroit Free Press*, Jan. 16, Feb. 23, Mar. 12, 15, and May 20, 22, 1864; *New York Tribune*, Feb. 16, 18, 1864; *Columbus Crisis*, Nov. 18, 25, 1863, and May 4, 1864; *Chicago Times*, Jan. 20, Feb. 6, and Mar. 4, 17, 1864; *Portland* (Maine) *Eastern Argus*, Jan. 7, 13, 15, 16, Feb. 11, Mar. 12, and June 22, 1864; and *New York Times*, Feb. 19, Mar. 31, and Apr. 22, 1864.

38. Ibid.; and Henry C. Lea (Philadelphia) to L. Myers, June 30, 1864, Leonard Myers Papers, HSP. Always at the forefront in attempting to reduce his state's levies, Governor John Andrew was informed that no matter how he computed his credits against assigned quotas, Massachusetts would still remain behind in meeting its obligations. See two letters of J. M. Forbes (Washington, D.C.) to Gov. Andrew, Apr. 7, 1864, Andrew Papers. Citizens lavished much praise on governors who managed to reduce quotas. See, for example, Ezra D. Fogg (Providence, R.I.) to T. A. Jenckes, Feb. 11, 1864, Thomas A. Jenckes Papers, LC; D. A. Odgen (Washington, D.C.) to Gov. Seymour, Mar. 2, 1864; and J. B. Young, Clerk, Board of Supervisors (New York City) to Gov. Seymour, Mar. 8, 1864, Letterbook 15, Horatio Seymour Papers, NYSL.

39. Capt. J. B. Merriweather (Jeffersonville, Ind.) to Col. Conrad Baker, June 4, 1864, and to Gov. Morton, June 22, 1864, Morton Papers; and H. Hagans and A. W. Hagans (Brandonsville, W.Va.) to Lt. Col. Joseph Darr, Jr., Mar. 21, 1864, Arthur I. Boreman Papers, WVAH.

40. See, for example, H. Parker [Avery?] ([n.p.]) to J. W. Longyear, June 23, 1864, Longyear Papers; and contract of John Ricole et al (Circleville, [Ohio]), May 14, 1864, Thomas J. Mendenhall Papers, OHS.

41. J. M. Williams (New York) to T. Jenckes, Apr. 6, 1864, Jenckes Papers. See also three letters from William H. Seward (Washington, D.C.) to E. Morgan, May 23, 25, and June 4, 1864, Edwin D. Morgan Papers, NYSL. For labor shortages and their relationship to governmental and manufacturing efforts in encouraging immigration during the war years, see Charlotte Erickson, *American Industry and the European Immigrant, 1860–1865* (New York: Russell & Russell, 1967), especially pp. 3–45.

42. Roy P. Basler, ed., *The Collected Works of Abraham Lincoln* (New Brunswick: Rutgers University Press, 1953), 7:312–13; and *OR*, ser. 3, 4:237–38. The five governors were John Brough of Ohio, Oliver P. Morton of Indiana, Richard Yates of Illinois, William M. Stone of Iowa, and James T. Lewis of Wisconsin.

43. One of the governors, Horatio Seymour of New York, attempted to have the individuals in these units declared exempt from the regular draft while in service, particularly after Lincoln had issued another call for five hundred thousand men on

July 18, 1864. See *OR*, ser. 3, 4:1266–67; and 5:649; and Governor Horatio Seymour, Albany, N.Y., July 19, 1864, to James B. Fry; and Governor Horatio Seymour, Albany, N.Y., July 21, 29, 1864, to C. W. Sandford, Letterbook 15, Seymour Papers.

44. These percentages are based on the information recorded in *OR*, ser. 3, 4:1266–67.

45. B. Mullen (Madison) to Hugh [D. Gallagher], Apr. 30, 1864, Miscellaneous Manuscripts, IHS. See also comments opposing this program in *Chicago Times*, Apr. 24 and May 10, 1864. Indiana men also were reluctant to leave for a hundred days because it would reduce the Home Guard, whose purpose it was to defend local areas against guerrilla activity. James H. McNeely (Evansville, Ind.) to Gov. Morton, June 13, 1864, Morton Papers.

46. Maggie G. Wade (Cleveland, Ohio) to Aunt, May 13, 1864, Benjamin F. Wade Papers, LC.

47. Father [Ira Fuller] (Warren) to Children, Apr. 26, 1864, Fuller Family Papers, KSU.

48. J. B. Armstrong (Bermuda Hundred, Va.) to W. H. Smith, June 18, July 4, 1864, William Henry Smith Papers, OHS. See also Lewis B. Gunckel (Dayton) to W. Smith, Aug. 18, 1864, Smith Papers.

49. *OR*, ser. 3, 4:1266–67.

50. Ibid., pp. 453–54.

51. Ibid. 5:649–50.

52. Stanton, in a conversation with a Massachusetts congressman, had mentioned his discussion with Lincoln on this matter. Samuel Hooper (Washington, D.C.) to John A. Andrew, May 1, 1864, Andrew Papers.

53. Basler, *Collected Works* 7:347–50.

54. Ibid., p. 344 and n. 1 for the interpretation that the president worried over the public reaction if he issued another draft call so soon after the bogus proclamation.

55. Ibid., p. 380; and *OR*, ser. 3, 4:421. Once all the returns were in, 72.6 percent of those held to service under the March call paid commutation, compared to 59.3 percent under the 1863 call. Based on the information recorded in the abridged version of Fry's *Final Report*, *OR*, ser. 3, 5:730, 733.

56. *OR*, ser. 3, 4:421; and Basler, *Collected Works* 7:380. The extant minutes from the House "Committee on Military Affairs and the Militia," HCMAM, RG 233, ser. HR38A–E8 NA, do not reveal any secret meeting with the president. However, Peskin, *Garfield*, pp. 231–32, 642, n. 19, refers to some of Garfield's "Biographical Notes," in which he recalled a secret meeting in June 1864. At this session, the president stated to the military committee that he needed a stronger draft law far more than he needed to be reelected the following fall.

57. For the text of the Smithers bill, see *CG*, 38th Cong., 1st sess., p. 3322.

58. One group of 149 Ohioans, for example, opposed any tampering with the fee. Another group of 12 individuals echoed this request with the added suggestion that any increase in the amount be calculated on the basis of a person's wealth. James LeRetillery et al (Coshocton County, Ohio) to House of Representatives, [June 1864], ser. HR38A–G12.13, "Various Subjects (May 30, 1864 . . . to . . . Feb. 13, 1865) and undated, Packet 2; and G. S. Goodhart et al (Hamilton County, Ohio) to House

of Representatives, [June 1864], ser. HR38A–H1.1, "Tabled Petitions and Memorials Relative to Amendment of the Conscription Law. . . . Dec. 7, 1863 . . . to . . . Mar. 3, 1865," HCMAM, RG 233, NA. For examples of letters in support of repeal, see H. P. Jones (Burlington, Mich.) to John W. Longyear, June 7, 1864, Longyear Papers; name illegible ([n.p.]) to T. A. Jenckes, June 14, 1864, Jenckes Papers; and James Smith (Washington, D.C.) to R. C. Schenck, June 20, 1864, Robert Cummings Schenck Papers, RBHL. Some individuals favored imposing a special tax on all persons who avoided service for whatever reason. See J. H. Pulte (Cincinnati) to S. P. Chase, June 21, 1864; and Henry A. [Lea?], Bounty Fund Commission (Philadelphia) to R. C. Schenck, June 28, 1864, Schenck Papers.

59. The morning after the Senate rejected H.R. 549, Chase discussed this turn of events with Garfield and Schenck. He suggested that Congress should now consider retaining the exemption fee ostensibly to save the conscription bill. Much to his pleasure, they appeared to be interested in his proposal. See entry for June 30, 1864, in David Donald, ed., *Inside Lincoln's Cabinet: The Civil War Diaries of Salmon P. Chase* (New York: Longmans, Green & Co., 1954), pp. 221–22.

60. From early May to mid-June 1864, the Army of the Potomac alone suffered over sixty thousand casualties. A few weeks before the House began its consideration of the draft bill, one influential Republican representative revealed his despair over the military reports that kept arriving from the battlefield. See George W. Julian (Washington, D.C.) to Laura, June 4, 1864, George W. Julian Papers, ISL-ID.

61. See, for example, George Hoadly (Cincinnati) to R. C. Schenck, June 13, 1864, Schenck Papers. As discussed in chapter 12, the exemption fee would be raised as an issue in 1864, but it had little or no influence in determining the war's outcome. After the war, an attempt to use Garfield's close association with a strong draft law against him was made when he ran for reelection. In the 1866 congressional election, conscription was referred to as "Garfield's law," but he was reelected by a 5 to 2 margin. See Peskin, *Garfield*, pp. 274–77.

62. *CG*, 38th Cong., 1st sess., pp. 2832, 3194–96, 3198.

63. Ibid., p. 3206. See also pp. 3487, 3489–91. Wilson also suggested allowing minors to enlist because they would reduce quotas and help to keep skilled workers in the factories. See ibid., pp. 3379–81. For an excellent overall discussion of Wilson's efforts to promote Southern recruitment to keep skilled workers at home, see Richard H. Abbott, "Massachusetts and the Recruitment of Southern Negroes, 1863–1865," *Civil War History* 14 (1968): 197–210.

64. Geary, "Lesson in Trial and Error," pp. 311–12. The nonappearances at the House caucus occurred prior to Schenck reporting the bill. See PERLEY, undated dispatch in *Boston Daily Journal*, June 20, 1864. See also PERLEY, dispatches dated June 23, 24, 1864, in *Boston Daily Journal*, for other comments on the caucuses.

65. *CG*, 38th Cong., 1st sess., pp. 3145–48.

66. Ibid., p. 3357.

67. Geary, "Lesson in Trial and Error," pp. 313–14.

68. *CG*, 38th Cong., 1st sess., pp. 2824, 3198–99, 3206, 3381–85, 3387.

69. Ibid., pp. 3272–75, 3279.

70. Ibid., p. 3279. Evidently there existed a serious problem with recruiters from

other areas in the District of Columbia in 1864. On various occasions, the *Washington, D.C. Evening Star* warned its readers that "If this District does not . . . protect itself by insisting that foreign recruiting agents shall stop their work here [in recruiting Negro male residents], it will have a time of it in filling up the heavy quota allotted to it." See editions for Jan. 15, 23, Feb. 17, and Mar. 3–5, 14, 16, 1864. Quote from Jan. 23 issue.

71. *CG*, 38th Cong., 1st sess., pp. 3432–45.

72. Ibid., pp. 3278–80, 3322, 3353–54, 3357, 3431–32. On June 28, PERLEY predicted in the *Boston Daily Journal*, June 29, 1864, that the combination of Southern recruitment and "high bounties" would ensure the passage of the Smithers bill.

73. *CG*, 38th Cong., 1st sess., pp. 3485–91.

74. Quote from Section 17 of the February 24 Amendatory Act, *U.S. Stats.* 13:6.

75. For the text of the July 4 Amendatory Act, see *U.S. Stats.* 13:379–81.

76. Peskin, *Garfield*, p. 226, relates a story of how Garfield offended some legislators by recommending the discontinuation of bounties in his first days as a congressman. Only later did he realize "that the draft was the most politically sensitive issue facing the Congress."

77. William Seward (Washington, D.C.) to Thurlow Weed, July 8, 1862, in *William Henry Seward* (New York: Derby and Miller, 1891), 3:115.

78. For example, 75 percent of the residents who enlisted from one New England town in 1865 were 19 and under. See Emily J. Harris, "Sons and Soldiers: Deerfield, Massachusetts and the Civil War," *Civil War History* 30 (1984): 168. In a study of four Ohio districts, Hugh G. Earnhart, "Commutation: Democratic or Undemocratic?" *Civil War History* 12 (1966): 137, finds that substitutes tended to be drawn from age groups that were "in their late teens and early twenties."

CHAPTER ELEVEN. COMMUTATION'S REPEAL AND CLASS DISCRIMINATION

1. Roy P. Basler, ed., *The Collected Works of Abraham Lincoln* (New Brunswick: Rutgers University Press, 1953), 6:447–48.

2. John G. Nicolay and John Hay, *Abraham Lincoln: A History* (New York: Century Co., 1886), 7:49.

3. Particularly among the Peace Democrats, the change in editorial opinion began months before Congress finally repealed the exemption fee. As early as October 28, 1863, Samuel Medary defended commutation by arguing that either its repeal or an increase in its price would definitely harm poor men. When Congress limited the exemption period in the February 24, 1864, Amendatory Act, Medary contended that it was discriminatory. See *Columbus Crisis*, Oct. 28, 1863, Jan. 20, Feb. 24, and Mar. 2, 1864. For similar charges by other Democratic editors, see, for example, *Chicago Times*, Feb. 20, 1864; and *Detroit Free Press*, Jan. 13 and Feb. 25, 1864.

4. *Chicago Times*, June 30 and July 1, 1864. See also editions for June 23, 27, 28, 1864.

5. *Detroit Free Press*, June 24, 1864. See also editions for May 26, June 15, 23, 24, 29, and July 7, 14, 1864.

6. *Columbus Crisis*, July 13, 1864. See also editions for June 15, 22, 29, 1864.

7. *Washington, D.C. Daily National Intelligencer*, June 20, 1864. See also editions for June 22, 23, 25, 27, 1864.

8. *Cleveland Plain Dealer*, June 6, 1864. See also editions for June 11, 14, 24, 27, 28, 30, and July 1, 6, 9, 19, 1864. No reliable evidence could be found to substantiate whether bounty brokers actually engaged in lobbying activities.

9. *New York Herald*, June 15 and July 4, 1864. See also *Portland,* (Maine) *Eastern Argus*, May 26 and June 13, 27, 1864.

10. *Cincinnati Daily Commercial*, June 4, 24, 25, 1864. See also editions for July 4, 7, 1864.

11. *New York Tribune*, June 22, 29, and July 4, 1864; and *Cleveland Leader*, June 14, 23, 28, and July 16, 1864.

12. *Boston Daily Journal*, June 16, 23, 25, 1864.

13. *Washington, D.C. Evening Star*, June 24, 29, 1864.

14. *(Washington, D.C.) Daily Morning Chronicle*, June 23, 24, 1864. See also editions for June 10 and July 9, 18, 1864.

15. *New York Times*, June 21, 22, 28, 30, 1864.

16. James W. Geary, "A Lesson in Trial and Error: The United States Congress and the Civil War Draft, 1862–1865" (Ph.D. diss., Kent State University, 1976), pp. 468–74.

17. Peter Levine, "Draft Evasion in the North during the Civil War, 1863–1865," *Journal of American History* 67 (1981): 818.

18. Fred A. Shannon, *The Organization and Administration of the Union Army, 1861–1865* (1928; reprint, Gloucester, Mass.: Peter Smith, 1965), 2:16, 19–22.

19. Robert E. Sterling, "Civil War Draft Resistance in the Middle West" (Ph.D. diss., Northern Illinois University, 1974), pp. 138, 149, 161–64, 659–60.

20. Eugene C. Murdock, "Was It a 'Poor Man's Fight'?" *Civil War History* 10 (1964): 241–45. For specific criticism of Murdock's methodology, see Michael H. Frisch, *Town into City: Springfield, Massachusetts, and the Meaning of Community, 1840–1880* (Cambridge: Harvard University Press, 1972), p. 69; and Sterling, "Civil War Draft Resistance in the Middle West," pp. 162–63.

21. Hugh G. Earnhart, "Commutation: Democratic or Undemocratic?" *Civil War History* 12 (1966): 132–42. For general criticism of Murdock's and Earnhart's studies, see Levine, "Draft Evasion," p. 818, n. 6.

22. Earnhart, "Commutation," p. 140.

23. Ibid., pp. 141–42.

24. Ibid., pp. 132–34, 138; Eugene C. Murdock, *One Million Men: The Civil War Draft in the North* (Madison: State Historical Society of Wisconsin, 1971), pp. 202–3; and Eugene C. Murdock, *Ohio's Bounty System in the Civil War* (Columbus: Ohio State University Press, 1963), p 6.

25. [J. Hewitt] (Cincinnati, Ohio) to Brother, [June 20?], 1864, Joseph Hewitt Papers, IHS.

26. These revised percentages are derived from the raw data in Earnhart, "Commutation," p. 139.

27. *Cincinnati Daily Commercial*, Oct. 22, 1864.

28. Prices taken from Murdock, *Ohio's Bounty System*, pp. 31, 36.

29. *Washington, D.C. Evening Star*, Mar. 10, 1865; and *Portland* (Maine) *Eastern Argus*, Mar. 16, 1865.

30. Earnhart, "Commutation," p. 136.

31. James Bamon ([Oil City, Pa.]) to H. Stroman, Apr. 5, 1865, Henry Stroman Papers, OHS.

32. *Detroit Free Press*, July 21, 27, 1864.

33. *New York Herald*, Feb. 14, 1865; and *New York Tribune*, Jan. 2, 1865.

34. *New York Herald*, Jan. 4, 1865.

35. *Boston Daily Journal*, July 27, 1864.

36. Substitute prices taken from Murdock, *Ohio's Bounty System*, p. 36; *Cleveland Leader*, July 14 and Sept. 1, 1864; and *Cleveland Plain Dealer*, July 25, 1864.

37. This percentage is based on revised calculations from the tables in Earnhart, "Commutation," pp. 141–42.

38. For a discussion of this law, see *Boston Daily Journal*, Feb. 16, 1865; *New York Herald*, Mar. 4, 1865; and *New York Tribune*, Feb. 16, 1865.

39. *New York Herald*, Feb. 18, 1865.

40. *Cleveland Plain Dealer*, May 31 and June 15, 1864; and *Portland* (Maine) *Eastern Argus*, June 17, 1864.

41. *Detroit Free Press*, Feb. 18 and Mar. 1, 5, 7, 10, 14, 1865; and *Chicago Times*, Jan. 9, 10, and Mar. 18, 1865.

42. *Washington, D.C. Daily Morning Chronicle*, Feb. 13, 1865; *Washington, D.C. Daily National Intelligencer*, Feb. 2, 3, 11, 16, 20 and Mar. 3, 10, 1865; and *Washington, D.C. Evening Star*, Jan. 3, 10, 24, Feb. 4, 7, 11, 15, 16, 20, and Mar. 8, 9, 10, 15, 1865. For prices in Ohio, see, for example, *Cleveland Plain Dealer*, Feb. 7, 9, 1865; *Cleveland Leader*, Sept. 3 and Dec. 30, 1864; and *Cincinnati Daily Commercial*, Mar. 1, 1865.

43. Contract of F. W. Hamilton et al (Indianapolis), Feb. 23, 1865, Lyndsey M. Brown Papers, ISL–ID. For comments on these organizations, see G. W. Miller (Washington, Pa.) to Sam, July 19, 1864, Samuel J. Randall Papers, UPL; and Wm. Allee (Akron, [Ohio]) to Bradley Reed, Feb. 17, 1865, William Allee Letter, Miscellaneous Manuscripts, OHS.

44. *New York Tribune*, Jan. 17, 1865; *New York Herald*, Feb. 14, 15, 22, 1865; and *New York Times*, Apr. 15, 1865.

45. *OR*, ser. 3, 4:1049; and N. G. Westler (Neseopeek), Sept. 22, 1864, to Hendrick B. Wright, Hendrick Bradley Wright Papers, HSP.

46. See, for example, E. G. Cure ([n.p.]) to Brother, July 7, 1864, John T. Wilder Letters, Miscellaneous Manuscripts, ISL-ID; and Matt Rhodes ([n.p.]) to John Rhodes, Sept. 14, 1864, John R. Rhodes Papers, RBHL.

47. *OR*, ser. 3, 5:730–39.

48. The three tables follow a version of the format that James B. McPherson developed. The raw data for Ohio is from Earnhart, "Commutation," pp. 138–42. It is rearranged and recalculated with the tabular format generally used elsewhere in the present study. For the data from Michigan and New York, see Michigan, Second District—"Descriptive Books of Drafted Men, 1863–1865," 3 vols., entry 5992; Michigan, Third District—"Descriptive Book of Drafted Men, 1863–1864 [1865?]," 1 vol.,

entry 6014; New York, Thirtieth District—"Descriptive Book of Drafted Men, Showing Exemptions, Aug. 1863–June 1864," 1 vol., entry 2991," and "Register of Drafted Men, Showing Men Who Were Exempted from Service and Men Who Failed to Report, Mar.-Apr. 1865," 1 vol., entry 2292. All sources are part of RG 110, NA.

49. R. T. Mead (Grant General Hospital, N.Y.) to Father, Feb. 21, 1865, Richard Titus Mead Papers, MHC-UM.

50. F. N. Field (Knoxville, Tenn.) to Brother, Sept. 15, 1864, Frederick N. Field Papers, MHC-UM.

51. Entry for Jan. 14, 1865, in Albert D. Baughman Diary, MHC-UM.

52. [Henry C. Lea], "Volunteering and Conscription," *United States Service Magazine* 1 (1864): 239–42; and "A Workingman's Ideas of Conscription," *Magazine of History* 16 (1917): 103–17 (reprint of 1863 article that appeared in *Fincher's Trade Review: The National Organ of the Producing Classes*).

CHAPTER TWELVE. ALIENATION AND THE DRAFT

1. Numerous excellent studies cover various aspects of the 1864 election. William Frank Zornow's *Lincoln and the Party Divided* (Norman: University of Oklahoma Press, 1954), remains unchallenged as the most thorough general history on the subject. It should be supplemented by at least a dozen articles that he wrote on various aspects of the contest. The best succinct treatment can be found in James M. McPherson's *Battle Cry of Freedom: The Civil War Era* (New York: Ballantine Books, 1988), pp. 774–806. It is particularly strong on military events leading up to the election and discusses the relative importance of certain subjects, such as the prisoner-of-war issue in the election. For divisions within the Republican party and the nascent peace movement in the summer of 1864, J. G. Randall and David Donald, *The Civil War and Reconstruction*, 2d ed. (Lexington: D. C. Heath & Co., 1969), pp. 469–79, also should be consulted. Of the numerous specialized studies, Joel H. Silbey's *A Respectable Minority: The Democratic Party in the Civil War Era, 1860–1868* (New York: W. W. Norton & Co., 1977), pp. 118–76, is particularly good on the splits within the party, its success in becoming more unified in 1864, and the defection of the War Democrats. For a work that emphasizes the cultural and symbolic dimensions of the election, and its more colorful aspects such as bond rallies and meetings, see Jean H. Baker, *Affairs of Party: The Political Culture of Northern Democrats in the Mid-Nineteenth Century* (Ithaca: Cornell University Press, 1983), pp. 269–316.

2. For a copy of this August 23 memorandum and a detailed discussion of Lincoln's plan to send a representative to meet with Jefferson Davis to negotiate a peace agreement, see Roy P. Basler, ed., *The Collected Works of Abraham Lincoln* (New Brunswick: Rutgers University Press, 1953), 7:514–19.

3. William Seward (Washington, D.C.) to Wife, Aug. 22, 1864, in Frederick W. Seward, *William Henry Seward* (New York: Derby & Miller, 1891), 3:240–41.

4. Carey S. Goodrich (Ulinhister, Ind.) to Gov. Morton, July 27, 1864; Miss E. C. Sims (Jefferson) to Gov. Morton, Aug. 15, 1864, Oliver P. Morton Papers, ISL-AD; James Haly (Napolean, Ohio) to R. K. Scott, July 14, 1864, Robert Kingston Scott

Papers, OHS; and Schuyler Colfax (South Bend, Ind.) to A. Lincoln, Sept. 26, 1864, Robert Todd Collection of the Papers of Abraham Lincoln, ser. 2, LC.

5. Quoted from *Detroit Free Press*, July 22, 1864. See also G. W. Miller (Washington, Pa.) to Sam, July 19, 1864, Samuel J. Randall Papers, UPL. For the origin and general activities of the Union Leagues, see Frank L. Klement, *Dark Lanterns: Secret Political Societies, Conspiracies, and Treason Trials in the Civil War* (Baton Rouge: Louisiana State University Press, 1984), pp. 34–63. He argues, albeit unconvincingly, that their propaganda "deserved a major share of the credit for the resounding Republican triumph" in the fall of 1864. The Union Leagues were only one aspect among many major factors, including military victories, that accounted for Republican success at the polls.

6. Frank L. Klement, *The Copperheads in the Middle West* (1960; reprint, Gloucester, Mass.: Peter Smith, 1972), pp. 198–208, and in a series of articles, contends that these organizations were largely a figment of the Republican imagination that had been created to convey the impression of Democratic disloyalty. He develops his thesis that these groups emanated largely from the "Republican world of make believe" in his later monograph, *Dark Lanterns* (quote from p. 144). For a critical assessment of Klement's thesis, see McPherson, *Battle Cry of Freedom*, pp. 782–84.

7. For the July 18 order, see Basler, *Collected Works*, 7:448–49. On the importance of the draft as a political issue in the summer of 1864, see Zornow, *Lincoln and the Party Divided*, p. 109.

8. For soldiers' letters, see Weldon R. R. Matteson ([n.p.]) to Sister, Sept. 4, 1864, Civil War Papers, BHS: Joseph R. Hawley (Bermuda Hundred, Va.) to W. A. Buckingham, Aug. 4, 1864, Special Folder, Lot D, William A. Buckingham Papers, CSL. For one soldier's opinion that Lincoln had made a mistake in ordering the July call, see Charlie [C. S. Medary] (Same old camp, Va.) to Father, July 20, 1864, Samuel Medary Papers, OHS. For civilians in favor of a draft call, see Horatio Woodman ([n.p.]) to Gov. Andrew, July 30, 1864, John Andrew Papers, MHS; and Issac N. Arnold (Chicago) to Montgomery Blair, July 13, 1864, Blair Family Papers, LC.

9. For a discussion of this speech, see chapter 1 of this study. On September 10, General Grant wrote Edwin Stanton to urge that the draft not be postponed, stating that only one in five new soldiers currently being recruited were arriving in the army because of "desertion." See *OR*, ser. 3, 4:706.

10. Ibid., ser. 3, 4:709–13.

11. Ibid., p. 715.

12. Schuyler Colfax (South Bend, Ind.) to the President, July 25, 1864, Lincoln Papers, ser. 2. For Colfax's concern over the possible repercussions of the draft on the forthcoming elections, see Schuyler Colfax (South Bend, Ind.) to Charles M. Heaton, Sr., July 22 and Aug. 9, Schuyler Colfax Letters, NIHS.

13. *OR*, ser. 3, 4:742–43. Despite Blaine's nervousness over the possible political consequences of the draft, he was aware of the military's view on the necessity for enforcing conscription. See Maj. Gen. O. Howard (Hq. Dept. and Army of the Tennessee before Atlanta, Ga.) to J. Blaine, Aug. 24, 1864, James G. Blaine Papers, LC.

14. McPherson, *Battle Cry of Freedom*, pp. 804–5; and Silbey, *Respectable Minority*, pp. 158–61. Lincoln did not limit his activities to soldiers. On October 10, 1864, he instructed Gideon Welles to cooperate with a representative who was trying to obtain the votes of sailors who were on duty with the Mississippi and blockading squadrons. See Basler, *Collected Works*, 8:43.

15. See *OR*, ser. 3, 5:735–37, for a breakdown of states that conducted a draft under this call.

16. On quotas, see, for example, W. R. Morrison (St. Louis) to A. Lincoln, Sept. 30, 1864, William Ralls Morrison Papers, ISHL; twelve letters and telegrams between Sept. 3, 1864, and Mar. 16, 1865, originating from Indianapolis in John H. Holliday Papers, ISL-ID; and W. M. Stone (Davenport, Iowa) to James B. Fry, Aug. 24, 1864, in *OR*, ser. 3, 4:636–38.

17. The draft was not a factor in most states, but it was in Pennsylvania. See Zornow, *Lincoln and the Party Divided*, pp. 191–94; and Arnold M. Shankman, *The Pennsylvania Antiwar Movement, 1861–1865* (Rutherford: Fairleigh Dickinson University Press, 1980), pp. 190–93.

18. Eugene C. Murdock, *One Million Men: The Civil War Draft in the North* (Madison: State Historical Society of Wisconsin, 1971), p. 202, discusses some of the Democratic press opposition to Fenton and Kellogg on the commutation issue.

19. United States Congress, *The Biographical Directory of the American Congress* (Washington, D.C.: Government Printing Office, 1971), pp. 935, 1219.

20. *OR*, ser. 3, 4:743.

21. Whiting was in ill health during the last year of the war and was unable to do much work. Indeed, the only written opinion that he issued between August 1, 1864, and the November election concerned how to interpret the crediting of a one-year recruit or drafted man against a three-year standard. See *OR*, ser. 3, 4:562–64. He did not issue a formal statement indicating that there would be no more drafts and, in his capacity as solicitor general, would have lacked the authority to do so anyway. Supposedly, he mentioned this possibility in October 1864, and it was reported as a "Special Dispatch" from Washington. However, it did not appear until November 5, 1864, when the *New York Times* merely reprinted the dispatch without comment, suggesting that Republican strategists may have fabricated the announcement. When Lincoln issued another troop call in December, after the elections were over, the Democrats cited Whiting's oral statement as just another example of how Lincoln and the Republican party were continuing to deceive the people. See, for example, *Cleveland Plain Dealer*, Jan. 20, 1865, and *Columbus Crisis*, Dec. 28, 1864, and Jan. 4, 1865.

22. *(Columbus) Crisis*, Oct. 5, 1864.

23. For a copy of the December 19 order, see Basler, *Collected Works*, 8:171–72; and Fry's orders of Dec. 23, 1864, and Jan. 2, 1865, in *OR*, ser. 3, 4:1008–9, 1035. After the war in his *Final Report to the Secretary of War by the Provost Marshal General*, Fry explained how he arrived at his computations. See *OR*, ser. 3, 5:640–46, 719–20.

24. See, for example, *OR*, ser. 3, 4:1010–11, 1039–42, 1050–53, 1090–91, 1100–1102, 1103–5, 1141–43, 1171–72, 1183–84; *Cleveland Plain Dealer*, Jan. 9 and Feb.

8, 1865; John T. Horner (St. Paul) to A. Ramsey, Jan. 10, 1865, Alexander Ramsey Papers, MIHS; H. A. Smith et al (Chelsea) to J. W. Longyear, Feb. 8, 1865; and petition of Citizens of Sylvan, Washtenaw Co., Mich., to Abraham Lincoln, Feb. 8, 1865, John Wesley Longyear Papers, MHC-UM; and D. D. Pratt (Logansport) to Governor Morton, Apr. 11, 1865, Morton Papers.

25. *OR*, ser. 3, 4:1045–48, 1061–65, 1073–75, 1092–96, 1122–28, 1144–46, 1171–72; and Basler, *Collected Works*, 8:231, 271–72.

26. *Cincinnati Daily Commercial*, Feb. 7, 1865.

27. *New York Herald*, Jan. 28 and Feb. 3, 1865; *Cleveland Plain Dealer*, Jan. 25 and Feb. 2, 1865; *Detroit Free Press*, Jan. 9 and Feb. 1, 1865; *Cincinnati Daily Commercial*, Feb. 4, 8, 13, 14, 1865; *New York Tribune*, Jan. 31 and Feb. 4, 1865; *Portland* (Maine) *Eastern Argus*, Feb. 6, 13, 1865; and *Chicago Times*, Feb. 10, 28, and Mar. 2, 1865.

28. *New York Herald*, Feb. 3, 1865; *Cleveland Plain Dealer*, Feb. 8, 17, 1865; and William E. Chandler (Philadelphia) to Montgomery Blair, Feb. 4, 1865, Blair Family Papers. For editors who tended to defend Fry, see *Washington, D.C. Daily Morning Chronicle*, Jan. 26, 30, 1865; and *New York Times*, Feb. 4, 17, 1865.

29. Gideon Welles (Navy Dept., Washington, D.C.) to Alexander H. Rice, Jan. 30, 1865, Chairman of the House Committee on Naval Affairs, HR38A–E13.11, "Letters Relating to Naval Recruiting Problems and Frauds," RG 233, NA. In this same series, see also Capt. J. P. McKinstry (USS *North Carolina*) to Rear Admiral Paulding, Jan. 14, 1865; E. Delafield Smith (U.S. District Attorney, N.Y.) to Rear Admiral Paulding, Jan. 18, 1865; and H. Paulding (New York) to Gideon Welles, Jan. 20, 1865. See also A. N. Smith (Washington, D.C.) to Gideon Welles, Feb. 11, 1865, entry 280, RG 24, NA; and *OR*, ser. 3, 4:1176–77. For a brief description of the naval frauds in New York City, see Eugene C. Murdock, *Patriotism Limited, 1862–1865: The Civil War Draft and the Bounty System* (Kent: Kent State University Press, 1967), pp. 134–35.

30. Basler, *Collected Works*, 8:264–65.

31. For one of the better general discussions of disillusionment in the Union army in 1864, see Gerald F. Linderman, *Embattled Courage: The Experience of Combat in the American Civil War* (New York: Free Press, 1987), especially pp. 216–34. See also Reid Mitchell, *Civil War Soldiers* (New York: Viking, 1988), pp. 56, 65–70.

32. By early 1865, for example, a three-year recruit in New York City could command as much as $1,526. The town of Turner, Maine, gave $500 to a man who enlisted for one year. Each recruit in Princeton, New Jersey, received $1,000. This sum was also given to a drafted man. Unlike those who were drafted earlier, he could not complain as much because Lincoln was now legally bound to conscript for one year only rather than three years. *New York Herald*, Feb. 15, 1865; *Portland* (Maine) *Eastern Argus*, Mar. 4, 1865; *Washington, D.C. Daily Morning Chronicle*, Feb. 27, 1865; and *U.S. Stats.* 13:379.

33. One town's "capacity to sacrifice her 'sons' was exhausted" as early as the summer of 1863. For some of the major trends that occurred in filling quotas with nonresidents after 1863, see Emily J. Harris, "Sons and Soldiers: Deerfield, Massachusetts and the Civil War," *Civil War History* 30 (1984): 157–71. For an excellent review

that covers many of the various effects of the war on the home front, see Phillip Shaw Paludan, *"A People's Contest": The Union and Civil War, 1861–1865* (New York: Harper & Row, 1988), especially pp. 32–38, 180–94, 324–32.

34. Hermon (Bermuda Hundred, Va.) to Father, Aug. 22, 1864; and Hermon (Petersburg) to Father, Sept. 1, 1864, in Harry F. Jackson and Thomas F. O'Donnell, eds., *Back Home in Oneida: Hermon Clarke and His Letters* (Syracuse: Syracuse University Press, 1965), pp. 154–58. For other examples of the soldiers' pay problem at this point of the war, see J. N. Barritt (Camp near White River, Ark.) to brother William M., Sept. 9 and Sept. 14, 1864, Miscellaneous Manuscripts, LC; and George Fowle (Petersburg, Va.) to Eliza, July 1 and Aug. 22, 1864, in Margery Greenleaf, ed., *Letters to Eliza from a Union Soldier, 1862–1865* (Chicago: Follett, 1970), pp. 111–13, 126–32. From Gov. John Andrew's pride and joy, the all-black Fifty-fourth Massachusetts, came a letter from a former Indiana resident who complained that he had not received any pay in over a year and a half. Wm. E. Erdington (Moris [sic] Island, N.C.) to Gov. Morton, Aug. 21, 1864, Morton Papers. On the absence of speedy payments to heirs, see, for example, Elizabeth A. Conley (New Thurker, R.I.) to T. A. Jenckes, Sept. 6, 1864, Thomas A. Jenckes Papers, LC; Sam S. Lacy (Lansing, Mich.) to J. W. Longyear, Dec. 7, 1864; and F. Russell (Detroit) to John Longyear, Feb. 28, 1865, Longyear Papers.

35. C. Thonssen (Cincinnati) to Lt. Gen. U. S. Grant, Jan. 26, 1865, entry 106 in "Letters Received by General Grant Concerning Exchanges of Prisoners, January 1865," RG 108, NA. On letters to congressmen, see, for example, F. G. Sherman (Providence, R.I.) to T. A. Jenckes, Dec. 10, 1864, Jenckes Papers; Nellie Carley (Michigan City, Ind.) to Schuyler Colfax, Sept. 28, 1864, Miscellaneous Manuscripts, RBHL; Lucius Fairchild (Madison) to J. Doolittle, Oct. 4, 1864, with Dec. 16, 1864, enclosures from Capt. Albert Grant, Nineteenth Wis. Vol. Inf. and Capt. J. D. Wood et al, C.S. Military Prison (Danville), to J. Doolittle, James Rood Doolittle Papers, SHSW-LD.

36. For the events leading up to the resumption of prisoner-of-war exchanges, see McPherson, *Battle Cry of Freedom*, pp. 798–801; and William Best Hesseltine, *Civil War Prisons: A Study in War Psychology* (1930; reprint, New York: Frederick Ungar Co., 1964), 220, 223–24, 229–32.

37. Maris A. Vinovskis, "Have Social Historians Lost the Civil War? Some Preliminary Demographic Speculations," *Journal of American History* 76 (1989): 36–39.

38. Estimates vary on the number of Union soldiers who perished during the war. Vinovskis, "Have Social Historians Lost the Civil War?" pp. 40–41, believes that one in six died; while Paludan, *"People's Contest,"* pp. 316–17, contends that the figure is closer to one in nine. For a succinct overview of the difficulties in determining the number of men in the Union army and casualties, see E. B. Long, *The Civil War Day by Day: An Almanac, 1861–1865* (Garden City, N.Y.: Doubleday & Company, 1971), pp. 705–13.

39. Harris, "Sons and Soldiers," p. 157.

40. Most recruiting drives that sought to raise bounty money through the private sector took place prior to July 1864. Murdock, *One Million Men*, p. 155, identifies the increasing reluctance to contribute voluntarily in the last months of the war, which

in turn led to a greater reliance on local taxes for raising bounty funds. For some examples of special assessments that were enacted by 1865, see Murdock, *One Million Men*, pp. 3–5, 166, 176–77. See pp. 166–69 for examples of private recruiting efforts in certain areas that continued in 1865, in conjunction with government-sponsored programs. See also *Cleveland Plain Dealer*, July 25, 1864, Jan. 17, and Feb. 7, 9, 1865; *Detroit Free Press*, Feb. 7, 18 and Mar. 11, 12, 14, 1865; *Cincinnati Daily Commercial*, Feb. 8 and Mar. 11, 1865; *New York Herald*, Mar. 4, 1865. Local committees received donations from all sectors of a community. In late 1864, 170 individuals in one small Ohio township contributed to the local bounty fund. Most gave $25, and a few gave $10, $50, or $100. Subscription List for Washington Township, Ohio [December 1864?], Charles W. Larsh Papers, OHS. Requests for donations were not necessarily confined to draft-liable men alone. In another rural Ohio township the local recruiting committee even approached a spinster, who felt compelled to donate to the bounty fund. See Betsey Cowles Diary, Austinburg, Ohio, entries for Feb. 7, 8, 13, 14, 1865, in Betsey Mix Cowles Papers, KSU.

41. *OR*, ser. 3, 4:1040–42.

42. After the war, Fry discussed the trend of paper credits, which became exacerbated during the last nine months of the war. He believed that some local recruiting committees had been "selected and instructed to 'fill the quota' . . . [and] to satisfy their fellow-citizens and relieve them from the draft, apparently lost sight of the wants of the service, and devoted themselves to securing credits to the exclusion of enlisting men." See *OR*, ser. 3, 5:652.

43. Michael H. Frisch, *Town into City: Springfield, Massachusetts, and the Meaning of Community, 1840–1880* (Cambridge: Harvard University Press, 1972), p. 64.

44. Richard H. Abbott, *Cobbler in Congress: The Life of Henry Wilson, 1812–1875* (Lexington: University Press of Kentucky, 1972), p. 141.

45. J. M. Forbes ([Washington, D.C.]) to Gov. Andrew, Apr. 7, 1864; Major Ware (Washington, D.C.) to Gov. Andrew, June 28, 1864; and J. M. Forbes (Boston) to Governor, July 2, 1864, Andrew Papers.

46. For Fry's negative assessment of this program, see *OR*, ser. 3, 5:662. For an excellent discussion of Massachusetts's involvement in this program, see Richard H. Abbott, "Massachusetts and the Recruitment of Southern Negroes, 1863–1865," *Civil War History* 14 (1968): 197–210.

47. N. L. Jeffries (Washington, D.C.) to R. C. Schenck, Feb. 25, 1865, with Feb. 25, 1865, enclosure from Col. R. D. Mussey (Nashville) to Gen. Fry, Robert Cummings Schenck Papers, RBHL; Gen. Joseph R. Hawley (Bermuda Hundred, Va.) to W. Buckingham, Aug. 4, 1864, Buckingham Papers; *Washington, D.C. Daily National Intelligencer*, July 9, 1864; *Detroit Free Press*, July 31, 1864; *New York Herald*, July 22, 1864; and *Cleveland Plain Dealer*, Jan. 14, 1865.

48. *Columbus Crisis*, Aug. 31, 1864.

49. *OR*, ser. 3, 4:631.

50. Ibid., ser. 1, vol. 43, p. 2, pp. 314, 360; and ser. 3, 4:644.

51. Ibid., ser. 3, 5:663–64.

52. Abbott, *Cobbler in Congress*, pp. 140–41, discusses this commission; and

A. N. Smith (Washington, D.C.) to Gideon Welles, Feb. 3, 1865, entry 280, "Fair Copies of Letters Sent to the Secretary of the Navy, Oct. 4, 1862–Mar. 1, 1870," 1 vol., RG 24, NA.

53. Wm. C. Kocher (Huntington, Ind.) to Gov. Morton, Apr. 11, 1865, Morton Papers; *CG*, 38th Cong., 2d sess., pp. 978–80, 1034–35; *U.S. Stats.* 13:7–8, 380.

54. *Cleveland Plain Dealer*, Feb. 15, 1865; *Washington, D.C. Evening Star*, July 22, 1864; *Washington, D.C. Daily National Intelligencer*, July 7, 25, 1864; and Capt. James Evans, Prov. Mar. for Second District, Grafton, W.Va., Aug. 26, 1864, to Gov. Boreman, Arthur I. Boreman Papers, WVAH. In the immediate wake of the Southern recruitment policy, West Virginia was one of several states that experienced a problem in keeping agents from other states away from its resident black population. In late July 1864, for example, Captain Evans began arresting these visitors, who were enticing physically fit blacks to leave West Virginia for the purpose of enlisting elsewhere as substitutes. See Evans, Grafton, W.Va., July 29, 1864, to Major [John N.] Showalter; and deposition of July 30, 1864, Boreman Papers.

55. *Washington, D.C. Daily Morning Chronicle*, Mar. 1, 2, 1865; *Chicago Times*, Feb. 16, 1865; *Portland* (Maine) *Eastern Argus*, Jan. 2, 1865; *Columbus Crisis*, Dec. 28, 1864; and *U.S. Stats.* 13:498–99.

56. Petitions of J. S. Rowley et al (Wirt, Allegany Co., N.Y.) to House of Representatives, Dec. 29, 1864; and M. Baxter et al (Grant County, Wis.) to Senate and House of Representatives, Jan. 14, 1865, in ser. HR 38A–G12.7, "Petitions and Memorials Relative to Amendment of the Conscription Law, Dec. 15, 1863 . . . to . . . Mar. 1865," HCMAM, RG 233, NA; and E. G. Ryan (Milwaukee, Wis.) to T. O. Howe, Dec. 17, 1864; and T. O. Howe (Washington, D.C.) to E. G. Ryan, Jan. 1865, Timothy Otis Howe Papers, SHSW-LD.

57. Desertions increased over 63 percent in the last nine months of the war. For the basis of this calculation, see chapter 2 of this study.

58. *New York Times*, Jan. 6, 1865, and editions for Feb. 9, 10, and Apr. 2, 1865. For other examples, see especially *Cleveland Leader*, Nov. 30, 1864, Jan. 5, and Feb. 1, 1865; *Cleveland Plain Dealer*, Jan. 7, 11, and Feb. 6, 1865; *Columbus Crisis*, Dec. 7, 28, 1864; *Washington, D.C. Daily Morning Chronicle*, Jan. 3 and Feb. 10, 1865; *Cincinnati Daily Commercial*, Jan. 9, 20, 1865; *Washington, D.C. Daily National Intelligencer*, Jan. 21, 27, Feb. 9, and Mar. 14, 1865; *New York Tribune*, Jan. 24 and Feb. 7, 9, 13, 1865; *Portland* (Maine) *Eastern Argus*, Feb. 11, 1865; and *Chicago Times*, Jan. 6, 17, 1865.

59. John Brough (Columbus, Ohio) to R. Schenck, Feb. 6, 9, 1865, Schenck Papers. For a similar letter from a governor who complained about certain features of the draft system and who proposed that authority to recruit needed to be returned to the states, see James T. Lewis (Madison) to E. M. Stanton, Jan. 10, 1865, in *OR*, ser. 3, 4:1040–42.

60. For examples of the numerous religious petitions that were sent to Congress, see Ernst Maurice Buerger, pastor of the German Lutheran Trinity Church (Washington, D.C.), Jan. 23, 1865. Various ministers in Perth Amboy, New Jersey, evidently met for the purpose of petitioning Congress in January 1865. See A. G. Lawson, pastor

of Baptist Church, James A. Little, pastor of Presbyterian Church, Alex Jones, rector of Episcopal Church, and J. Reeves Daniels, pastor of Methodist Church. There are at least four other packets containing similar petitions from ministers whose congregations were located in places such as Hillsborough, Ohio, and Stroudsburg, Pennsylvania. See ser. 38A–H10.2, SCMAM, RG 46, NA; and ser. HR38A–G12.8, HCMAM, RG 233, NA.

61. *U.S. Stats.* 13:9, 380; and John Butler's Oct. 1, 1864, journal entry, John Butler Papers, WRHS.

62. This story is recounted in Murdock, *One Million Men*, p. 215. The *Detroit Free Press* in its editions of July 14 and 16, 1864, supported exemptions for the Catholic clergy but opposed extending them to New England ministers who had "perverted the duties of their sacred calling." One state provost marshal recommended the removal of all religious exemptions because the privilege was being abused in Pennsylvania. He complained that the "Quakers, Dunkards, and Mennonites are having more than a revival" because draft-liable men were rushing to join these "non-combatant sects" in order to continue avoiding conscription through the payment of commutation. Richard I. Dodge (Harrisburg) to James B. Fry, Dec. 12, 1864, in *OR*, ser. 3, 4:990–94.

63. For the letters and endorsement, see *OR*, ser. 3, 3:844–45; and John Sherman (Washington, D.C.) to E. M. Stanton, Dec. 22, 1864, with Dec. 19, 1864, enclosure from Ellen Sherman (South Bend) to John, Records of the Office of the Secretary of War, "Letters Received," Irregular Series, RG 107, NA.

64. Richard M. Williams (Rockville, [Md.]) to Senate, Feb. 17, 1865; and Peter Cooper (New York, N.Y.) to Senate, Jan. 9, 1865, both in ser. 38A–H10.2, SCMAM, RG 46, NA; J. C. Smith (Brooklyn) to DeWitt C. Littlejohn, Jan. 5, 1865, ser. HR38A–E12.7, HCMAM, RG 233, NA; Thomas Fountain et al (Bremer County, Iowa) to House of Representatives, Jan. 5, 1865, ser. HR38A–G12.13, packet 2, HCMAM, RG 233, NA; and J. H. Alexander (Baltimore) to R. Schenck, Dec. 7, 1864; and S. Brewer (Cortland, N.Y.) to R. Schenck, Jan. 3, 1865, both in Schenck Papers.

65. Joseph Frease (Canton, Ohio) to J. Garfield, Dec. 30, 1864; petition of James Bull et al ([Canandaigua?], N.Y.) to Senate and House of Representatives [Jan. 1865]; and "A Citizen" ([n.p.]) to House Military Committee, [Jan. 1865]. All three are in ser. HR38A–G12.7, HCMAM, RG 233, NA. See also William Lawrence (Bellefontaine, Ohio) to R. Schenck, Jan. 7, 1865; J. Alexander (Baltimore) to R. Schenck, Dec. 20, 1864; and A. C. Duell (Urbana, Ohio) to R. C. Schenck, Jan. 26, 1865, all in the Schenck Papers.

66. *CG*, 38th Cong., 2d sess., pp. 1076, 1158; and *U.S. Stats.* 13:491. For Fry's objections to this recruiting scheme, see *OR*, ser. 3, 4:1042–44. After Congress approved this policy, Attorney General James Speed issued an opinion that essentially allowed these organizations to use federal bounties in obtaining recruits. See *OR*, ser. 3, 4:1234–37.

67. Ezra B. Hunt (Elizabeth, N.J.) to R. Schenck, Jan. 13, 1865; J. H. Alexander (Baltimore) to R. Schenck, Dec. 7, 1864; George S. Boutwell (Washington, D.C.) to R. C. Schenck, Dec. 12, 1864, all in Schenck Papers; and petition of Horace Binney

et al (Philadelphia) to Senate and House of Representatives, [Jan. 1865], ser. HR38A–G12.13, HCMAM, RG 233, NA.

68. Gideon Welles (Washington, D.C.) to Alexander H. Rice, Jan. 30, 1865, with enclosure; and E. Delafield Smith, U.S. District Attorney (New York) to Rear Admiral Paulding, Jan. 18, 1865, ser. HR38A–E13.11, RG 233, NA.

69. A. N. Smith (Washington, D.C.) to Gideon Welles, Jan. 20, 1864 [1865], entry 280 in "Fair Copies of Letters Sent to the Secretary of the Navy, Oct. 4, 1862–Mar. 1, 1870," RG 24, NA; and OR, ser. 3, 4:1155–56.

70. For the individual roll call votes and a detailed chronicle of the journey of the March 3, 1865, Amendatory Act through Congress, see my "A Lesson in Trial and Error: The United States Congress and the Civil War Draft, 1862–1865" (Ph.D. diss., Kent State University, 1976), pp. 415–59. For information on the statistical methodolgy used for the Thirty-eighth Congress, see pp. 482–502.

71. In discussing the disillusionment that gripped the Union army in the last year of the war, historians tend to overlook why certain soldiers who enlisted in 1862 were dissatisfied. On July 21, 1862, Secretary of War Edwin Stanton had authorized Governor John Andrew to enlist men into his old regiments with the understanding that they would be discharged with their unit rather than have to spend a full three-year term. Apparently Stanton did not extend this same privilege to all state governors; but they, in the absence of a directive, merely assumed that the policy applied to their citizens as well. Beginning in mid-August 1862 when the government wanted men for units already in the field, many governors used the promise of a reduced term of service to entice men to join the old regiments. Once the tattered remnants of these units began heading home in the spring of 1864, governors and congressmen alike were besieged with angry protests from the men who had been left behind because they had not spent a full three years in uniform. In response to a congressional inquiry later that year, the War Department replied that it had ordered the release only of those soldiers who had clearly not enlisted for a three-year term as reflected in the "muster-in-rolls." See OR, ser. 3, 2:240; and Journal of the House of Representatives, 38th Cong., 2d sess., 1865, H. Exec. Doc. 43 (Serial 1223), pp. 1–3.

72. For Senate action on this bill, see CG, 38th Cong., 2d sess., pp. 604–16, 632–42, 1237, 1294–96, 1378–79, 1386.

73. For voting behavior on this conscription bill, see Geary, "Lesson in Trial and Error," pp. 423–24, 426, 429–31, 438, 441–42, 444–48, 450–52, 456–58. In the second session of the Thirty-eighth Congress, the Senate consisted of 37 Republicans, 9 Democrats, and 3 Unionists. There were 103 Republicans, 75 Democrats, and 5 Unionists in the House. The major addition to the membership consisted of two senators and one representative from Nevada, which resulted from Nevada's admission to statehood on October 31, 1864.

74. For House action on this bill, see CG, 38th Cong., 2d sess., pp. 7, 45, 47, 79, 98, 116, 149, 175, 247, 257, 276, 280, 291, 297–98, 338, 350, 451, 500, 539, 616, 618, 653–54, 665, 691–92, 778, 795, 827, 838, 928–29, 974, 976–80, 1025, 1034–36, 1074–75, 1077–85, 1114–23, 1154–61, 1332, 1335, 1398–1405, 1412–13.

75. U.S. Stats. 13:487–91.

76. OR, ser. 3, 4:1263.

CONCLUSION

1. One recent study provides an excellent comparative analysis of the different emphases of the debates over the draft in 1940 and during the Vietnam War era. Based largely on a changing society, including the "material prosperity" of the post–World War II era, the debates during the Vietnam War concentrated more on the draft's effect on individuals rather than how it would impact society as a whole. James Burk, "Debating the Draft in America," *Armed Forces and Society* 15 (1989): 431–48.

2. For the diverse demands and challenges directed at the Selective Service System from its inception in 1917 to its quasi-retirement in 1973 when it was replaced by the All Volunteer Force, see the studies by John Whiteclay Chambers II, *To Raise an Army: The Draft Comes to Modern America* (New York: Free Press, 1987); J. Garry Clifford and Samuel R. Spencer, Jr., *The First Peacetime Draft* (Lawrence: University Press of Kansas, 1986); George Q. Flynn, *Lewis B. Hershey: Mr. Selective Service* (Chapel Hill: University of North Carolina Press, 1985); and George Q. Flynn, "The Draft and College Deferments during the Korean War," *Historian* 50 (1988): 369–85. Chambers's and Clifford's works are particularly good on the influence that certain civilians such as Grenville Clark had on the legislation that created the Selective Service System.

3. See, for example, Michael Useem, "Conscription and Class," *Society* 18 (1981): 28–30; James B. Jacobs, "Punishment or Obligation?" *Society* 18 (1981): 54–57; and Myra McPherson, *Long Time Passing: Vietnam and the Haunted Generation* (Garden City, N.Y.: Doubleday & Co., 1984), pp. 104–5.

4. For the occupational distribution of these hardship exemptions, refer to table 7 in chapter 8 of this study.

5. Only 5 percent of World War I conscripts had college deferments, which increased to 11 percent for those in World War II. In the closing days of World War II, scientists brought the issue of expanding deferments to the forefront. By the Korean War, the base had broadened to include demands that all postgraduate disciplines be included. See Flynn, "College Deferments," pp. 369–85. According to McPherson, *Long Time Passing*, pp. 35–36, deferments increased by 900 percent between 1951 and 1966. On the difficulties encountered when college protesters lost their deferments and were reclassified during the Vietnam War, see Flynn, *Lewis B. Hershey*, pp. 234–39.

6. Useem, "Conscription and Class," 29–30; Sam C. Sarkesian, "Who Serves?" *Society* 18 (1981): 57–60; and McPherson, *Long Time Passing*, pp. 28–44. McPherson draws heavily on oral interviews in addition to published sources. Her work is particularly useful for its coverage of the inequalities and general operations of the conscription system, and of the problems encountered by those who served and those who did not during the Vietnam War.

7. James A. Stegenga, "Cleaning up Conscription," *Society* 18 (1981): 52–54; and Sarkesian, "Who Serves?" p. 60.

8. Jacobs, "Punishment or Obligation?" 54–57; and Sarkesian, "Who Serves?" pp. 59–60.

9. James M. McPherson, *Battle Cry of Freedom: The Civil War Era* (New York: Ballantine Books, 1988), p. 608.

10. On a broader scale, Chambers, *To Raise an Army*, p. 276, reaches a similar conclusion that the "military obligation of American citizenship remains ill defined."

11. *OR*, ser. 3, 5:803–42.

12. Ibid., pp. 825–41.

13. David M. Kennedy, *Over Here: The First World War and American Society* (New York: Oxford University Press, 1980), pp. 150–53.

14. Chambers, *To Raise an Army*, p. 253.

15. Ibid., p. 254.

16. George W. Peck, *How Private Geo. W. Peck Put Down the Rebellion . . .* (Chicago: Belford, Clarke, & Co., 1887), pp. 13–14.

17. Albert Burton Moore, *Conscription and Conflict in the Confederacy* (New York: Macmillan, 1924), pp. 359–61, finds that "there is no ground for assuming that any system could have at this time produced material results." In his estimation, neither a reliance on volunteering nor a draft system that functioned through the state governments was a realistic alternative in raising troops for the Confederate army.

18. *OR*, ser. 3, 5:842.

19. Most historians share the opinion that the draft "worked," but they usually arrive at this judgment on assumptions only. Accordingly, the draft was successful because it stimulated men to enlist, but its more important influence in forcing communities to raise bounty funds is understated. A few assume it worked because over one million men were raised in the last two years of the war. Consistent with this opinion, the draft has been deemed so successful that it is sometimes placed on a par with the superior leadership of General Ulysses S. Grant and Abraham Lincoln in explaining the North's ultimate victory. The draft's importance in other areas, particularly in encouraging the greater use of black troops, is overlooked. See, for example, Eugene C. Murdock, *One Million Men: The Civil War Draft in the North* (Madison: State Historical Society of Wisconsin, 1971), pp. 344–45; Fred A. Shannon, *The Organization and Administration of the Union Army, 1861–1865)* (1928; reprint, Gloucester, Mass.: Peter Smith, 1965), 2:60, 137–38; Jack Franklin Leach, *Conscription in the United States: Historical Background* (Tokyo: Charles B. Tuttle Co., 1952), pp. 468–69; and Allan Nevins, *The War for the Union* (New York: Charles Scribner's Sons, 1960), 1:465.

20. For a discussion of the importance of the federal draft in stimulating the use of black troops and the relative numbers of blacks who served in the Union army and navy, refer to chapter 3 of this study.

PRIMARY SOURCES

Manuscript and Archival Collections

Albany Institute of History and Art, Albany, New York
 John O. Cole Papers
 Erastus Corning Papers
Brown University Library, Providence, Rhode Island
 Samuel Sullivan Cox Papers
Buffalo and Erie County Historical Society, Buffalo, New York
 Civil War Papers
Connecticut Historical Society, Hartford
 Gideon Welles Papers
Connecticut State Library, Hartford
 William A. Buckingham Papers
Historical Society of Pennsylvania, Philadelphia
 Alexander Henry Papers
 Leonard Myers Papers
 Hendrick Bradley Wright Papers
Historical Society of Western Pennsylvania, Pittsburgh
 John Covode Papers
Illinois State Historical Society, Springfield
 William Ralls Morrison Papers
 Lyman Trumbull Papers
Indiana Historical Society, Indianapolis
 George Edwards Papers
 Michael Frash Diary
 Joseph Hewitt Papers
 Horace Hobart Papers
 William Houghton Papers
 Henry S. Lane Papers
 Miscellaneous Manuscripts
 Thomas Prickett Papers
 William Steele Papers
 James S. Thomas Papers
 Lew Wallace Papers
Indiana State Library, Archives Division, Indianapolis
 Oliver P. Morton Papers

Indiana State Library, Indiana Division, Indianapolis
    Lyndsey M. Brown Papers
    W. W. Carey Papers
    John H. Holliday Papers
    George W. Julian Papers
    Miscellaneous Manuscripts
Indiana University, Manuscripts Department, Lilly Library, Bloomington
    Henry S. Lane Papers
Iowa State Historical Society, Iowa City
    Samuel J. Kirkwood Papers, Letterbook
Kansas Historical Society, Topeka
    Charles and Sara T. D. Robinson Papers
Kent State University, American History Research Center, Kent, Ohio
    Betsey Mix Cowles Papers
    Fuller Family Papers
Library of Congress, Manuscripts Division, Washington, D.C.
    James G. Blaine Papers
    Blair Family Papers
    John C. Covode Papers
    Ethan Allan Hitchcock Papers
    Thomas A. Jenckes Papers
    Abraham Lincoln Papers (Robert Todd Lincoln Collection)
    Miscellaneous Manuscripts
    John Sherman Papers
    William T. Sherman Papers
    Edwin M. Stanton Papers
    Lyman Trumbull Papers
    Benjamin F. Wade Papers
    Israel Washburn Papers
    Henry Wilson Papers
Massachusetts Historical Society, Boston
    John Andrew Papers
    James Schouler Papers
Minnesota Historical Society, Minneapolis
    Alexander Ramsey Papers
National Archives and Records Administration, Washington, D.C.
    Records of the Bureau of Naval Personnel, Record Group 24. Entry 280, "Fair
        Copies of Letters Sent to the Secretary of the Navy, Oct. 4, 1862– Mar. 1,
        1870," 1 vol.
    Records of the United States Senate, Record Group 46.
        Committee on Military Affairs and the Militia:
        (1) Series 37A–J6, "Petitions of Various Subjects . . . Jan. 10, 1862 . . . to
        . . . Feb. 25, 1863."
        (2) Series 38A–H10.2, "Petitions and Memorials Relative to the Amendment
        of the Conscription Law . . . Dec. 8, 1863 . . . to . . . Feb. 1865."

Records of the Adjutant General's Office, Record Group 94. Entry 398, "Drafted Bureau, Letters Sent," 3 vols.

Records of the Office of the Secretary of War, Record Group 107. "Letters Received," Irregular Series.

Records of the Headquarters of the Army, Record Group 108. Entry 106, "Letters Received by General Grant Concerning Exchanges of Prisoners, January 1865."

Records of the Provost Marshal General's Bureau, Record Group 110:

(1) Delaware—"Descriptive Books of Drafted Men, Aug. 1863–Mar. 1865," 3 vols. (entry 3782).

(2) Iowa, First District—"Descriptive Book of Drafted Men, Oct.–Dec. 1864," 1 vol. (entry 6397); Second District— "Medical Register of Examinations of Drafted Men, Nov. 1864–May 1865," 1 vol. (entry 6413); Third District— "Descriptive Book of Drafted Men and Substitutes, Sept. 1864–Feb. 1865," 1 vol. (entry 6429) and "Medical Register of Examinations of Enrolled Men, 1864–65," 1 vol. (entry 6428); Fourth District—"Medical Register of Drafted Men, Sept. 1864–Feb. 1865," 1 vol. (entry 6450); Fifth District—"Descriptive Book of Drafted Men [undated]," 1 vol. (entry 6470); and Sixth District—Untitled source, part of records for Fort Dodge and Marshalltown, 1 vol. (entry 6495).

(3) Kansas, Northern District—"Descriptive Book of Drafted Men, Feb.–Mar. 1865," 1 vol. (entry 6551); and Southern District—"Descriptive Book of Drafted Men, Feb.–Mar. 1865," 1 vol. (entry 6552).

(4) Michigan, Second District—"Descriptive Books of Drafted Men, 1863–1865," 3 vols. (entry 5992); and Third District—"Descriptive Book of Drafted Men, 1863-1864 [1865?]," 1 vol. (entry 6014).

(5) New Hampshire, First District—"Descriptive Books of Drafted Men and Substitutes Exempted from Service, 1863–65," 2 vols. (entry 645); Second District—"Descriptive Book of Drafted Men, Aug. 1863–Mar. 1865," 1 vol. (entry 667); and Third District—"Descriptive Books of Drafted Men, Sept. 1863–Mar. 1865," 1 vol. (entry 681).

(6) New York, Thirtieth District—"Descriptive Book of Drafted Men, Showing Exemptions, Aug. 1863–June 1864," 1 vol. (entry 2291), and "Register of Drafted Men, Showing Men Who Were Exempted from Service and Men Who Failed to Report, Mar.–Apr. 1865," 1 vol. (entry 2292).

(7) Rhode Island, First District—"Register of Drafted Men, 1863," 1 vol. (entry 1331); and Second District—"Descriptive Book of Drafted Men, 1863," 1 vol. (entry 1348).

Records of the United States House of Representatives, Record Group 233. Committee on Military Affairs and the Militia:

(1) Series HR38A–E8, "Minutes of the Committee on Military Affairs."

(2) Series HR38A–E12.7, "Various Subjects . . . Dec. 13, 1863 . . . to . . . Jan. 24, 1865."

(3) Series HR38A–E13.11, "Letters Relating to Naval Recruiting Problems and Frauds."

(4) Series HR38A–G12.7, "Petitions and Memorials Relative to Amendment of the Conscription Law, Dec. 15, 1863 . . . to . . . Mar. 1865."

(5) Series HR38A–G12.8, "Exemption of Ministers of the Gospel from Military Duty."

(6) Series HR38A–G12.13, "Various Subjects . . . Dec. 12, 1863 . . . to . . . May 11, 1864," and "May 30, 1864 . . . to . . . Feb. 13, 1865."

(7) Series HR38A–H1.1, "Tabled Petitions and Memorials Relative to Amendment of the Conscription Law . . . Dec. 7, 1863 . . . to . . . Mar. 3, 1865."

(8) Series HR38A–H1.7, "Exemption of Ministers and Aliens from Military Service."

New Hampshire Historical Society, Concord
> Joseph Gilmore Papers
> John P. Hale Papers

New York Public Library
> James Rood Doolittle Papers

New York State Library, Albany
> Edwin D. Morgan Papers
> Horatio Seymour Papers

Northern Indiana Historical Society, South Bend
> Schuyler Colfax Letters

Ohio Historical Society, Columbus
> Joel Brigham Papers
> John Brough Papers
> Patrick Keran Papers
> Charles W. Larsh Papers
> Samuel Medary Papers
> Thomas J. Mendenhall Papers
> Miscellaneous Manuscripts
> Alexander St. Clair Boys Papers
> Robert Kingston Scott Papers
> William Henry Smith Papers
> William James Smith Papers
> Henry Stroman Papers

Oregon Historical Society, Portland
> Addison C. Gibbs Papers

Pennsylvania State University Library, Pennsylvania Historical Collections, State College
> Thomas O. Crowl Papers

Rutherford B. Hayes Library, Fremont, Ohio
> Miscellaneous Manuscripts
> Warren P. Noble Papers
> John R. Rhodes Papers
> Robert Cummings Schenck Papers
> William Zackman Papers

State Historical Society of Wisconsin, Archives Division, Madison

Records of the Office of the Executive, General Letterbooks
Records of the Office of the Executive, Incoming Letters from Individuals Representing Governmental Departments
State Historical Society of Wisconsin, Library Division, Madison
 James Rood Doolittle Papers
 Timothy Otis Howe Papers
 John Fox Potter Papers
 William and Jesse M. Roberts Papers
University of Michigan, Bentley Library, Michigan Historical Collections, Ann Arbor
 Albert D. Baughman Diary
 Charles Butler Papers
 Frederick N. Field Papers
 Claudius Buchanan Grant Papers
 James Houghton Journal
 Daniel Kent Papers
 John Wesley Longyear Papers
 John C. Love Papers
 Edwin J. March Papers
 Richard Titus Mead Papers
 John W. Nichoson Papers
 Henry Albert Potter Papers
 Sligh Family Papers
University of Pennsylvania Library, Special Collections, Philadelphia
 Samuel J. Randall Papers
West Virginia Department of Archives and History, Charleston
 Arthur I. Boreman Papers
West Virginia University Library, Morgantown
 Waitman T. Willey Papers
Western Reserve Historical Society, Cleveland, Ohio
 John Butler Papers
 Darius Cadwell Papers
 Albert Gallatin Riddle Papers
 Samuel Williamson, Jr., Papers

Published Letters and Collections

Barnes, David M. *The Draft Riots in New York, July, 1863*. New York: Baker and Godwin, 1863.

Basler, Roy P., ed. *The Collected Works of Abraham Lincoln*. 9 vols. New Brunswick: Rutgers University Press, 1953.

Bauer, K. Jack, ed. *Soldiering: The Civil War Diary of Rice C. Bull, 123rd New York Volunteer Infantry*. San Rafael: Presidio Press, 1977.

Beale, Howard K., ed. *The Diary of Edward Bates, 1859–1866*. Vol. 4 of the *Annual Report of the American Historical Association for the Year 1930*. Washington, D.C.: Government Printing Office, 1933.

————. *Diary of Gideon Welles*. Vol. 1 New York: W. W. Norton & Co., 1960.

Berlin, Ira, et al., eds. *Freedom: A Documentary History of Emancipation, 1861–1867*. The Black Military Experience Series, no. 2. Cambridge: Cambridge University Press, 1982.

Brooks, Noah. *Washington, D.C. in Lincoln's Time*. Edited by Herbert Mitgang. 1896. Reprint. Chicago: Quadrangle Books, 1971.

Byrne, Frank L., ed. *The View from Headquarters: Civil War Letters of Harvey Reid*. Madison: State Historical Society of Wisconsin, 1965.

Cutler, Julia Perkins. *Life and Times of Ephraim Cutler Prepared from His Journals and Correspondence, with Biographical Sketches of Jervis Cutler and William Parker Cutler*. Cincinnati: Robert Clarke & Co., 1890.

Donald, David., ed. *Inside Lincoln's Cabinet: The Civil War Diaries of Salmon P. Chase*. New York: Longmans, Green & Co., 1954.

Gould, Benjamin Apthorp, comp. *Investigations in the Military and Anthropological Statistics of American Soldiers*. Cambridge: U.S. Sanitary Commission, 1869.

Greenleaf, Margery, ed. *Letters to Eliza from a Union Soldier, 1862–1865*. Chicago: Follett, 1970.

Hills, Osmer C. (Easthampton, Conn.) to Brother, August 12, 1862, letter reprinted in *Lincoln Lore*, 1564 (1968): 4. Original at Lincoln National Life Foundation.

Hughes, Sarah Forbes, ed. *Letters and Recollections of John Murray Forbes*. 2 vols. Boston: Houghton, Mifflin Company, 1899.

Jackson, Harry F., and Thomas F. O'Donnell, eds. *Back Home in Oneida: Hermon Clarke and His Letters*. Syracuse: Syracuse University Press, 1965.

[Lea, Henry C.] "Volunteering and Conscription." *United States Service Magazine* 1 (1864): 239–42.

[Lieber, Francis]. "Conscription and Volunteering as Methods of Recruiting National Armies." *Brownson's Quarterly Review* 25 (1863): 55–77.

[Locke, David Ross]. *The Struggles (Social, Financial, and Political) of Petroleum V. Nasby*. Boston: I. N. Richardson & Co., 1872.

McPherson, James M., ed. *The Negro's Civil War: How American Negroes Felt and Acted during the War for the Union*. New York: Vintage Books, 1964.

Pease, Theodore Calvin, and James G. Randall, eds. *The Diary of Orville Hickman Browning*. Vol. 1 of 2, vol. 20 of *The Collections of the Illinois State Historical Library*. Springfield: Illinois State Historical Library, 1927.

O'Sullivan, John, and Alan M. Meckler, eds. *The Draft and Its Enemies: A Documentary History*. Urbana: University of Illinois Press, 1974.

Richardson, James D., comp. *The Messages and Papers of Jefferson Davis and the Confederacy, Including Diplomatic Correspondence, 1861–1865*. Rev. ed. Vol. 1. New York: Chelsea House—Robert Hector, 1966.

Seward, Frederick W. *William Henry Seward*. Vol. 3. New York: Derby & Miller, 1891.

Thorndike, Rachael Sherman, ed. *The Sherman Letters: Correspondence between General Sherman and Senator Sherman from 1837 to 1891*. 1894. Reprint. New York: DaCapo Press, 1969.

The Tribune Almanac for the Years 1838 to 1868 Inclusive: Comprehending the Politicians Register and the Whig Almanac. Containing Annual Election Returns by States and Counties. . . . New York: *New York Tribune*, 1868.

Vallandigham, Clement L. *The Record of Hon. C. L. Vallandigham on Abolition, the Union, and the Civil War.* Cincinnati: J. Walter & Co., 1863.

———. *Speeches, Arguments, Addresses, and Letters of Clement L. Vallandigham.* New York: J. Walter & Co., 1864.

"A Workingman's Ideas of Conscription." *Magazine of History* 16 (1917): 103–7 (reprint of 1863 article that appeared in *Fincher's Trade Review: The National Organ of the Producing Classes*).

Newspapers

Ashtabula (Ohio) *Sentinel*, 1862–63.

Boston Daily Journal, 1863–65.

Canton Ohio Repository, 1862–63.

Chicago Times, 1862–65.

Cincinnati Daily Commercial, 1862–65.

Cincinnati Enquirer, 1862–63.

Cleveland Leader, 1862–65.

Cleveland Plain Dealer, 1862–65.

Columbus Crisis, 1862–65.

Columbus Daily Ohio State Journal, 1862–63.

Detroit Free Press, 1862–65.

New York Herald, 1862–65.

New York Times, 1862–65.

New York Tribune, 1862–65.

Portland (Maine) *Eastern Argus*, 1862–65.

Washington, D.C. Daily Morning Chronicle, 1862–65.

Washington, D.C. Daily National Intelligencer, 1862–65.

Washington, D.C. Evening Star, 1862–65.

Government Documents

United States Congress. *Congressional Globe.* 37th Cong., 2d and 3d sess.; and 38th Cong., 1st and 2d sess.

———. *Journal of the House of Representatives.* 38th Cong., 1st sess., Serial 1179.

———. *Journal of the House of Representatives.* 38th Cong., 2d sess., H. Exec. Doc. 43. Serial 1223.

———. *Journal of the House of Representatives. Final Report to the Secretary of War by the Provost Marshal General.* 39th Cong., 1st sess., H. Exec. Doc. no. 1, vol. 4. Serials 1251–1252.

———. *Journal of the Senate.* 37th Cong., 3d sess., Serial 1148.

———. *United States Statutes at Large.* vols. 1, 12–13.

United States War Department. *The War of the Rebellion: A Compilation of the Official Records of the Union and Confederate Armies.* 128 vols. (Washington D.C.: Government Printing Office, 1880–1901), ser. 1, 3, and 4, passim.

SECONDARY SOURCES

Books, Dissertations, and Collected Works

Abbott, Richard H. *Cobbler in Congress: The Life of Henry Wilson, 1812–1875.* Lexington: University Press of Kentucky, 1972.

Baker, Jean H. *Affairs of Party: The Political Culture of Northern Democrats in the Mid-Nineteenth Century.* Ithaca: Cornell University Press, 1983.

Belz, Herman. *Emancipation and Equal Rights: Politics and Constitutionalism in the Civil War Era.* New York: W. W. Norton & Co., 1978.

————. *Reconstructing the Union: Theory and Policy during the Civil War.* Ithaca: Cornell University Press, 1969.

Bernstein, Iver Charles. *The New York City Draft Riots: Their Significance for American Society and Politics in the Age of the Civil War.* New York: Oxford University Press, 1990.

Berry, Mary Frances. *Military Necessity and Civil Rights Policy: Black Citizenship and the Constitution, 1861–1868.* Port Washington, N.Y.: Kennikat Press, 1977.

Blackman, Emily C. *History of Susquehanna County, Pennsylvania: From a Period Preceding Its Settlement to Recent Times. . . .* Philadelphia: Claxton, Remsen & Haffelfinger, 1873.

Bogue, Allan G. *The Congressman's Civil War.* Cambridge: Cambridge University Press, 1989.

————. *The Earnest Men: Republicans of the Civil War Senate.* Ithaca: Cornell University Press, 1981.

Brock, Peter. *Pacifism in the United States from the Colonial Era to the First World War.* Princeton: Princeton University Press, 1968.

Brown, D. Alexander. *The Galvanized Yankees.* Urbana: University of Illinois Press, 1963.

Burton, William L. *Melting Pot Soldiers: The Union's Ethnic Regiments.* Ames: Iowa State University Press, 1988.

Chambers, John Whiteclay, II. *To Raise an Army: The Draft Comes to Modern America.* New York: Free Press, 1987.

Clifford, J. Garry, and Samuel R. Spencer, Jr. *The First Peacetime Draft.* Lawrence: University Press of Kansas, 1986.

Cook, Adrian. *The Armies of the Streets: The New York City Draft Riots of 1863.* Lexington: University Press of Kentucky, 1974.

Cornish, Dudley Taylor. *The Sable Arm: Negro Troops in the Union Army, 1861–1865.* New York: W. W. Norton & Co., 1966.

Curry, Leonard P. *Blueprint for Modern America: Nonmilitary Legislation of the First Civil War Congress.* Nashville: Vanderbilt University Press, 1968.

Erickson, Charlotte. *American Industry and the European Immigrant, 1860–1865.* 1957. Reprint. New York: Russell & Russell, 1967.

Evans, G. N. D., ed. *Allegiance in America: The Case of the Loyalists.* Reading, Mass.: Addison-Wesley Co., 1969.

Faulkner, Harold Underwood. *American Economic History.* 7th ed. New York: Harper & Row, 1954.

Fite, Emerson D. *Social and Industrial Conditions in the North during the Civil War.* New York: Macmillan Co., 1910.

Flynn, George Q. *Lewis B. Hershey: Mr. Selective Service.* Chapel Hill: University of North Carolina Press, 1985.

Foner, Eric. *Politics and Ideology in the Age of the Civil War.* New York: Oxford University Press, 1980.

Franklin, John Hope. *The Emancipation Proclamation.* New York: Doubleday & Co., 1963.

Fredrickson, George M. *The Inner Civil War: Northern Intellectuals and the Crisis of the Union.* New York: Harper & Row, 1965.

Frisch, Michael H. *Town into City: Springfield, Massachusetts, and the Meaning of Community, 1840–1880.* Cambridge: Harvard University Press, 1972.

Geary, James W. "A Lesson in Trial and Error: The United States Congress and the Civil War Draft, 1862–1865." Ph.D. diss., Kent State University, 1976.

Glatthaar, Joseph T. *Forged in Battle: The Civil War Alliance of Black Soldiers and White Officers.* New York: Free Press, 1990.

Hammond, Bray. *Sovereignty and an Empty Purse: Banks and Politics in the Civil War.* Princeton: Princeton University Press, 1970.

Hancock, Harold Bell. *Delaware during the Civil War.* Wilmington: Historical Society of Delaware, 1961.

Hattaway, Herman, and Archer Jones. *How the North Won: A Military History of the Civil War.* Urbana: University of Illinois Press, 1983.

Hesseltine, William Best. *Civil War Prisons: A Study in War Psychology.* 1930. Reprint. New York: Frederick Ungar Co., 1964.

———. *Lincoln and the War Governors.* 1948. Reprint. Gloucester, Mass.: Peter Smith, 1972.

Higginbotham, Don. *The War of American Independence: Military Attitudes, Policies, and Practice, 1763–1789.* New York: Macmillan Co., 1971.

Hyman, Harold M. *A More Perfect Union: The Impact of the Civil War and Reconstruction on the Constitution.* New York: Alfred A. Knopf, 1973.

Klement, Frank L. *The Copperheads in the Middle West.* 1960. Reprint. Gloucester, Mass.: Peter Smith, 1972.

———. *Dark Lanterns: Secret Political Societies, Conspiracies, and Treason Trials in the Civil War.* Baton Rouge: Louisiana State University Press, 1984.

Jimerson, Randall C. *The Private Civil War: Popular Thought during the Sectional Conflict.* Baton Rouge: Louisiana State University Press, 1988.

Kennedy, David M. *Over Here: The First World War and American Society.* New York: Oxford University Press, 1980.

Leach, Jack Franklin. *Conscription in the United States: Historical Background.* Tokyo: Charles B. Tuttle Co., 1952.

Linderman, Gerald F. *Embattled Courage: The Experience of Combat in the American Civil War.* New York: Free Press, 1987.

Long, Clarence D. *Wages and Earnings in the United States, 1860–1890.* A Study by the National Bureau of Economic Research, New York. Princeton: Princeton University Press, 1960.

Long, E. B., with Barbara Long. *The Civil War Day by Day: An Almanac, 1861–1865.* Garden City, N.Y.: Doubleday & Co., 1971.

Lonn, Ella. *Desertion during the Civil War.* 1928. Reprint. Gloucester, Mass.: Peter Smith, 1966.

McCague, James. *The Second Rebellion: The Story of the New York City Draft Riots.* New York: Dial Press, 1968.

McPherson, James M. *Battle Cry of Freedom: The Civil War Era.* New York: Ballantine Books, 1988.

———. *Ordeal by Fire: The Civil War and Reconstruction.* New York: Alfred A. Knopf, 1982.

McPherson, Myra. *Long Time Passing: Vietnam and the Haunted Generation.* Garden City, N.Y.: Doubleday & Co., 1984.

Malone, Dumas, ed. *The Dictionary of American Biography.* New York: Charles Scribner's Sons, 1936.

Mitchell, Memory F. *Legal Aspects of Conscription and Exemption in North Carolina, 1861–1865.* Chapel Hill: University of North Carolina Press, 1965.

Mitchell, Reid. *Civil War Soldiers.* New York: Viking, 1988.

Moore, Albert Burton. *Conscription and Conflict in the Confederacy.* New York: Macmillan, 1924.

Murdock, Eugene C. *Ohio's Bounty System in the Civil War.* Columbus: Ohio State University Press, 1963.

———. *One Million Men: The Civil War Draft in the North.* Madison: State Historical Society of Wisconsin, 1971.

———. *Patriotism Limited, 1862–1865: The Civil War Draft and the Bounty System.* Kent: Kent State University Press, 1967.

Nevins, Allan. *The War for the Union.* 2 vols. New York: Charles Scribner's Sons, 1960.

Nicolay, John G., and John Hay. *Abraham Lincoln: A History.* 10 vols. New York: Century Co., 1886.

Palladino, Grace. "The Poor Man's Fight: Draft Resistance and Labor Organization in Schuylkill County, Pennsylvania, 1860–1865." Ph.D. diss., University of Pittsburgh, 1983.

Paludan, Phillip Shaw. *"A People's Contest": The Union and Civil War, 1861–1865.* New York: Harper & Row, 1988.

Parish, Peter J. *The American Civil War.* New York: Holmes & Meier, 1975.

Peck, George W. *How Private Geo. W. Peck Put Down the Rebellion, or the Funny Experiences of a Raw Recruit.* Chicago: Belford, Clarke & Co., 1887.

Peskin, Allan. *Garfield.* Kent: Kent State University Press, 1978.

Randall, James G. *Constitutional Problems under Lincoln.* Rev. ed. Urbana: University of Illinois Press, 1951.

Randall, J. G., and David Donald. *The Civil War and Reconstruction.* 2d ed. Lexington: D. C. Heath & Co., 1969.

Rhodes, James Ford. *History of the United States from the Compromise of 1850. . . .* 8 vols. New York: Macmillan Co., 1899.

Shankman, Arnold M. *The Pennsylvania Antiwar Movement, 1861–1865.* Rutherford: Fairleigh Dickinson University Press, 1980.

Shannon, Fred A. *The Organization and Administration of the Union Army, 1861– 1865.* 1928. Reprint. 2 vols. Gloucester, Mass.: Peter Smith, 1965.

Silbey, Joel H. *A Respectable Minority: The Democratic Party in the Civil War Era, 1860–1868.* New York: W. W. Norton & Co., 1977.

Sterling, Robert E. "Civil War Draft Resistance in the Middle West." Ph.D. diss., Northern Illinois University, 1974.

Thomas, Benjamin P., and Harold M. Hyman. *Stanton: The Life and Times of Lincoln's Secretary of War.* New York: Alfred A. Knopf, 1962.

United States Congress. *The Biographical Directory of the American Congress.* Washington, D.C.: Government Printing Office, 1971.

Upton, Emory. *The Military Policy of the United States.* Washington, D.C.: Government Printing Office, 1904.

Valuska, David Lawrence. "The Negro in the Union Navy." Ph.D. diss., Lehigh University, 1973.

Voegeli, V. Jacque. *Free but Not Equal: The Midwest and the Negro during the Civil War.* Chicago: University of Chicago Press, 1967.

Warner, Ezra J. *Generals in Blue: Lives of the Union Commanders.* Baton Rouge: Louisiana State University Press, 1964.

Weigley, Russell F. *History of the United States Army.* New York: Macmillan Co., 1967.

Wiley, Bell Irvin. *The Life of Billy Yank: The Common Soldier of the Union.* Baton Rouge: Louisiana State University Press, 1971.

———. *The Road to Appomattox.* New York: Atheneum, 1968.

Williams, Lorraine Anderson. "The Civil War and Intellectuals of the North." Ph.D. diss., American University, 1953.

Winks, Robin W. *Canada and the United States: The Civil War Years.* Baltimore: Johns Hopkins University Press, 1960.

Wright, Edward Needles. *Conscientious Objectors in the Civil War.* 1931. Reprint. New York: A. S. Barnes & Co., 1961.

Wubben, Hubert H. *Civil War Iowa and the Copperhead Movement.* Ames: Iowa State University Press, 1980.

Zornow, William Frank. *Lincoln and the Party Divided.* Norman: University of Oklahoma Press, 1954.

Article-length Studies

Abbott, Richard H. "Massachusetts and the Recruitment of Southern Negroes, 1863– 1865." *Civil War History* 14 (1968): 197–210.

Auman, William T. "Neighbor against Neighbor: The Inner Civil War in the Randolph Country Area of Confederate North Carolina." *North Carolina Historical Review* 61 (1984): 59–92.

Baker, Jean H. "A Loyal Opposition: Northern Democrats in the Thirty-seventh Congress." *Civil War History* 25 (1979): 139–55.

Barnett, James. "The Bounty Jumpers of Indiana." *Civil War History* 4 (1958): 429– 36.

Belz, Herman. "Law, Politics, and Race in the Struggle for Equal Pay during the Civil War." *Civil War History* 22 (1976): 197–213.

Bernstein, J. L. "Conscription and the Constitution: The Amazing Case of Kneedler *v.* Lane." *American Bar Association Journal* 53 (1967): 708–12.

Billings, Elden E. "The Civil War and Conscription." *Current History* 54 (1968): 333–38.

Blassingame, John W. "The Recruitment of Colored Troops in Kentucky, Maryland, and Missouri, 1863–1865." *Historian* 29 (1967): 633–45.

Burk, James. "Debating the Draft in America." *Armed Forces and Society* 15 (1989): 431–48.

Cain, Marvin R. "A 'Face of Battle' Needed: An Assessment of Motives and Men in Civil War Historiography." *Civil War History* 28 (1982): 5–27.

Curry, Leonard P. "Congressional Democrats: 1861–1863." *Civil War History* 12 (1966): 213–29.

Earnhart, Hugh G. "The Administrative Organization of the Provost Marshal General's Bureau in Ohio, 1863–1865." *Northwest Ohio Quarterly* 37 (1966): 87–99.

———. "Commutation: Democratic or Undemocratic?" *Civil War History* 12 (1966): 132–42.

Flynn, George Q. "The Draft and College Deferments during the Korean War." *Historian* 50 (1988): 369–85.

Geary, James W. "Blacks in Northern Blue: A Select Annotated Bibliography of Afro-Americans in the Union Army and Navy during the Civil War." *Bulletin of Bibliography* 45 (1988): 183–93.

———. "Civil War Conscription in the North: A Historiographical Review." *Civil War History* 32 (1986): 208–28.

———. "The Enrollment Act in the Thirty-seventh Congress." *Historian* 46 (1984): 562–82.

———. "Examining Societal Attitudes through Satire: Petroleum Vesuvius Nasby Fights the Civil War." *Illinois Quarterly* 44 (1982): 29–37.

———. "Manpower Mobilization." In *The Civil War in the North: A Selective Annotated Bibliography*, edited by Eugene C. Murdock. New York: Garland, 1987.

Haller, John S. "Civil War Anthropometry: The Making of a Racial Ideology." *Civil War History* 16 (1970): 309–24.

Hallock, Judith Lee. "The Role of the Community in Civil War Desertion." *Civil War History* 29 (1983): 123–34.

Hamer, Marguerite B. "Luring Canadian Soldiers into Union Lines during the War Between the States." *Canadian Historical Review* 27 (1946): 150–62.

Harris, Emily J. "Sons and Soldiers: Deerfield, Massachusetts and the Civil War." *Civil War History* 30 (1984): 157–71.

Haynes, Henry. "Henry Wilson." In *Dictionary of American Biography*, edited by Dumas Malone. New York: Charles Scribner's Sons, 1936.

Hershberg, Theodore et al. "Occupation and Ethnicity in Five Nineteenth-Century Cities: A Collaborative Inquiry." *Historical Methods Newsletter* 7 (1973): 174–216.

Hershberg, Theodore, and Robert Dockhorn. "Occupational Classification." *Historical Methods Newsletter* 9 (1976): 59–98.

Hess, Earl J. "The 12th Missouri Infantry: A Socio-Military Profile of a Union Regiment." *Missouri Historical Review* 76 (1981): 53–77.

Imholte, John Quinn. "The Legality of Civil War Recruiting: U.S. *versus* Gorman." *Civil War History* 9 (1963): 422–29.

Jacobs, James B. "Punishment or Obligation?" *Society* 18 (1981): 54–57.

Kessel, Reuben, and Arman Alchian. "Real Wages in the North during the Civil War: [Wesley Frank] Mitchell's Data Reinterpreted." *Journal of Law and Economics* (1959): 95–113.

Larsen, Lawrence H. "Draft Riot in Wisconsin, 1862." *Civil War History* 7 (1961): 421–27.

Levine, Peter. "Draft Evasion in the North during the Civil War, 1863–1865." *Journal of American History* 67 (1981): 816–34.

Lofton, Williston H. "Northern Labor and the Negro during the Civil War." *Journal of Negro History* 34 (1949): 251–73.

Man, Albon P., Jr. "Labor Competition and the New York Draft Riots of 1863." *Journal of Negro History* 36 (1951): 375–405.

Marvel, William. "New Hampshire and the Draft, 1863." *Historical New Hampshire* 36 (1981): 58–72.

Murdock, Eugene C. "Was It a 'Poor Man's Fight'?" *Civil War History* 10 (1964): 241–45.

Peterson, Robert L., and John A. Hudson. "Foreign Recruitment for Union Forces." *Civil War History* 7 (1961): 176–89.

Purcell, Douglas Clare. "Military Conscription in Alabama during the Civil War." *Alabama Review* 34 (1981): 94–106.

Raney, William F. "Recruiting and Crimping in Canada for the Northern Forces, 1861–1865." *Mississippi Valley Historical Review* 10 (1923): 21–33.

Riggs, David F. "Sailors of the U.S.S. *Cairo*: Anatomy of a Gunboat Crew." *Civil War History* 28 (1982): 266–73.

Ripley, C. Peter. "The Black Family in Transition: Louisiana, 1860–1865." *Journal of Southern History* 41 (1975): 369–80.

Rorabaugh, W. J. "Who Fought for the North in the Civil War? Concord, Massachusetts, Enlistments." *Journal of American History* 73 (1986): 695–701.

Sandburg, Carl. "Lincoln and Conscription." *Illinois State Historical Society Journal* 32 (1939): 5–19.

Sarkesian, Sam C. "Who Serves?" *Society* 18 (1981): 57–60.

Shaw, William L. "The Confederate Conscription and Exemption Acts." *American Journal of Legal History* 6 (1962): 368–405.

Smith, John David. "The Recruitment of Negro Soldiers in Kentucky, 1863–1865." *Kentucky Historical Society Register* 72 (1974): 364–90.

Stegenga, James A. "Cleaning up Conscription." *Society* 18 (1981): 52–54.

Useem, Michael. "Conscription and Class." *Society* 18 (1981): 28–30.

Vinovskis, Maris A. "Have Social Historians Lost the Civil War? Some Preliminary Demographic Speculations." *Journal of American History* 76 (1989): 34–58.

Walker, Mack. "The Mercenaries." *New England Quarterly* 39 (1966): 390–98.

Weddle, Kevin J. "Ethnic Discrimination in Minnesota Volunteer Regiments during the Civil War." *Civil War History* 35 (1989): 239–59.

Wright, William C. "New Jersey's Military Role in the Civil War Reconsidered." *New Jersey History* 92 (1974): 197–210.

INDEX